access to history

Den
and
Ger

GEOFF LAYT

SECOND

-45

D1494771

HODDER
EDUCATION
AN HACHETTE UK COMPANY

To Janet, my wife. Many thanks for your help and guidance.

The Publishers would like to thank the following for permission to reproduce copyright material:

Photo credits: p3 Library of Congress, LC-DIG-ggbain-30813; **p9** http://commons.wikimedia.org/wiki/File:Rosa_Luxemburg.jpg; **p14** Berliner Verlag/Archiv/dpa/Corbis; **p52** Library of Congress, LC-USZ62-103826; **p60** World History Archive/TopFoto; **p65** Library of Congress, LC-DIG-ggbain-36337; **p80** http://commons.wikimedia.org/wiki/File:Field_Marshal_Paul_von_Hindenburg.jpg; **p90** Fine Art Images/HIP/TopFoto; **p101** Library of Congress, LC-USZ62-48839; **p103** bpk/Kunstbibliothek, SMB; **p110** Bundesarchiv, Bild 119-1721/CC-BY-SA; **p125** Bundesarchiv, Bild 119-2600/CC-BY-SA; **p129** http://commons.wikimedia.org/wiki/File:Papen_attach%C3%A90001.jpg; **p141** The Granger Collection/TopFoto; **pp147, 151** ullsteinbild/TopFoto; **p166** Bundesarchiv, Bild 102-15282A/o.Ang./CC-BY-SA; **p173** Topham Picturepoint; **p192** Austrian Archives/Corbis; **p193** Bundesarchiv, Bild 102-12733/CC-BY-SA; **p195** Bundesarchiv, Bild 102-13805/CC-BY-SA; **p214** TopFoto/AP; **p218** Bundesarchiv, Bild 146-1968-101-20A/Heinrich Hoffmann/CC-BY-SA; **p226** Topham Picturepoint; **p245** Fine Art Images/HIP/TopFoto; **p269** RIA Novosti/TopFoto.; **p275** Bundesarchiv, Bild 183-R99621/CC-BY-SA; **p276** Keystone/Hulton Archive/Getty Images; **p281** ullsteinbild/TopFoto; **p283** 'Ein Kampf, ein Wille, ein Ziel: Sieg um jeden Preis!', BANC PIC 2005.009:181--D, The Bancroft Library, University of California, Berkeley. Courtesy of The Bancroft Library, University of California, Berkeley.

The publishers would like to thank the following for permission to reproduce material in this book: J. Noakes and G. Pridham, editors, *Nazism 1919–45*, volumes 1 and 2, University of Liverpool Press, 1988

Acknowledgements: Allen Lane, *Hitler, 1889–36: Hubris* by I. Kershaw, 1998. Ashgate Publishing, *Who's Afraid of Children? Children, Conflict and International Relations* by H. Brocklehurst, 2006. Bachmann & Turner, *Weimar Eyewitness* by E. Larsen, 1976. Berg, *The German Empire, 1871–1918* by H.-U. Wehler, 1985. Cambridge University Press, *Modern Germany* by V.R. Berghahn, 1987. GHIL Bulletin, *'A Very German Settlement'? The Post-1918 Settlement Revaluated* by C. Fischer, 2006. Grove Press, *Berlin in Lights: The Diaries of Count Harry Kessler 1918–37* by H. Kessler, 2001. Hamish Hamilton, *German History in Marxist Perspective. The East German Approach* by A. Dorpalen, 1985. Harper Perennial, *Nazi Germany and the Jews* by S. Friedländer, 1998. Heinemann, *Germany 1919–45* by M. Collier and P. Pedley, 2000. Hodder, *A History of Germany 1815–1990* by W. Carr, 1991; *From Bismarck to Hitler* by G. Layton, 2002; *Imperial and Weimar Germany* by J. Laver, 1992; *Nazi Germany 1933–45* by J. Laver, 1991; *Weimar and the Rise of Nazi Germany* by G. Layton, 2005. Hurst & Blackett, *Mein Kampf* by A. Hitler, 1939. John Murray, *Weimar and Nazi Germany* by C. Hinton and J. Hite, 2000. Longman, *From Bismarck to Hitler* by J.C.G. Röhl, 1970; *The Hitler State* by M. Broszat, 1981; *The Weimar Republic* by J.W. Hiden, 1974. Macmillan, *National Socialism in Germany* by N. Rothnie, 1987; *The Meaning of Hitler* by S. Haffner, 1979. New Perspective, 'Life in the Third Reich', in *New Perspective*, volume 2, number 3, March by H. Metelmann, 1998. Oswald Wolff, *Upheaval and Continuity: A Century of German History* by E.J. Feuchtwanger, ed., 1973. Oxford University Press, *Assize of Arms* by J.H. Morgan, 1945; *From Weimar to Auschwitz* by H. Mommsen, 1991; *The Speeches of Adolf Hitler (1922–39)* by N. Baynes, trans & ed., 1942. Princeton University Press, *The Political Education of Arnold Brecht: An Autobiography* by A. Brecht, 1970. Routledge, *The Weimar Republic* by E. Kolb, 1988; *The Weimar Republic* by S. Lee, 1998. Secker & Warburg, *The Rise and Fall of the Third Reich* by W.H. Shirer, 1960. Weidenfeld & Nicolson, *Account Settled* by H. Schacht, 1949; *Plotting Hitler's Death* by J. Fest, 1994; *Weimar: Why Did German Democracy Fail?* by I. Kershaw, ed., 1990.

Every effort has been made to trace all copyright holders, but if any have been inadvertently overlooked the Publishers will be pleased to make the necessary arrangements at the first opportunity.

Although every effort has been made to ensure that website addresses are correct at time of going to press, Hodder Education cannot be held responsible for the content of any website mentioned in this book. It is sometimes possible to find a relocated web page by typing in the address of the home page for a website in the URL window of your browser.

Hachette UK's policy is to use papers that are natural, renewable and recyclable products and made from wood grown in sustainable forests. The logging and manufacturing processes are expected to conform to the environmental regulations of the country of origin.

Orders: please contact Bookpoint Ltd, 130 Milton Park, Abingdon, Oxon OX14 4SE. Telephone: +44 (0)1235 827720. Fax: +44 (0)1235 400454. Lines are open 9.00a.m.–5.00p.m., Monday to Saturday, with a 24-hour message answering service. Visit our website at www.hoddereducation.co.uk

© 2015 Geoff Layton

First published in 2015 by
Hodder Education
An Hachette UK Company
Carmelite House, 50 Victoria Embankment
London EC4Y 0DZ

Impression number	10	9	8	7	6	5	4	3	2
Year	2019	2018	2017	2016					

Cover photo © Illustrated London News/Mary Evans Picture Library
Produced, illustrated and typeset in Palatino LT Std by Gray Publishing, Tunbridge Wells
Printed and bound by CPI Group (UK) Ltd, Croydon CR0 4YY

A catalogue record for this title is available from the British Library

ISBN 978 1471839122

Contents

Dedication

Keith Randell (1943–2002)

The *Access to History* series was conceived and developed by Keith, who created a series to 'cater for students as they are, not as we might wish them to be'. He leaves a living legacy of a series that for over 20 years has provided a trusted, stimulating and well-loved accompaniment to post-16 study. Our aim with these new editions is to continue to offer students the best possible support for their studies.

CHAPTER 1

The establishment of the Weimar Republic 1918–19

The purpose of this chapter is to consider the events that occurred in Germany during the final days of the First World War and the challenges faced by the new democratic Germany during its first months. These were dramatic but difficult times for German politicians and the German people. The main points are considered through the following sections:

★ The collapse of Imperial Germany

★ The German Revolution

★ The National Assembly and the Weimar constitution

The key debate on *page 24* of this chapter asks the question: Was the German Revolution a failure?

Key dates

1918	**Sept.**	Ludendorff conceded that Germany was defeated
	Oct. 3	Prince Max of Baden appointed chancellor
	Nov. 2	Grand Fleet mutiny at Kiel
	Nov. 3–9	Rebellions spread – soldiers' and workers' councils formed
	Nov. 8	Bavaria proclaimed a socialist republic
	Nov. 9	Kaiser abdicated and fled to Netherlands
		Ebert appointed chancellor
		Germany proclaimed a republic
	Nov. 10	Ebert–Groener agreement

1918	**Nov. 11**	Armistice signed with Allies at Compiègne
1919	**Jan. 1**	German Communist Party founded
	Jan. 5–11	Spartacist uprising in Berlin
	Jan. 15	Murder of Karl Liebknecht and Rosa Luxemburg
	Feb. 6	National Assembly met at Weimar
	Feb.–May	Disturbances, strikes and riots in many parts of Germany
	July 31	Weimar constitution adopted by the National Constituent Assembly

The collapse of Imperial Germany

▶ *What were the problems faced by Imperial Germany in 1918?*

▶ *Were the changes of the October reform a 'revolution from above'?*

When war broke out in 1914 it was assumed in Germany, as well as by all the Great Powers, that the conflict would not last very long. However, by late September 1918, after four years of bloody war, Germany faced military defeat. The reasons for its eventual collapse go right back to the early days of August 1914, but the pressures had developed over the years that followed. The main factors can be identified as follows:

- *Germany's failure to achieve rapid victory in the summer of 1914.* The German High Command's strategy was built on the notion of a quick victory in order to avoid a long drawn-out conflict with the **Allies**. By the autumn of 1914 the **Schlieffen Plan** had failed to gain a rapid victory.
- *Stalemate.* Germany was forced to fight the war on two fronts: the east and the west. The balance of military power resulted in a war of stalemate that put immense pressures on **Imperial Germany**. The situation was made particularly difficult for Germany by the Allies' naval blockade, which seriously limited the import of all supplies. And, although the German policy of **unrestricted submarine warfare** at first seriously threatened Britain, it did not decisively weaken it.
- *Strengths of the Allies.* Britain and France were major colonial powers and could call on their overseas empires for personnel, resources and supplies. Furthermore, from April 1917, the Allies were strengthened by the USA's entry into the war, which resulted in the mobilisation of 2 million men.
- *Limitations of the German war economy.* Imperial Germany was totally unprepared for the economic costs of a prolonged war. It made efforts to increase arms production, but the economy was seriously dislocated, by the disruption to finance and the collapse of trade.
- *Failure of the final offensive, March 1918.* A chance for Germany to escape from the military defeat came when Russia surrendered in March 1918. This immediately enabled Germany to launch a final major offensive on the Western Front. However, it was unable to maintain the momentum and, by August, German troops were being forced to retreat. At the same time, its own allies, Austria, Turkey and Bulgaria, were collapsing.

The socio-economic effects of the First World War

In 1914 the vast majority of Germans supported the war and there were no signs of the country's morale and unity breaking down until the winter months

KEY TERMS

Allies The nations who were allied against Germany and Austria-Hungary during the First World War. They were Russia, France, Great Britain and later others, including the USA.

Schlieffen Plan Its purpose was to avoid a two-front war by winning victory on the Western Front before dealing with the threat from Russia. It aimed to defeat France within six weeks by a massive German offensive in northern France and Belgium.

Imperial Germany Germany from its unification in 1871 until 1918. Also referred to as the Second Reich (Empire).

Unrestricted submarine warfare Germany's policy of attacking all military and civilian shipping in order to sink supplies going to Britain.

of early 1917. Then, the accumulation of shortages, high prices and the **black market**, as well as the bleak military situation, began to affect the public mood. Social discontent thereafter grew markedly because of:

- *Food and fuel shortages.* The exceptionally cold winter of 1916–17 contributed to severe food and fuel shortages in the cities. It was nicknamed the 'turnip winter' because the failure of the potato crop forced the German people to rely heavily on turnips, which were normally grown for animal fodder.
- *Civilian deaths.* The number of civilian deaths from starvation and hypothermia increased from 121,000 in 1916 to 293,000 in 1918.
- *Infant mortality (children under one year of age).* The number of child deaths increased by over 50 per cent in the course of the war years.
- *The influenza epidemic.* In 1918 Europe was hit by the 'Spanish flu', which killed between 20 million and 40 million people – a figure higher than the casualties of the First World War. It has been cited as the most devastating epidemic recorded, probably because people's resistance to disease was lowered by the decline in living conditions.
- *Inflation.* Workers were forced to work even longer hours, but wages fell below the inflation rate. Average prices doubled in Germany between 1914 and 1918, whereas wages rose by only 50–75 per cent.

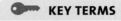

KEY TERMS

Black market
The underground economy where goods are sold at unregulated prices.

Putsch The German word for an uprising. Normally, a *putsch* means the attempt by a small group to overthrow the government.

General Staff A body within the German Army which was responsible for all military planning.

Chancellor Prime minister of the German government.

Erich Ludendorff

1865	Born in the Polish Prussian province of Posen
1914	Appointed chief-of-staff to Hindenburg on the Eastern Front
1916	Transferred to Western Front. Promoted to the post of quartermaster general, as virtual military dictator up until 1918
1917	Responsible for the dismissal of Chancellor Bethmann-Hollweg
1918	Masterminded the German final offensive
	Tried to direct the constitutional October reform, but soon dismissed
1920	Took part in the Kapp *putsch* (see page 46)
1923–9	Collaborated with Hitler and was involved in the Munich *putsch* (see page 48)
1937	Died. Hitler attended his funeral

Ludendorff rose quickly in the army to join the **General Staff** at the age of 30, where he worked closely with Schlieffen. In the campaign in Belgium and northern France he showed considerable initiative and was sent, as chief-of-staff, to serve with Hindenburg on the Eastern Front. Here he played an important part in the major victories over the Russians.

In 1916 Ludendorff and Hindenburg were posted to the Western Front and during the years that followed they were able to assume supreme command of the German war effort. Ludendorff strongly supported unrestricted submarine warfare: he also secured the military victory over Russia. By the end of the war, he was effectively the wartime dictator of Germany, but when it became clear that Germany had lost the war, he failed in his attempt to direct the constitutional reform in October 1918 (see page 5).

Ludendorff proved himself to be a soldier of considerable ability, energy and enthusiasm, yet his right-wing politics later shaped his ambitions. He supported the Kapp *putsch* and early activities of Hitler's Nazi Party, whose racial views he shared. However, he became disenchanted with Hitler and in his latter years declared himself a pacifist. On the occasion of Hitler's appointment as **chancellor**, he said: 'I solemnly prophesy that this accursed man will cast our Reich into the abyss and bring our nation to inconceivable misery.'

SOURCE A

? How does the photo in
Source A show the
domestic impact of the
war on Germany's
children?

Children's free food programme. Children enjoying a free meal in a soup kitchen in 1917.

- *Casualties.* About 2 million Germans were killed, with a further 6 million wounded, many suffering disability. The emotional trauma for all these soldiers and their families was not so easy to put into statistics.

Social discontent, therefore, grew markedly in the final two years of the war. Considerable anger was expressed against the so-called 'sharks' of industry, who had made vast profits from the war. Resentment grew in the minds of many within the middle classes because they felt that their social status had been lowered as their income declined. Above all, opposition began to grow against the political leaders, who had urged **total war**. Faced with the worsening situation on the domestic front and the likelihood of defeat on the Western Front, the military leaders, Generals Ludendorff and Hindenburg (see above and page 80), recognised the seriousness of Germany's position and decided to seek peace with the Allies.

The October reform

Once Ludendorff came to appreciate that an Allied invasion of Germany would lead to destructive internal disturbances, he pushed for political change. Ever since Imperial Germany had been created in 1871, it had been an **autocracy**. Now Ludendorff wanted to change Germany into a **constitutional monarchy** through the **Kaiser**'s handing over political power to a civilian government. In other words, he aimed to establish a more democratic government, while maintaining the German monarchy.

KEY TERMS

Total war Involves the whole population in war, economically and militarily.

Autocracy A system where one person (usually a hereditary sovereign) has absolute rule.

Constitutional monarchy Where the monarch has limited power within the lines of a constitution.

Kaiser Emperor. The last Kaiser of Germany was Wilhelm II, 1888–1918.

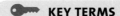

Ludendorff's political turnaround had two aims. First, he wanted to secure for Germany the best possible peace terms from the Allies – it was believed that the Allied leaders would be more sympathetic to a democratic regime in Berlin. Secondly, he hoped the change would prevent the outbreak of political revolutionary disturbances. However, Ludendorff had a third and a more cynical ulterior motive. He saw the need to shift the responsibility for Germany's defeat away from the military leadership and the conservative forces, which had dominated Imperial Germany, such as landowners and the army. Instead, he intended to put the responsibility and blame for the defeat on the new leadership. Here lay the origins of the **'stab in the back' myth**, which was later to play such a vital part in the history of the **Weimar Republic**.

The 'stab in the back' myth was a theme soon taken up by sympathisers of the political right wing. The Bavarian military attaché reported in October 1918:

SOURCE B

Report of the Bavarian military attaché, quoted in V.R. Berghahn, *Modern Germany*, Cambridge University Press, 1987, p. 59.

On the domestic political situation one often hears the opinion expressed that it is a good thing that the left-wing parties will have to incur the odium for peace. The storm of indignation of the people will fall on them … One hopes that then one can get back into the saddle and continue to govern according to the old recipe.

It was against this background that on 3 October 1918 **Prince Max of Baden**, a moderate conservative, was appointed chancellor. He had democratic views and also a well-established international reputation because of his work with the Red Cross. In the following month a series of constitutional reforms came into effect, which turned Germany into a **parliamentary democracy**:

- Wilhelm II gave up his powers over the army and the navy to the *Reichstag*.
- The chancellor and his government were made accountable to the *Reichstag*, instead of to the Kaiser.
- At the same time, **armistice** negotiations with the Allies were opened.

What pushed Germany, in such a short space of time, from political reform towards revolution was the widespread realisation that the war was lost. The shock of defeat, after years of hardship and optimistic propaganda, hardened popular opinion. By early November it was apparent that the creation of a constitutional monarchy would not defuse what had become a revolutionary situation.

'A revolution from above'?

The changes of the October reform have traditionally been portrayed as 'a revolution from above'. This suggests that they were brought about by those in power and not forced as a result of 'a revolution from below'. The historian

Hans-Ulrich Wehler regards the events of October 1918 as proving the view that Germany had long been controlled and manipulated by the conservative traditional forces (1985): 'The conservative bastions of the monarchy and the Army were to be preserved as far as possible behind the facade of new arrangements intended to prevent the radical overthrow of the system and prove acceptable to the Allies.'

Some historians, however, like E. Kolb, have suggested that the steps taken by the military leaders coincided with increasing pressure from the *Reichstag* to bring about political change. The most telling evidence supporting this interpretation is the resolution passed (on the same day as Ludendorff's recommendation for an armistice) demanding 'the creation of a strong government supported by the confidence of a majority of the *Reichstag*'. Furthermore, Prince Max was appointed only after consultation with the majority parties in the *Reichstag*.

The idea that it was the *Reichstag* that brought about these changes certainly cannot be ignored but, on balance, it would be wrong to read too much into its actions. Over the years the German *Reichstag* had shown no real inclination to seize the initiative. This still applied in 1918. The *Reichstag* suspended proceedings on 5 October and went into recess until 22 October, when it adjourned again until 9 November. These were hardly the actions of an institution that wished to control events decisively. It seems that the October reform was shaped 'from above' and the *Reichstag* was happy to go along with this. However, it would be an exaggeration to see these events as a constitutional revolution. The forces that had dominated Imperial Germany were still firmly in position at the end of the month.

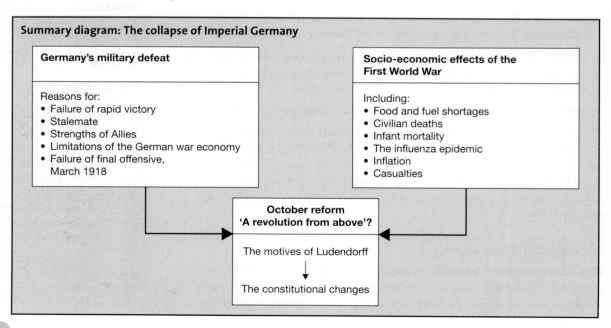

Summary diagram: The collapse of Imperial Germany

Germany's military defeat

Reasons for:
- Failure of rapid victory
- Stalemate
- Strengths of Allies
- Limitations of the German war economy
- Failure of final offensive, March 1918

Socio-economic effects of the First World War

Including:
- Food and fuel shortages
- Civilian deaths
- Infant mortality
- The influenza epidemic
- Inflation
- Casualties

October reform 'A revolution from above'?

The motives of Ludendorff

↓

The constitutional changes

The German Revolution

▶ *How and why did the October reform fail to prevent the November revolution?*

▶ *Why were the consequences of the divisions in the left-wing movement so significant?*

On 29 October a mutiny began to spread among some sailors who refused to obey orders at Wilhelmshaven, near Kiel. Prince Max's government quickly lost control of the political situation and, by 2 November, sailors had gained control of other major ports, such as Kiel and Hamburg. These mutinies had been prompted by a real fear among the sailors that their officers were planning a suicide attack on the British fleet, in order to restore the honour of the German navy. The news of the Kiel mutiny fanned the flames of discontent to the other ports of Bremen and Lübeck and soon throughout Germany. By 6 November numerous workers' and soldiers' councils, similar to the **soviets** that had been set up by the **Bolshevik Revolution** in Russia, were established in the major cities of Berlin, Cologne and Stuttgart. In **Bavaria**, the last member of the House of Wittelsbach, King Louis III, was deposed and the socialist Kurt Eisner proclaimed Bavaria an independent democratic **socialist republic**.

By the end of the first week of November it was clear that the October reform had failed to impress the German people. The popular discontent was turning into a more fundamental revolutionary movement whose demands were for an immediate peace and the abdication of Kaiser Wilhelm II. The disturbances were prompted by:

- the realisation by troops and sailors that the war was lost and nothing was to be gained by carrying on
- the sense of national shock when the news came of Germany's military defeat – propaganda and censorship had delayed the reality for too long
- the increasing anger and bitterness over socio-economic conditions.

Prince Max would certainly have liked to preserve the monarchy, and possibly even Wilhelm II himself, but the Emperor's delusions that he could carry on without making any more political changes placed the chancellor in a difficult position. In the end, Prince Max became so worried by the revolutionary situation in Berlin that on 9 November he announced that the Kaiser would renounce the throne and that a left-wing provisional **coalition government** would be formed by Friedrich Ebert:

- 'provisional' as it was short term until a national election was held to vote for a National Assembly (parliament)
- 'coalition' as it was a combination of parties, the SPD and the USPD (see page 9).

 KEY TERMS

Soviet A Russian word meaning an elected council.

Bolshevik Revolution The term 'Bolshevik' means majority – which was used by Lenin as the leader of the majority Russian Socialist Party from 1903. In October 1917 Lenin and the Bolsheviks seized power to create a communist government.

Bavaria One of the oldest states in Europe and part of Imperial Germany, which maintained its kingdom until November 1918.

Socialist republic A system of government without a monarchy that aims to introduce social changes for collective benefit.

Coalition government Usually formed when a party does not have an overall majority in parliament; it then combines with more parties and shares government positions.

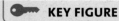

It was in this chaotic situation that **Philipp Scheidemann**, one of the provisional government's leaders, appeared on the balcony of the *Reichstag* building and proclaimed Germany a republic. (Actually, an hour later Germany was also declared a '**soviet republic**' by Karl Liebknecht – a statement crucial for the shaping of the next few months of the German Revolution.) It was only at this point in the evening of 9 November that the Kaiser, who was in Belgium, accepted the advice of leading generals to abdicate. However, in effect, the Kaiser did not formally abdicate, he simply walked away and went into exile voluntarily in the Netherlands.

The left-wing movement

A genuinely revolutionary situation existed in Germany in early November 1918. However, the revolutionary wave that swept Germany was not a united force. In fact, the left-wing movement behind it consisted of three main strands (see Table 1.1).

Table 1.1 The German left-wing movement

	Moderate socialists	**Radical socialists**	**Revolutionary socialists**
Party name	SPD (German Social Democratic Party)	USPD (German Independent Social Democratic Party)	Spartacists (Spartacus League)
Aim	To establish a socialist republic by the creation of parliamentary democracy	To create a socialist republic governed by workers' and soldiers' councils in conjunction with a parliament	To create a soviet republic based on the rule of the workers' and soldiers' councils
Leaders	Friedrich Ebert and Philipp Scheidemann	Karl Kautsky and Hugo Haase	Rosa Luxemburg and Karl Liebknecht

The SPD (German Social Democratic Party)

The SPD represented moderate socialist aims and was led by Friedrich Ebert and Philipp Scheidemann. It dated from 1875. In the election of 1912 it had become the largest party in the *Reichstag* with a membership of over a million people. Its fundamental aim was to create a socialist republic, but being wholly committed to parliamentary democracy, it totally rejected anything that might have been likened to Soviet-style communism.

The Spartacists

On the extreme left stood the Spartacus League (otherwise known as the Spartacists), led by Karl Liebknecht and the Polish-born Rosa Luxemburg (see her profile on page 9).

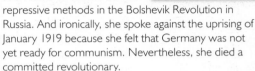

Rosa Luxemburg

1871	Born in Poland of Jewish origins, badly disabled and endured continuous pain
1905	Took part in the revolutionary troubles in Russia and founded, with Liebknecht, the Spartacus League
1914–18	Imprisoned for the duration of the war
1918	Freed from prison and helped to create the KPD (German Communist Party) from the Spartacus League
1919	Murdered in police custody in Berlin

In 1905 'Red Rosa' was one of the founders of the Spartacus League and championed the cause of armed revolution that would sweep the capitalist system away.

Even from prison during the war she campaigned secretly for a revolutionary end to the conflict. However, she soon came to criticise Lenin's repressive methods in the Bolshevik Revolution in Russia. And ironically, she spoke against the uprising of January 1919 because she felt that Germany was not yet ready for communism. Nevertheless, she died a committed revolutionary.

After her death, Luxemburg was described as 'arguably one of the finest political theorists of the twentieth century', who famously said, 'Freedom is always for the person who thinks differently.' In contrast to the brutality of the Bolsheviks in Russia, she presented a humane and optimistic view of communism.

The Spartacists had been formed in 1905 as a minor faction of the SPD and by 1918 they had a national membership of about 5000. From 1914 the Spartacists had opposed the war and they were deeply influenced by Lenin and Bolshevism. They had come to believe that Germany should follow the same path as communist Russia. The fundamental aim of the Spartacists was to create a soviet republic based on the rule of the **proletariat** through workers' and soldiers' councils.

The USPD (Independent German Social Democratic Party)

The USPD had been formed in 1917 as a breakaway group from the SPD. It was led by Hugo Haase and Karl Kautsky. Although the USPD was in a minority in the assembly in the *Reichstag* it had a substantial following of 300,000 members.

The USPD demanded radical social and economic change as well as political reforms. However, as a political movement, it was far from united and internal divisions and squabbles seriously curtailed its influence. The main disagreement was between those who sympathised with the creation of a parliamentary democracy and those who advocated a much more revolutionary democracy based on the workers' councils.

Ebert's coalition government

Because of the different aims and methods of the socialist movement, there was a lack of unity in Ebert's coalition government. Moreover, it should also be remembered that German society was in a chaotic state of near collapse, so the leading political figures at the time had little room to manoeuvre when they had to make hasty and difficult decisions.

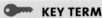

KEY TERM

Proletariat The industrial working class who, in Marxist theory, would ultimately take power in the state.

Table 1.2 Ebert's main problems

Socio-economic	Left-wing opposition	Right-wing opposition	Military
1. Inflation. Wages were falling behind prices, which was increasing social discontent	1. Strikes. From the autumn of 1918 the number of strikes and lock-outs increased markedly	1. *Freikorps*. A growing number of right-wing, nationalist soldiers were forming paramilitary units	1. Demobilisation. About 1.5 million soldiers had to be returned home to Germany
2. Shortages. From the winter of 1916–17 fuel and food shortages were causing real hardship in the cities	2. German communists. Inspired by the events of 1917–18 in Russia, communists aimed to bring about a revolution in Germany	2. The army. The army was generally conservative, but deeply embittered by the military defeat	2. Allied blockade. The Allies maintained the naval blockade even after the Armistice. Shortages, causing social distress, were not relieved until June 1919
3. Flu epidemic. The 'Spanish flu' killed thousands. It was the most serious flu epidemic of the twentieth century	3. Workers' and soldiers' councils. Hundreds of councils were created and many wanted changes to the army and industry	3. Nationalists. Nationalist-conservatives were deeply against the abdication of the Kaiser and did not support the creation of the new republic	3. Peace terms. The Armistice was when they agreed to stop fighting, but there was great public concern about the terms and actual effects of the peace treaty

Ebert himself was a moderate and was frightened that the political situation in Germany could easily run out of control. The nature of Ebert's major problems can be seen in Table 1.2.

Ebert's main worry was that the extreme left would gain the upper hand. He recognised the growing number of workers' councils and feared that they might threaten his policy of gradual change. He was determined to maintain law and order to prevent the country collapsing into civil war. He also feared that the return of millions of troops after the Armistice agreement, which was eventually signed on 11 November, would create enormous social and political problems. These were the main concerns in the minds of Ebert and the SPD leadership in the months that followed and were the main reasons why they made agreements with the army and industrialists.

Ebert–Groener agreement

On 10 November, the day after the declaration of the republic, General **Wilhelm Groener**, Ludendorff's successor, telephoned Chancellor Ebert, which was later revealed in the former's memoirs (see Source C).

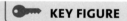 **KEY FIGURE**

Wilhelm Groener (1867–1939)

Politician and soldier, who succeeded Ludendorff. Worked hard with Ebert to prevent revolutionary disturbances in Germany 1918–19. Committed to the Weimar Republic and served as defence minister 1928–32.

SOURCE C

**From the memoirs of General Groener, written in the 1930s, quoted in
J.C.G. Röhl, *From Bismarck to Hitler*, Longman, 1970, pp. 87–8.**

*In the evening [10 November 1918] I telephoned the Reich Chancellery and told
Ebert that the Army put itself at the disposal of the government, that in return
for this the Field Marshal and the officer corps expected the support of the
government in the maintenance of order and discipline in the Army. The officer
corps expected the government to fight against Bolshevism and was ready for
the struggle. Ebert accepted my offer of an alliance …*

According to Groener in
Source C what did the
two men agree on and
why did the deal have
important implications for
the new republic?

The Ebert–Groener telephone conversation was very significant. The Supreme
Army Command agreed to support the new government and to use troops
to maintain the stability and security of the new republic. In return, Ebert
promised to oppose the spread of revolutionary socialism and to preserve the
authority of the army officers. The deal agreed has become known simply as the
Ebert–Groener agreement.

Stinnes–Legien agreement

A few days later, on 15 November, Karl Legien, leader of the trade unions,
and Hugo Stinnes, leader of the industrial employers, held another significant
discussion. The Stinnes–Legien agreement was, in effect, a deal where the trade
unions made a commitment not to interfere with private ownership and the
free market, in return for workers' committees, an eight-hour working day and
full legal recognition. Ebert's provisional government endorsed this because the
German trade unions were a powerful movement and traditionally closely tied
with the SPD.

These two agreements with the army and industry, however, have been severely
criticised over the years, particularly by the left wing. Critics have accused Ebert
of having supported compromises with the forces of conservatism. The army
was not reformed at all and it was not really committed to democracy. Employers
resented the concessions and were unsympathetic to the Weimar system.
Nevertheless, there is a counter-argument that Ebert and the SPD leadership
were motivated by the simple desire to guarantee stability and a peaceful
transition.

Left-wing divisions

By the final days of 1918 it was clear that the SPD had become distanced from its political 'allies' on the left and their conflicting aims resulted in fundamental differences over strategy and policies.

SPD

The SPD government became increasingly isolated. It moved further to the political right and grew dependent on the civil service and the army to maintain effective government.

Aim

- To establish a socialist republic by the creation of parliamentary democracy.

Strategy

- To make arrangements for a democratic *Reichstag* election leading to a National Assembly.
- To introduce moderate changes, but to prevent the spread of communist revolution.

Policies

- To maintain law and order by running the country with the existing legal and police systems.
- To maintain the traditional German Army.
- To introduce welfare benefits.

USPD

In late December 1918 the USPD members of Ebert's government resigned over the shooting of some Spartacists by soldiers. However, the split had really emerged over the USPD's desire to introduce fundamental social and economic changes that the SPD did not want to adopt.

Aim

- To create a socialist republic governed by workers' and soldiers' councils in conjunction with a parliament.

Strategy

- To introduce radical social and economic changes.

Policies

- To reform the army fundamentally.
- To nationalise key industries.
- To introduce welfare benefits.

Spartacists

On 1 January 1919 the Spartacists formally founded the *Kommunistische Partei Deutschlands* (KPD) – the German Communist Party. It refused to participate in the parliamentary elections, preferring instead to place its faith in the workers' councils.

Aim

- To create a soviet republic based on the rule of the workers' and soldiers' councils.

Strategy

- To oppose the creation of a National Assembly and to take power by strikes, demonstrations and revolts leading to fundamental social and economic changes.

Policies

- To replace the army by local militias of workers.
- To carry out extensive nationalisation of industries and land.
- To introduce welfare benefits.

SOURCE D

From an article in *Vorwärts*, the SPD newspaper, published on 24 December 1918, quoted in John Laver, *Imperial and Weimar Germany*, Hodder & Stoughton, 1992, p. 39.

It was hunger that forced the Russian people under the yoke of militarism. Russia's workers went on strike, destroyed the economy through over-hasty socialisation, deprived themselves of the means of making a living through unrealisable demands, and sacrificed their freedom to militarism. Bolshevik militarism is the violent despotism of a clique ... .

Let the Russian example be a warning. Do we want another war? Do we want terror, the bloody reign of a caste? NO! We want no more bloodshed and no militarism. We want to achieve peace through work. We want peace, in order not to degenerate into a militarism dictated by the unemployed, as in Russia. Bolshevik bums call the armed masses into the streets, and armed masses, bent on violence, are militarism personified. But we do not want militarism of the right or of the left.

Bolshevism, the lazy man's militarism, knows no freedom or equality. It is vandalism and terror by a small group that arrogates power. So do not follow the Spartacists, the German Bolsheviks, unless you want to ruin our economy and trade.

In what ways did the SPD editorial in Source D deride the Spartacists? How does it underline the differences in the aims of the SPD and the Spartacists?

The Spartacist revolt

In January 1919 the Spartacists decided that the time was ripe to launch an armed rising in Berlin with the aim of overthrowing the provisional government in order to create a soviet republic.

On 5 January they occupied public buildings, called for a general strike and formed a revolutionary committee. They denounced Ebert's provisional government and the coming elections, which in their eyes were betraying the revolution. However, they had little chance of success. There were three days of savage street fighting and over 100 were killed. The Spartacist coup was easily defeated and afterwards, controversially, Liebknecht and Luxemburg were brutally murdered while in police custody.

The uprising of January 1919 showed that the Spartacists were strong on policies, but detached from political realities. They had no real strategy and their 'revolutionaries' were mainly just workers with rifles. By contrast, the government, led by the defence minister, **Gustav Noske**, had not only the backing of the army's troops, but also 120 'irregular' military-style groups, ***Freikorps***, with about 400,000 soldiers. He placed his trust in the generals in charge to use unrestrained force against disturbances.

 KEY FIGURE

Gustav Noske (1868–1946)

Born a basket-maker, he became a trade unionist and SPD member. He was the first defence minister in the early Weimar governments, 1918–20.

 KEY TERM

Freikorps 'Free corps.' Right-wing, nationalist soldiers who acted as paramilitaries and were only too willing to use force to suppress communist activity.

These events created a very troubled atmosphere in the following few months. The elections for the National Assembly duly took place in February 1919 (see page 17), although the continuation of strikes and street disorder in Berlin meant that, for reasons of security, the Assembly's first meeting was switched to the town of Weimar. More serious trouble in Bavaria in April resulted in a short-lived soviet-type republic being established there (see page 41). The *Freikorps* brought the disturbances under control though, in each case, at the cost of hundreds of lives. The infant republic had survived the traumas of its birth.

SOURCE E

What is the battle portrayed in this cartoon in Source E?

'What does Spartacus want? Fighting the new militarism, capitalism and landowners.' A KPD poster from 1919.

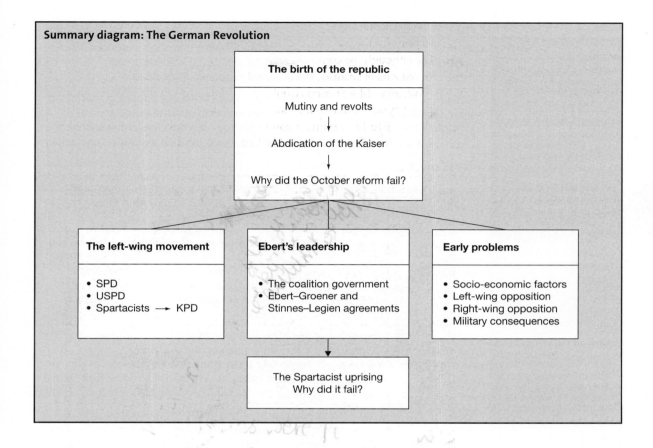

Summary diagram: The German Revolution

The birth of the republic

Mutiny and revolts

↓

Abdication of the Kaiser

↓

Why did the October reform fail?

The left-wing movement

• SPD
• USPD
• Spartacists → KPD

Ebert's leadership

• The coalition government
• Ebert–Groener and Stinnes–Legien agreements

Early problems

• Socio-economic factors
• Left-wing opposition
• Right-wing opposition
• Military consequences

The Spartacist uprising
Why did it fail?

3 The National Assembly and the Weimar constitution

▶ *Were the elections for the National Assembly and the Weimar constitution an achievement for democracy?*

▶ *How fundamental were the changes brought about by the German Revolution?*

Despite the disturbances across Germany, in the months after the collapse of Imperial Germany, the new republic was still able to hold its first elections for a National Assembly on 19 January 1919. Most political parties took the opportunity to retitle themselves, but new names did not disguise the fact that there was considerable continuity in the structure of the party system (see Table 1.3, page 16).

The election results (see Figure 1.1, page 17) quickly led to the creation of the National Assembly on 6 February.

Table 1.3 The major political parties in the Weimar Republic

BVP: *Bayerische Volkspartei* (Bavarian People's Party)	Leader: Heinrich Held	The BVP was a regional party formed from elements of the ZP in 1919 in order to uphold Bavaria's local interests. It was conservative, but generally supported the republic
DDP: *Deutsche Demokratische Partei* (German Democratic Party)	Leaders: Walther Rathenau and Hugo Preuss	Formed from the National Liberals in the old *Reichstag*, it attracted support from the professional middle classes, especially the intellectuals and some of the businessmen. The party supported the democratic republic and was committed to constitutional reform
DNVP: *Deutschnationale Volkspartei* (German National People's Party)	Leaders: Karl Helfferich and Alfred Hugenberg (see page 79)	The DNVP was a right-wing party formed from the old conservative parties and some of the racist, anti-Semitic groups, such as the Pan-German League. It was monarchist and anti-republican. Generally, it was closely tied to the interests of heavy industry and agriculture, including landowners and small farmers
DVP: *Deutsche Volkspartei* (German People's Party)	Leader: Gustav Stresemann (see page 65)	A new party founded by Stresemann, who was a conservative and monarchist. At first suspicious of the Weimar Republic and voted against the new constitution. From 1921, under Stresemann's influence, the DVP became a supporter of parliamentary democracy. It attracted support from the Protestant middle and upper classes
KPD: *Kommunistische Partei Deutschlands* (German Communist Party)	Leader: Ernst Thälmann (see page 125)	The KPD was formed in January 1919 by the extreme left wing (Spartacists). It was anti-republican in the sense that it opposed Weimar-style democracy and supported a revolutionary overthrow of society. Most of its supporters were from the working class and it was strengthened by the defection of many USPD members in 1920
NSDAP: *Nationalsozialistische Partei Deutschlands* (National Socialist German Workers' Party – Nazi Party)	Leader: Adolf Hitler (see page 101)	Extreme right-wing party formed in 1919. It was anti-republican, anti-Semitic and strongly nationalist. Until 1930 it remained a fringe party with support from the lower middle classes
SPD: *Sozialdemokratische Partei Deutschlands* (German Social Democratic Party)	Leaders: Friedrich Ebert (see page 52) and Philipp Scheidemann	The moderate wing of the socialist movement, it was very much the party of the working class and the trade unions. It strongly supported parliamentary democracy and was opposed to the revolutionary demands of the more left-wing socialists
USPD: *Unabhängige Sozialdemokratische Partei Deutschlands* (Independent German Social Democratic Party)	Leaders: Karl Kautsky and Hugo Haase	The USPD broke away from the SPD in April 1917. It included many of the more radical elements of German socialism and, therefore, sought social and political change. About half its members joined the KPD during 1919–20 while by 1922 most of the others had returned to the ranks of the SPD
ZP: *Zentrumspartei* (Centre Party)	Leaders: Matthias Erzberger and Heinrich Brüning (see page 125)	The ZP had been created in the nineteenth century to defend the interests of the Roman Catholic Church. It continued to be the major political voice of Catholicism and enjoyed a broad range of supporters from aristocratic landowners to Christian trade unionists. Most of the ZP was committed to the republic. From the late 1920s it became more sympathetic to the right wing

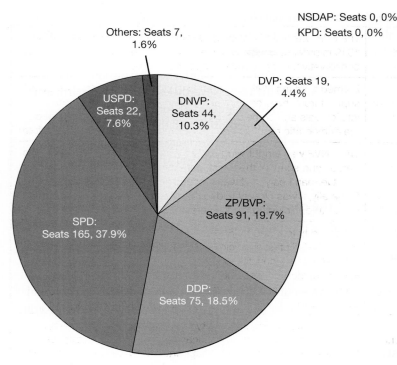

Figure 1.1 *Reichstag* election result January 1919. Turnout 83 per cent and the total number of seats was 423.

In many respects the election results represented a major success for the forces of parliamentary democracy:

- The high turnout of 83 per cent in the election suggested faith in the idea of democracy.
- 76.1 per cent of the electorate voted for pro-democratic parties.
- The solid vote for the three main democratic parties, the SPD, the DDP and the ZP, made it straightforward to form a coalition government, which became known as the 'Weimar Coalition'.

However, it should be borne in mind that:

- Although the DNVP gained only 10.3 per cent, it had backing from important conservative supporters, for example, landowners, army officers and industrialists.
- The DVP and its leader, Stresemann, did not support the Weimar Republic in 1919 because they wanted Germany to have a constitutional monarchy.

The Weimar constitution

Back in November 1918, Ebert invited the liberal lawyer Hugo Preuss to draw up a new **constitution** for Germany and a draft was outlined by the time the National Assembly was established in February 1919. Preuss worked closely

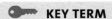 **KEY TERM**

Constitution The principles and rules that govern a state.

on the draft with a constitutional committee of 28 members over the next six months, although their discussions were deeply overshadowed by the dispute about the Treaty of Versailles (see pages 31–9).

The proposals for the new constitution were influenced by the long-established democratic ideas of Britain and the USA. Nevertheless, Germany's particular circumstances and traditions were not ignored as, for example, in the introduction of **proportional representation** and the creation of a **federal structure**. Eventually, on 31 July 1919, the *Reichstag* voted strongly in favour of the constitution (262 for and 75 against) and on 11 August President Ebert ratified it.

The key terms of the constitution

The main features of the constitution are outlined below and in Figure 1.2.

Definition

Germany was declared a 'democratic state', although it retained the title of 'Reich' (empire). It was a republic (all monarchies were ended). It had a federal structure with seventeen *Länder* (regional states), for example, Prussia, Bavaria, Saxony.

President

The people elected the president every seven years. He enjoyed considerable powers, such as:

- The right to dissolve the *Reichstag*.
- The appointment of the chancellor. (Although the president was not obliged, he tended to choose as chancellor the leader of the largest party in the *Reichstag*. In order to form a workable coalition government, it was necessary for the chancellor to negotiate with the leaders of other political parties.)
- The position of supreme commander of the armed forces.
- The capacity to rule by decree at a time of national emergency (**Article 48**) and to oversee the *Reichstag*.

These powers created a very complex relationship between the roles of the president and the *Reichstag*/chancellor.

Parliament

There were two houses in the German parliament:

- The *Reichstag* was the main representative assembly and law-making body of the parliament. It consisted of deputies elected every four years on the basis of a system of proportional representation. The proportional representation system allocated members to parliament from the official list of political party candidates. They were distributed on the basis of one member for every 60,000 votes in an electoral district.

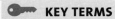

KEY TERMS

Proportional representation A system that allocates parliamentary seats in proportion to the total number of votes.

Federal structure Where power and responsibilities are shared between central and regional governments, for example, the USA.

Article 48 Gave the Weimar president the power to rule by decree in an emergency.

- The *Reichsrat* was the less important house in the parliament. It was made up of representatives from all of the seventeen state regional governments (*Länder*), which all held local responsibilities such as education, police and so on. But the *Reichsrat* could only initiate or delay proposals, and the *Reichstag* could always overrule it.

Bill of Rights

The constitution also drew up a range of individual rights. It outlined broad freedoms, for example:

- personal liberty and the right to free speech
- freedom from censorship
- equality before the law of all Germans
- religious freedom (and no state Church was allowed).

In addition to this, the Bill of Rights upheld a range of social rights, for example to provide welfare and the protection of labour.

Supreme Court

In order to settle different interpretations of law, a Supreme Court was created.

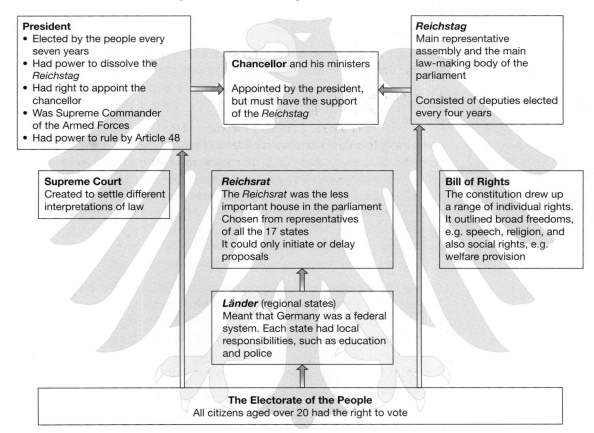

President
- Elected by the people every seven years
- Had power to dissolve the *Reichstag*
- Had right to appoint the chancellor
- Was Supreme Commander of the Armed Forces
- Had power to rule by Article 48

Chancellor and his ministers

Appointed by the president, but must have the support of the *Reichstag*

Reichstag
Main representative assembly and the main law-making body of the parliament

Consisted of deputies elected every four years

Supreme Court
Created to settle different interpretations of law

Reichsrat
The *Reichsrat* was the less important house in the parliament
Chosen from representatives of all the 17 states
It could only initiate or delay proposals

Bill of Rights
The constitution drew up a range of individual rights. It outlined broad freedoms, e.g. speech, religion, and also social rights, e.g. welfare provision

Länder (regional states)
Meant that Germany was a federal system. Each state had local responsibilities, such as education and police

The Electorate of the People
All citizens aged over 20 had the right to vote

Figure 1.2 The Weimar constitution.

The issues

Since the Weimar Republic lasted only fourteen crisis-ridden years, it is hardly surprising that its written constitution has been the focus of considerable attention. Some historians have gone so far as to argue that the real causes of the collapse of the republic and the success of the Nazis can be found in its clauses. Such claims are based on three aspects of the constitution:

- The introduction of proportional representation.
- The relationship between the president and the *Reichstag* and, in particular, the emergency powers available to the president under Article 48.
- The fact that the traditional institutions of Imperial Germany were allowed to continue.

Proportional representation

The introduction of proportional representation became the focus of criticism after 1945 because, it was argued, it had encouraged the formation of many new, small splinter parties, the Nazis, for example. This made it more difficult to form and maintain governments.

In Weimar Germany it was virtually impossible for one party to form a majority government, and so coalitions were required – sometimes of three and even four parties. Furthermore, it was argued that all the negotiations and compromises involved in forming governments contributed to the political instability of Weimar. It is for these reasons that many critics of Weimar felt that a voting political system based on two major parties, like in Britain (or the USA), which favoured the so-called '**first past the post**' model, would have created more political stability.

Having said this, it is difficult to see how an alternative voting system, without proportional representation, could have made for a more effective parliamentary democracy in early twentieth-century Germany. The main problem was the difficulty of creating coalitions among the main parties, which had been well established in the nineteenth century. The parties were meant to reflect the different political, religious and geographical views and so a system of proportional representation was the only fair way. By comparison, the existence of all the splinter parties was a relatively minor issue.

There is also the view that, after the economic and political crisis of 1929–33 (see pages 116–19), proportional representation encouraged the emergence of political extremism. However, it now seems clear that the changes in the way people voted and the way they changed their allegiance from one party to another were just too volatile to be kept in check. It may also have been the case that a 'first past the post' system would have actually helped the rise of Nazism and communism.

KEY TERM

First past the post
An electoral system that simply requires the winner to gain one vote more than the second placed candidate. In a national election it tends to give the most successful party disproportionately more seats than its total vote merits.

The relationship between the president and the *Reichstag*

The relationship created between the *Reichstag* and the president in the Weimar constitution was meant to have a fair system of checks and balances, but this was very complex. It was intended to lessen the fears that an unrestricted parliament would become too powerful. Fear of an over-powerful parliament was strong on the right wing, and within liberal circles. It therefore aimed to create a presidency that could provide leadership 'above the parties' and limit the powers of the *Reichstag*. The president's powers were seen as amounting to those of an *Ersatzkaiser*, a substitute emperor. When the power of the president is compared with the authority of the *Reichstag*, it seems that the attempt to prevent too much power being placed in the hands of one institution resulted in massive power being granted to another. As a result, there was uncertainty in constitutional matters from the start.

The framers of the constitution struggled to keep a balance of power between the president and the *Reichstag*. Was the ultimate source of authority in the democratic republic vested in the representative assembly of the people – the *Reichstag* – or in the popularly elected head of state – the president?

Article 48

Matters were made more difficult by the powers conferred on the president by Article 48. This provision provided the head of state with the authority to suspend civil rights in an emergency and restore law and order by the issue of presidential decrees. The intention was to create the means by which government could continue to function in a crisis. However, the effect was to override the power of the *Reichstag* in what the historian Gordon Craig referred to as 'a constitutional anomaly'. Fears of the emergency powers were actively expressed by some deputies in the constitutional debate of 1919, and they later assumed a particular importance during the crisis that brought Hitler to power in 1933. However, it should be remembered that in the crisis of 1923 the presidential powers were used as intended and to very good effect (see pages 64–6).

The continuity of traditional institutions

Although the Weimar constitution introduced a wide range of democratic rights and civil liberties, it made no provision to reform the old traditional institutions of Imperial Germany, such as:

- The civil service was well educated and professional, but tended to conform to the conservative values of Imperial Germany.
- The judiciary continued to enjoy its traditional independence under the Weimar constitution, but the hearts of many judges did not lie with the Weimar Republic.

- The army enjoyed great status and many of the generals were socially linked with the Prussian landowners. It sought to maintain its influence after 1918 and was generally not sympathetic to democratic Germany. It was the only real authority that had military capacity.
- Universities were very proud of their traditional status and generally more sympathetic to the old political ideas and rules.

In Weimar's difficult early years effective use was made of the established professional skills and educated institutions of the state. However, the result was that powerful conservative forces were able to exert great influence. This was at odds with the left wing's wishes to extend civil rights and to create a modern, democratic society. So, while the spirit of the Weimar constitution was democratic and progressive, many of the institutions remained dedicated to the values of Imperial Germany.

What kind of revolution?

By mid-1919 a degree of stability had returned to Germany. The revolution had run its course and the Weimar Republic had been established. However, serious doubts remain about the nature and real extent of these revolutionary changes.

Undoubtedly, there existed the possibility of revolution in Germany as the war came to an end. The effects of war and the shock of defeat shook the faith of large numbers of people used to the old order. Imperial Germany could not survive, so Wilhelm II and the other princes stood down and parliamentary democracy was introduced. These were important changes.

Moreover, it should be remembered that the new constitution was a great improvement on the previous undemocratic constitution of Imperial Germany and a very large majority voted in favour of it. Indeed, Weimar was initially seen as 'the most advanced democracy in the world'. What the constitution could not control were the conditions and circumstances in which it had to operate. And the Weimar Republic had other, more serious, issues than just the constitution, such as the Treaty of Versailles and its socio-economic problems. Theodor Heuss, the first president of the German Federal Republic in 1949, is quoted in Source F.

SOURCE F

Heuss addressing the *Bundestag* (the *Reichstag*'s successor) in 1949, quoted in E.J. Feuchtwanger, editor, *Upheaval and Continuity: A Century of German History*, Oswald Wolff, 1973, p. 106.

It is now fashionable … to denigrate the Weimar Constitution. It is now customary to say that because Hitler's turn came and the provisions of the Weimar Constitution did not stop him, therefore this constitution was bad. The historical process does not work in quite so primitive a manner.

In what ways did Heuss defend the Weimar constitution in his speech in Source F?

The democracy of Weimar was so slow in getting off the ground and never got properly into gear because Germany never conquered democracy for herself. Democracy came to Germany … in the wake of defeat … and in the shadow of the wretched crime of the stab-in-the-back myth. These things were much more decisive in governing the operation of the Weimar constitution than the technical formulation of this or that constitutional paragraph, even if we may today consider some of them less than perfect.

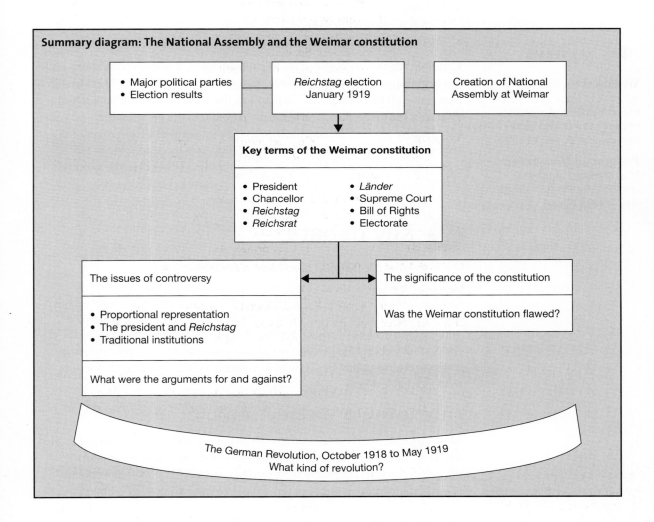

Summary diagram: The National Assembly and the Weimar constitution

- Major political parties
- Election results

Reichstag election January 1919

Creation of National Assembly at Weimar

Key terms of the Weimar constitution

- President
- Chancellor
- *Reichstag*
- *Reichsrat*

- *Länder*
- Supreme Court
- Bill of Rights
- Electorate

The issues of controversy

- Proportional representation
- The president and *Reichstag*
- Traditional institutions

What were the arguments for and against?

The significance of the constitution

Was the Weimar constitution flawed?

The German Revolution, October 1918 to May 1919
What kind of revolution?

It seems unrealistic to imagine that any piece of paper could have resolved all Germany's problems after 1918. The Weimar constitution had weaknesses, but it was not fatally flawed.

In the end, however, the German Revolution was strictly limited in scope. Society was left almost untouched by these events, for there was no attempt to reform the key institutions:

- The civil service, judiciary and army all remained essentially intact.
- Similarly, the power and influence of Germany's industrial and commercial leaders remained unchanged.
- There were no changes in land ownership.

Certainly, plans were outlined for the improvement of working conditions and the beginnings of a **welfare state** by the government, but the SPD leadership hoped that all the changes would follow in the wake of constitutional reform. As it was, the divisions on the left really played into the hands of the conservative forces, who became increasingly influential in German politics. In the words of the historian M. Hughes (1988), 'it is more accurate to talk of a potential revolution which ran away into the sand rather than the genuine article'.

KEY TERMS

Welfare state The idea of the state playing a key role in the protection and promotion of the economic and social well-being of its people.

Proletarian dictatorship Marxist theory of a state created in which the working class control power.

 # Key debate

 Was the German Revolution a failure?

At first, Weimar itself was not a subject of extensive research by historians. If they did study it, they concentrated on the final years regarding its collapse and the Nazi seizure of power. It was not really until the 1950s (in the wake of the Nazi defeat and the division of Germany in 1949 into two politically very different regimes) that the German Revolution 1918–19 became the focus of more academic debate.

An achievement? The liberal democratic view

Most historians in West Germany, such as E. Eyck and K.D. Erdmann, assumed that there had only ever been two possible options available to Germany at the end of the war: the people were torn between a communist dictatorship and a parliamentary republic in the style of Weimar. In this light, Ebert's decisions were portrayed as those of a heroic figure whose actions had created a parliamentary democracy and saved Germany from Bolshevism. Erdmann in the 1950s succinctly stated that there was a clear choice between: 'social revolution in line with forces demanding a **proletarian dictatorship** and parliamentary republic in line with the conservative elements like the German officer corps'.

A tragic disaster? The Marxist view

In contrast, historians in communist East Germany viewed the German Revolution as an unsuccessful proletarian revolution. Partly this was because the masses had not yet been sufficiently organised, because the Communist Party was not founded until early 1919. Additionally, they saw the actions of the SPD betraying the left-wing movement. Even worse, they felt that Ebert had decided to collaborate with the traditional forces of the army and industry. In their view, the real heroes were the Spartacists, who had stuck to their true revolutionary ideas and died on the barricades in Berlin.

EXTRACT 1

From A. Dorpalen, *German History in Marxist Perspective. The East German Approach*, Hamish Hamilton, 1985, pp. 314–15.

The immediate policies of the Ebert government drove the state along this dangerous road. To anyone viewing revolutions as engines of social progress, Ebert's concern with restoring order carried little conviction. It seemed a manoeuvre to salvage the old power apparatus in open betrayal of the revolution and the government's own supporters. In its blind struggle against the revolution … the new regime did not purge the bureaucracy of its non-democratic elements, but retained the old imperial officials right up to the minister level. In the same vein, Ebert entered an alliance with the old militarist forces – those mortal enemies of the nation – thus shielding the officer corps from all revolutionary aspirations inside and outside the Army. Similarly the government sanctioned a pact between labour unions and the private capitalist employers.

In Extract 1, what are the criticisms of Ebert and the SPD?

A failed compromise? The revised view of social historians

Yet, the view of an influential group of social historians in the 1970s in West Germany was that the social base for change in Germany was wider than it had been previously believed. The analysis by E. Kolb and R. Rürup (1988) about the workers' councils movement has shown that very few fell under the control of the extreme revolutionary left. The vast majority were led by the SPD with USPD support and the threat from the revolutionary communists was grossly exaggerated. They may well have been vocal in putting forward their revolutionary plans, but their actual base of support was minimal. So, according to their interpretations, the revolution still amounted to little more than a political and constitutional revolution, which fell short of bringing about any radical changes in the social and economic structure of Germany.

EXTRACT 2

From H.A. Winkler, quoted in E. Kolb, *The Weimar Republic*, Routledge, 1988, p. 145.

First: the governing Social Democrats could not, without provoking chaos, avoid some degree of co-operation with leading elements of the old regime. Secondly: the extent of that co-operation … was considerably greater than the situation required. In other words, if the Social Democrats had shown a greater degree of political will, they could have altered more and would not have had to preserve so much.

According to Extract 2, what was wrong with the level of co-operation shown by the SPD with the old order?

'A very German revolution'? In opposition to the received view

More recently, the New Zealand historian C. Fischer (2006) has come to criticise the long-established dominant view that the German Revolution had failed to achieve fundamental social change. He proposes that it is too simple to denounce the revolution as a weak compromise, judged by some social historians as a failure when matched against the model of normal revolutions. Instead, he believes that in the circumstances of Germany's defeat, the revolution was in many respects a remarkable achievement.

EXTRACT 3

From C. Fischer, *'A Very German Settlement'? The Post-1918 Settlement Revaluated*, GHIL Bulletin, 2006, pp. 31–2.

1918 was, indeed, a very German revolution, but then, on the whole countries tend to get the revolutions they have earned. On these terms Germany's revolutionary settlement was sufficiently practical yet visionary to offer the country a viable future, for it represented a readiness on each side to accommodate the other, and thus was a triumph of moderation over utopian extremism in all its forms.

In spite of this, Weimar failed, but in 1920 the reasons for this lay as much in the future as in Germany's legacy, and international forces would play as great a part in this disaster as domestic factors.

According to Extract 3, what was so successful about the German Revolution?

Chapter summary

By the summer of 1918 it was clear to the military leadership that the war was lost. Ludendorff then initiated proposals with the October reform in the hope of preserving Imperial Germany. Yet, they were not enough to satisfy the people; the social discontent led rapidly to populist opposition and the abdication of the Kaiser and the declaration of a republic. Clearly, therefore, the German Revolution was a crucial historical development. By summer 1919 Ebert's new regime had stood up for a parliamentary democracy and successfully held national elections. Moreover, the Weimar constitution was passed convincingly and the government had overcome some powerful opposition from the revolutionary left wing. However, from the very start it had also decided to make important concessions to the ultra-conservative forces and it faced a range of fundamental problems.

Refresher questions

Use these questions to remind yourself of the key material covered in this chapter.

1 Why did Germany lose the First World War?

2 How did the war affect the living and working conditions of the German people?

3 Why did Ludendorff support constitutional reform?

4 What is the 'stab in the back' myth and why was it so significant?

5 What were the main features of the constitutional changes in the October reform?

6 How and why did the October reform fail to prevent revolution in November?

7 In what ways was the left-wing movement divided?

8 What were the main leadership problems faced by Ebert's government?

9 Why did the Spartacist revolt fail?

10 Was the election for the National Assembly an achievement for democracy?

11 What were the most significant terms of the Weimar constitution?

12 What were the arguments for and against the terms of the Weimar constitution?

13 To what extent was the Weimar constitution fatally flawed?

14 How fundamental were the changes brought about by the German Revolution?

Question practice

ESSAY QUESTIONS

1 'The revolution in Germany broke out in autumn 1918 because many German people in the cities were starving.' Explain why you agree or disagree with this view.

2 'By mid-1919 the German Revolution had brought about remarkably little change.' Assess the validity of this view.

3 To what extent was the German Revolution a failure?

SOURCE ANALYSIS QUESTIONS

1 With reference to Sources 1 and 2 (below), and your understanding of the historical context, which of these two sources is more valuable in explaining why Germany faced upheaval at the end of the First World War?

2 With reference to Sources 1, 2 and 3 (below), and your understanding of the historical context, assess the value of these sources to a historian studying the threat of communism to the newly formed republic.

SOURCE 1

From the memoirs of General Groener, written in the 1930s and published after his death, quoted in J.C.G. Röhl, *From Bismarck to Hitler*, Longman, 1970, pp. 87–8.

The duty of the Army command was now to lead the rest of the Army speedily and in an orderly fashion, and above all sound in mind and body, back to the homeland …

The officer corps, however, could only cooperate with a government willing to take up the struggle against radicalism and Bolshevism. Ebert accepted this, but he was in grave danger of losing control and close to being overrun by the Independents and the Liebknecht group …

In the evening [10 November 1918] I telephoned the Reich Chancellery and told Ebert that the Army put itself at the disposal of the government, that in return for this the Field Marshal and the officer corps expected the support of the government in the maintenance of order and discipline in the Army. The officer corps expected the government to fight against Bolshevism and was ready for the struggle. Ebert accepted my offer of an alliance …

At first, of course, we had to make concessions, for developments in the Army and in the homeland had taken such a turn as to make the vigorous issuing of commands by the High Command impossible for the time being. The task was to contain and render harmless the revolutionary movement.

SOURCE 2

From an article in *Vorwärts*, the SPD newspaper, published on 24 December 1918, quoted in John Laver, *Imperial and Weimar Germany*, Hodder & Stoughton, 1992, p. 39.

It was hunger that forced the Russian people under the yoke of militarism. Russia's workers went on strike, destroyed the economy through over-hasty socialisation, deprived themselves of the means of making a living through unrealisable demands, and sacrificed their freedom to militarism. Bolshevik militarism is the violent despotism of a clique …

Let the Russian example be a warning. Do we want another war? Do we want terror, the bloody reign of a caste? NO! We want no more bloodshed and no militarism. We want to achieve peace through work. We want peace, in order not to degenerate into a militarism dictated by the unemployed, as in Russia. Bolshevik bums call the armed masses into the streets, and armed masses, bent on violence, are militarism personified. But we do not want militarism of the right or of the left.

Bolshevism, the lazy man's militarism, knows no freedom or equality. It is vandalism and terror by a small group that arrogates power. So do not follow the Spartacists, the German Bolsheviks, unless you want to ruin our economy and trade.

SOURCE 3

From *The Spartacus League Programme*, published on 31 December 1918, quoted in John Laver, *Imperial and Weimar Germany*, Hodder & Stoughton, 1992, p. 40.

The question today is not democracy or dictatorship. The question that history has put on the agenda reads: bourgeois democracy or socialist democracy? For the dictatorship of the proletariat is democracy in the socialist sense of the word. Dictatorship of the proletariat does not mean bombs, putsches, riots and anarchy, as the agents of capitalist profits deliberately and falsely claim. Rather, it means using all instruments of political power to achieve socialism, to expropriate [dispossess of property] the capitalist class, through and in accordance with the will of the revolutionary majority of the proletariat.

CHAPTER 2

Weimar's early years of crisis 1919–24

Although the German Revolution had resulted successfully in the establishment of a parliamentary democracy, the young republic faced a myriad of problems. Germany was obliged to sign the Treaty of Versailles, imposed by the Allies, and that document was to scar the post-war years. On top of that, the country faced severe political and economic difficulties, resulting in very high levels of inflation in 1923 when Germany's currency became totally worthless. Not surprisingly, some Germans lost confidence in the government, which, at times, threatened the very existence of the republic in 1919–24. This chapter examines the crises faced by the Weimar Republic through the following themes:

★ The Treaty of Versailles
★ Threats from the extreme left
★ Threats from the extreme right
★ 'A republic without republicans'?
★ The economic crisis
★ The consequences of the Great Inflation
★ Stresemann's 100 days

Key dates

1919	April–May	'Red Bavaria': crushed by *Freikorps*
	June 28	Treaty of Versailles signed
1920	March	Kapp *putsch*
1921	May 5	Allies fixed reparations at £6600 million (132 billion gold marks)
	Aug. 26	Murder of Erzberger
1922	June 24	Murder of Rathenau
1923	Jan. 11	Franco-Belgian occupation of the Ruhr (not ended until 1925)
1923	Jan. 13	Passive resistance proclaimed by the German government
	Jan.–Nov.	Period of hyperinflation
	Aug. 12	Stresemann made chancellor of Germany; state of emergency declared
	Aug.–Nov.	Stresemann's 100 days
	Autumn	The 'German October' in Saxony: overthrown by army
	Nov. 9	Munich Beer Hall *putsch*
	Nov. 15	Introduction of *Rentenmark*
1924	April	Dawes Plan proposed and accepted

The Treaty of Versailles

▶ *What were the most significant terms of the Treaty of Versailles?*

▶ *Why has the Treaty of Versailles been so controversial?*

For most Germans the **Paris Peace Settlement** of 1919 was a far more controversial issue than the new constitution. It had been generally assumed among German public opinion that the peace treaty would be fair. This was partly because defeat had never really been expected, even as late as the summer of 1918, and partly because it was generally assumed that it would be based mainly on US President Wilson's 'Fourteen Points' (see below).

It soon became clear that the peace treaty would not be open for discussion with Germany's representatives. When the draft terms were presented in May 1919 there was national shock and outrage in Germany. In desperation, the first Weimar government led by Scheidemann resigned. The Allies were not prepared to negotiate, which obliged an embittered *Reichstag* finally to accept the Treaty of Versailles by 237 votes to 138 in June. This was because Germany simply did not have the military capacity to resist. And so, on 28 June 1919, the German representatives, led by Hermann Müller, signed the treaty in the Hall of Mirrors at Versailles near Paris.

The aims of the 'Big Three'

The Treaty of Versailles was a compromise, but only in the sense that it was a compromise *between* the Allied powers. So the really decisive negotiations were between the so-called 'Big Three':

- Woodrow Wilson, president of the USA
- Georges Clemenceau, prime minister of France
- David Lloyd George, prime minister of Great Britain.

Woodrow Wilson

Woodrow Wilson has traditionally been portrayed as an idealist, as he had a strong religious background. Initially, he had been an academic, but he was drawn into politics when he had campaigned against corruption. At first he had opposed the USA's entry into the war. Once he declared war against Germany in April 1917 he drew up the Fourteen Points in the hope of creating a more just world. His main aims were:

- to reduce armaments
- to apply the principle of **self-determination**
- to create a **League of Nations** in order to maintain international peace.

KEY TERMS

Paris Peace Settlement
The meeting by the Allies in Paris, 1919–20, which resulted in five peace treaties with the defeated enemies and the creation of the League of Nations. The Versailles Treaty was signed with Germany on 28 June 1919 and the St-Germain Treaty with Austria-Hungary on 10 September 1919.

Self-determination
The right of people of the same nation to decide their own form of government. In effect, it is the principle of each nation ruling itself. Wilson believed that it was integral to the peace settlement and would lead to long-term peace.

League of Nations
The international body to encourage disarmament and to prevent war.

Georges Clemenceau

Georges Clemenceau was an uncompromising French nationalist. Germany had invaded France twice in his lifetime and he was deeply influenced by the devastation from the war in northern France. He was motivated by revenge and he was determined to gain financial compensation and to satisfy France's security concerns. His main aims were:

- to annex the Rhineland and to create a '**buffer state**'
- to impose major disarmament on Germany
- to impose heavy **reparations** on Germany in order to weaken it and to get recompense for the damage of the war to finance rebuilding.

David Lloyd George

David Lloyd George was a pragmatist. He was keen to uphold British national interests and initially he played on the idea of revenge. However, he recognised that there would have to be compromise. In particular, he saw the need to restrain Clemenceau's revenge. His main aims were:

- to guarantee British military security – especially, to secure naval supremacy
- to keep communism at bay
- to limit French demands because he feared that excessively weakening Germany would have serious economic consequences for the European economy.

The terms of the Treaty of Versailles

The key terms of the Treaty of Versailles can be listed under the following headings: territorial arrangements, war guilt, reparations, disarmament and maintaining peace.

Territorial arrangements

- Eupen-Malmedy. Subject to a **plebiscite**, the districts of Eupen and Malmedy to be handed over to Belgium.
- Alsace-Lorraine. Germany to return these provinces to France. (Mainly French speaking and some rich iron deposits. Previously annexed by Germany in 1871.)
- North Schleswig. Subject to a plebiscite, Germany to hand over North Schleswig to Denmark.
- West Prussia and Posen. Germany to surrender West Prussia and Posen to Poland, thus separating East Prussia from the main part of Germany and creating the 'Polish Corridor'. (Mixed population, but mainly Polish except for the big towns.)
- Upper Silesia. A plebiscite to be held in the province of Upper Silesia. (As a result, in 1921 it was divided between Poland and Germany, which caused great acrimony, as the population was mixed and the area rich in resources.)

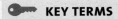

KEY TERMS

Buffer state The idea of separating two rival countries by leaving a space between them.

Reparations Payment of money (and gold) and the transfer of property and equipment from the defeated to the victor after war.

Plebiscite A vote by the people on one specific issue – like a referendum.

Table 2.1 German losses resulting from the Treaty of Versailles

Type of loss	Percentage of loss
Territory	13%
Population	12% (6.5 million)
Agricultural production	15%
Iron ore	48%
Coal	15%

- Danzig and Memel. The German coastal cities of Danzig (Gdańsk in Polish) and Memel made international 'free cities' under the control of the League of Nations.
- Austria. The reunification (**Anschluss**) of Germany with Austria was forbidden. (Although the empires of Germany and Austria had been independent states, they were both German speaking and there were demands for some kind of union after 1918. The Allies prevented this as it would make a greater Germany stronger.)
- Kiel Canal and rivers. All major rivers to be open for all nations and to be run by an international commission.
- Saar area. Placed under the control of the League of Nations for fifteen years, which was 'administered' by France. (A very rich industrial area, but mainly German. Voted to return to Germany in 1935.)
- Rhineland. The Rhineland to be **demilitarised** from the French frontier to a line 50 km (32 miles) east of the Rhine. (The Rhineland remained part of Germany, but no fortifications allowed and no military forces to be garrisoned within the area.)
- Germany's colonies. All German colonies distributed as **mandates**, under control of countries supervised by the League of Nations, for example Britain took responsibility for German East Africa.

KEY TERMS

Anschluss Usually translated as 'union'. Although the population of Austria was wholly German the Versailles Treaty outlawed any political union between Germany and Austria.

Demilitarisation
The removal of military personnel, weaponry or forts.

Mandates The name given by the Allies to the system created in the Peace Settlement for the supervision of all the former colonies of Germany (and Turkey) by the League of Nations.

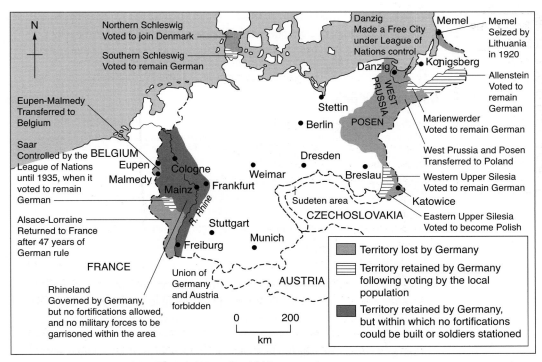

Figure 2.1 The terms of the Treaty of Versailles 1919.

War guilt

Germany was forced to sign the War Guilt clause (Article 231); see Source A.

Why did the Allies impose the clause in Source A and why was it accepted by the German delegation?

> **SOURCE A**
>
> **From Article 231 of the Treaty of Versailles, 1919.**
>
> *The Allied Governments affirm and Germany accepts the responsibility of Germany and her allies for causing all the loss and damage to which the Allied governments and their peoples have been subjected as a result of the war imposed by the aggression of Germany and her allies.*

Reparations

- The reparations sum was to be fixed later by the Inter-Allied Reparations Commission (IARC). In 1921 the sum was fixed at £6600 million.
- Germany to make substantial payments in kind, for example in coal.
- All coal production in the Saar region was to be given to France.

Disarmament

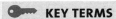

KEY TERMS

Conscription Compulsory enlistment to military service by the state.

Diktat A dictated peace. The Germans felt that the Treaty of Versailles was imposed without negotiation.

- Germany to abolish **conscription** and to reduce its army to 100,000. No tanks or large calibre guns were allowed.
- Rhineland demilitarised zone (see above).
- Germany allowed no military aircraft.
- German navy limited to six battleships, six cruisers, twelve destroyers and twelve torpedo boats. No submarines were allowed. (The German fleet surrendered to Britain in 1918, but sank its own ships at Scapa Flow in the Orkney Islands on 28 June 1919.)

Maintaining peace

The treaty also set out the Covenant of the League of Nations, which included the aims and organisation of the League. Germany had to accept the League, but it was initially not allowed to join.

The *Diktat*

No other political issue produced such total agreement within Weimar Germany as the rejection and condemnation of the Treaty of Versailles. The treaty's terms were seen as unfair and were simply described as a ***Diktat***. Germany's main complaints were as follows:

- The treaty was considered to be very different from Wilson's Fourteen Points. Most obviously, many Germans found it impossible to understand how and why the guiding principle of self-determination was *not* applied in a number of cases.
- Many Germans viewed the following areas as 'German', but they were excluded from the new German state and placed under foreign rule: Austria,

Danzig, Posen and West Prussia, Memel, Upper Silesia, Sudetenland and Saar.

- Similarly, the loss of Germany's colonies was not in line with the fifth of Wilson's Fourteen Points, which had called for 'an impartial adjustment of all colonial claims'. Instead, they were passed on to the care of the Allies as mandates.
- Germany found it impossible to accept the War Guilt clause (Article 231), which was the Allies' justification for demanding the payment of reparations. Most Germans argued that Germany could not be held solely responsible for the outbreak of the war. They were convinced that the war of 1914 had been fought for defensive reasons because their country had been threatened by 'encirclement' from the Allies in 1914.
- Germans considered the Allied demand for extensive reparations totally unreasonable. Worryingly, the actual size of the reparations payment was not stated in the Treaty of Versailles – it was left to be decided at a later date by the IARC. From a German viewpoint this amounted to their being forced to sign a 'blank cheque'.
- The imposition of the disarmament clauses was seen as grossly unfair, as Britain and France remained highly armed and made no future commitments to disarm. It seemed as if Germany had been **unilaterally disarmed**, whereas Wilson had spoken in favour of universal disarmament.
- Germany's treatment by the Allies was viewed as undignified and unworthy of a great power. For example, Germany was excluded from the League of Nations but, as part of the treaty, was forced to accept the rules of its Covenant. This simply hardened the views of those Germans who saw the League as a tool of the Allies rather than as a genuine international organisation.

Altogether, the treaty was seen as a *Diktat*. The Allies maintained a military blockade on Germany until the treaty was signed. This had significant human consequences such as increasing food shortages. Furthermore, the Allies threatened to take further military action if Germany did not co-operate. Source B states the thoughts of a liberal lawyer, Hugo Preuss, who drew up the Weimar constitution, written in 1923.

SOURCE B

From H. Preuss, *Deustchlands Republikanische Reichsverfassung*, 1923, quoted in J.C.G. Röhl, *From Bismarck to Hitler*, Longman, 1970, pp. 103–4.

… the German Republic was born out of terrible defeat. This … cast, from the first, a dark shadow on the new political order … initially the belief still predominated that the new order was necessary for the rebirth of Germany.

That is why the democratic clauses of the Weimar constitution met with relatively little resistance, despite the unrivalled severity of the armistice terms. For everyone still expected a peace settlement in accordance with Wilson's

 **KEY TERM**

Unilateral disarmament
The disarmament of one party. Wilson pushed for general (universal) disarmament after the war, but France and Britain were more suspicious. As a result, only Germany had to disarm.

What are Preuss's criticisms of the Versailles Treaty in Source B? Do you think this was a balanced view?

14 Points, which all the belligerent countries had bindingly accepted as the basis for the peace … The criminal madness of the Versailles Diktat was a shameless blow in the face to such hopes based on international law and political common sense. The Reich constitution was born with this curse upon it …

SOURCE C

? How did the German magazine cartoon in Source C effectively condemn the Treaty of Versailles?

A cartoon drawn in July 1919 from the German newspaper *Kladderatsch*, which portrays Georges Clemenceau as a vampire.

Versailles: a more balanced view

In the years 1919–45 most Germans regarded the Treaty of Versailles as a *Diktat*. In Britain, too, there developed a growing sympathy for Germany's position. However, this was not the case in France, where the treaty was generally condemned as being too lenient. It was only after the Second World War that a more balanced view of the Treaty of Versailles emerged. As a result, recent historians have tended to view the peacemakers of 1919 more sympathetically.

Earlier German criticisms of the treaty are no longer as readily accepted as they once were.

Of course, at the Paris peace conferences, Allied statesmen were motivated by their own national self-interests, and the representatives of France and Britain were keen to achieve these at the expense of Germany. However, it is now recognised that it was the situation created by the war that shaped the terms of the treaty and not just anti-German feeling. The aims and objectives of the various Allies differed and achieving agreement was made more difficult by the complicated circumstances of the time. It should be remembered that the Paris Peace Settlement was not solely concerned with Germany, so Austria-Hungary, Bulgaria and Turkey were forced to sign separate treaties. In addition, other problems had to be dealt with. For example, Britain had national interests to look after in the Middle East as a result of the collapse of the Turkish Empire. At the same time, the Allies were concerned by the threat of Soviet Russia and were motivated by a common desire to contain the Bolshevik 'menace'.

In the end, the Treaty of Versailles was a compromise. It was not based on Wilson's Fourteen Points as most Germans thought it would be, but equally it was not nearly so severe as certain sections of Allied opinion had demanded. It should be borne in mind that:

- Clemenceau, the French representative, was forced to give way over most of his country's more extreme demands, such as the creation of an independent Rhineland and the **annexation** of the Saar.
- The application of self-determination was not nearly so unfair as many Germans believed:
  - Alsace-Lorraine would have voted to return to France anyway, as it had been French before 1871.
  - Plebiscites were held in Schleswig, Silesia and parts of Prussia to decide their future.
  - Danzig's status under the League was the result of Woodrow Wilson's promise to provide 'Poland with access to the sea'.
  - The eastern frontier provinces of Posen and West Prussia were rather more mixed in ethnic make-up than Germans were prepared to admit (in these provinces Germans predominated in the towns, whereas the Poles did so in the countryside – which made it very difficult to draw a clear frontier line).
  - Austria and Sudetenland had never been part of Germany before 1918, anyway.
- Germany was not physically occupied and, as a result, the real damage was suffered on foreign soil (France and Belgium).
- The Treaty of Versailles appeared relatively moderate in comparison to the severity of the terms imposed by the Germans on the Russians at the Treaty of Brest-Litovsk in 1918, which annexed large areas of Poland and the Baltic states.

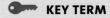 **KEY TERM**

Annexation Taking over of another country against its will.

The significance of the Treaty of Versailles

The historical significance of the Treaty of Versailles goes well beyond the debate over its fairness. It raises the important issue of its impact on the Weimar Republic and whether it acted as a serious handicap to the establishment of long-term political stability in Germany.

The economic consequences of reparations were undoubtedly a genuine concern. The English economist John Maynard Keynes feared in 1919 that the reparations would fundamentally weaken the economy of Germany with consequences for the whole of Europe. However, Germany's economic potential was still considerable. It had potentially by far the strongest economy in Europe and still had extensive industry and resources. As will be seen later, the republic's economic problems cannot be blamed on the burden of reparations alone. And it should also be remembered that by 1932, because reparations had been scaled back, Germany actually received more in loans under the Dawes Plan (see page 84) than it paid in reparations.

It is not really possible to maintain that the treaty had weakened Germany politically. In some respects, Germany in 1919 was in a stronger position than in 1914. The great empires of Russia, Austria-Hungary and Turkey had gone, creating a power vacuum in central and eastern Europe that could not be filled, at least in the short term, by a weak and isolated Soviet Russia or by any other state. In such a situation, cautious diplomacy might have led to the establishment of German power and influence at the heart of Europe. However, on another level, the treaty might be considered more to blame because, in the minds of many Germans, it was regarded as the real cause of the country's problems and they really believed that it was totally unfair. In the war German public opinion had been strongly shaped by nationalist propaganda and then deeply shocked by the defeat. Both the Armistice and Versailles were closely linked to the 'stab in the back' myth that the German Army had not really lost the First World War in 1918 (see page 5). It may have been a myth, but it was a very powerful one.

As a result, although the war had been pursued by Imperial Germany, it was the new democracy of Weimar that was forced to take the responsibility and the blame for the First World War. Therefore, Weimar democracy was deeply weakened by Versailles, which fuelled the propaganda of the republic's opponents over the years. Even for sympathetic democrats like Hugo Preuss, Versailles only served to disillusion many into thinking that the gains of the revolution were undone (see Source B, page 36). In this way, the Treaty of Versailles contributed to the internal political and economic difficulties that emerged in Germany after 1919.

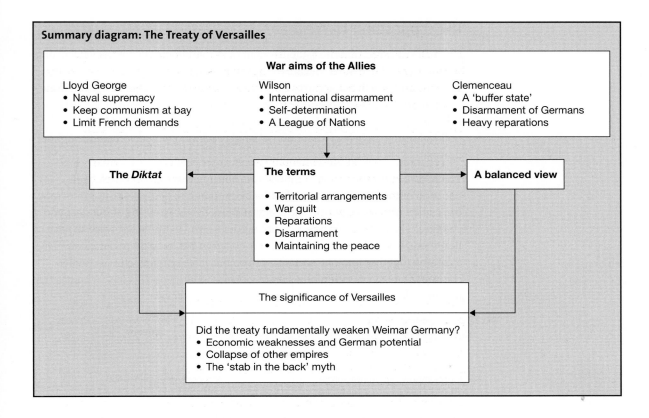

Summary diagram: The Treaty of Versailles

War aims of the Allies

Lloyd George
- Naval supremacy
- Keep communism at bay
- Limit French demands

Wilson
- International disarmament
- Self-determination
- A League of Nations

Clemenceau
- A 'buffer state'
- Disarmament of Germans
- Heavy reparations

The *Diktat*

The terms
- Territorial arrangements
- War guilt
- Reparations
- Disarmament
- Maintaining the peace

A balanced view

The significance of Versailles

Did the treaty fundamentally weaken Weimar Germany?
- Economic weaknesses and German potential
- Collapse of other empires
- The 'stab in the back' myth

② Threats from the extreme left

▶ *How serious was the opposition of the extreme left to the Weimar Republic?*

After the German Revolution of 1918–19 the left-wing movement at first remained in a state of confusion:

- The moderate socialists of the SPD were committed to parliamentary democracy.
- The Communists (the KPD) pressed for a workers' revolution.
- The USPD stood for the creation of a radical socialist society, but within a democratic framework.

This situation became clearer when, in 1920, the USPD disbanded and the vast majority of its members joined either the KPD or the SPD. So, from that time there were two left-wing alternative parties, but with fundamental differences.

KPD opposition to Weimar

The KPD believed that the establishment of parliamentary democracy fell a long way short of its real aims. It wanted the revolution to proceed on Marxist lines with the creation of a one-party communist state and the major restructuring of Germany both socially and economically (see box). As a result of the 1917 Russian Revolution, many German communists were encouraged by the political unrest to believe that international revolution would spread throughout Europe.

The KPD's opposition to the republic was nothing less than a complete rejection of the Weimar system. It was not prepared to be part of the democratic opposition or to work within the parliamentary system to bring about desired changes. The differences between the moderate and extreme left were so basic that there was no chance of political co-operation between them, let alone a coming together into one socialist movement. The extreme left was totally committed to a very different vision of German politics and society, whereas the moderate left was one of the pillars of Weimar democracy.

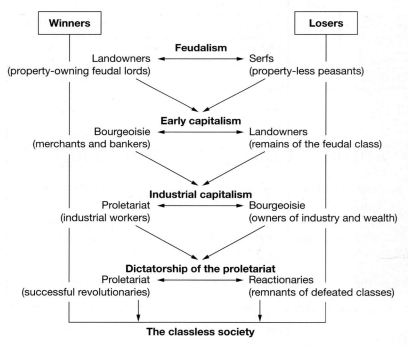

Figure 2.2 A visual representation of the Marxist notion of the workings of the dialectic.

Marxism

Karl Marx (1818–83) was a German revolutionary who expressed his ideology in two major books, *The Communist Manifesto* and *Capital*, in which he outlined his scientific analysis of human society. He claimed that history was a continuous struggle of the classes between those who had economic and political power and those who did not. This continuous process of class struggle was known as the dialectic.

Marxists in the nineteenth century were inspired by the belief that the industrial age would culminate in a revolution in which the proletariat (working classes) would overthrow the bourgeoisie (industrial classes) by revolution and create a classless society.

Revolutionary disturbances

The KPD was indeed a reasonable political force in the years 1919–23. It enjoyed the support of ten to fifteen per cent of the electorate and there were continuous revolutionary disturbances – protests, strikes and uprisings (see Table 2.2).

Table 2.2 Major communist uprisings 1919–23

Date	Place	Action	Response
January 1919	Berlin	Spartacist uprising to seize power (see page 13)	Crushed by German Army and *Freikorps*
March 1919	Bavaria	Creation of soviet republic 'Red Bavaria' (see below)	Crushed by the *Freikorps*
March 1920	Ruhr	Formation of the Ruhr Army by 50,000 workers to oppose the Kapp *putsch*	Crushed by German Army and *Freikorps*
March 1921	Merseburg and Halle	'March Operation'. Uprising of strikes organised by the KPD	Put down by police
Summer 1923	Saxony and Thuringia	'German October'. A wave of strikes and the creation of an SPD/KPD state government. Plans for a military uprising by the Communists (see below)	Overthrown by German Army

The most significant disturbances were 'Red Bavaria' and the 'German October'.

'Red Bavaria'

After the collapse of the Bavarian monarchy (see page 7), the USPD leader Kurt Eisner took the political lead. However, he struggled to unite the socialist parties to implement reforms and was assassinated on 21 February 1919. In the wake, confusion broke out. A Bavarian soviet republic with a 'Red Army' of workers was set up by Eugen Leviné and proposed radical political and economic changes. Yet, after a month the *Freikorps* and the army moved in and brutally crushed the republic with 1000 deaths in May, which became known as the **White Terror**. This traumatic episode in a conservative, agricultural Catholic area shifted politics to the right wing and it became a haven for extremists.

The 'German October'

In the crisis of 1923 (see pages 64–7), left-wing revolutionary actions came to a head in central Germany. The KPD and SPD had formed coalitions in the regional governments of Saxony and Thuringia, but the Communists went further and made military preparations for an uprising with 'Proletarian Hundreds' (defence units). In response, Stresemann's government, by rapid and determined action, foiled the plan for the 'German October' revolution – the army crushed the units and the regional governments were re-created without communists.

The Red threat?

These actions by the extreme left gave the impression that Germany was really facing a Bolshevik-inspired **Red threat**. And, as a result of right-wing propaganda, many Germans began to have exaggerated fears about the possibility of impending revolution.

Yet, looking back, it is clear that the extreme left posed much less of a threat to Weimar than was believed. Despite all the disturbances, the revolutionary left was never really likely to seize political power. The main reasons for their failure lay in a combination of their own weaknesses and the effective resistance of the Weimar governments:

- Bad co-ordination. Even during the chaos and uncertainty of 1923, the activities of the extreme left proved incapable of mounting a unified attack on Weimar democracy.
- Poor leadership. The repression the extreme left suffered at the hands of the *Freikorps* removed some of its ablest and most spirited leaders, for example, Liebknecht and Luxemburg (see page 13). The later leadership suffered from internal divisions and disagreements on tactics.
- Concessions. The Weimar governments played on the differences within the extreme left by making concessions which split it, for example over the Kapp *putsch* in March 1920 (see page 46).
- Repression. The authorities systematically repressed the rebels with considerable brutality.

In the end, the extreme left was just not powerful enough to lead a revolution against the Weimar Republic.

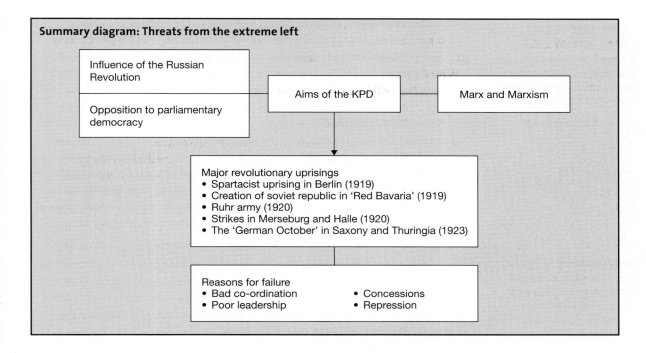

Summary diagram: Threats from the extreme left

Influence of the Russian Revolution

Opposition to parliamentary democracy

Aims of the KPD

Marx and Marxism

Major revolutionary uprisings
- Spartacist uprising in Berlin (1919)
- Creation of soviet republic in 'Red Bavaria' (1919)
- Ruhr army (1920)
- Strikes in Merseburg and Halle (1920)
- The 'German October' in Saxony and Thuringia (1923)

Reasons for failure
- Bad co-ordination
- Poor leadership
- Concessions
- Repression

③ Threats from the extreme right

▶ *What were the aims and objectives of the extreme right?*

▶ *Who were the plotters in the Kapp* putsch *and the Munich Beer Hall* putsch, *and why did they both fail?*

Opposition from the extreme right was very different both in its form and in its extent to that of the extreme left. On the right wing there was a very mixed collection of opponents to the republic and their resistance found expression in different ways.

The extreme right in theory

In contrast to Marxist socialism, the extreme right did not really have an alternative organised ideology (apart from a shared intense **nationalism**). It was simply drawn together by a growing belief in the following:

- Anti-democracy. It was united by its rejection of the Weimar system and its principles. It aimed to destroy the democratic constitution because it was seen as weak, which it believed had contributed to Germany's problems.
- **Anti-Marxism**. Even more despised than democracy was the fear of communism. It was seen as a real threat to traditional values and the ownership of property and wealth – and when Russian communism was established, it reinforced the idea that communism was anti-German.

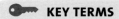 **KEY TERMS**

Nationalism In general, the belief in – and support for – a national identity. The spirit of German nationalism helped to unify the German states in the nineteenth century. But many nationalists wanted to create a Greater Germany of all German speakers.

Anti-Marxism Opposition to the ideology of Karl Marx.

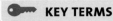

KEY TERMS

Authoritarianism A broad term meaning government by strong non-democratic leadership.

November criminals Those who signed the November Armistice and a term of abuse to vilify all those who supported the democratic republic.

Völkisch Nationalist views associated with Aryan racism (especially anti-Semitism).

Anti-Semitism Hatred of Jews. It became the most significant part of Nazi racist thinking. For Hitler, the 'master-race' was the pure Aryan (the people of northern Europe).

Reactionary Opposing change and supporting a return to traditional ways.

- **Authoritarianism**. The extreme right favoured the restoration of some authoritarian, dictatorial regime – although in the early 1920s there was no real consensus on what kind of strong government and leadership would be established.
- Nationalism. Nationalism was at the core of the extreme right, but Germany's national pride had been deeply hurt by the events of 1918–19. Not surprisingly, from the time of the Treaty of Versailles, this conservative-nationalist response reinforced the ideas of the 'stab in the back' myth and the '**November criminals**'. The war, it was argued, had been lost not because of any military defeat suffered by the army, but as a result of the betrayal by unpatriotic forces within Germany. These were said to include pacifists, socialists, democrats and Jews. Right-wing politicians found a whole range of scapegoats to take the blame for German acceptance of the Armistice.

Worse still, these 'November criminals' had been prepared to overthrow the monarchy and establish a republic. To add insult to injury, they had accepted the 'shameful peace' of Versailles. The extreme right accepted such interpretations, distorted as they were. They not only served to remove any responsibility from Imperial Germany, but also acted as a powerful stick with which to beat the leaders of Weimar Germany.

Organisations of the extreme right

The extreme right appeared in various forms. It included a number of political parties and was also the driving force behind the activities of various paramilitary organisations.

DNVP

The DNVP (German National People's Party) was a coalition of nationalist-minded old imperial conservative parties and included such groups as the Fatherland Party and the Pan-German League. From the very start, it contained extremist and racist elements. Although it was still the party of landowners and industrialists, it had a broad appeal among some of the middle classes. It was by far the largest party in the *Reichstag* on the extreme right and was able to poll 15.1 per cent in the 1920 election.

Racist nationalism

The emergence of racist nationalism, or *völkisch* nationalism, was clearly apparent before 1914, but the effects of the war and its aftermath increased its attraction for many on the right. By the early 1920s there were probably about 70 relatively small splinter nationalist parties, which were also racist and **anti-Semitic**, for example the Nazi Party.

Bavaria became a particular haven for such groups, since the regional state government was sufficiently **reactionary** to tolerate them. One such group was the German Workers' Party, originally founded by Anton Drexler. Adolf Hitler joined the party in 1919 and within two years had become its leader. However, during the years 1919–24, regional and policy differences divided such groups and attempts to unify the nationalist right ended in failure. When, in 1923, Hitler and the Nazis attempted to organise an uprising with the Munich Beer Hall *putsch*, it ended in fiasco (see pages 47–50). It was not until the mid-1920s that Hitler began to bring the different groups together under the leadership of the NSDAP.

Freikorps

The *Freikorps* that flourished in the post-war environment attracted the more brutal and ugly elements of German militarism. As a result of the demobilisation of the armed forces there were nearly 200 **paramilitary units** around Germany by 1919.

The *Freikorps* were employed by the government in a crucial role to suppress the threats from the extreme left but became a law unto themselves. Since the *Freikorps* were anti-republican and committed to the restoration of authoritarian rule, they had no respect for the Weimar governments and were quite prepared to use acts of violence and murder to intimidate others. Indeed, after their bloody action in 'Red Bavaria' (see page 41), they became key players in the 'White Terror'.

Consul Organisation

From 1920 the Weimar governments tried to control the actions of the *Freikorps*, but a new threat emerged from the right wing in the form of political assassination. In the years 1919–22 there were 376 political murders: 22 by the left and 354 by the right. The most notorious terrorist gang was known as the 'Consul Organisation' because it was responsible for the assassination of a number of key republican politicians:

- **Matthias Erzberger**. Murdered because he was a Catholic and a member of the ZP who had signed the Armistice.
- **Walther Rathenau**, foreign minister 1921–2 (who drew up the Rapallo Treaty with the USSR). Murdered because he was Jewish and was committed to democracy.
- Karl Gareis, leader of the USPD. Murdered on 9 June 1921 because he was a committed socialist.

Extreme right uprisings

Hostility from the extreme right against Weimar democracy came to a head with two uprisings:

- the Kapp *putsch*
- the Munich Beer Hall *putsch*.

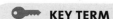

KEY TERM

Paramilitary units Informal non-legal military squads.

KEY FIGURES

Matthias Erzberger (1875–1921)

A democrat and strong Catholic member of the ZP. Proposed the peace resolution in 1917 and signed the Armistice on 11 November 1918. Finance minister in the Weimar governments of 1919–20, but forced to resign following an infamous legal case. Assassinated by paramilitaries.

Walther Rathenau (1867–1922)

Jewish businessman and politician who rose to prominence in the First World War. Pro-democrat and founder of the DDP in 1919. Served as minister of reconstruction and later foreign minister. Assassinated by the Organisation Consul.

KEY FIGURES

Wolfgang Kapp (1858–1922)

Prussian civil servant who helped to found the right-wing German Fatherland Party. Campaigned for the restoration of the monarchy, but the *putsch* was a fiasco.

Hans von Seeckt (1866–1936)

German general and monarchist who became head of army command, 1920–6. His attitude towards the republic was ambivalent, though he served it better than many other generals.

? According to Source D, why did Seeckt take no action in the Kapp *putsch*? What were the implications of his decision?

The Kapp *putsch*

The *Freikorps* played a central role in the first attempt by the extreme right wing to seize power from the constitutional government. This was because by early 1920 there was considerable unease within the ranks of the *Freikorps* at the demands to reduce the size of the German Army according to the terms of the Versailles Treaty (see page 34).

When it was proposed to disband two brigades of the army, the Ehrhardt Marine Brigade and the Baltikum that were stationed in the Berlin area, **Wolfgang Kapp** and General Lüttwitz decided to exploit the situation. They encouraged 12,000 troops to march on Berlin and seize the main buildings of the capital virtually unopposed, where they installed a new government.

Significantly, the German Army did not provide any resistance to this *putsch*. In spite of requests from Ebert and the chancellor to put down the rebellious forces, the army was not prepared to become involved with either side. Although it did not join those involved in the *putsch*, it failed to support the legitimate government. **General von Seeckt**, the senior officer in the Defence Ministry, spoke to many colleagues and his reputed declaration on the outbreak of the *putsch* on 13 March 1920:

SOURCE D

Seeckt's words of 13 March 1920, quoted in William Carr, *A History of Germany 1815–1990*, fourth edition, Hodder Arnold, 1991, p. 263.

Troops do not fire on troops. So, you perhaps intend, Herr Minister, that a battle be fought before the Brandenburger Tor between troops that have fought side by side against a common enemy? When Reichswehr fires on Reichswehr then all comradeship within the officers corps will have vanished.

The army's decision to put its own interests before its obligation to defend the government forced the latter to flee the capital and move to Stuttgart. However, the *putsch* collapsed. Before leaving Berlin, the SPD members of the government had called for a general strike, which paralysed the capital and quickly spread to the rest of the country. After four days, Kapp and his government exerted no real authority and they fled the city.

The aftermath of the Kapp *putsch*

At first sight, the collapse of the Kapp *putsch* could be viewed as a major success for the Weimar Republic. In the six days of crisis, it had retained the backing of the people of Berlin and had effectively withstood a major threat from the extreme right. However, what is significant is that the Kapp *putsch* had taken place at all. In this sense, the Kapp *putsch* highlights clearly the weakness of the Weimar Republic. The army's behaviour at the time of the *putsch* was typical of its right-wing attitudes and its lack of sympathy for the republic. During the months after the coup, the government failed to confront this problem.

The army leadership had revealed its unreliability. Yet, amazingly, at the end of that very month Seeckt was made chief of the army command (1920–6). He was appointed because he enjoyed the confidence of his fellow officers, even though his support for the republic was lukewarm. Under Seeckt's influence, the organisation of the army was remodelled and its status redefined:

- Seeckt imposed very strict military discipline and recruited new troops, increasingly at the expense of the *Freikorps*.
- Seeckt was determined to uphold the independence of the army. He believed it held a privileged position that placed it beyond direct government control. For example, he turned a blind eye to the Versailles disarmament clauses in order to increase the size of the army with more modern weapons.

Many within its ranks believed that the army served some higher purpose to the nation as a whole. It had the right to intervene as it saw fit without regard to its obligations to the Republic. All this suggests that the aftermath of the Kapp *putsch*, the Ebert–Groener Pact (see page 10) and the constitution's failure to reform the structures of army had made it a '**state within a state**'.

The judiciary also continued with the old political values that had not changed since imperial times. It enjoyed the advantage of maintaining its independence from the Weimar constitution, but it questioned the legal rights of the new republic and reached some dubious and obviously biased decisions. Those involved in the *putsch* of 1920 never felt the full rigour of the law:

- Kapp died awaiting trial.
- Lüttwitz was granted early retirement.
- Only one of the 705 prosecuted was actually found guilty and sentenced to five years' imprisonment.

The Munich Beer Hall *putsch*

Although the Munich Beer Hall *putsch* was one of the threats faced by the young republic in the year 1923, the event is also a crucial part of the rise of Hitler and the Nazis. The details of the events also relate to Chapter 4 on pages 102–4.

It should be noted that the government of Bavaria (of which Munich was the capital) was under the control of the ultra-conservative Gustav von Kahr, who blamed most of Germany's problems on the national government in Berlin. Like Hitler, he wished to destroy the republican regime, although his long-term aim was the creation of an independent Bavaria. By October 1923 General von Lossow, the army's commander in Bavaria, had fallen under Kahr's spell and had even begun to disobey orders from the defence minister from Berlin. So it was both of these ultra-conservatives who plotted with Hitler and the Nazis to 'March on Berlin' (see Table 2.3, page 48).

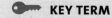 **KEY TERM**

State within a state
A situation where the authority and government of the state are threatened by a rival power base.

Table 2.3 The plotters in the Munich Beer Hall *putsch*

Name	Position	Background/attitude	Involvement
Erich von Ludendorff	Retired general	Took part in Kapp *putsch*. Opposed to democracy (see also page 3)	Collaborated with Hitler and supported the *putsch* on 8–9 November
Gustav von Kahr	Leader of the Bavarian state government	Deeply anti-democratic and sympathetic to many of the right-wing extremists. Committed to the restoration of the monarchy in an independent Bavaria	Planned with Hitler and Lossow to seize power, but became wary. Forced to co-operate with his rally on 8 November, though did not support the *putsch* on 9 November
Otto von Lossow	Commander of the Bavarian section of the German Army	Despised Weimar democracy and supported authoritarian rule. Very conservative	Planned with Hitler and Kahr to seize power, but became wary. Forced to co-operate in the rally on 8 November, though did not support the *putsch* on 9 November
Adolf Hitler	Leader of the Nazi Party	Extremist: anti-Semitic, anti-democratic and anti-communist. Backed by the Nazi SA	Planned and wholly committed to seize power. Forced the hands of Kahr and Lossow and carried on with the *putsch* on 9 November
Hans von Seeckt	General. Chief of the Army Command, 1920–6	Unsympathetic to democracy and keen to preserve the interests of the army, but suspicious of Hitler and the Nazis (see page 47)	Initially ambiguous attitude in early November. But in the crisis he used his powers to command the armed forces to resist the *putsch*

By the first week of November 1923 Kahr and Lossow, fearing failure, decided to abandon the plan. However, Hitler was not so cautious and preferred to press on rather than lose the opportunity. On 8 November, when Kahr was addressing a large audience in one of Munich's beer halls, Hitler and the Nazis took control of the meeting and declared a 'national revolution'. Under pressure, Kahr and Lossow co-operated and agreed to proceed with the uprising. However, the tables were turned when Seeckt used his powers to command the armed forces to resist the *putsch*.

When, on the next day, the Nazis attempted to take Munich they had insufficient support and the Bavarian police easily crushed the *putsch*. Fourteen Nazis were killed and an injured Hitler was arrested on a charge of treason.

The aftermath of the Munich Beer Hall *putsch*

On one level, the inglorious result of the Nazi *putsch* was encouraging for Weimar democracy. It withstood a dangerous threat in what was a difficult year. Most significantly, Seeckt and the army did not throw in their lot with the Nazis, which upset Hitler so much that he described him as a 'lackey of the Weimar Republic'. However, once again it was the dealings of the judiciary that raised so much concern:

- Hitler was sentenced to a mere five years (the minimum stipulation for treason). His imprisonment at Landsberg provided quite reasonable conditions and he was released after less than ten months.
- Ludendorff was acquitted on the grounds that although he had been present at the time of the *putsch*, he was there 'by accident'!

The judiciary in Weimar Germany

Although the judiciary enjoyed independence under the Weimar constitution, the hearts of many judges did not lie with the Weimar Republic. As was seen with the legal cases after the two *putsches*, they were biased and tended to favour the extreme right and condemn the extreme left. Indeed, during the years 1919–22:

- Out of the 354 right-wing assassins only 28 were found guilty and punished, but no-one was executed.
- Of the 22 left-wing assassins ten were sentenced to death.
- In a famous legal case in 1920, Erzberger accused the leader of the DNVP, Helfferich, of libel. But although Helfferich was condemned by the judge for his allegations and had to pay a small fine, Erzberger himself was so discredited that he had to resign. The judge's prejudiced handling of the case revealed his political sympathies.

SOURCE E

In what ways does the cartoonist in Source E try to deride the judiciary? And what concerns does he raise about the trial and the sympathies of the German judiciary for Weimar Germany?

In a 1924 cartoon about the trial of Hitler and Ludendorff, a judge says: 'High treason? Rubbish! The worst we can charge them with is breaking by-laws about entertaining in public.'

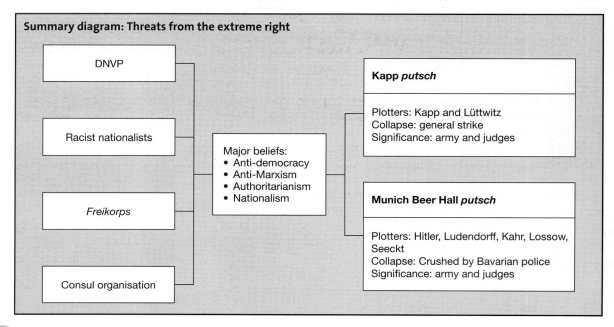

Summary diagram: Threats from the extreme right

DNVP

Racist nationalists

Freikorps

Consul organisation

Major beliefs:
• Anti-democracy
• Anti-Marxism
• Authoritarianism
• Nationalism

Kapp *putsch*

Plotters: Kapp and Lüttwitz
Collapse: general strike
Significance: army and judges

Munich Beer Hall *putsch*

Plotters: Hitler, Ludendorff, Kahr, Lossow, Seeckt
Collapse: Crushed by Bavarian police
Significance: army and judges

'A republic without republicans'?

▶ *Why did it become increasingly difficult for the new republic to function as a democracy?*

The optimism of the first election of the republic (see page 17) gave way to concerns in the election of June 1920.

The results of the 1920 election can be seen in Table 2.4 and they raise several key points:

- The combined support for the three main democratic parties declined dramatically:
  - 1919: 76.1 per cent
  - 1920: 48.0 per cent.
  (The figures do not include the DVP under the leadership of Stresemann which voted against the Weimar constitution at first, but became committed to the Republic from 1921.)
- The performance for each of the pro-democratic parties was as follows:
  - the SPD declined sharply from 37.9 to 21.7 per cent
  - the DDP declined catastrophically from 18.5 to 8.3 per cent
  - the ZP dropped slightly from 19.75 to 18.0 per cent.
- The support for the extreme left and right increased, especially the DNVP:
  - the DNVP increased from 10.3 to 15.1 per cent
  - the KPD/USPD increased from 7.6 to 20.0 per cent.

Table 2.4 Weimar *Reichstag* election results 1919–20 (see major political parties on page 16)

	Turnout	NSDAP	DNVP	DVP	ZP/BVP	DDP	SPD	USPD/KPD	Others
January 1919									
Seats	423	–	44	19	91	75	165	22	7
%	83.0	–	10.3	4.4	19.7	18.5	37.9	7.6	1.6
June 1920									
Seats	459	–	71	65	85	39	102	88	9
%	79.2	–	15.1	13.9	18.0	8.3	21.2	20.0	2.9

The Weimar Republic faced overt opposition not only from both the extremes but also from its democratic supporters who struggled with the practical problem of creating and maintaining workable government coalitions. In the four years 1919–23 Weimar had six governments, the longest of which lasted just eighteen months (see Table 2.5).

Friedrich Ebert

1871	Born in Heidelberg of humble background and trained as a saddler
1889	Became a trade union organiser and SPD member
1912	Elected as a member of the *Reichstag*
1916	Chosen as leader of the SPD
1918	Made chancellor of the provisional government when Imperial Germany collapsed
1919	Chosen as the country's first president, a position he held until his death
1925	Died at the age of 54 of a ruptured appendix

As a young apprentice Ebert became quickly involved in trade union work and his written and spoken skills were soon recognised by the SPD leadership. He quickly advanced through the party, covering a range of full-time political jobs, and in 1912 he entered the *Reichstag*. Although the First World War divided the SPD fundamentally, Ebert worked really hard to reconcile the different views in the party and in 1916 he was chosen as leader. However, it proved impossible to overcome the differences, which led a year later to the party splitting and the creation of the USPD.

When Germany collapsed in autumn 1918, Ebert wanted a democratic parliamentary government with a constitutional monarchy, but when events got out of hand the monarchy stood down and he accepted the chancellorship. It was a major success to manage to hold the first truly democratic German elections, which led to the National Assembly and the creation of the Weimar constitution. However, Ebert himself was attacked for endorsing the use of the army and the *Freikorps* to brutally suppress the more radical elements of the left.

From a humble background, Ebert was chosen to be the country's first president in February 1919, a position he held until his death. He oversaw the years of crisis and applied the emergency decrees of Article 48 with success. Yet, he became the focus of scurrilous criticism from the extreme right. He was a man of great integrity and decency, who was a patriot and served his office with distinction and correctness. His character and achievements shaped the development of Weimar.

Table 2.5 Governments of the Weimar Republic 1919–23

Period in office	Chancellor	Make-up of the coalition
1919	Philipp Scheidemann	SPD, ZP, DDP
1919–20	Gustav Bauer	SPD, ZP, DDP
1920	Hermann Müller	SPD, Centre, DDP
1920–1	Konstantin Fehrenbach	ZP, DDP, DVP
1921–2	Joseph Wirth	SPD, DDP, ZP
1922–3	Wilhelm Cuno	ZP, DDP, DVP

Conclusion

The success of the democratic parties in the *Reichstag* elections of January 1919 at first disguised some of Weimar's fundamental problems in its political structure. But opposition to the republic ranged from indifference to brutal violence and, as early as 1920, democratic support for Weimar began to switch to the extremes. This is shown by the results of the first election after the Treaty of Versailles.

The extent of the opposition from the extreme right to democracy was not always appreciated. Instead, President Ebert and the Weimar governments overestimated the threat from the extreme left and they came to rely on the forces of reaction for justice and law and order. This was partly because the conservative forces successfully exploited the image of the left as a powerful threat. So, in many respects, it was the persistence of the old attitudes in the major traditional national institutions that represented the greatest long-term threat to the republic. The violent forces of counter-revolution, as shown by the *putsches* of Kapp and Hitler, were too weak and disorganised to seize power in the early years. But the danger of the extreme right was just below the surface; it was the real growing threat to Weimar democracy.

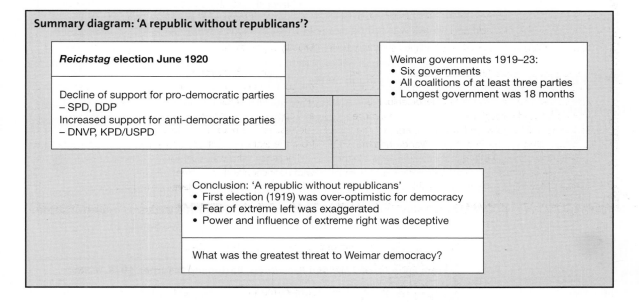

Summary diagram: 'A republic without republicans'?

Reichstag election June 1920

Decline of support for pro-democratic parties – SPD, DDP
Increased support for anti-democratic parties – DNVP, KPD/USPD

Weimar governments 1919–23:
• Six governments
• All coalitions of at least three parties
• Longest government was 18 months

Conclusion: 'A republic without republicans'
• First election (1919) was over-optimistic for democracy
• Fear of extreme left was exaggerated
• Power and influence of extreme right was deceptive

What was the greatest threat to Weimar democracy?

5 The economic crisis

▶ *How did the First World War weaken the German economy?*

▶ *Why did Germany suffer hyperinflation?*

In the twenty years before the First World War the German economy grew immensely. By 1914 it had become arguably the most powerful economy on the Continent and it was in a position to compete with Britain's supremacy. These strengths were based on the following:

• extensive natural resources, for example, coal and iron ore
• an advanced and well-developed industrial base, for example, engineering, chemicals, electrical equipment

- a well-educated population, with special technical skills
- an advanced banking system.

However, the result of four years of total war seriously dislocated the German economy. So, although the economy still had many natural strengths and great potential, by 1919 it faced fundamental economic problems. The most notable of these were the following:

- The loss of resources from such territories as the Saar, Alsace-Lorraine and Silesia which, for example, resulted in a sixteen per cent decline in coal production, thirteen per cent decline in arable agricultural land and 48 per cent loss of iron ore (see page 32).
- The cost of paying reparations (set at £6600 million in 1921).
- The growing increase in prices. Between 1914 and 1918 the real value of the mark was falling against other currencies, while the prices of basic goods increased nearly four-fold.
- The increase in national debt to 144,000 million marks by 1919 compared with 5000 million marks in 1914.

Significantly, Germany had always depended on its ability to export to achieve economic growth. However, between 1914 and 1918 world trade had collapsed and even after 1919 it remained very sluggish.

The causes of the Great Inflation

Germany's growing economic problems came to a head in 1923 when prices soared and money values spiralled down. This is referred to as **hyperinflation**. And it led to 1923 becoming an extraordinary year (see Source F).

SOURCE F

From Egon Larsen, *Weimar Eyewitness*, Bachmann & Turner, 1976, p. 58.

You went into a cafe and ordered a cup of coffee at the prices shown on the blackboard over the service hatch: an hour later, when you asked for the bill, it had gone up by a half or even doubled … Bartering became more and more widespread.

Professional people including lawyers accepted food in preference to cash fees. A haircut cost a couple of eggs, and craftsmen such as watchmakers displayed in their shop windows: 'Repairs carried out in exchange for food'. Once I was asked at the box-office of our local fleapit cinema if I could bring some coal as the price of two seats … A student I knew had sold his gallery ticket at the State Opera for one dollar to an American; he could live on that money for a whole week … In the summer of that inflation year my grandmother found herself unable to cope. So she asked one of her sons to sell her house. He did so for I don't know how many millions of marks. The old woman decided to keep the money under her mattress and buy food with it as the need arose – with the result that nothing was left except a pile of worthless paper when she died a few months later.

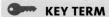

KEY TERM

Hyperinflation In Germany in 1923 this meant that prices spiralled out of control because the government increased the amount of money being printed. As a result, it displaced the whole economy.

What picture emerges from these anecdotes of 1923 in Source F? Of what value is this source to a historian?

Although prices had been rising since the early months of the war, many Germans came to assume that this was a result of the Treaty of Versailles and particularly the reparations. Others blamed the situation on the financial greed and corruption of the Jews. However, with hindsight, it is clear that the fundamental cause of the inflation was the huge increase in the amount of paper money in circulation, as a result of the government's printing more and more notes to pay off the interest on its massive debts. The causes of the Great Inflation can be divided into three phases:

- The long term: the military demands of the First World War (1914–18) led to an enormous increase in financial costs.
- The medium term: the costs of introducing social reforms and welfare and the pressure to satisfy the demands for reparation payments from 1921.
- The short term: the French occupation of the Ruhr in 1923 resulted in financial and political crisis and the government of Wilhelm Cuno encouraged a policy of **passive resistance**.

Long term

Not surprisingly, Germany had made no financial provision for a long drawn-out war. However, despite the increasing cost of the war, the Kaiser's government had decided, for political reasons, against increases in taxation. Instead, it had borrowed massive sums by selling **war bonds** to the public. When this proved insufficient from 1916, it simply allowed the national debt to grow bigger and bigger.

The result of Imperial Germany's financial policies was that by the end of 1918 only sixteen per cent of war expenditure had been raised from taxation – 84 per cent had been borrowed. Victory would doubtless have allowed Imperial Germany to settle its debts by claiming reparations from the Allies, but defeat meant the reverse.

Another factor was that although the war years had seen almost full employment, the economy had concentrated on the supply of military weapons. Since production was necessarily military based, it did not satisfy the growing requirements of the civilian consumers. Consequently, the high demand for, and the shortage of, consumer goods began to push prices up.

The Weimar Republic had to cope with the massive costs of war. By 1919 Germany's finances were described by Volker Berghahn as 'an unholy mess'.

Medium term

The government of the Weimar Republic (like any government with a large deficit) could control inflation only by narrowing the gap between the government's income and expenditure through:

- increasing taxation in order to raise its income
- cutting government spending to reduce its expenditure.

KEY TERMS

Passive resistance Refusal to work with occupying forces.

War bonds To pay for the war, Imperial Germany encouraged people to invest in government funds in the belief they were helping to finance the war and their savings would be secure.

However, in view of Germany's domestic situation neither of these options was particularly attractive, as both would alienate the people and cause political and social difficulties, such as increased unemployment and industrial decline.

From 1919 the Weimar government guided by Matthias Erzberger, the finance minister, extensively increased taxation on profits, wealth and income. However, it decided not to go so far as aiming to **balance the budget**. It decided to adopt a policy of **deficit financing** in the belief that it would:

- give the people more money to spend and so increase the demand for goods and thereby create work
- overcome the problems of demobilising millions of returning troops – a booming economy would ensure there were plenty of jobs for the returning soldiers and sailors
- cover the cost of public spending on an extensive welfare state, for example, health insurance, housing and benefits for the disabled and orphans (see pages 72–3).

Unfortunately, an essential part of this policy was to allow inflation to continue.

The reparations issue should be seen as only a contributory factor to the inflation. It was certainly not the primary cause. Nevertheless, the sum drawn up by the Reparations Commission added to the economic burden facing the Weimar government because the reparation payments had to be in **hard currency**, like dollars and gold (not inflated German marks). In order to pay their reparations, the Weimar governments proceeded to print larger quantities of marks and sell them to obtain the stronger currencies of other countries. This was not a solution. It was merely a short-term measure that had serious consequences. The value of the mark went into sharp decline and inflation climbed even higher (see Table 2.6).

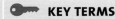

KEY TERMS

Balanced budget
A financial programme in which a government does not spend more than it raises in revenue.

Deficit financing
The financial policy of a government to spend more than it receives as revenue, in order to stimulate the economy. In this way, it gives the people more money to spend and so, in theory, increases the demand for goods and thereby creates work.

Hard currency A currency that the market considers to be strong because its value does not depreciate. In the 1920s the hardest currency was the US dollar.

Table 2.6 The Great Inflation: exchange rate and wholesale prices

Date	Exchange rate of German marks against the US dollar	Wholesale price index. The index is created from a scale of prices starting with 1 for 1914
1914 July	4.2	1
1919 January	8.9	2
1920 January	14.0	4
1921 January	64.9	14
1922 January	191.8	37
1923 January	17,792	2,785
1923 July	353,412	74,787
1923 September	98,860,000	23,949,000
1923 November	200,000,000,000	750,000,000,000

Short term

Germany had already been allowed to postpone several instalments of its reparations payments in early 1922, but an attempt to resolve the crisis on an international level by calling the Genoa Economic Conference was ill fated. When, in July 1922, the German government made another request for a 'holiday' from making reparations payments, the final stage of the country's inflationary crisis set in.

The French government, at this time led by Raymond Poincaré, suspected German intentions and was determined to secure what was seen as France's rightful claims. Therefore, when in December 1922 the Reparations Commission declared Germany to be in default, Poincaré ordered French and Belgian troops to occupy the industrial Ruhr, to make Germany pay in kind for what it had not paid in capital. In the next few months the inflationary spiral ran out of control.

The government, led by Wilhelm Cuno, embarked on a policy of 'passive resistance' and in a way the invasion did help to unite the German people. It urged the workers to go on strike and refuse to co-operate with the French authorities, although it also promised to carry on paying their wages. At the same time, the government was unable to collect taxes from the Ruhr area and the French prevented the delivery of coal to the rest of Germany, thus forcing the necessary stocks of fuel to be imported.

In this situation, the government's finances collapsed and the mark fell to worthless levels. By autumn 1923 it cost more to print a bank note than the note was worth and the *Reichsbank* was forced to use newspaper presses to produce sufficient money. The German currency ceased to have any real value and the German people had to resort to barter (see Table 2.7).

Table 2.7 Prices in the Great Inflation (in German marks)

Items for sale	1913	Summer 1923	November 1923
1 kg of bread	0.29	1,200	428,000,000,000
1 kg of butter	2.70	26,000	6,000,000,000,000
1 kg of beef	1.75	18,800	5,600,000,000,000
1 pair of shoes	12.00	1,000,000	32,000,000,000,000

Conclusion

The fundamental cause of the Great Inflation is to be found in the mismanagement of Germany's finances from 1914 onwards. Certainly, the inflationary spiral did not increase at an even rate and there were short periods, as in the spring of 1920 and the winter of 1920–1, when it did actually slacken. However, at no time was there willingness by the various German governments to bring spending and borrowing back within reasonable limits.

Until the end of 1918 the cost of waging war was the excuse, but in the immediate post-war period the high levels of debt were allowed to continue. It has been argued by some that the inflation remained quite modest in the years 1914–22 and perhaps acceptable in view of all the various difficulties facing the new government. However, the payment of reparations from 1921 simply added to an already desperate situation and the government found it more convenient to print money than to tackle the basic problems facing the economy.

By the end of 1922 hyperinflation had set in. Cuno's government made no effort to deal with the situation. Indeed, it could be said that Cuno deliberately deepened the economic crisis and played on the nationalist fervour brought about by the popular decision to encourage 'passive resistance'. It was only in August 1923 when the German economy was on the verge of complete collapse that a new coalition government was formed under Gustav Stresemann. He found the will to introduce an economic policy which was aimed at controlling the amount of money in circulation.

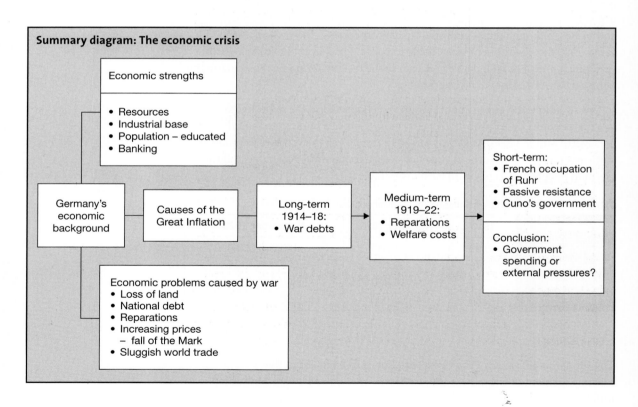

Summary diagram: The economic crisis

Economic strengths
- Resources
- Industrial base
- Population – educated
- Banking

Germany's economic background

Causes of the Great Inflation

Long-term 1914–18:
- War debts

Medium-term 1919–22:
- Reparations
- Welfare costs

Short-term:
- French occupation of Ruhr
- Passive resistance
- Cuno's government

Conclusion:
- Government spending or external pressures?

Economic problems caused by war
- Loss of land
- National debt
- Reparations
- Increasing prices – fall of the Mark
- Sluggish world trade

6 The consequences of the Great Inflation

▶ *Why did some Germans lose and some win?*

▶ *How disastrous was the inflation?*

It has been claimed that the worst consequence of the inflation was the damage done to the German middle class. Stresemann himself said as much in 1927. Later on in the 1930s it was generally assumed that the reason a large proportion of the middle class voted for the Nazis was because of their economic sufferings in 1923. In the light of recent historical research, such assumptions have come to be questioned and a much more complex interpretation has emerged about the impact of the inflation on the whole of society.

The key to understanding who gained and who lost during the period of the hyperinflation lies in considering each individual's savings and their amount of debt. However, it was not always clearly linked to class differences. So what did this mean in practice?

Winners and losers

The real winners were those sections of the community who were able to pay off their debts, mortgages and loans with inflated and worthless money. This obviously worked to the advantage of such groups as businessmen and homeowners, which included members of the middle class. Those who recognised the situation for what it was exploited it by making massive gains from buying up property from those financially desperate. Some businessmen profited from the situation by borrowing cheaply and investing in new industrial enterprises. Among these, one of the most notorious examples was Hugo Stinnes who, by the end of 1923, controlled twenty per cent of German industry.

At the other extreme were those who depended on their savings. Any German who had money invested in bank accounts with interest rates found their real value had eroded. Most famously, millions who had bought and invested in war bonds now could not get their money back. The bonds were worth nothing. Those living on fixed incomes, such as pensioners, found themselves in a similar plight. Their savings quickly lost value, since any increase was wiped out by inflation (see Table 2.8, page 60).

Table 2.8 Financial winners and losers

Financial winners and losers	Explanation of gains or losses
Mortgage holders	Borrowed money was easily paid off in valueless money
Savers	Money invested was eroded
Exporter	Sales to foreign countries were attractive because of the rate of exchange
Those on fixed incomes	Income declined in real terms dramatically
Recipients of welfare	Depended on charity or state. Payments fell behind the inflation rate
Long-term renters/landlords	Income was fixed in the long term and so it declined in real terms
The German state	Large parts of the government debt were paid off in valueless money (but not reparations)

SOURCE G

? How does the photo in Source G show the effects of the Great Inflation?

Children playing with blocks of worthless banknotes in 1923.

The human consequences

The material impact of the hyperinflation has recently been the subject of considerable historical research in Germany and, as a result, our understanding of this period has been greatly increased and many previous conclusions have been revised. However, it should be remembered that the following discussion of the effects of the hyperinflation on whole classes deals with broad categories, for example, region and age, rather than individual examples. Two people from the same social class could be affected in very different ways depending on their individual circumstances.

Peasants

In the countryside the peasants coped reasonably well as food remained in demand. They depended less on money for the provision of the necessities of life because they were more self-sufficient.

Mittelstand

The ***Mittelstand***, including shopkeepers and craftsmen, also seem to have done reasonably good business, especially if they were prepared to exploit the demands of the market.

Industrial workers

Workers' **real wages** and standard of living improved until 1922. It was in the chaos of 1923 that, when the trade unions were unable to negotiate wage settlements for their members, wages could not keep pace with the rate of inflation and a very real decline took place. However, as they had fewer savings, they lost proportionally less than those living on saved income. Unemployment did go up to 4.1 per cent in 1923, but it was still at a relatively low level.

Civil servants

The fate of public employees is probably the most difficult to analyse. Their income fell sharply in the years 1914–20, but they made real gains in 1921–2. They suffered again in the chaos of 1923 because they depended on fixed salaries, which fell in value before the end of each month. They tended to gain – if they were buying a property on a mortgage – but many had been attracted to buying war bonds and so lost out.

Retired people

Elderly people generally suffered badly because they depended on fixed pensions and savings.

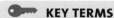 **KEY TERMS**

Mittelstand Translated as 'the middle class', but in Germany it represents the lower middle classes: shopkeepers, craft workers and clerks.

Real wages The actual purchasing power of income when set against prices, taking into account inflation/ deflation and also the effect of deductions.

Business people

Generally, they did well because they bought up property with worthless money and they paid off mortgages. They also benefited if they made sales to foreign countries, as the rate of exchange was very attractive.

Other social effects

By merely listing the financial statistics of the Great Inflation, there is a danger of overlooking the very real human dimension. As early as February 1923, the health minister announced:

SOURCE H

Extract from F. Bumm speaking to the *Reichstag*, February 1923, quoted in J.W. Hiden, *The Weimar Republic*, Longman, 1974, p. 87.

… we do have a preliminary mortality rate for towns with 100,000 or more inhabitants. After having fallen in 1920–1, it has climbed again for the year 1921–2, rising from 12.6 to 13.4 per thousand inhabitants … thus, oedema [an unpleasant medical condition which occurs when water accumulates in parts of the body] is reappearing, this so-called war dropsy, which is a consequence of a bad and overly watery diet. There are increases in stomach disorders and food poisoning, which are the result of eating spoiled foods. There are complaints of the appearance of scurvy, which is a consequence of an unbalanced and improper diet. From various parts of the Reich, reports are coming in about an increase in suicides … More and more often one finds 'old age' and 'weakness' listed in the official records as the cause of death; these are equivalent to death through hunger.

> **?** According to the health minister in Source H, what were the health and social consequences of the economic crisis?

Even more interesting than the health minister's description about Germany's declining health were the possible effects on behaviour, as people began to resort to desperate measures:

- a decline in law and order and an increase in crime
- a decline in 'morality', for example, more prostitution
- a growth in suicides
- an increase in prejudice and a tendency to find scapegoats, for example, Jewish people.

It has often been suggested that such social problems contributed to people's lack of faith in the republican system. The connection is difficult to prove, as it is not easy to assess the importance of morality and religious codes in past societies. However, it would be foolish to dismiss out of hand their effects on German society and its traditional set of values. At the very least, the loss of some old values led to increased tensions. Even more significantly, when another crisis developed at the end of the decade, the people's confidence in the ability of Weimar to maintain social stability was eventually lost. In that sense, the inflation of 1923 was not the reason for the Weimar Republic's decline, but it caused psychological damage that continued to affect the republic in future years.

Conclusion

Traditionally, the Great Inflation has been portrayed as a catastrophe with damaging consequences that paved the way for the collapse of the Weimar Republic and the rise of Nazism. However, a number of economic historians from the 1980s have perceived the issue differently.

The historian C.-L. Holtfrerich, writing in the 1980s, maintains that in the years up to the end of 1922 Weimar's economic policy amounted to a 'rational strategy ... in the national interest'. His interpretation is that by not reducing the budget deficits, the Weimar Republic was able to maintain economic growth and increase production. He argues that the German economy compared favourably with other European economies that also went into recession in 1920–1:

- Low unemployment. Whereas Britain had an unemployment rate of seventeen per cent in 1921, Germany had nearly full employment with only 1.8 per cent unemployed.
- Rising wage levels. The real wages of industrial workers increased between 1918 and 1922.
- Growing foreign investment. Foreigners' capital, particularly from the USA, provided an important stimulus to economic activity.
- Industrial production. This nearly doubled from 1919 to 1922 (albeit from a low base because of the war).

Holtfrerich does not accept that the policy was a disaster. In fact, he sees it as the only way that could have ensured the survival of the Weimar Republic. He argues that, in the early years of 1921–2, any policy that required cutting back spending would have resulted in the most terrible economic and social consequences, and perhaps even the collapse of the new democracy. In this sense, the inflation up to 1923 was actually beneficial.

This interpretation remains controversial and many have found it difficult to accept. Holtfrerich has been criticised for drawing an artificial line at 1922 – as if the years up to 1922 were those of modest and 'good' inflation, whereas the year 1923 marked the start of hyperinflation with the problems arising from that date. This seems a rather doubtful way of looking at the overall development of the Great Inflation, bearing in mind the long-term build-up and the nature of its causes. It also tends to separate the inflation from the drastic measures that were eventually required to solve it. Finally, an assessment of the Great Inflation must consider other important factors, such as the social and psychological. There is always a danger for economic historians to rely largely on a study of economic and financial data.

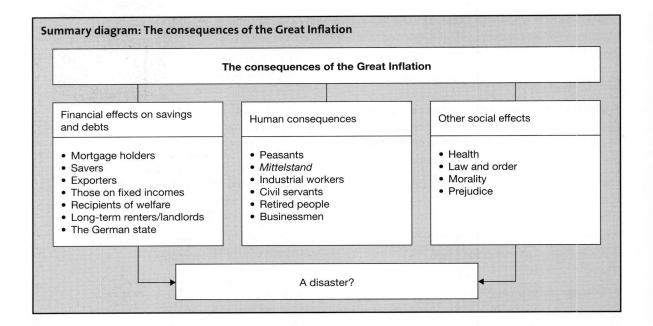

Summary diagram: The consequences of the Great Inflation

The consequences of the Great Inflation

Financial effects on savings and debts	Human consequences	Other social effects
• Mortgage holders • Savers • Exporters • Those on fixed incomes • Recipients of welfare • Long-term renters/landlords • The German state	• Peasants • *Mittelstand* • Industrial workers • Civil servants • Retired people • Businessmen	• Health • Law and order • Morality • Prejudice

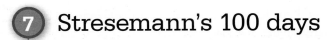

A disaster?

7 Stresemann's 100 days

▶ *How did the Weimar Republic survive the crisis of 1923?*

In the summer of 1923 the problems facing the Weimar Republic came to a head and it seemed close to collapse:

- The German currency had collapsed and hyperinflation had set in.
- French and Belgian troops were occupying the Ruhr.
- The German government had no clear policy on the occupation, except for 'passive resistance'.
- There were various left-wing political disturbances across the country: in Saxony the creation of an SPD/KPD regional state government resulted in an attempted Communist uprising (page 42).
- The ultra-conservative state government in Bavaria was defying the national government: this finally resulted in the Munich Beer Hall *putsch* (see pages 48–50).

Yet, only a few months later, a semblance of calm and normality returned. The Weimar Republic's remarkable survival illustrates the telling comment of the historian D. Peukert that even 1923 shows 'there are no entirely hopeless situations in history'.

Gustav Stresemann

1878	Born in Berlin, the son of a publican and brewer
1914–18	Nationalist and supporter of Ludendorff and Hindenburg
1919	Formed the DVP and became its leader 1919–29
1921	Despite opposing Weimar democracy at first, he and the DVP decided to support it
1923	'Stresemann's 100 days' as chancellor of Germany
1923–9	Foreign minister in all governments
1926	Awarded the Nobel Peace Prize
1929	Died of a stroke at the age of 51

After graduating with an economics degree from Berlin University and having run a successful business career, Stresemann was elected, at 29, the youngest member of the *Reichstag*. He was a committed monarchist and nationalist who strongly supported the expansionist policies of Imperial Germany.

Stresemann was appalled by Germany's defeat and the Treaty of Versailles and, in his heart, he remained a monarchist who hoped to create a constitutional monarchy. In 1919 he formed the DVP and opposed the Weimar Republic. However, by 1921 he came to recognise the political reality and finally committed himself and his party to the republic.

In the 1923 crisis Stresemann was made chancellor, and it is generally recognised by historians that it marked the climax of his career. All the problems were confronted: the occupation of the Ruhr, the hyperinflation and the opposition from left- and right-wing extremists. Although his term in office lasted for just three months (which became known as 'Stresemann's 100 days'), it laid the basis for the recovery of 1924–9.

Stresemann was foreign minister in all the Weimar governments from 1923 to 1929; in effect, he was the architect of Weimar foreign policy. He showed a strength of character and a realism which allowed him to negotiate with the Allies and to improve Germany's international position. Nevertheless, he failed to generate real domestic support for Weimar. Indeed, his long-term reputation remains arguable, as he failed to revise the Versailles Treaty fundamentally. It is also questionable whether he could have saved the Weimar Republic from Nazism.

Stresemann's achievements

It is important to recognise that, during the summer of 1923, things had just been allowed to slide under Chancellor Cuno. Nevertheless, the appointment of Gustav Stresemann as chancellor in August 1923 resulted in the emergence of a politician who was actually prepared to take difficult political decisions. Stresemann led a broad coalition of DVP, DDP, ZP and SPD and aimed to resolve Germany's economic plight and also tackle the problem of its weakness internationally.

Within a few weeks Stresemann introduced a series of crucial initiatives:

- First, in September, he called off the 'passive resistance' in the Ruhr and promised to resume the payment of reparations. He needed to conciliate the French in order to evoke some international sympathy for Germany's economic position.
- Under the guidance of Finance Minister Hans Luther the government's expenditure was sharply cut in order to reduce the deficit. Over 700,000 public employees were sacked.

- The leading financial expert Hjalmar Schacht was appointed to oversee the introduction of a new German currency. In December 1923 the trillions of old German marks were replaced and a new stable currency, the *Rentenmark,* was established.
- Stresemann evoked some sympathy from the Allies for Germany by the 'miracle of the *Rentenmark*' and his conciliatory policy. He therefore asked the Allies to hold an international conference to consider Germany's economic plight and, as a result, the Dawes Committee was established. Its report, the Dawes Plan, was published in April 1924. It did not reduce the overall reparations bill, but for the first five years it fixed the payments in accordance with Germany's ability to pay (see pages 84–5).
- The extremists of the left and the right were defeated.

The survival of Weimar

Although Stresemann's resolute action in tackling the problems might help to explain why the years of crisis came to an end, on its own it does not help us to understand why the Weimar Republic was able to come through. The republic's survival in 1923 was in marked contrast to its collapse ten years later when challenged by the Nazis.

Why, then, did the republic not collapse during the crisis-ridden months before Stresemann's emergence on the political scene? The following factors provide clues to an answer:

- Popular anger was directed more towards the French and the Allies than towards the Weimar Republic itself.
- Despite the effects of inflation, workers did not suffer to the same extent as they did during the mass unemployment of the 1930s.
- Some business people did very well out of the inflation, which made them tolerant of the republic.

If these suggestions about public attitudes towards the republic are correct, then it seems that, although there was distress and disillusionment in 1923, hostility to the Weimar Republic had not yet reached unbearable levels – as it was to do ten years later.

Moreover, in 1923 there was no obvious political alternative to Weimar. The extreme left had not really recovered from its divisions and suppression in the years 1918–21 and in its isolated position it did not enjoy enough support to overthrow Weimar. The extreme right, too, was not yet strong enough. It was similarly divided and had no clear plans. The failure of the Kapp *putsch* served as a clear warning of the dangers of taking hasty action and was possibly the reason why the army made no move in 1923.

Summary diagram: Stresemann's 100 days

Germany's problems at the time of Stresemann's appointment in August 1923:	Stresemann's achievements:
• Hyperinflation • Franco-Belgian occupation of Ruhr • 'Passive resistance' effects • Communist uprising in Saxony • Extreme right opposition in Bavaria	• Passive resistance called off • Government spending reduced • Asked for Schacht to introduce new currency • Conciliatory policy with Allies • Extremists defeated

Weimar's survival in 1923. Can it be explained?

Chapter summary

The German Revolution had created a parliamentary democracy, but the republic faced many problems and it was threatened from the extreme left and the extreme right. Both sides could not tolerate the democracy and were quite prepared to resort to various forms of political violence. As for the Treaty of Versailles, the terms were not actually so damning, but their severity as perceived in the German mind added fuel to Weimar's critics, especially from the influence of powerful conservative institutions such as the army and the judiciary.

On top of that, hyperinflation brought things to a head in 1923. Certainly, a minority was able to pay off their debts with borrowed money in useless notes, whereas those with savings and set incomes were hit very badly – with profound human consequences.

Yet, quite surprisingly, Weimar did survive 1923 – in contrast to the 1930s. In his 100 days Stresemann showed resolution with his political and economic initiatives, while the political extremists revealed their limitations. The question was whether after the trauma of those years the new republic really could stabilise and develop into a mature democracy.

Refresher questions

Use these questions to remind yourself of the key material covered in this chapter.

1 In what ways did the Allies differ over war aims?

2 Why did the Germans view the Treaty of Versailles as unfair?

3 To what extent was the Treaty of Versailles mainly motivated by anti-German feeling?

4 Did the Treaty of Versailles fundamentally weaken Weimar Germany?

5 Was the failure of the extreme left caused by its own weaknesses?

6 What did the extreme right stand for and how did it manifest itself?

7 What was the significance of the Kapp *putsch* and the Munich Beer Hall *putsch* and why did they both fail?

8 Why did Weimar democracy struggle to form workable governments?

9 In what ways was the German economy weakened by the First World War?

10 What were the long-, medium- and short-term causes of the inflation?

11 Who were the winners and the losers in the inflation?

12 In what ways did the Great Inflation affect people's lives?

13 How could the inflation perhaps be viewed as not so disastrous?

14 How did Stresemann's 100 days resolve the year of crisis?

15 How did Weimar manage to survive the crisis of 1923, unlike 1933?

 Question practice

ESSAY QUESTIONS

1 'The main problem faced by Weimar Germany in the years 1919–23 was reparations payments.' Explain why you agree or disagree with this view.

2 To what extent would you agree that Weimar's early problems were fundamentally economic?

3 'The main threat to the Weimar Republic in the period 1919–23 was the extreme right.' How far do you agree with this judgement?

Question practice

SOURCE ANALYSIS QUESTIONS

1 With reference to Sources 2 and 3, and your understanding of the historical context, which of these two sources is more valuable in explaining why the Kapp *putsch* failed?

2 With reference to Sources 1, 2 and 3, and your understanding of the historical context, assess the value of these sources to a historian studying the Kapp *putsch* and its failure.

SOURCE 1

From the proclamation of Wolfgang Kapp, published on 13 March 1920, quoted in John Laver, *Imperial and Weimar Germany*, Hodder & Stoughton, 1992, p. 43.

The Reich and the nation are in grave danger. With terrible speed we are approaching the complete collapse of the State and of law and order. The people are only dimly aware of the approaching disaster. Prices are rising unchecked. Hardship is growing. Starvation threatens. Corruption, usury, nepotism and crime are cheekily raising their heads. The government, lacking in authority, impotent and in league with corruption is incapable of overcoming the danger …

What are the tasks facing the new government? …

The government will ruthlessly suppress strikes and sabotage. Everyone should go peacefully about his work. Everyone willing to work is assured of our firm protection: striking is treason to the nation, the Fatherland and the future. The government will … not be a one-sided capitalist one. It will rather save German workers from the hard fate of slavery to international big business and hopes by such measures to put an end to the hostility of the working classes to the State … We shall govern not according to theories but according to the practical needs of the State and the nation as a whole. In the best German tradition the State must stand above the conflict of classes and parties. It is the objective arbiter in the present conflict between capital and labour. We reject the granting of class-advantage to the Right or the Left. We recognise only German citizens. Everyone must do his duty! The first duty of every man is to work. Germany must be a moral working community!

SOURCE 2

Arnold Brecht was a lawyer and civil servant in the Weimar Republic. He recalls the Kapp *putsch* in his autobiography. A. Brecht, *The Political Education of Arnold Brecht: An Autobiography*, Princeton University Press, 1970, pp. 180–3.

After a few days Kapp had to admit defeat. The quick collapse of his putsch was due in equal measure to the shallowness of the whole venture, the resistance of the working classes, and the loyalty of most state secretaries in the federal and state ministries. These officials were not faced with the dilemma, as they were twelve years later under Papen's and Hitler's regimes, that the constitutional President himself had appointed the new Chancellor. On the contrary, the Kapp putsch was directed against the constitutional President …

There were three main problems to be solved: first, finding out which military units in Germany had remained loyal, which had gone over to Kapp, and which were wavering, and how they could be kept on our side; second, deciding whether we ought to negotiate with Kapp … and third, bringing the struggles which had flared up, especially on the Ruhr, between Communists and the army, to an end. All ministers agreed that there should be no negotiations with Kapp.

SOURCE 3

Brigadier Morgan, working in the Inter-Allied Reparations Commission 1920–4, recalls the Kapp *putsch*, quoted in J.H. Morgan, *Assize of Arms*, Oxford University Press, 1945, pp. 67–8.

At seven o'clock on the Sunday morning I returned … to my quarters at the [Hotel] Adlon. I went into the bathroom to wash my hands and turned on the tap. There was a gurgling sound … but no water appeared … The next moment the electric light went out … I was vaguely conscious of something peculiar about my room. Normally, a faint light, like early dawn, suffused it even in the watches of the night … A wall of blackness seemed to shut in the hotel like a fog.

I recall the confident prophecy of my chauffeur that the workers would have something to say about the Kappists. The trade unions had now struck and struck heavily. They had proclaimed a general strike with the gloves off. No 'essential services' had been exempted. Water, light, power, communications, the very arteries of life completely cut off.

CHAPTER 3

Weimar's golden age

It is generally held that after the turmoil of the early 1920s, the years 1924–9 were a time of recovery and stability in German history. Indeed, it is quite common to refer to the period as the 'golden twenties'. The purpose of this chapter is to consider the accuracy of this picture by examining the following sections:

★ The German economic recovery

★ Political stability

★ Gustav Stresemann's foreign policy

★ Culture

★ Weimar 1924–9: an overview

Key dates

1922		Treaty of Rapallo	1926		Germany joined the League of Nations
1923–9		Stresemann as foreign minister			
1924	April	Dawes Plan for reparations	1928	May	Müller's Grand Coalition
1925	Feb. 28	Death of Ebert		Aug.	Kellogg–Briand Pact
	April	Hindenburg elected president	1929	June	Proposals of the Young Plan for reparations
	Oct.	Locarno Conference		Oct.	Death of Stresemann

 ## The German economic recovery

▶ *How much did the Weimar economy really recover in the 'golden twenties'?*

It is often claimed that after the hyperinflation, the introduction of the new currency – the *Rentenmark* – and the measures brought about by the Dawes Plan ushered in five years of economic growth and affluence. Certainly, the period stands out between the economic chaos of 1922–3 and the **Great Depression** of 1929–33. So, for many Germans looking back from the end of the 1920s, it seemed as if Germany had made a remarkable recovery.

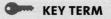 **KEY TERM**

Great Depression The severe economic crisis of 1929–33 that started in the USA with the Wall Street Crash. Marked by mass unemployment, falling prices and a lack of spending.

The strengths of the German economy

In spite of the loss of resources as a result of the Treaty of Versailles, heavy industry was able to recover reasonably quickly and, by 1928, production levels had reached those of 1913. This was the result of the use of more efficient methods of production, particularly in coal-mining and steel manufacture, and also because of increased investment. Foreign bankers were particularly attracted by Germany's high interest rates. And even the large US corporations, such as Ford and General Motors, invested massively in factories with more efficient methods of mass production.

At the same time, German industry had the advantage of being able to lower costs because of the growing number of **cartels**, which had better purchasing power than smaller industries. For example, IG Farben, the chemicals giant, became the largest manufacturing enterprise in Europe, while Vereinigte Stahlwerke combined the coal, iron and steel interests of Germany's great industrial companies and grew to control nearly half of all production.

Between 1925 and 1929 German exports rose by 40 per cent. Such economic progress brought social benefits as well. Hourly wage rates rose every year from 1924 to 1930 and by as much as five to ten per cent in 1927 and 1928.

Social welfare

Although the state of Imperial Germany had introduced social care in the 1880s, the Weimar Republic made striking improvements in the provision of welfare. The Weimar constitution incorporated basic social rights and aimed to address social provision through the creation of a welfare state. Significantly, in the hope of creating a more equal society, Matthias Erzberger, as finance minister, had aimed clearly to offset the costs by implementing a series of **progressive taxes** including increasing taxes on capital and an increase in the highest income tax from four per cent to 60 per cent.

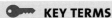

KEY TERMS

Cartels An arrangement between businesses to control markets by exercising a monopoly.

Progressive tax A tax system in which those who earn higher incomes pay a higher percentage of their income than those with lower incomes.

Social legislation

Working conditions. As a result of the Stinnes–Legien Agreement (see page 11), various laws were introduced restricting the maximum working week to 48 hours and introducing a state scheme for compulsory arbitration in strikes.

War victims. Benefits and pensions for widows and the wounded were included from 1920 in the welfare scheme.

Youth. National Youth Welfare Law (1922). Programmes for the young from poor backgrounds were established, as well as provision for youth clubs and sports facilities.

Health and pensions. The new national insurance code extended welfare in various laws (1923–5):

- more standardised pensions
- an improved health insurance scheme provided by doctors and the insurance funds
- accident insurance for occupational diseases, for example in the chemical industry and the mines.

Unemployment. The Unemployment Insurance Law of 1927 created a system covering 17 million workers which offered benefit at 75 per cent of pay for three-quarters of a year (the largest scheme in the world).

In addition, large state subsidies were provided for the construction of local amenities such as education, hospitals, parks, schools, sports facilities and, especially, council housing. Over 2 million houses were built between 1924 and 1931 – and a further 200,000 renovated – so that the figure of homelessness was reduced by 60 per cent in the decade. All these developments, alongside the more obvious signs of wealth, for example the increase in the number of cars, supported the view that the Weimar Republic's economy was enjoying boom conditions. However, revenue did not match the expenditure, meaning that the social costs had serious financial implications for the economy of the Weimar Republic (see page 74).

The weaknesses in the German economy

From the statistics for 1924–9 it is easy to get an impression that there was a 'golden age'. However, the actual rate of German recovery was less clear:

- The economic growth was uneven, and in 1926 production actually declined. In overseas trade, the value of imports always exceeded that of exports.
- Unemployment never fell below 1.3 million in this period. And even before the effects of the USA's financial crisis began to be felt, the number of unemployed workers averaged 1.9 million in 1929.
- In agriculture, grain production was still only three-quarters of its 1913 figure and farmers, many of whom were in debt, faced falling incomes. By the late 1920s, income per head in agriculture was 44 per cent below the national average.

Fundamental economic problems

The economic indicators listed above suggest that the German economy had fundamental problems in this period and it is therefore important to appreciate the broader view by looking at the following points:

- World economic conditions did not favour Germany. Traditionally, Germany had relied on its ability to export to achieve economic growth, but world trade did not return to pre-war levels. German exports were hindered by protective **tariffs** in many parts of the world. They were additionally handicapped by the loss of valuable resources in territories such as Alsace-Lorraine and Silesia (see pages 32–3) as a result of the Versailles Treaty.
- German agriculture. The German peasantry made up one-third of the national population and found itself in difficulties because of worldwide pressures. The fall in world prices from the mid-1920s placed a great strain on farmers, who were simply failing to make a profit. Support in the form of government financial aid and tariffs could help only partially to reduce the problems. This decline in income reduced the spending power of a large section of the population and this led to a fall in demand within the economy as a whole.

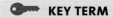 **KEY TERM**

Tariffs Taxes levied by an importing nation on foreign goods coming in, and paid by the importers.

- The changing balance of the population. From the mid-1920s there were more school leavers because of the high pre-war birth rate. The available workforce increased from 32.4 million in 1925 to 33.4 million in 1931. This meant that, even without a recession, there was always likely to be an increase in unemployment in Germany.
- Savings and investment discouraged. Savers had lost a great deal of money in the Great Inflation and, after 1924, there was less enthusiasm to invest money again. As a result, the German economy came to rely on investors from abroad, for example the USA, who were attracted by the prospect of higher interest rates than those in their own countries. Germany's economic well-being became ever more dependent on foreign investment.
- Government finances raised concern. Although the government succeeded in balancing the budget in 1924, from 1925 it continually ran into debt. It continued to spend increasing sums of money and by 1928 public expenditure had reached 26 per cent of **GNP**, which was double the pre-war figure. The government found it difficult to encourage domestic savings and was forced to rely more and more on international loans. Such a situation did not provide the basis for solid future economic growth.

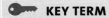

KEY TERM

GNP Gross national product is the total value of all goods and services in a nation's economy (including income derived from assets abroad).

'A sick economy'?

It has been suggested that the problems faced by the German economy *before* the world depression of 1929 were disguised by the flood of foreign capital and exacerbated by the development of an extensive social welfare system. The German economy was in a poor state because:

- Foreign loans made it liable to suffer from any problems that arose in the world economy.
- Investment was too low to encourage growth.
- The cost of the welfare state could be met only by the government's taking on increasing debts.
- The agricultural sector faced serious problems from the mid-1920s and various sectors of the German economy had actually started to slow down from 1927.

Source A gives a report from Deutsche Bank in 1928.

SOURCE A

? What weaknesses did the Deutsche Bank identify in the economy? To what extent is Source A of value to a historian?

From the annual report of the Deutsche Bank, quoted in Ian Kershaw, editor, *Weimar: Why Did German Democracy Fail?*, Weidenfeld & Nicolson, 1990, p. 163.

[It referred to] … the complete inner weakness of our economy. It is so overloaded with taxes required by the excessively expensive apparatus of the state, with over-high social payments, and particularly with the reparations sum now reaching its 'normal' level [as laid down by the Dawes Plan] that any healthy growth is constricted. Development is only possible to the extent that these restrictive chains are removed.

Whether the above weaknesses are enough to support the view of Weimar
Germany as 'an abnormal, in fact a sick economy', as claimed by the historian
K. Borchardt, writing in the 1970s, remains controversial, and it is hard to assess
what might have happened without the world economic crisis. However, it is
interesting that Stresemann wrote in 1928, 'Germany is dancing on a volcano.
If the short-term credits are called in, a large section of our economy would
collapse.' So, on balance, the evidence suggests that by 1929 the Weimar
Republic was facing serious difficulties and was already heading for a major
economic downturn of its own making.

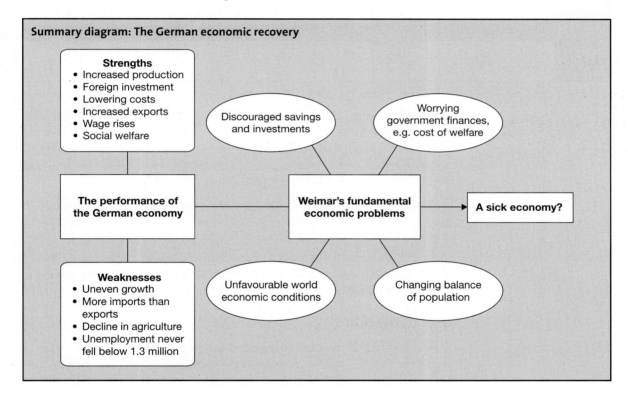

2 Political stability

▶ *How politically stable was Weimar in the years 1924–9?*

The election results during the middle years of the Weimar Republic gave
grounds for cautious optimism about its survival (see Table 3.1). The extremist
parties of both left and right lost ground and altogether they polled less than
30 per cent of the votes cast:

- The DNVP peaked in December 1924 with 103 seats (20.5 per cent of the vote)
  and fell back to 73 (14.2 per cent) in May 1928.

Table 3.1 Weimar *Reichstag* election results 1924 and 1928. (See also major political parties on page 16.)

	Turnout	NSDAP	DNVP	DVP	ZP/BVP	DDP	SPD	KPD	Others
May 1924									
Seats	472	32	95	45	81	28	100	62	29
%	77.4	6.5	19.5	9.2	15.6	5.7	20.5	12.6	10.3
December 1924									
Seats	493	14	103	51	88	32	131	45	29
%	78.8	3.0	20.5	9.2	17.3	6.3	26.0	9.0	7.8
May 1928									
Seats	491	12	73	45	78	25	153	54	51
%	75.6	2.6	14.2	8.7	15.2	4.9	29.8	10.8	14.0

- The Nazis lost ground in both elections and were reduced to only twelve seats (2.6 per cent) by 1928.
- The KPD, although recovering slightly by 1928 with 54 seats (10.6 per cent), remained below their performance of May 1924 and well below the combined votes gained by the KPD and USPD in June 1920 (see page 51).

In comparison, the parties sympathetic to the republic maintained their share of the vote and the SPD made substantial gains, winning 153 seats (29.8 per cent) in 1928. As a result, following the 1928 election, a 'Grand Coalition' of the SPD, DDP, DVP and Centre was formed under Hermann Müller, the leader of the SPD. It enjoyed the support of over 60 per cent of the *Reichstag* and it seemed as if democracy was at last beginning to emerge in Weimar politics.

Coalition politics

The election of 1928 must not be regarded as typical in Weimar history, and it should not hide the basic weaknesses of the German parliamentary system. These included not only the problems created by proportional representation (see page 20), but also the ongoing difficulty of creating and maintaining coalitions from the various parties. In such a situation each party tended to put its own self-interests before those of the government.

The parties tended to reflect their traditional interests: religion and class. So attempts to widen their appeal made little progress. As a result, the differences between the main parties meant that opportunities to form workable coalitions were very limited:

- There was never any possibility of a coalition including both the SPD and the DNVP because the former believed in parliamentary democracy whereas the latter fundamentally rejected the Weimar political system.
- The Communists, KPD, remained totally isolated.

- A right–centre coalition of Centre, DVP and DNVP created a situation in which the parties tended to agree on domestic issues, but disagree on foreign affairs.
- On the other hand, a broad coalition of SPD, DDP, DVP and Centre meant that these parties agreed on foreign policy, but differed on domestic issues.
- A minority government of the political centre, including the DDP, DVP and Centre, could only exist by seeking support from either the left or right. It was impossible to create a coalition with a parliamentary majority that could also consistently agree on both domestic and foreign policy.

In this situation, there was little chance of democratic government being able to establish lasting political stability. Of the seven governments between 1923 and 1930 (see Table 3.2), only two had majorities and the longest survived for just 21 months. In fact, the only reason governments lasted as long as they did was that the opposition parties were also unable or unwilling to unite. More often than not, it was conflicts within the parties that formed the coalition governments that led them to collapse.

Table 3.2 Governments of the Weimar Republic 1923–30

Period in office	Chancellor	Make-up of the coalition
1923–4	Wilhelm Marx	Centre, DDP, DVP
1924–5	Wilhelm Marx	Centre, DDP, DVP
1925	Hans Luther	Centre, DVP, DNVP
1926	Hans Luther	Centre, DDP, DVP
1926	Wilhelm Marx	Centre, DDP, DVP
1927–8	Wilhelm Marx	Centre, DDP, DNVP
1928–30	Hermann Müller	SPD, DDP, Centre, DVP

The responsibility of the parties

The attitude of the Weimar Republic's political parties towards parliamentary government was irresponsible. This may well have been a legacy from the imperial years. In that time the parties had expressed their own narrow interests in the knowledge that it was the Kaiser who ultimately decided policy. However, in the 1920s parliamentary democracy needed the political parties to show a more responsible attitude towards government. The evidence suggests that no such attitude existed, even in the most stable period of the republic's history.

The SPD

Until 1932 the SPD remained the largest party in the *Reichstag*. However, although firm in its support of the republic, the party was divided between its desire to uphold the interests of the working class and its commitment to democracy. Some members, and especially those connected with the trade unions, feared that joining coalitions with other parties would lead to a weakening of their principles. Others, the more moderate, wanted to participate in government in order to influence it. At the same time, the party was hindered by the old argument between those committed to a more extreme left-wing socialist programme and those who favoured moderate, gradual reform.

As a result, during the years of the republic 1920–8, the SPD did not join any of the fragile government coalitions. This obviously weakened the power base of those democratic coalitions from 1924 to 1928. The SPD remained the strongest party during those years: although it was committed to democracy, it was not prepared to take on the responsibility of government until 1928.

The Centre Party

Real political leadership in Weimar politics, therefore, had to be provided by the Centre Party. The ZP electoral support was solid and the party participated in all the coalition governments from 1919 to 1932 by taking ministerial posts. However, its support did not increase because its appeal was restricted to traditional Catholic areas. Further, its social and economic policies, which aimed at bridging the gaps between the classes, led to internal quarrels.

In the early years, such differences had been put to one side under the strong left-wing leadership of Matthias Erzberger and Josef Wirth. However, during the 1920s the party moved decisively to the right and the divisions within the party widened. In 1928 the leadership eventually passed to Ludwig Kaas and Heinrich Brüning, who appealed more to the conservative partners of the coalition than to the liberal or social democratic elements. This was a worrying sign both for the future of the Centre Party and for Germany itself.

The liberal parties

The position of the German liberals was not a really strong one. The DDP and DVP joined in all the coalition governments of this period and in Gustav Stresemann, the leader of the DVP, they possessed the republic's only really capable statesman. However, this hid some worrying trends. Their share of the vote, though constant in the mid-1920s, had nearly halved from 22 per cent in 1920 to 14 per cent by 1928. Indeed, Stresemann himself addressed the DVP executive committee on 26 February 1928 (see Source B).

SOURCE B

Stresemann's speech to the DVP in 1928, quoted in S. Lee, _The Weimar Republic_, Routledge, 1998, p. 75.

Let us not fool ourselves about this: we are in the midst of a parliamentary crisis that is already more than a crisis of conscience. The crisis has two roots: one the caricature that has become the parliamentary system in Germany; secondly the complete false position of parliament in relation to its responsibilities to the nation.

? What are the main points of Stresemann's political message in Source B? And why is the context – date and audience – of the source so significant?

The reasons for the liberals' eventual collapse after 1930 were already established beforehand. This decline was largely a result of the divisions within both parties. The DDP lacked clear leadership and its membership was involved in internal bickering over policy. The DVP was also divided and, despite Stresemann's efforts to bring unity to the party, this remained a source of conflict. It is not really surprising that moves to bring about some kind of united liberal party came to nothing. As a result, German liberalism failed to gain popular support; and after 1929 its position declined dramatically.

The DNVP

One promising feature of German party politics came unexpectedly from the conservative DNVP. Since 1919 the DNVP had been totally opposed to the republic and it had refused to take part in government. In electoral terms, it had enjoyed considerable success, and in December 1924 gained 103 seats (20.5 per cent). However, as the republic began to recover after the 1923 crisis, it became increasingly clear that the DNVP's hopes of restoring a more right-wing government were diminishing. The continuous opposition policy meant that the party had no real power and achieved nothing. Some influential groups within the DNVP realised that if they were to have any influence on government policy, then the party had to be prepared to participate in government. As a result, in 1925 and 1927 the DNVP joined government coalitions. This more sympathetic attitude towards the Weimar Republic was an encouraging development.

That more conciliatory policy was not popular, however, with all groups within the party. When, in the 1928 election, the DNVP vote fell by a quarter, the more extreme right wing asserted its influence. Significantly, it elected **Alfred Hugenberg**, an extreme nationalist, as the new leader. Hugenberg was Germany's greatest media tycoon: he owned 150 newspapers and a publishing house, and had interests in the film industry. He utterly rejected the idea of a republic based on parliamentary democracy. He now used all his resources to promote his political message. The DNVP reverted to a programme of total opposition to the republic and refused to be involved in government. A year later, his party was working closely with the Nazis against the Young Plan (see pages 86 and 120).

President Hindenburg

A presidential election was due in 1925. It was assumed that President Friedrich Ebert would be re-elected, so his unexpected death in February 1925 created political problems. There was no clear successor in the first round of the election and so a second round was held. It did result in the choice of Hindenburg as president, but the figures clearly underlined the divisions in German society (see Table 3.3).

 KEY FIGURE

Alfred Hugenberg (1865–1951)

A civil servant, banker and industrialist, who opposed the Weimar Republic. He also became Germany's greatest media tycoon. He was appointed leader of the DNVP in 1928 and then funded Hitler's political campaign.

Table 3.3 Presidential election, second round, 26 April 1925

Candidate (party)	Votes (millions)	Percentage
Paul von Hindenburg (DNVP)	14.6	48
Wilhelm Marx (ZP)	13.7	45
Ernst Thälmann (KPD)	1.9	6

The appointment of President Hindenburg has remained controversial. On the one hand, on Hindenburg's coming to power there was no immediate swing to the right. The new president proved totally loyal to the constitution and carried out his presidential duties with correctness. Those nationalists who had hoped that his election might lead to the restoration of the monarchy, or the creation of a military-type regime, were disappointed. Indeed, it has been argued that Hindenburg as president acted as a true substitute kaiser or ***Ersatzkaiser*** (so, although Wilhelm II had abdicated and Germany had lost its monarchy, Hindenburg was seen by monarchists as, in effect, fulfilling the role of sovereign). In that sense, the status of Hindenburg as president at last gave Weimar some respectability in conservative circles.

KEY TERM

Ersatzkaiser 'Substitute emperor.' After Hindenburg was elected president, he provided the *ersatzkaiser* figure required by the respectable right wing: he was a conservative, a nationalist and a military hero.

Paul von Hindenburg

1847	Born of a Prussian noble family in Posen and served his whole career in the Prussian army
1914	Won the victory of the Battle of Tannenberg on the Eastern Front
1916	Promoted to field marshal and military dictator 1916–18
1918	Accepted the defeat of Germany and retired
1925	Elected president of Germany
1930–2	Appointed Brüning, Papen and Schleicher as chancellors
1932	Re-elected president
1933	Persuaded to appoint Hitler as chancellor
1934	Died and given a national funeral

Hindenburg was regularly promoted, but his career was seen as 'steady rather than exceptional'. In 1914 he was recalled from retirement and his management of the campaign on the Eastern Front earned him distinction. However, Hindenburg did not have great military skills

and was outshone in his partnership with Ludendorff. During the years 1916–18, the two men were effectively the military dictators of Germany.

Although Hindenburg served as president of Germany (1925–34), he accepted the post only reluctantly. He was not a democrat and looked forward to the return of the monarchy. Nevertheless, he took up the responsibility of his office and performed his duties correctly.

From 1930 Hindenburg's significance increased in the political crisis. As president, he was responsible for the appointment of all the chancellors from 1930 to 1934 and he became a crucial player in the political intrigue of the competing forces. Given his authority, Hindenburg was held ultimately responsible for the events that ended with the appointment of Hitler, but he was very old and easily influenced by Papen and Schleicher. He had no respect for Hitler, but he did not have the will and determination to make a stand against Nazism.

On the other hand, it is difficult to ignore the pitfalls resulting from the appointment of an old man. In his heart, Hindenburg had no real sympathy for the republic or its values. Those around him were mainly made up of anti-republican figures, many of them from the military. He preferred to include the DNVP in government and, if possible, to exclude the SPD. From the start, Hindenburg's view was that the government should move towards the right, although it was really only after 1929 that the serious implications of his outlook became fully apparent for Weimar democracy. As the historian A.J. Nicholls, writing in 1968, put it: 'he refused to betray the republic, but he did not rally the people to its banner'.

The limitations of the political system

During this period the parliamentary and party political system in Germany failed to make any real progress. It just coped as best it could. Government carried out its work but with only limited success. There was no *putsch* from left or right and the anti-republican extremists were contained. Law and order were restored and the activities of the various paramilitary groups were restricted.

These were only minor and negative successes. Moreover, despite the good intentions of certain individuals and groups, there were no signs of any real strengthening of the political structure. Stable government had not been established. One coalition government collapsed in 1926 over a minor issue about the use of the national flag and the old imperial flag; another one fell over the creation of religious schools.

Even more significant for the future was the growing contempt and cynicism shown by the people towards party politics, particularly over the negotiating and bargaining involved in the creation of most coalitions. The turnout of the elections declined in the mid-1920s compared to 1919 and 1920. There was also an increasing growth of small fringe parties. The apparent stability of these years was really a deception, a mirage. It misled some people into believing that a genuine basis for lasting stable government had been achieved. It had not.

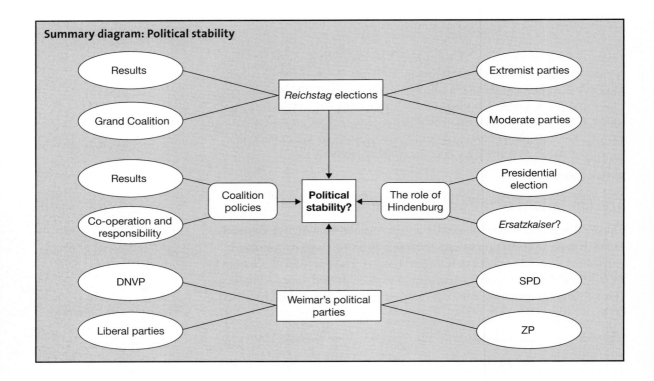

Summary diagram: Political stability

3 Gustav Stresemann's foreign policy

▶ *What were Stresemann's aims in foreign policy and to what extent was he successful?*

Before 1921–2 there was little to suggest that Stresemann was to become the mainstay of Weimar democracy. In the years before 1914 his nationalism found expression in his support of the Kaiser's **Weltpolitik** and from the start of the First World War, Stresemann was an ardent supporter of the **Siegfriede**. He campaigned for unrestricted submarine warfare and opposed supporters of peace in 1917.

By 1918 Stresemann's support for the military regime and the Treaty of Brest-Litovsk had earned him the title of 'Ludendorff's young man' (see page 3). And when the war came to an end in defeat, Stresemann was deliberately excluded from the newly created DDP and, so, was left no real option but to form his own party, the DVP. At first, his party was hostile to the revolution of 1918 and the republic and campaigned for the restoration of the monarchy.

Stresemann's turning point

Indeed, it was only after the failed Kapp *putsch* and the murders of Erzberger and Rathenau (page 45) that Stresemann led his party into adopting a more sympathetic approach towards the Weimar Republic. His sudden change of heart has provided plenty of evidence for those critics who have regarded his support of the Weimar Republic as sham. This charge is not entirely fair. Despite the conservatism of his early years, Stresemann's subsequent career shows that he was a committed supporter of constitutional government.

Stresemann's ideal was a constitutional monarchy. But that was not to be. By 1921 he had become convinced that the republic and its constitution provided Germany with its only chance of preventing a dictatorship of either left or right. This was a realistic assessment of the situation and why he was referred to as a *Vernunftrepublikaner*, a rational republican, rather than a convinced one.

Stresemann's aims

From the time Stresemann became responsible for foreign affairs, at the height of the 1923 crisis, his foreign policy was shaped by a deep understanding of the domestic and international situations. Stresemann recognised, unlike many nationalists, that Germany had been militarily defeated and not simply 'stabbed in the back'. He also rejected the solutions of those hardliners who failed to understand the circumstances that had brought Germany to its knees in 1923.

Stresemann's main aims were to free Germany from the limitations of Versailles and to restore his country to the status of a great power, the equal of Britain and France. Offensive action was ruled out by Stresemann and so his only choice was diplomacy. As he himself once remarked, he was backed up only by the power of German cultural traditions and the German economy. So, at first, he worked towards his main aims in the 1920s by pursuing the following objectives:

- To recognise that France did rightly have security concerns and that France also controlled the balance of power on the Continent. He regarded Franco-German friendship as essential to solving outstanding problems.
- To play on Germany's vital importance to world trade in order to earn the goodwill and co-operation of Britain and the USA. The sympathy of the USA was also vital so as to attract US investment into the German economy.
- To maintain the Rapallo-based friendship with the USSR. He rejected out of hand those 'hardliners' who desired an **alliance** with Soviet Russia and described them as the 'maddest of foreign policy makers'. Stresemann's strategy was in the tradition of Wirth's **fulfilment**.
- To encourage co-operation and peace, particularly with the Western powers. This was in the best interests of Germany to make it the leading power in Europe once again.

 KEY TERMS

Vernunftrepublikaner
'A rational (pragmatic) republican.' Used in the 1920s to define those people who really wanted Germany to have a constitutional monarchy but who, out of necessity, came to support the democratic Weimar Republic.

Alliance An agreement where members promise to support the other(s), if one or more of them is attacked.

Fulfilment The policy of conforming to the terms of Versailles Treaty, while aiming for moderate revision of the terms. It was initiated by Joseph Wirth in 1921–2, and later pursued by Stresemann.

Stresemann and foreign affairs 1923–9

The Dawes Plan

The starting point of Stresemann's foreign policy was the issue of reparations. As chancellor, he had called off 'passive resistance' and agreed to resume the payment of reparations. The result of this was the US-backed Dawes Plan (see Figure 3.1), which has been described as 'a victory for financial realism'. Despite opposition from the right wing it was accepted in April 1924.

THE DAWES PLAN 1924

The reorganisation of German currency
- One new *Rentenmark* was to be worth one billion of the old marks.
- The setting up of a German national bank, the *Reichsbank*, under Allied supervision.

An international loan of 800 million gold marks to aid German economic recovery
- The loan was to be financed mainly by the USA.

New arrangements for the payment of reparations
- Payment to be made annually at a fixed scale over a longer period.

Figure 3.1 The Dawes Plan.

Although the Dawes Plan left the actual sum to be paid unchanged, the monthly instalments over the first five years were calculated according to Germany's capacity to pay. Furthermore, it provided for a large loan to Germany to aid economic recovery. For Stresemann, its advantages were many:

- For the first time since the First World War, Germany's economic problems received international recognition.
- Germany gained credit for the cash-starved German economy by means of the loan and subsequent investments.
- It resulted in a French promise to evacuate the Ruhr during 1925.

In the short term, the Dawes Plan was a success. The German economy was not weakened, since it received twice as much capital from abroad as it paid out in reparations. The mere fact that reparations were being paid regularly contributed to the improved relations between France and Germany during these years. However, the whole system was dangerously dependent on the continuation of US loans, as can be seen in Figure 3.2. In attempting to break out of the crisis of 1923, Stresemann had linked Germany's fortunes to powerful external forces, which had dramatic effects after 1929.

The Locarno Pact

The ending of the occupation of the Ruhr and the introduction of the Dawes Plan showed that the Great Powers were prepared to take Germany's interests seriously. However, Stresemann continued to fear that Anglo-French friendship could lead to a military alliance. In order to ease this concern, Stresemann

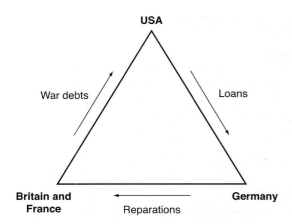

Figure 3.2 The reparations triangle in the 1920s.

proposed an international security pact for Germany's western frontiers. Although France was at first hesitant, Britain and the USA both backed the idea.

In October 1925 a series of treaties was signed which became known as the Locarno Pact. The main points were:

- A **mutual guarantee agreement** accepted the Franco-German and Belgian-German borders. These terms were guaranteed by Britain and Italy. All five countries renounced the use of force, except in self-defence.
- The demilitarisation of the Rhineland was recognised as permanent.
- **Arbitration** treaties between Germany, Poland and Czechoslovakia agreed to settle future disputes peacefully – but the existing frontiers were not accepted as final.

To see the territories affected by the Treaty of Locarno, refer to the map on page 33.

The Locarno treaties represented an important diplomatic development. Germany was freed from its isolation by the Allies and was again treated as an equal partner. Stresemann had achieved a great deal at Locarno at very little cost. He had confirmed the existing frontiers in the west, since Germany was in no position to change the situation. In so doing he had also limited France's freedom of action since the occupation of the Ruhr or the possible annexation of the Rhineland was no longer possible. Moreover, by establishing the beginnings of a solid basis for Franco-German understanding, Stresemann had lessened France's need to find allies in eastern Europe. The Poles viewed the treaties as a major setback, since Stresemann had deliberately refused to confirm the frontiers in the east.

Further diplomatic progress

Stresemann hoped that further advances would follow Locarno, such as the restoration of full German rule over the Saar and the Rhineland, a reduction in

KEY TERMS

Mutual guarantee agreement An agreement between states on a particular issue, but not an alliance.

Arbitration treaty An agreement to accept the decision by a third party to settle a conflict.

reparations, and a revision of the eastern frontier. However, although there was further diplomatic progress in the years 1926–30 it remained limited:

- Germany had originally been excluded from the League of Nations (see page 34) but, in 1926, it was invited to join the League and was immediately recognised as a permanent member of the Council of the League.
- Two years later, in 1928, Germany signed the Kellogg–Briand Pact, a declaration that outlawed 'war as an instrument of national policy'. Although of no real practical effect it showed that Germany was co-operating with 68 nations.
- In 1929 the Allies agreed to evacuate the Rhineland earlier than intended, in return for a final settlement of the reparations issue. The result was the Young Plan, which further revised the scheme of payments. Germany now agreed to continue to pay reparations until 1988, although the total sum was reduced to £1850 million, only one-quarter of the figure demanded in 1921 (see page 34).

The Treaty of Berlin

Although Stresemann viewed friendship with the West as his priority, he was not prepared to drop the Rapallo Treaty. He was still determined to stay on good terms with the USSR. As a result, the two countries signed the Treaty of Berlin in April 1926 in order to continue the basis of a good Russo-German relationship. This was not double-dealing by Stresemann, but was simply a recognition that Germany's defence needs in the heart of Europe meant that she had to have understanding with both the East and the West. The treaty with the Soviet Union therefore reduced strategic fears on Germany's Eastern Front and placed even more pressure on Poland to give way to German demands for frontier changes. It also opened up the possibility of a large commercial market and increased military co-operation.

Assessment of Stresemann: success or failure?

In 1926 Stresemann was awarded the Nobel Peace Prize (along with his British and French counterparts Aristide Briand and Austen Chamberlain). Only three years later, at the early age of 51, he died suddenly of a stroke. The socialist newspaper *Vorwärts* wrote an obituary column for him (see Source C).

SOURCE C

According to the newspaper's obituary, what were Stresemann's achievements? To what extent is Source C of value to a historian?

From *Vorwärts*, 6 October 1929, quoted in Geoff Layton, *From Bismarck to Hitler*, Hodder Education, 1995, p. 125.

Stresemann's achievement was in line with the ideas of the international socialist movement. He saw that you can only serve your people by understanding other peoples. To serve collapsed Germany he set out on the path of understanding. He refused to try to get back land which had gone forever. He offered our former enemies friendship. Being a practical man he saw that any other path would have left Germany without any hope of recovery. He covered the long distance from being a nationalist politician of conquest to being a champion of world peace. He fought with great personal courage for the ideals in which he believed … It is no wonder that right-wingers watched with horror as he went from his original camp to the opposite one. They could not accept him because doing so involved accepting that the Republic created by the workers had brought Germany from devastation to recovery.

Stresemann has always been the focus of debate. He has been regarded by some as a fanatical nationalist and by others as a 'great European' working for international reconciliation. He has been praised for his staunch support of parliamentary government, but condemned for pretending to be a democrat. He has also been portrayed as an idealist on the one hand and an opportunist on the other.

SOURCE D

'He looks to the right, he looks to the left – he will save me'. (It is worth noting that the little boy is the 'German Michael' – a stereotype for the naïve German.) A cartoon drawn in 1923 about Stresemann.

> According to the cartoonist in Source D, how is Stresemann portrayed?

Stresemann achieved a great deal in a short time to change both Germany's domestic and international positions. Moreover, the improvement had been achieved by peaceful methods. When one also considers the dire situation he inherited in 1923 with forces, both internal and external, stacked against him, it is perhaps not surprising that his policy has been described as 'astonishingly successful' (E. Kolb, 1982) and he has been referred to as 'Weimar's greatest statesman' (J. Wright, 2004).

Nevertheless, it should be borne in mind that the circumstances in the years 1924–9 were working strongly in Stresemann's favour. M. Walsdorff, writing in 1971, was more critical of Stresemann for failing to achieve his fundamental aims to revise Versailles. He argues, first, that Stresemann overestimated his ability to establish friendly relations with other powers. Secondly, he suggests that the limits and slow pace of the changes had resulted in a dead end – and there was no hint of any revision of the Polish frontier.

Also, Stresemann's policies failed to generate broad enough domestic support for Weimar. The right wing was always totally against 'fulfilment' and, although a minority, they became increasingly loud and influential so that, by the time of Stresemann's death, the nationalist opposition was already mobilising itself against the Young Plan (see page 120). Even more significantly, it seems that the silent majority had not really been won over by Stresemann's policy of conciliation. Consequently, by 1929 his policy had not had time to establish itself and generate sufficient support to survive the difficult circumstances of the 1930s.

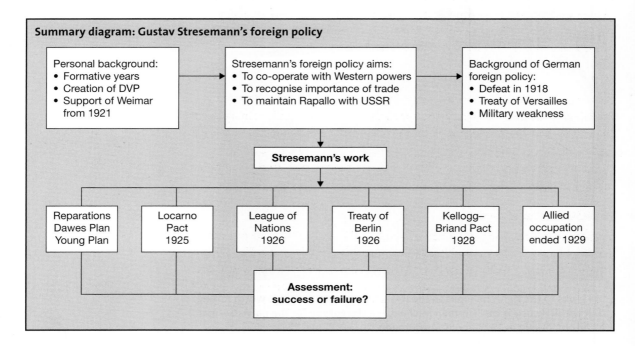

Summary diagram: Gustav Stresemann's foreign policy

Personal background:
- Formative years
- Creation of DVP
- Support of Weimar from 1921

Stresemann's foreign policy aims:
- To co-operate with Western powers
- To recognise importance of trade
- To maintain Rapallo with USSR

Background of German foreign policy:
- Defeat in 1918
- Treaty of Versailles
- Military weakness

Stresemann's work

| Reparations Dawes Plan Young Plan | Locarno Pact 1925 | League of Nations 1926 | Treaty of Berlin 1926 | Kellogg–Briand Pact 1928 | Allied occupation ended 1929 |

Assessment: success or failure?

4 Culture

> ▶ *In what ways were the 1920s a culturally rich period?*
> ▶ *Why was there a conflict of cultures in Weimar Germany?*

The Weimar years witnessed an explosion of culture that affected many aspects of German life. Its roots pre-dated 1914, but Imperial Germany had in the main been conservative, authoritarian and conformist. In contrast, in the wake of the war and defeat, the Weimar Republic became a more liberal society that upheld **toleration** and reduced censorship. This also coincided with dramatic changes in communication: the emergence of film and the radio. All this encouraged many cultural artists to express themselves openly in Weimar Germany and contributed to the label of the 'golden years', as described in the 1920s by William Shirer, the European correspondent of the US newspaper the *Chicago Tribune*:

> *A wonderful ferment was working in Germany. Life seemed more free, more modern, more exciting than in any place I had ever seen. Nowhere else did the arts or the intellectual life seem so lively … In contemporary writing, painting, architecture, in music and drama, there were new currents and fine talents.*

The new cultural ferment

The term generally used to reflect the cultural developments in Weimar Germany was ***Neue Sachlichkeit***, which can be translated as 'new practicality' or 'new functionalism', which means essentially a desire to show reality and objectivity. These words are best explained by researching and looking at some of the major examples of different art forms.

Art

Artists in favour of the 'new objectivity' broke away from the traditional nostalgia of the nineteenth century. They wanted to understand ordinary people in everyday life, and through their art they aimed to comment on the state of society. This approach was epitomised by Georg Grosz and Otto Dix, whose paintings and caricatures in a seedy and aggressive style had strong political and social messages.

Architecture and design

One of the most striking artistic developments in Weimar Germany was the Bauhaus school led by the architect Walter Gropius, which was established in 1919 in the town of Weimar itself. The Bauhaus movement was a new style that influenced all aspects of design: furniture, urban planning, pottery, textiles and graphics. Its approach was functional and it emphasised the close relationship between art and technology, which is underlined by its motto 'Art and

KEY TERMS

Toleration Acceptance of alternative political, religious and cultural views.

Neue Sachlichkeit A form of art that developed in post-war Germany which tried to express reality with a more objective view of the world.

SOURCE E

? In the painting in Source E, how does Kirchner reflect the glamour and decadence of Berlin society?

Street, Berlin – a painting of two well-dressed prostitutes and their furtive customers by the German artist Ernst Ludwig Kirchner. His work was branded as 'degenerate' by the Nazis and he killed himself in 1938.

Technology – a new unity'. It used materials such as steel, cement and plastic, in geometric designs. It was profoundly resisted among more conservative circles.

KEY TERMS

Expressionists Artists who focus on expressing feelings through symbolism, exaggeration or distortion.

Avant garde A general term suggesting new ideas and styles in art.

Literature

It is impossible to categorise the rich range of writing which emerged in Weimar Germany. Not all writers were **expressionists** influenced by the *Neue Sachlichkeit*. For example, the celebrated Thomas Mann, who won the Nobel Prize for literature, was not part of that movement. In fact, the big sellers were the authors who wrote traditional nostalgic literature, such as Hans Grimm. In the more *avant garde* style were the works of Arnold Zweig and Peter Lampel, who explored a range of social issues growing out of the distress and misery of working people in the big cities. Two particular books to be remembered are: the pacifist *All Quiet on the Western Front*, published in 1928 by Erich Maria Remarque, an ex-soldier critical of the First World War; and *Berlin Alexanderplatz*, written by Alfred Döblin, which examined the life of a worker in Weimar society.

Theatre

In drama, *Neue Sachlichkeit* developed into what was called *Zeittheater* (theatre of the time) that introduced new dramatic methods often with explicit left-wing sympathies, and were most evident in the plays of Bertolt Brecht and Erwin Piscator. They used innovative techniques such as banners, slogans, film and slides, and adopted controversial methods to portray characters' behaviour in their everyday lives.

Mass culture

The 1920s were a time of dramatic changes that saw the emergence of a modern mass culture. Germany was no exception. It saw the development of mass communication methods and international influences, especially from USA, such as jazz music and consumerism.

Film

During the 1920s the German film industry became the most advanced in Europe and there were more cinemas in the country than elsewhere in Europe. German film-makers were also well respected for their high-quality work. Most notable of the films of the time were:

- *Metropolis* (1926) by the film-maker Fritz Lang: a sci-fi classic that raised frightening issues about the direction of modern industrialised society.
- *King Frederick the Great* (1922): a traditional, patriotic epic.
- *Blue Angel* (1930): with the young actress Marlene Dietrich – the first big German 'talkie' which openly played on female glamour and touched on sexual issues.

Although the German film market was very much dominated by the organisation UFA, run by Alfred Hugenberg (see page 79), from the mid-1920s US 'movies' quickly made an exceptional impact. The popular appeal of the comedy of Charlie Chaplin shows that Weimar culture was part of an international mass culture and was not exclusively German.

Radio

Radio also emerged very rapidly as another mass medium. The German Radio Company was established in 1923 and, in the following year, a radio network and nine companies were set up to serve different regions across the country. By 1932, despite the depression, one in four Germans owned a radio.

Cabaret

Berlin had all the traditional features of high culture but in the 1920s a vibrant nightlife also developed. Cabaret clubs opened up with a permissiveness that mocked the conventions of the old Germany: satirical comedy, jazz music and women dancers (and even wrestlers) in varying degrees of nudity. At parties there was an interest in sexual experimentation that included transvestism and homosexuality.

The conflict of cultures

It is easy to assume that Weimar was an exciting and vibrant era which celebrated its liberal creativity and culture. There were some respected conservative intellectuals, like Arthur Möller and Oswald Spengler, who condemned the new democratic and industrial society. Moreover, many of the writers in the 1920s opposed pacifism and proudly glorified the sacrifices of the First World War.

Much of the reaction against *Neue Sachlichkeit* simply reflected the broader doubts and tensions in Weimar society. Berlin was not typical of Germany, but it left a very powerful impression – both positive and negative. Some could enjoy and appreciate the cultural experimentation, but most Germans were horrified by what they saw as the decline in established moral and cultural standards.

It has also been suggested that Weimar culture never established a genuinely tolerant attitude. The *avant garde* and the conservatives were clearly at odds with each other. Ironically, although both sides took advantage of the freedoms and permissiveness of Weimar liberalism they still remained critical of each other. Weimar society was becoming increasingly **polarised** before the onset of the political and economic crisis in 1929.

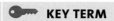

KEY TERM

Polarised The division of society into distinctly opposite views (the comparison is to the north and south poles).

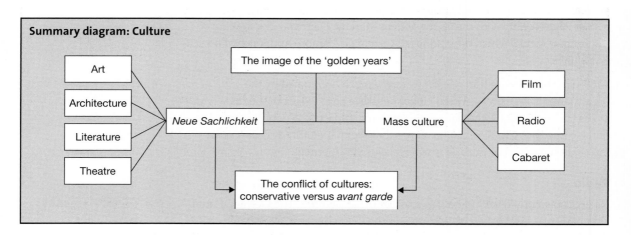

(5) Weimar 1924–9: an overview

▶ *To what extent had Weimar stabilised in the years 1924–9?*

The years 1924–9 marked the high point of the Weimar Republic. By comparison with the periods before and after, these years do appear stable. The real increase in prosperity experienced by many, and the cultural vitality of the period, gave support to the view that these years were indeed the 'golden years'. However, historians have generally tended to question this stability because it was in fact limited in scope. This is the reason why the historian D. Peukert, writing in 1987, describes these years as a 'deceptive stability'.

A weak economy?

Germany's economic recovery was built on poor foundations that created a false idea of prosperity. Problems persisted in the economy and they were temporarily hidden only by an increasing reliance on credit from abroad. Consequently, Germany's economy became tied up with powerful external forces over which it had no control. Hindsight now allows historians to see that, in the late 1920s, any disruption to the world's trade or finance markets was bound to have a particularly damaging effect on the uncertain German economy.

A divided society?

German society was still divided by deep class differences that prevented the development of national agreement and harmony. The introduction of the state scheme for compulsory arbitration in strikes in 1919 did not fully overcome concerns between employers and their workers. Its procedure was used as a matter of course, whereas the intention had been that it would be the exception, not the rule. As a result, there was arbitration in some 76,000 industrial disputes between 1924 and 1932. In 1928 workers were locked out from their place of work in the Ruhr ironworks when the employers refused to accept the arbitration award. It was the most serious industrial confrontation of the Weimar period. A compromise solution was achieved, but it showed the extent of bitterness and division in industrial relations, even before the start of the depression. Even social welfare, which was meant to be integrating for society, was not so well received: the employers were concerned at the growing cost of their contributions; while the peasantry grew resentful as they did not benefit.

A fractured political system?

Tension was also evident in the political sphere, where the parliamentary system had failed to build on the changes of 1918–19. The original ideals of the constitution had not been developed and there was little sign that it had produced a stable and mature system. In particular, the main democratic parties had still not recognised the necessity of working together in a spirit of compromise. It was not so much the weaknesses of the constitution, but the failure to establish a shared political outlook that led to its instability. Even the successes of Stresemann in the field of foreign affairs were offset by the fact that significant numbers of his fellow countrymen rejected his policy out of hand and pressed for a more hardline approach.

In reality, the middle years of the Weimar Republic were stable only in comparison with the periods before and after. The fundamental problems inherited from the war and the years of crisis had not been fully resolved. In that sense, Weimar's condition in 1929 raised the question: was it strong enough to withstand a storm?

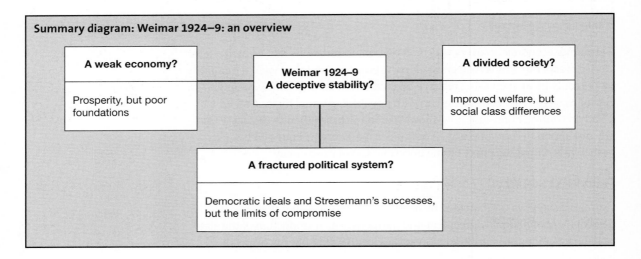

Summary diagram: Weimar 1924–9: an overview

A weak economy?	Weimar 1924–9 A deceptive stability?	A divided society?
Prosperity, but poor foundations		Improved welfare, but social class differences

A fractured political system?

Democratic ideals and Stresemann's successes, but the limits of compromise

Chapter summary

In contrast to the chaotic early years of crisis, the 'golden age' afterwards can be seen as a welcome improvement. The restoration of a solid currency with the *Rentenmark* and the decline of political extremists were significant factors in creating a calmer environment. However, all the features of the 'recovery' or the 'stability' were relative. The economy did grow markedly, but the prosperity was built on poor foundations, especially because of the dependence on US loans. The democratic governments did manage to function more effectively and Stresemann could trumpet his diplomatic successes, but the compromises were not generally celebrated. Cultural life thrived, but although welfare improved, the fundamental class divisions in society were not overcome. Therefore, it is questionable whether the economic social and political changes amounted to real long-term success for the Weimar Republic by the end of the decade.

Refresher questions

Use these questions to remind yourself of the key material covered in this chapter.

1 What were the strengths and the weaknesses of the German economy in the 'golden twenties'?

2 Did Weimar's social welfare provision make Germany a more equal society?

3 Was the Weimar economy fundamentally sick?

4 Did the general election results of 1924–8 suggest optimism for the Weimar Republic?

5 What were the problems/weaknesses faced by the main parties?

6 Why did the political parties find it so difficult to co-operate?

7 Was the appointment of Hindenburg as president a good or a bad sign for Weimar democracy?

8 What were Stresemann's aims and objectives?

9 What were the strengths and weaknesses of the Dawes Plan?

10 Why were the Locarno treaties so significant?

11 Did Stresemann fail or succeed?

12 What was *Neue Sachlichkeit* and how did it express itself?

13 In what ways did Weimar culture reach out to ordinary people?

14 Who reacted against *Neue Sachlichkeit* and why?

15 Were the years of Weimar's golden age a time of deceptive stability?

 # Question practice

ESSAY QUESTIONS

1 'Weimar Germany in the 1920s was seen as culturally rich primarily because of its writers.' Explain why you agree or disagree with this view.

2 How important was the part played by Gustav Stresemann in the establishment of stability within Germany between 1923 and 1929?

3 'By 1929 the Weimar Republic had a good chance of survival.' Assess the validity of this view.

4 How accurate is it to describe the years 1924–9 in Germany as a period of deceptive stability?

SOURCE ANALYSIS QUESTIONS

1 With reference to Sources 1 and 2 (on page 96), and your understanding of the historical context, which of these two sources is more valuable in explaining why Stresemann pursued his policy of fulfilment?

2 With reference to Sources 1, 2 and 3 (on pages 96–7), and your understanding of the historical context, assess the value of these sources to a historian studying the aims and achievements of Stresemann as foreign minister 1923–9.

SOURCE I

Letter of 7 September 1925 sent by Stresemann to the ex-Crown Prince, quoted in J.C.G. Röhl, *From Bismarck to Hitler*, Longman, 1970, p. 112.

In my opinion there are three great tasks that confront German foreign policy in the more immediate future:

In the first place the solution of the Reparations question in a sense tolerable for Germany and the assurance of peace, which is an essential premise for the recovery of our strength.

Secondly, the protection of Germans abroad, those 10 to 12 millions of our kindred who now live under a foreign yoke in foreign lands.

The third great task is the readjustment of our eastern frontiers; the recovery of Danzig, the Polish corridor, and a correction of the frontier in Upper Silesia.

In the background stands the union with German Austria, although I am quite clear that this not merely brings no advantages to Germany, but seriously complicates the problem of the German Reich …

The question of a choice between east and west does not arise as the result of our joining the League. Such a choice can only be made when backed by military force. That, alas we do not possess. We can neither become a continental spear-head for England, as some believe, nor can we involve ourselves in an alliance with Russia. I would utter warning against any utopian ideas of coquetting with Bolshevism.

SOURCE 2

Stresemannn's speech on 10 September 1926 to the League of Nations, two days after Germany's accession, quoted in S. Lee, *The Weimar Republic*, Routledge, 1998, p. 87.

… the German government may well speak for the great majority of the German race when it declares that it will wholeheartedly devote to the duties devolving upon the League of Nations …

Germany's relations to the League are not, however, confined exclusively to the possibilities of co-operation in general aims and issues. In many respects the League is the heir and executor of the Treaties of 1919. Out of these treaties there have arisen in the past, I may say frankly, many differences between the League and Germany. I hope that our co-operation within the League will make it easier in future to discuss these questions. In this respect mutual confidence will, from a political point of view, be found a greater creative force than anything else.

SOURCE 3

Memorandum of 6 March 1926 by Colonel Stülpnagel (and approved by Seeckt) sent to the Foreign Office, quoted in J.C.G. Röhl, *From Bismarck to Hitler*, Longman, 1970, p. 111.

The immediate aim of German policy must be the regaining of full sovereignty over the area retained by Germany, the firm acquisition of those areas at present separated from her, and the re-acquisition of those areas essential to the German economy. That is to say:

1. The liberation of the Rhineland and the Saar area.

2. The abolition of the Corridor and the regaining of Polish Upper Silesia.

3. The Anschluss of German Austria.

4. The abolition of the Demilitarised Zone.

These immediate political aims will produce conflict primarily with France and Belgium and with Poland which is dependent on them, then with Czechoslovakia and finally also with Italy …

The above exposition of Germany's political aims … clearly shows that the problem for Germany in the next stages of her political development can only be the re-establishment of her position in Europe, and that the regaining of her world position will be a task for the distant future. Re-establishing a European position is for Germany a question in which land forces will almost exclusively be decisive, for the opponent of this resurrection is in the first place France. It is certainly to be assumed that a reborn Germany will eventually come into conflict with the American-English powers in the struggle for raw materials and markets, and that she will then need adequate maritime forces. But this conflict will be fought out on the basis of a firm European position, after a new solution to the Franco-German problem has been achieved through either peace or war.

CHAPTER 4

Hitler and Nazism

In the 1920s Hitler and the Nazi Party enjoyed a chequered history and they did not make any real political impact until the onset of the Great Depression. However, Nazism did take root. The purpose of this chapter is to examine the role of the Nazis in Germany in the 1920s through the following sections:

★ Hitler and the creation of the Nazi Party

★ Nazi ideology

★ Nazi fortunes in the 1920s

Key dates

1919	Creation of German Workers' Party (DAP) by Anton Drexler		1924	Hitler in Landsberg prison. *Mein Kampf* written
1920 Feb.	Party name changed to NSDAP (National Socialist German Workers' Party)		1925 Feb.	NSDAP refounded in Munich
	25-Points party programme drawn up by Drexler and Hitler		1926 Feb.	Bamberg conference: Hitler's leadership of the party re-established
1923 Nov. 8–9	Beer Hall *putsch* in Munich		1928 May	*Reichstag* election result

1 Hitler and the creation of the Nazi Party

▶ *How did Hitler become involved in politics?*

▶ *Why did the Beer Hall* putsch *fail?*

There was little in the background of Adolf Hitler to suggest that he would become a powerful political figure. Hitler was born at Braunau-am-Inn in 1889 in what was then the Austro-Hungarian Empire. He failed to impress at school, and after the death of his parents he moved to Vienna in 1907. There he applied unsuccessfully for a place as a student at the Academy of Fine Arts. For the next six years he led an aimless and unhappy existence in the poorer districts of the city. It was not until he joined the Bavarian Regiment on the outbreak of war in

1914 that he found a real purpose in life. He served bravely throughout the war and was awarded the Iron Cross, first class.

When the war ended, Hitler was in hospital recovering from a British gas attack. By the time he had returned to Bavaria in early 1919 he had already framed in his mind the core of what was to become National Socialism:

- fervent German nationalism
- support of authoritarianism and opposition to democracy and socialism
- a racially inspired view of society which exhibited itself most obviously in a rabid anti-Semitism and a veneration of the German *Volk* as the master race.

Such a mixture of ideas in a man whose personal life was much of a mystery – he had no close family and few real friends – has excited some historians to resort to psychological analysis leading to extraordinary speculation. Did his anti-Semitism originate from contracting syphilis from a Jewish prostitute? Could his authoritarian attitude be explained by his upbringing at the hands of an old and repressive father? Such psychological diagnoses – and there are many – may interest the student, but the supporting evidence for such explanations is at best flimsy. Or perhaps the influences came from further afield. One clue to his fierce anti-Semitism could be his encounters with **White Russian** émigrés who had fled Russia after the 1917 Bolshevik Revolution. They were extreme right-wing nationalists who saw Bolshevism as a part of a Jewish conspiracy for world domination. Many of them had been members of the notoriously violent Black Hundreds organisation, which had been involved in the worst of the **pogroms** in tsarist Russia. Yet, such suggestions are all highly speculative and do not really help to explain the key question of how and why Hitler became such an influential political force.

The creation and emergence of the Nazi Party

It was because of his committed right-wing attitudes that Hitler was employed in the politically charged atmosphere of 1919 as a kind of spy by the political department of the Bavarian section of the German Army. One of his investigations brought him into contact with the DAP (*Deutsche Arbeiterpartei* – German Workers' Party), which was not a movement of the revolutionary left as Hitler had assumed on hearing its name, but one committed to nationalism, anti-Semitism and **anti-capitalism**. Hitler joined the tiny party and immediately became a member of its committee. His energy, oratory and propaganda skills soon made an impact on the small group and it was Hitler who, with the party's founder, Anton Drexler, drew up the party's 25-points programme in February 1920 (see Source A). At the same time, it was agreed to change the party's name to the NSDAP, the National Socialist German Workers' Party. (For analysis of Nazi ideology, see pages 104–8.)

By mid-1921 it was clear that Hitler was the driving force behind the party. Although he still held only the post of propaganda chief, it was his powerful

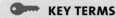

KEY TERMS

Volk Often translated as 'people', although it tends to suggest a nation with the same ethnic and cultural identities and with a collective sense of belonging.

White Russians Opponents of the Bolsheviks after the creation of the Soviet state.

Pogrom An organised or encouraged massacre of innocent people. The term originated from the massacres of Jews in Russia.

Anti-capitalism Rejects an economic system based on private property and profit.

speeches that had impressed local audiences and had helped to increase party membership to 3300. He had encouraged the creation of the armed squads to protect party meetings and to intimidate the opposition, especially the Communists. It was his development of early propaganda techniques – the Nazi salute, the swastika, the uniform – that had done so much to give the party a clear and easily recognisable identity.

SOURCE A

From the programme of the NSDAP, quoted in N. Baynes, translator and editor, *The Speeches of Adolf Hitler (1922–39)*, Oxford University Press, 1942, pp. 102–7.

1. We demand the union of all Germans in a Greater Germany on the basis of the right of national self-determination.

2. We demand equality of rights for the German People in its dealings with other nations, and the revocation of the peace treaties of Versailles and Saint Germain.

3. We demand land and territory (colonies) to feed our people and to settle our surplus population.

4. Only members of the Volk (nation) may be citizens of the State. Only those of German blood, whatever their creed may be members of the nation. Accordingly no Jew may be a member of the nation. …

7. We demand that the State shall make it its primary duty to provide a livelihood for its citizens. If it should prove impossible to feed the entire population, non-citizens must be deported from the Reich. …

10. It must be the first duty of every citizen to perform physical or mental work. The activities of the individual must not clash with the general interest, but must proceed within the framework of the community and be for the general good. …

14. We demand profit sharing in large industrial enterprises.

15. We demand the extensive development of insurance for old age. …

18. We demand the ruthless prosecution of those whose activities are injurious to the common interest. Common criminals, usurers, profiteers must be punished with death, whatever their creed or race. …

25. We demand the creation of a strong central power of the Reich.

> **?** In what ways did the NSDAP programme in Source A attempt to appeal to the fears and prejudices of the German people?

Alarmed by Hitler's increasing domination of the party, Drexler and some other members of the committee tried to limit his influence. However, it was here, for the first time, that Hitler showed his political ability to manoeuvre and to gamble. He was by far the most influential speaker and the party knew it, so, shrewdly, he offered to resign. In the ensuing power struggle he was quickly able to mobilise support at two meetings in July 1921. He was invited back triumphant. Embarrassed, Drexler resigned and Hitler became chairman and *Führer* (leader) of the party.

Adolf Hitler

1889	Born in Braunau-am-Inn, Austria. Left school with no real qualifications
1914–18	Served the German Army and awarded the Iron Cross, first class
1921	Appointed leader of the NSDAP
1923–4	Beer Hall *putsch*. Sentenced to five years in prison for treason; wrote *Mein Kampf*
1925–33	Restructured the party and committed the party to a 'legality policy'
1933	Appointed German chancellor by Hindenburg
	Given dictatorial powers by the Enabling Law
1934	Ordered the purge of the SA, known as the Night of the Long Knives
	Death of Hindenburg: Hitler assumed the joint offices of chancellor and president and the title of *Führer*
1938	Blomberg–Fritsch crisis. Purge of army generals and other leading conservatives
1939	Ordered the invasion of Poland on 1 September (resulting in the declaration of war by Britain and France)
1941	Ordered the invasion of the USSR on 22 June
1944	Survived assassination in the Stauffenberg Bomb Plot
1945	Killed himself in the ruins of Berlin

Hitler's outlook on life was shaped by his unhappy years in Vienna (1907–13) when he failed to become an art student. It was here, too, that the core of his political ideas was established: anti-Semitism, German nationalism, anti-democracy and anti-Marxism. Hitler found a real purpose only in the war of 1914–18.

His nationalism and the camaraderie of the troops gave him direction, but the shock of Germany's surrender confirmed his prejudices.

In post-war Germany Hitler was drawn to the NSDAP, which remained a fringe political party in Bavaria in the 1920s. The depression created the environment in which he could exploit his political skills: his charisma, his rhetoric and his advanced use of propaganda. Nevertheless, although he became the leader of the largest party by 1932, he was only invited to be chancellor in January 1933 as part of a coalition with other nationalists and conservatives.

The Nazi dictatorship was established with immense speed and Hitler was personally given unlimited powers. He was portrayed as the all-powerful dictator, but there has been great debate about his direction of daily affairs (see pages 171–5). Nevertheless, Hitler's leadership controlled German events through:

- creating a one-party state
- supporting the racial policy that culminated in genocide
- pursuing an expansionist foreign policy.

Below the surface Hitler's regime was chaotic, but the cult of the *Führer* was upheld by Goebbels' propaganda machine, as well as by the diplomatic and military successes of 1935–41. However, winter 1942–3 marked the 'turn of the tide' and Hitler, increasingly deluding himself, refused to consider surrender. It was only when the Red Army closed in on Berlin that the spell of the *Führer*'s power was finally broken – by Hitler killing himself in his bunker.

Having gained supreme control over the party in Munich, Hitler aimed to subordinate all the other right-wing groups under his party's leadership and certainly, in the years 1921–3, the party was strengthened by a number of significant developments:

- The armed squads were organised and set up as the **SA** in 1921 as a paramilitary unit led by Ernst Röhm (see page 161). It was now used to organise planned thuggery and violence. Most notoriously, the conflict in the town of Coburg degenerated into a pitched battle between the Communists and the SA, but it showed how politically vital it was to win to control of the streets.

 KEY TERM

SA *Sturmabteilung*, became known in English as the Brownshirts after the colour of their uniform. They supported the radical socialist aspects of Nazism.

- The party established its first newspaper in 1921, the *Völkischer Beobachter* (*People's Observer*).
- In 1922 Hitler won the backing of Julius Streicher, who previously had run a rival right-wing party in northern Bavaria. Streicher also published his own newspaper, *Der Stürmer,* which was overtly anti-Semitic with a range of seedy articles devoted to sex and violence.
- Hitler was also fortunate to win the support of the influential Hermann Göring, who joined the party in 1922 (see page 196). He was born into a Bavarian landowning family, while his wife was a leading Swedish aristocratic. They made many very helpful social contacts in Munich, which gave Hitler and Nazism respectability.

By 1923 the party had a membership of about 20,000. Hitler certainly enjoyed an impressive personal reputation and, as a result, Nazism successfully established an influential role on the extreme right in Bavaria. However, despite Nazi efforts, it still proved difficult to control all the radical right-wing political groups, which remained independent organisations across Germany. The Nazi Party was still very much a fringe party, limited to the region of Bavaria.

The Beer Hall *Putsch* 1923

The successful takeover of power by **Mussolini** in Italy in October 1922, combined with the developing internal crisis in Germany, convinced Hitler that the opportunity to seize power had arrived. Indeed, a leading Nazi introduced Hitler at one of his speeches in Munich by saying: 'Germany's Mussolini is called Adolf Hitler'. However, the Nazis were far too weak on their own to stage any kind of political takeover and Hitler himself was still seen merely as a 'drummer' who could stir up the masses for the national movement. It was the need for allies which led Hitler into negotiations with Kahr and the Bavarian state government and the Bavarian section of the German Army under Lossow (see page 48).

It was with these two men that Hitler plotted to 'March on Berlin' (in the style of Mussolini's coup which, only the previous year, had become known as the 'March on Rome'). They aimed to mobilise all the military forces from Bavaria – including sections of the German Army, the police, the SA and other paramilitaries – and then, by closing in on Berlin, to seize national power. With hindsight, Hitler's plan was unrealistic and doomed because:

- He grossly overestimated the level of public support for a *putsch* – despite the problems faced by Weimar's democratic government in 1923.
- He showed a lack of real planning.
- He relied too heavily on the promise of support of Ludendorff.
- Most significantly, at the eleventh hour, Kahr and Lossow, fearing failure, decided to hold back.

Hitler was not so cautious and preferred to press on rather than lose the opportunity. On 8 November, when Kahr was addressing a large audience in

KEY FIGURE

Benito Mussolini (1883–1945)

Journalist and at first a socialist. Became leader of the National Fascist Party in 1919 and seized power in the 'March on Rome' in 1922. He ruled Italy as a dictator known as *Il duce* (the leader) 1925–43.

one of Munich's beer halls, Hitler and the Nazis took control of the meeting, declared a 'national revolution' and forced Kahr and Lossow to support it. The next day Hitler, Göring, Streicher, Röhm (and Ludendorff) marched into the city of Munich with 2000 SA men, but they had no real military backing, and the attempted takeover of Munich was easily crushed by the Bavarian police. Fourteen Nazis were killed and Hitler was arrested on a charge of treason.

The consequences

In many respects the *putsch* was a farce. Hitler and the *putschists* were arrested and charged with treason and the NSDAP itself was banned. However, Hitler gained significant political advantages from the episode:

SOURCE B

'Hitler's entry into Berlin.' A cartoon published by the *Simplicissimus* magazine in April 1924 just after Hitler's trial.

In Source B, how are Hitler and Ebert portrayed?

- He turned his trial into a great propaganda success both for himself and for the Nazi cause. He played on all his rhetorical skills and evoked admiration for his patriotism. For the first time he made himself a national figure.
- He won the respect of many other right-wing nationalists for having had the courage to act.
- The leniency of his sentence – five years, the minimum stipulated by the Weimar constitution and actually reduced to ten months – seemed like an act of encouragement on the part of the judiciary.
- He used his months in prison to write and to reassess his political strategy (see below), including dictating *Mein Kampf*.

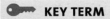

KEY TERM

Mein Kampf 'My struggle.' The book written by Hitler in 1924, which expresses his political ideas.

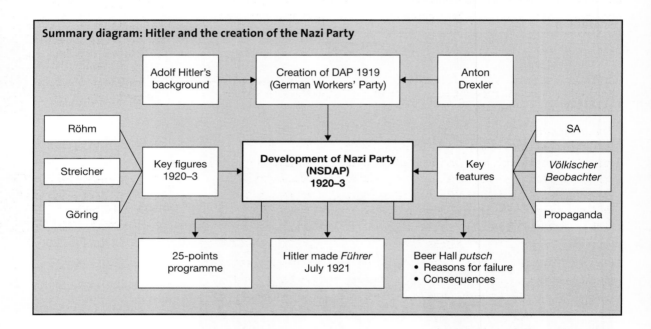

Summary diagram: Hitler and the creation of the Nazi Party

2 Nazi ideology

▶ *What were the main elements of Nazi thinking?*

▶ *Was Nazism an original German ideology?*

Nazism always emphasised the importance of action over thought. However, while in Landsberg prison, Hitler dictated the first part of *Mein Kampf* which, in the following years, became the bible of National Socialism. Together with the 25-points programme of 1920, it provided the basic framework of Nazi ideology.

Racism

Hitler's ideas were built on his concept of race. He believed that humanity consisted of a hierarchy of races and that life was no more than 'the survival of the fittest'. He argued that **Social Darwinism** necessitated a struggle between races, just as animals fought for food and territory in the wild. Furthermore, he considered it vital to maintain racial purity, so that the blood of the weak would not undermine the strong.

It was a crude philosophy, which appears even more simplistic when Hitler's analysis of the races is considered. The *Herrenvolk* (master-race) was the **Aryan** race and was exemplified by the Germans. It was the task of the Aryan to remain pure and to dominate the inferior races. At the lower end of his racial pyramid Hitler placed the Slavs, gypsies and negroes and the particular focus of his hatred, the Jews. In the following extract from *Mein Kampf* Hitler writes:

SOURCE C

From Adolf Hitler, *Mein Kampf*, Hurst & Blackett, 1939, p. 248. (See also the 25-points programme, page 100: points 4 and 7.)

The adulteration of the blood and racial deterioration conditioned thereby are the only causes that account for the decline of ancient civilisations; for it is never by war that nations are ruined, but by the loss of their powers of resistance, which are exclusively a characteristic of pure racial blood. In this world everything that is not of sound stock is like chaff. Every historical event in the world is nothing more, nor less, than a manifestation of the instinct of racial self-preservation, whether for weal or woe [for better or for worse].

Hitler's anti-Semitism was violent and irrational. The Jew became the universal scapegoat for the Nazis, responsible for all Germany's problems past and present. Hitler saw the Jewish community as a kind of cancer within the German political body – a disease that had to be cut out. However, he was the product, not the creator, of a society that was permeated by such prejudices. There was a long tradition of anti-Semitism in European history. It was not the preserve of the Nazis, and it certainly has never been a purely German phenomenon. It was rooted in the religious hostility of Christians towards the Jews (as being responsible for the death of Christ) that could be traced back to medieval Europe. There had emerged in Germany, in the course of the nineteenth century, a more clearly defined anti-Semitism based on racism and national resentment. By 1900 a number of specifically anti-Semitic *völkisch* political parties were winning seats in the *Reichstag* and, although they were comparatively few, their success shows that anti-Semitic ideas were becoming more prevalent and generally more respectable.

KEY TERMS

Social Darwinism
A philosophy that portrayed the world as a 'struggle' between people, races and nations. Hitler viewed war as the highest form of 'struggle' and was deeply influenced by the theory of evolution based on natural selection.

Aryan Defined by the Nazis as the non-Jewish people of northern Europe. Technically, refers to people whose language has an Indian/European root.

According to Hitler in Source C, what were the reasons for the rise and fall of nations?

Anti-democracy

In Hitler's opinion, there was no realistic alternative to strong dictatorial government. Ever since his years in Vienna he had viewed parliamentary democracy as weak and ineffective. It went against the German historical traditions of militarism and the power of the state. Furthermore, it encouraged the development of an even greater evil, communism.

More specifically, Hitler saw Weimar democracy as a betrayal. In his eyes, it was the democratic and socialist politicians of 1918, the 'November criminals', who had stabbed the German Army in the back, by accepting the armistice and establishing the republic. Since then, Germany had lurched from crisis to crisis.

In place of democracy Hitler wanted an all-embracing one-party state that would be run on the **Führerprinzip**, which rejected representative government and liberal values. Thus, the masses in society were to be controlled for the common good, but an individual leader was to be chosen in order to rouse the nation into action, and to take the necessary decisions. (See also the 25-points programme, page 100: point 25.)

Nationalism

A crucial element in Nazi thinking was an aggressive nationalism, which developed out of the particular circumstances of Germany's recent history. The armistice of 1918 and the subsequent Treaty of Versailles had to be overturned, and the lost territories had to be restored to Germany (see pages 32–3). But Hitler's nationalism called for more than a mere restoration of the 1914 frontiers. It meant the creation of an empire (*Reich*) to include all those members of the German *Volk* who lived beyond the frontiers of Imperial Germany: the Austrian Germans; the Germans in the Sudetenland; the German communities along the Baltic coast; all were to be included within the borderlands of Germany.

Yet, Hitler's nationalist aims did not end there. He dreamed of a Greater Germany, a superpower, capable of competing with the British Empire and the USA. Such an objective could be achieved only by territorial expansion on a grand scale. This was the basis of Hitler's demand for **Lebensraum** for Germany. Only by the conquest of Poland, the Ukraine and Russia could Germany obtain the raw materials, cheap labour and food supplies so necessary for continental supremacy. The creation of his 'New Order' in eastern Europe also held one other great attraction: namely, the destruction of the USSR, the centre of world communism. In *Mein Kampf*, Hitler wrote (Source D):

SOURCE D

From Adolf Hitler, *Mein Kampf*, , Hurst & Blackett, 1939, p. 17. (See also the 25-points programme, page 100: points 1–3.)

The German people must be assured the territorial area which is necessary for it to exist on earth … People of the same blood should be in the same Reich. The

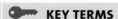

KEY TERMS

Führerprinzip 'The leadership principle.' Hitler upheld the idea of a one-party state, built on an all-powerful leader.

Lebensraum 'Living space.' Hitler's aim to create an empire by establishing German supremacy over the eastern lands in Europe.

According to Source D, what were Hitler's main political aims?

German people will have no right to engage in a colonial policy until they shall have brought all their children together in one state. When the territory of the Reich embraces all the Germans and finds itself unable to assure them a livelihood, only then can the moral right arise, from the need of the people, to acquire foreign territory … Germany will either become a World Power or will not continue to exist at all. … The future goal of our foreign policy ought to be an Eastern policy, which will have in view the acquisition of such territory as is necessary for our German people.

The socialist aspect of Nazism

A number of points in the 1920 programme demanded socialist reforms and, for a long time, there existed a faction within the party that emphasised the anti-capitalist aspect of Nazism, for example:

- profit sharing in large industrial enterprises
- the extensive development of insurance for old age
- the nationalisation of all businesses.

Hitler accepted these points in the early years because he recognised their popular appeal but he himself never showed any real commitment to such ideas. As a result, they were the cause of important differences within the party and were not really dropped until Hitler had fully established his dominant position by 1934. (See also the 25-points programme, page 100: points 10, 14 and 15.)

What Hitler and Goebbels later began to promote was the concept of the *Volksgemeinschaft* (people's community). This remained the vaguest element of the Nazi ideology, and is therefore difficult to define precisely. First, it was intended to overcome the old differences of class, religion and politics. But secondly, it aimed to bring about a new collective national identity by encouraging people to work together for the benefit of the nation and by promoting 'German values'. Such a system could of course benefit only those who racially belonged to the German *Volk* and who willingly accepted the loss of individual freedoms in an authoritarian system (see pages 210–55).

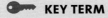

KEY TERM

Volksgemeinschaft
'A people's community.' Nazism stressed the development of a harmonious, socially unified and racially pure community.

The ideology of National Socialism

Early historians and biographers of Hitler simply saw him as a cynical opportunist motivated by the pursuit of power. Others have now generally come to view him as a committed political leader influenced by certain key ideas that he used to lay the basis of a consistent Nazi programme.

To describe Hitler's thinking, or Nazism, as an ideology is really to flatter it. An 'ideology' suggests a coherent thought-through system or theory of ideas, as found, for example, in Marxism. Nazism lacked coherence and was intellectually superficial and simplistic. It was not genuinely a rational system of thought, just a random collection of ideas. It was not in any positive sense original – every aspect of Hitler's thinking was to be found in the nationalist and racist writings of the nineteenth century:

- Hitler's nationalism was an outgrowth of the fervour generated in the years leading up to Germany's unification of 1871.
- Hitler's idea of an all-German *Reich* was a simple repetition of the demands for the 'Greater Germany' made by those German nationalists who criticised the limits of the 1871 unification.
- Even the imperialism of *Lebensraum* had already found expression in the programme of 'Germanisation' supported by those writers who saw the German race as somehow superior.
- The growing veneration for the *Volk* had gone hand-in-hand with the development of racist ideas, and in particular of anti-Semitism.

Thus, even before Hitler and other leading Nazis were born, the core of what would become Nazism was already current in political circles. It was to be found in the cheap and vulgar pamphlets sold to the masses in the large cities; in the political programme of respectable pressure groups, such as the **Pan-German League**; within the corridors of Germany's great universities; and in the creative works of certain cultural figures, such as the composer Richard Wagner.

Despite these links, one must avoid labelling Nazi ideology as the logical result of German intellectual thinking. It is all too easy to emphasise those elements that prove the linkage theory, while ignoring the host of other evidence that points to entirely different views, for example the strong socialist tradition in Germany. Moreover, it is well to remember that a number of countries, but especially Britain and France, also witnessed the circulation of very similar ideas at this time. In that sense, nationalism and racism were an outgrowth of nineteenth-century European history. Nazi ideology may not have been original, but it should not therefore be assumed that it was an inevitable result of Germany's past.

KEY TERM

Pan-German League
A movement founded in the late nineteenth century, which campaigned for the uniting of all Germans into one country.

Summary diagram: Nazi ideology

Racism:
- Social Darwinism
- Anti-Semitism

Anti-democracy:
- *Führerprinzip*
- One-party state

Key Nazi ideas expressed in:
- 25-points programme
- *Mein Kampf*

Nationalism:
- Restoration of German territories
- *Lebensraum*

Socialist aspects:
- Anti-capitalism
- *Volksgemeinschaft*

Nazi ideology

Was Nazism an original German ideology?

Nazi fortunes in the 1920s

▶ *In what ways was the Nazi Party revitalised and how strong was it by 1929?*

When Hitler left prison in December 1924 the future for Nazism looked bleak. The party was in disarray; its leading members were split into factions and the membership was in decline. More significantly, the atmosphere of crisis that had prevailed in the early years of the republic had given way to a period of political and economic calm (see pages 71–94). Nevertheless, the party was officially refounded on 27 February 1925 and at the same time Hitler wrote a lengthy editorial for the *Völkischer Beobachter* with the heading 'A new beginning'.

Strategy and leadership

In Landsberg prison Hitler, reflecting on the failure of the 1923 *putsch*, became convinced of two vital points: first, that he must re-establish his own absolute control over the party, and secondly, that an armed coup was no longer an appropriate tactic. Therefore, a new policy was necessary, as Hitler told Ludecke when he received a visit from him in prison (see Source E).

SOURCE E

From K. Ludecke, quoted in J. Noakes and G. Pridham, editors, *Nazism 1919–45*, volume 1, University of Liverpool Press, 1988, p. 37.

I must have looked at him incredulously. 'Oh yes', he continued, 'I am not going to stay here much longer. When I resume active work it will be necessary to pursue a new policy. Instead of working to achieve power by armed conspiracy, we shall have to hold our noses and enter the Reichstag against the Catholic and Marxist deputies. If out-voting them takes longer than our shooting them, at least the result will be guaranteed by their own Constitution! Any lawful process is slow.

> According to Source E, how and why did Hitler aim to work within the constitution?

The Nazi Party remained deeply divided in a number of ways:

- Not everyone agreed with the new policy of legality.
- Traditional regional hostilities continued to exist, particularly between the party's power base in Bavaria and the branches in northern Germany.
- Most importantly, policy differences had become more pronounced between the nationalist and anti-capitalist wings of the party (see page 107).

For over a year Hitler struggled with this internal friction. The problem was highlighted by the power and influence of Gregor Strasser and also his brother Otto. Gregor Strasser joined the NSDAP in 1920 and stood loyally next to Hitler in the Munich *putsch*, but he epitomised the opposing standpoint within the party. He favoured the more socialist anti-capitalist policies for the workers and he was, in effect, the leader of the movement in northern Germany.

Gregor Strasser

1892	Born in Bavaria and trained as a pharmacist
1920	Joined the NSDAP and supported the anti-capitalist, socialist faction
1923	Took part in the Munich Beer Hall *putsch*
1926	Defeated by Hitler over the party's leadership at the party conference in Bamberg
1926–32	Responsible for building the mass movement of the party
	Led the NSDAP in northern Germany
1932	Offered the post of vice-chancellor by Chancellor Schleicher
	Expelled from the party by Hitler
1934	Murdered in the Night of the Long Knives

Gregor Strasser was a significant figure in the rise of Nazis. He was, in effect, second to Hitler until 1932. He was always a supporter of the anti-capitalist 'left-wing' socialist faction, which became increasingly disillusioned when Hitler courted big business (see page 148). Like Hitler, an inspiring political speaker, he also showed the administrative skills to develop a mass movement for the party. (He should not be confused with his brother, Otto, who initially supported the party but left it in 1930.)

Eventually, in February 1926, the ideological and personality differences within the party came to a head at a special party conference in Bamberg. On the one hand, it was a significant victory for Hitler, as he mobilised sufficient support to re-establish his supremacy. The Nazi Party was to be run according to the *Führerprinzip* and there was to be no place for disagreements. On the other hand, the party declared that the original 25 points of the programme with its socialist elements remained unchangeable. So, although Hitler had cleverly outmanoeuvred his greatest threat and he had re-established a degree of unity within the party, there were still significant rivalries and differences.

The creation of the party structure

The most significant development in the years before the Great Depression lay in the reorganisation of the party structure. The whole of Germany was divided into regions (*Gaue*), which reflected the electoral geography of Weimar's system of proportional representation. The control of each region was placed in the hands of a **Gauleiter**, who then had the responsibility of creating district (*Kreis*) and branch (*Ort*) groups. In this way, a vertical party structure was created throughout Germany, which did not detract from Hitler's own position of authority as leader.

Perhaps the most renowned of the *Gauleiter*s was the holder of the Berlin post, Joseph Goebbels. Goebbels had originally been a sympathiser of Strasser's socialist ideas, but from 1926 he transferred his support to Hitler. He was then rewarded by being given the responsibility for winning over the capital, a traditionally left-wing stronghold of the SPD. He showed a real interest in propaganda and created the newspaper, *Der Angriff* (*The Attack*), but was not appointed chief of party propaganda until 1930 (see page 218).

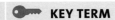 **KEY TERM**

Gauleiter 'Leader of a regional area.' The Nazi Party was organised into 35 regions from 1926.

The Nazis also founded a number of new associated Nazi organisations that were geared to appeal to the specific interests of particular groups of Germans. Among these were:

- the **Hitler Youth**
- the Nazi Teachers' Association
- Union of Nazi Lawyers
- the Order of German Women.

Strasser was mainly responsible for building up an efficient party structure and this was reflected in its increasing membership during these years (see Table 4.1).

One other significant initiative in these years was the creation of the **SS**. It was set up in 1925 as an elite body of black-shirted guards, sworn to absolute obedience to the *Führer*. In 1929 it had only 200 members. At first, it was just Hitler's personal bodyguard, although, when it was placed under the control of Himmler later that year, it soon developed its own identity.

The *Reichstag* election of May 1928

By 1928 it can be seen clearly that the party had made progress and was really an effective political machine, most obviously because:

- The structure was effectively organised.
- The membership had increased four-fold since 1925.
- Hitler's leadership was authoritative and secure (despite the ongoing challenge from the Strasser faction).

As a result, the Nazi Party had also successfully absorbed many of the other right-wing racist groups in Germany. Such advances, however, could not compensate for Nazi disappointment after the *Reichstag* election in May 1928. When the votes were counted, the party had won only 2.6 per cent of the vote and a mere twelve seats (see page 76). It seemed as if Hitler's policy of legality had failed to bring political success, whereas in the favourable socio-economic circumstances Weimar democracy had managed to stabilise its political position. So, Nazism may have taken root, but there was no real sign that it could flourish in Germany.

If this evidence confirmed the belief of many that Hitler was nothing more than an eccentric without the personal leadership to establish a really broad national appeal, there was just one development which ran counter to this. In the election, the party made significant gains in the northern part of Germany among the rural middle and lower-middle classes of areas such as Schleswig-Holstein.

This trend was reflected in the regional state elections of 1929, which suggested that the fall in agricultural prices was beginning to cause discontent – demonstrations and protests were giving way to bankruptcies and violence.

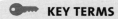

KEY TERMS

Hitler Youth The Nazi youth organisation. In German: *Hitlerjugend* (*HJ*).

SS *Schutz Staffel* (Protection Squad); became known as the Blackshirts after their uniform.

Table 4.1 NSDAP membership

Year	Membership
1925	27,000
1926	49,000
1927	72,000
1928	108,000

Most significantly, in the province of Thuringia, in central Germany, the Nazi Party trebled its vote in regional elections and broke the ten per cent barrier for the first time, recording 11.3 per cent. Such figures suggested that the Nazis could exploit the increasingly difficult economic times of the Great Depression.

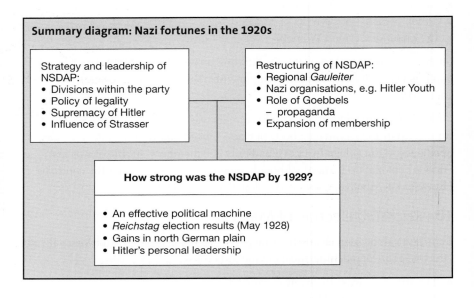

Summary diagram: Nazi fortunes in the 1920s

Strategy and leadership of NSDAP:
- Divisions within the party
- Policy of legality
- Supremacy of Hitler
- Influence of Strasser

Restructuring of NSDAP:
- Regional *Gauleiter*
- Nazi organisations, e.g. Hitler Youth
- Role of Goebbels – propaganda
- Expansion of membership

How strong was the NSDAP by 1929?

- An effective political machine
- *Reichstag* election results (May 1928)
- Gains in north German plain
- Hitler's personal leadership

Chapter summary

Hitler emerged from an obscure background. He and the Nazi Party were the clear products of the difficulties of post-war Germany. Nazi ideology grew out of an uncompromising rejection of Weimar democracy and socialism; instead, fervent nationalism and racism, especially anti-Semitism, were embraced.

The strategy of seizing power in the Munich *putsch* of 1923 was a disaster and Hitler's imprisonment could have ended his political ambitions once and for all. Nevertheless, once he was released, the party was revitalised. The restructuring of the many Nazi organisations and the dynamic propaganda led by Goebbels helped to lay better foundation stones for the party.

Despite successful exploitation of the discontent in the rural areas as the agricultural recession set in, Nazi results were very disappointing in the 1928 *Reichstag* election.

Refresher questions

Use these questions to remind yourself of the key material covered in this chapter.

1 How did Hitler become involved in politics?

2 What was Hitler's aim in the *putsch* and why did it fail?

3 How did Hitler manage to turn the failure of the Munich Beer Hall *putsch* to his advantage?

4 Explain the main elements of Nazi thinking in relation to the following: racism, anti-democracy, nationalism and socialism.

5 Was Nazism an original ideology?

6 In what ways was the Nazi Party revitalised from 1925?

7 How strong was the Nazi Party by the end of the 1920s?

Question practice

ESSAY QUESTIONS

1 'The Nazi Party was of no importance in the years 1920–9.' Explain why you agree or disagree with this view?

2 To what extent is it right to describe the Nazi Party as weak in the years before 1929?

3 'Weimar's economic recovery is the main reason for the failure of Hitler and the Nazi Party in the years 1920–9.' Assess the validity of this view.

SOURCE ANALYSIS QUESTIONS

1 With reference to Sources 1 and 2 (below and on page 114), and your understanding of the historical context, which of these two sources is more valuable in explaining why Hitler and the NSDAP gained support in the early 1920s?

2 With reference to Sources 1, 2 and 3 (below and on page 114), and your understanding of the historical context, assess the value of these sources to a historian studying whether the NSDAP had become a significant party by 1928.

SOURCE 1

Hitler describing early Nazi public meetings in 1920, quoted in Adolf Hitler, *Mein Kampf*, Hurst & Blackett, 1939, p. 389.

The meetings nearly always started with the subject of War guilt, about which nobody then bothered, and then went on to the Peace Treaties; violent methods of speech were found suitable and, indeed necessary.

In those days, if a public mass meeting, at which ordinary workers were present, dealt with the Versailles Treaty, it was taken as being an attack on the Weimar Republic. The moment Versailles was criticised, there would regularly be interruptions; 'And Brest-Litovsk?' The crowd would continue to shout until it persuaded them. We felt inclined to dash our heads against the wall with despair at such people! They would not understand that Versailles was a shame and a disgrace, or that a dictated peace was a frightening plundering of our nation.

SOURCE 2

A report on events in Munich in November 1923 written by Paul Gierasch, a journalist, quoted in M. Collier and P. Pedley, *Germany 1919–45*, Heinemann, 2000, p. 153.

The National Socialists are neither Socialist or in any true sense national. The named 'socialist' is used a bait to the working men for a movement that has anti-communism as its inspiration. To Hitler's party flock young people of the feather-brained, unbalanced type – students, clerks and others who have lost their economic security. In his speeches Hitler asked that the German nation be cleansed of all non-Aryan elements. He says that Germany would be free of all ills if Jewish economic power were destroyed. However, he argues that first of all, accounts must be settled with what he calls the traitorous Jewish Socialist leaders who have plunged the German people into misery.

SOURCE 3

A speech by Nazi deputy Wilhelm Kube to the rural population of Oldenburg in north-west Germany in 1928, quoted in Geoff Layton, *Weimar and the Rise of Nazi Germany*, Hodder Murray, 2005, p. 118.

We have recognised that the distress of agricultural is inseparably bound up with the political misery of the whole German people; the parliamentarism, which is corrupt through and through and a weak government are unable to overcome the German political and economic emergency.

Let us do away with this Marxist-capitulation extortion system that has made Germany, our homeland, powerless, without honour, defenceless, and that has turned free German farmers and middle class people into poor, misused slaves of the world stock exchange …

Only when Germany is reborn in power, freedom and honour, led by unselfish German men who are not burdened by the contemptible policy of the last few years, only then will the German farmer stand as a free man on free soil serving the great German community as the backbone of our people.

CHAPTER 5

The collapse of democracy

In the 1920s Hitler and Nazism took root, but they did not make any real political impact. It was the onset of the world depression which precipitated a political and economic crisis in Germany. This chapter prompts two key inextricably linked questions: 'Why did Weimar democracy fail?' and 'Why did the Nazis take power?' These issues will be examined in the following sections:

★ The world economic crisis

★ The breakdown of parliamentary government

★ Brüning: presidential government

★ Papen's 'Cabinet of Barons'

★ The death of Weimar democracy

★ The Nazi mass movement

★ Nazi political methods

★ Political intrigue and the appointment of Hitler

★ The Nazi 'legal revolution'

The key debate on *page 155* of this chapter asks the question: Was the creation of the Nazi dictatorship an inevitable product of German history?

Key dates

1929	Oct.	Wall Street Crash and onset of global depression	1932	May	Resignation of Brüning. Papen appointed as chancellor
1930	March	Collapse of Müller's government and Brüning appointed as chancellor		July	*Reichstag* election: Nazis emerged as largest party
	Sept.	*Reichstag* election: Nazis emerged as second largest party		Sept.	*Reichstag* passed a massive vote of no confidence in Papen's government
	Dec.	Brüning's economic measures imposed by presidential decree		Dec.	Papen dismissed and replaced by Schleicher as chancellor
1931	July	Five leading German banks failed	1933	Jan. 30	Schleicher dismissed and Hitler appointed as chancellor
1932	Jan.	Unemployment peaked at 6.1 million		Feb. 27	*Reichstag* fire: communists blamed
	April	Re-election of Hindenburg as president of Germany		March 5	Final elections according to Weimar constitution
				March 23	Enabling Law passed

1 The world economic crisis

▶ *What were the political, economic and social effects of the world economic crisis on Germany?*

There is no dispute among historians that the economic crisis known as the Great Depression was an event of major significance. Its effects were felt throughout most of the world.

Germany undoubtedly felt it in a particularly savage way. It suffered the consequences of the **Wall Street Crash** perhaps more than any other country. Almost immediately, US loans and investment dried up and this was quickly followed by demands for the repayment of those short-term loans. At the same time, the crisis caused a further decline in the price of food and raw materials as industrialised nations reduced their imports. As demand for exports collapsed, so world trade slumped. In this situation, German industry could no longer pay its way. Without overseas loans and with its export trade falling, prices and wages fell and the number of bankruptcies increased.

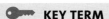

KEY TERM

Wall Street Crash The collapse of share prices on the New York Stock Exchange in October 1929.

Table 5.1 Economic effects of the world economic crisis on Germany

Economic effects	Key features
Trade	
Slump in world trade. Demand for German exports fell rapidly, for example steel, machinery and chemicals	Exports value fell by 55% 1929 = £630 million 1932 = £280 million
Employment	
Workers laid off – mass unemployment	Number of registered unemployed (annual averages) 1929 = 1.8 million 1932 = 5.6 million
Industry	
Industrial production declined sharply	Production (1928 = 100%) 1929 = 100% 1932 = 58%
Agriculture	
Wages and incomes fell sharply. Many farms sold off	Agricultural prices (1913 = 100%) 1927 = 138% 1932 = 77%
Finance	
Banking sector dislocated by loss of confidence	Five major banks collapsed in 1931; 50,000 businesses bankrupted

It is, however, all too easy to put Germany's economic crisis down to the Wall Street Crash. It should be borne in mind that there were fundamental weaknesses in the German economy *before* the crash:

- The **balance of trade** was in the red, that is, it was in debt.
- The number of unemployed averaged 1.9 million in 1929, even before the Wall Street Crash.
- Many farmers were already in debt and had been facing falling incomes since 1927.
- German government finances from 1925 were continually run in deficit.

Although the Wall Street Crash contributed to Germany's economic problems, it is *probable* that the German economy faced a chance of a serious depression without it. This suggests that the world economic crisis should really be seen as simply the final push that brought the Weimar economy to collapse. In that sense, it could be said that the Wall Street Crash was merely the occasion, not the cause of Germany's economic crisis.

The human effects of the Great Depression

During the winter of 1929–30 unemployment rose above 2 million and only twelve months after the crash it had reached 3 million. By January 1932 it stood at 6.1 million, which did not substantially fall until the spring of 1933. On their own, such figures can provide only a limited understanding of the effects of a depression of this magnitude. Unemployment figures, for example, do not take into account those who did not register. Nor do they record the extent of part-time working throughout German industry.

Most significantly, statistics fail to convey the extent of the human suffering that was the consequence of this disaster because the depression in Germany affected virtually everyone; few families escaped its effects.

Many manual industrial workers, both skilled and unskilled, faced the prospect of long-term unemployment. For women, there was the impossible task of trying to feed families and keep homes warm on the money provided by limited social security benefits.

Such problems were not to be limited to the working classes. This depression dragged down the middle classes. From the small shopkeepers to the professionals in law and medicine, people struggled to survive in a world where there was little demand for their goods and services. For such people, the decline in their economic position and the onset of poverty were made more difficult by the loss of pride and respectability.

The situation in the countryside was no better than in the towns. As world demand fell further, the agricultural depression deepened, leading to widespread rural poverty. For some **tenant farmers** there was even the ultimate humiliation of being evicted from their homes, which had often been in their families for generations.

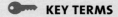

KEY TERMS

Balance of trade The difference in value between exports and imports. If the value of the imports is above that of exports, the balance of the payments has a deficit that is often said to be 'in the red'.

Tenant farmer A farmer who works land owned by someone else and pays rent either in cash or in a share of the produce.

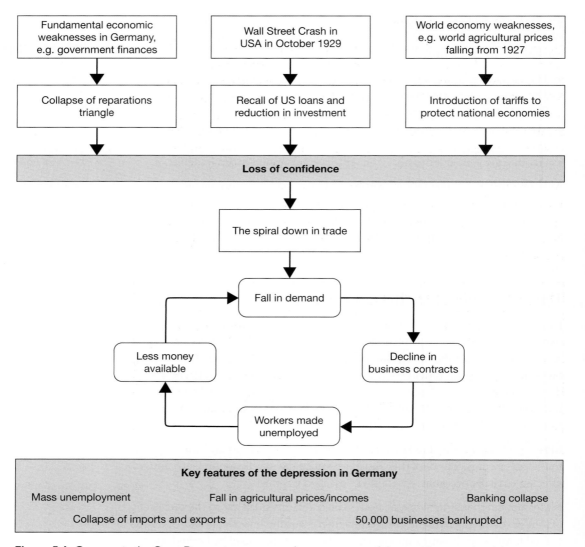

Figure 5.1 Germany in the Great Depression: causes and consequences of the world economic crisis.

Today it is difficult to appreciate the scale of the suffering that struck German people in the early 1930s. The city of Cologne could not pay the interest on its debts, banks closed their doors and, in Berlin, large crowds of unemployed youngsters were kept occupied with open-air games of chess and cards. To many ordinary respectable Germans it seemed as if society itself was breaking down uncontrollably. It is not surprising that many people lost faith in the Weimar Republic, which seemed to offer no end to the misery, and began to see salvation in the solutions offered by political extremists. This was why the economic crisis in Germany quickly degenerated into a more obvious political crisis.

The political implications

The impact of the depression in Germany was certainly more severe than in either Britain or France, but it was equivalent to the US experience. By 1932 in Germany, one in three workers was unemployed and industrial production had fallen by 42 per cent of its 1929 level. In the USA, the comparable figures were one in four and 46 per cent. However, in Germany the economic crisis quickly became a political crisis, simply because there was a lack of confidence that weakened the republic's position in its hour of need. Britain, France and the USA were all well-established democracies and did not face the possibility of a wholesale collapse of their political systems.

Taken together, these two points suggest that the depression hastened the end of the Weimar Republic, but only because its economy was already in serious trouble, and the democratic basis of its government was not sufficiently well established.

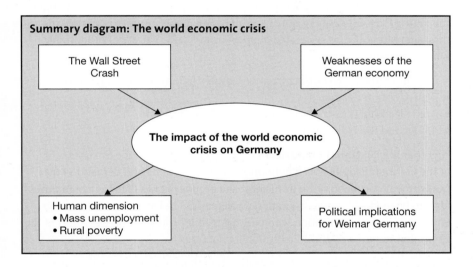

Summary diagram: The world economic crisis

The Wall Street Crash

Weaknesses of the German economy

The impact of the world economic crisis on Germany

Human dimension
• Mass unemployment
• Rural poverty

Political implications for Weimar Germany

2 The breakdown of parliamentary government

▶ *Why did the Grand Coalition eventually break up?*

▶ *How did the leadership of Brüning weaken democracy?*

In 1929 the German government was in the hands of Hermann Müller's Grand Coalition, which had been formed after the general election of May 1928 (see page 76). Yet, at the time when unity and firm government were required, the Weimar Republic was torn apart by the re-emergence of the emotive issue of reparations.

The Young Plan and the National Opposition

The Dawes Plan successfully overcame the reparations crisis by rescheduling payments but, from the outset, it was seen as a temporary measure until Germany regained its economic strength (see page 84). In 1929 the Inter-Allied Reparations Commission (IARC) formed a committee of financiers under the chairmanship of the US banker Owen Young and its report suggested a new scheme of payments. Germany was to continue paying reparations until 1988, but the final sum was reduced to £1850 million (only one-quarter of the figure demanded in 1921). After some negotiation, the German government, shortly before Stresemann's death, accepted the Young Plan.

In German right-wing circles, however, Stresemann's diplomacy was seen as another betrayal of national interests to the Allies. In their view, any payment of reparations was based upon the 'lie' of the War Guilt clause and the new scheme, therefore, had to be opposed. A national committee, created by Alfred Hugenberg and the new leader of the DNVP (see page 79), was formed to fight the Young Plan. Hugenberg now used all his media resources to promote his message. Moreover, he generated support from a wide variety of other right-wing nationalist factions:

- *Stahlhelm* (the largest ex-servicemen's organisation), led by Franz Seldte
- Pan-German League
- some leading industrialists, for example, Fritz Thyssen
- Hitler and the Nazi Party.

KEY TERM

National Opposition
A title given to a group of various political forces that was forged out of the Young Plan in 1929 to oppose all reparations payments.

Together this **National Opposition** drafted a Law Against the Enslavement of the German People, which denounced any reparations and demanded the punishment of collaborating ministers. The proposal gained enough signatures for it to be made the issue of a national referendum in December 1929. In the end, the National Opposition won only 5.8 million votes, a long way short of the 21 million required by the constitution for success.

The campaign of the National Opposition had, however, stirred nationalist emotions. It had brought together many right-wing opponents of the Republic. For Hitler, the campaign also showed clear-cut benefits:

- Party membership grew to 130,000 by end of 1929.
- Nazism really gained a national standing for the first time.
- The main party rally at Nuremberg had been a great propaganda success on a much more grandiose scale than any before.
- Hitler made influential political contacts on the extreme right wing.
- It brought the opportunity of having access to Hugenberg's media empire.

The collapse of Müller's Grand Coalition

Müller's coalition government successfully withstood the attack from the National Opposition. However, it was not so successful in dealing with its own internal divisions. Müller, a Social Democrat, struggled to hold the coalition together, and it was an issue of finance which finally brought down the government in March 1930.

The sharp increase in unemployment had created a large deficit in the new national insurance scheme (see page 72) and the four major parties in the coalition could not agree on how to tackle it. The SPD, as the political supporters of the trade unions, wanted to increase the contributions and to maintain the levels of welfare payments. The DVP, on the other hand, had strong ties with big business and insisted on reducing benefits. Müller could no longer maintain a majority and he had no option but to tender the resignation of his government.

The appointment of Heinrich Brüning

President Hindenburg granted the post of chancellor to Heinrich Brüning. At first sight, this appeared an obvious choice, since he was the parliamentary leader of the ZP, the second largest party in the *Reichstag*. However, with hindsight, it seems that Brüning's appointment marked a crucial step towards the end of true parliamentary government. This was for two reasons. First, he was manoeuvred into office by a select circle of political intriguers, who surrounded the ageing President Hindenburg:

- Otto Meissner, the president's state secretary
- Oskar von Hindenburg, the president's son
- Major General **Kurt von Schleicher**, a leading general.

All three were conservative nationalists and had limited faith in the democratic process. Instead, they looked to the president and the emergency powers of Article 48 of the constitution (see page 21) as a means of creating a more authoritarian government. In Brüning, they saw a respectable, conservative figure who could offer firm leadership.

Secondly, Brüning's response to the growing economic crisis led to a political constitutional crisis. His economic policy was to propose cuts in government expenditure, so as to achieve a balanced budget and prevent the risk of reviving inflation. However, the budget was rejected in the *Reichstag* by 256 votes to 193 in July 1930. When, despite this, Brüning put the proposals into effect by means of an emergency decree, signed by the president according to Article 48, the *Reichstag* challenged the decree's legality and voted for its withdrawal. Deadlock had been reached. Brüning therefore asked Hindenburg to dissolve the *Reichstag* and to call an election in September 1930.

Nazi breakthrough

Brüning had hoped that in the developing crisis the people would be encouraged to support the parties of the centre-right, from which a coalition could be formed. However, the election results proved him wrong (see Table 5.2), as explained by Count Harry Kessler in his diary entry (see Source A).

 KEY FIGURE

Kurt von Schleicher (1882–1934)

Professional soldier and civil servant. Defence minister in Papen's presidential government and chancellor from December 1932 to January 1933. Murdered in the Night of the Long Knives.

To what extent do you think that Kessler's analysis in Source A was accurate?

SOURCE A

From Harry Kessler, *Berlin in Lights: The Diaries of Count Harry Kessler 1918–37*, Grove Press, 2001, p. 381.

A black day for Germany. The Nazis have increased their representation tenfold, they have risen from 12 to 107 seats and have thus become the second largest party in the Reichstag. The impression abroad is bound to be catastrophic, the aftermath, both diplomatically and financially will be dreadful. With 107 Nazis, 41 Hugenbergers, and over 70 Communists, that is to say, some 220 deputies who radically rejected the present German state and seek to overthrow it by revolutionary means, we are confronted with a political crisis which can only be mastered by the formation of a strong united front of all those forces which support or at least tolerate the Republic. ...

National Socialism is the feverish symptom of the dying German petty bourgeoisie; but this poison of its illness can bring misery to Germany and Europe for decades to come. This class cannot be saved; but in its death-throes it can bring terrible new suffering to Europe.

Table 5.2 *Reichstag* election results for 1928 and 1930. (See also major political parties on page 16.)

	Turnout	NSDAP	DNVP	DVP	ZP/BVP	DDP	SPD	USPD/KPD	Others
May 1928									
Seats	491	12	73	45	78	25	153	54	51
%	75.6	2.6	14.2	8.7	15.2	4.9	29.8	10.8	14.0
September 1930									
Seats	577	107	41	30	87	20	143	77	72
%	82.0	18.3	7.0	4.5	14.8	3.8	24.5	13.1	13.8

The key features about the performance of the political parties are as follows:

- Nazis: with 107 seats and 18.3 per cent, the NSDAP became the second largest political party in Germany.
- Nationalists: the vote of the DNVP was halved from 14.2 to 7 per cent, largely benefiting the Nazis.
- Middle-class democratic parties: the DDP and the DVP lost twenty seats between them.
- Left-wing parties: the vote of the SPD declined from 29.8 to 24.5 per cent, although in contrast the vote of the KPD, the Communists, increased from 10.8 to 13.1 per cent.

As the result of the 1928 *Reichstag* election had been so disappointing, not even Hitler could have expected the dramatic gains of 1930. Nevertheless, there are several key factors to explain the Nazi breakthrough:

- Since 1928 the Nazi leaders had deliberately directed their propaganda at rural and middle-class/lower middle-class audiences. Nazi gains were at the expense of the DNVP, DVP and DDP.
- Nazi success cannot just be explained by these 'protest votes'. Nearly half of the Nazi seats were won by the party's attracting 'new' voters:
  - The electorate had grown by 1.8 million since the previous election because a new generation of voters had been added to the roll.
  - The turnout had increased from 75.6 to 82 per cent.

It would seem that the Nazis had not only picked up a fair proportion of these young first-time voters, but also persuaded many people who had not previously participated in elections to support their cause.

The implications of the 1930 *Reichstag* election were profound. It meant that the left and right extremes had made extensive gains against the pro-democratic parties. This now made it very difficult for proper democratic parliamentary government to function.

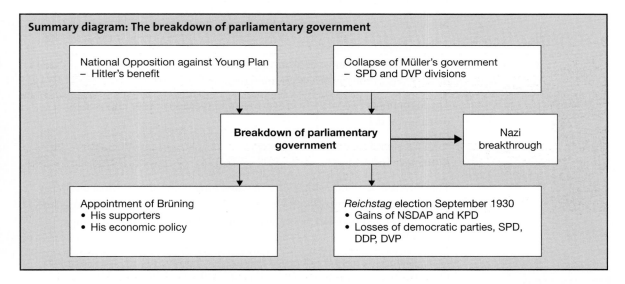

Summary diagram: The breakdown of parliamentary government

National Opposition against Young Plan
– Hitler's benefit

Collapse of Müller's government
– SPD and DVP divisions

Breakdown of parliamentary government

Nazi breakthrough

Appointment of Brüning
• His supporters
• His economic policy

Reichstag election September 1930
• Gains of NSDAP and KPD
• Losses of democratic parties, SPD, DDP, DVP

③ Brüning: presidential government

▶ *Was Brüning economically incompetent, or simply a victim of the circumstances?*

Brüning's political position after the election was undoubtedly difficult. His plan of reinforcing his parliamentary support from the centre-right had not succeeded. Instead, he faced the committed opposition of the more powerful extremes of both left and right. However, Brüning was not dismissed as chancellor; he still enjoyed the support of Hindenburg and his government was 'tolerated' by the SPD. Although the SPD did not join the government, it resolved not to oppose in *Reichstag* the emergency decrees of Article 48 because of the threat now facing the republic from the extremists.

In this way, true parliamentary democracy gave way to 'presidential government' with some backing from the *Reichstag*. From 1930 to 1932 Brüning remained as chancellor and he governed Germany by the use of Article 48 through President Hindenburg. He was almost a semi-dictator, as can be seen from his growing use of presidential decrees (see Table 5.3).

Table 5.3 Presidential government 1930–2

	1930	1931	1932
Presidential decree laws (Article 48)	5	44	66
Reichstag **laws**	98	34	5
Sitting days of the *Reichstag*	94	42	13

Economic policy

Brüning's economic policy was at least consistent in pursuing his aims:

- to balance the budget
- to prevent the chance of restarting inflation
- to get rid of the burden of German reparations

Throughout his two years in office, his main measures were imposed by presidential decree:

- to cut spending drastically
- to raise taxes.

This lowered demand, which led to a worsening of the slump. Most obviously, there was a large increase in the number of unemployed and a serious decline in welfare state provision. Soon he was mocked with the title 'the Hunger Chancellor'.

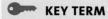

KEY TERM

Public works Employment schemes financed by the state to provide jobs.

Many historians have condemned Brüning's economic regime for sticking to his policy of reducing expenditure, for seriously worsening the situation and enabling the rise of the Nazis. He was criticised particularly for his failure in the summer of 1931 to introduce economic measures, such as **public works** in the construction industry. These might just have been enough to lessen the worst effects of the depression during 1932.

It could be argued that Brüning had limited economic alternatives. This was because the German economy had entered the depression with such severe weaknesses from the 1920s (see page 73) that economic failure was unavoidable. On these grounds, therefore, it could be argued that no chancellor would have been in a position to expand the economy and that Brüning was at the mercy of other forces.

Heinrich Brüning

1885	Born into a Catholic trading family
1904–11	Attended Munich University and awarded a doctorate in economics
1915–18	Volunteered in the war and won the Iron Cross, first class
1924–33	Elected to the *Reichstag* as ZP deputy – and party leader from 1929
1930	Appointed as chancellor by Hindenburg in March
	His July budget was rejected by the *Reichstag* resulting in the *Reichstag* election of September 1930
1932	Proposed land reform of the Prussian estates
	Dismissed as chancellor by Hindenburg
1934	Fled to the Netherlands and emigrated to the USA
1970	Died in the USA

Brüning was a political and economic conservative. He was very much on the right wing of the ZP, with a hostility towards socialism, which made it difficult for him to work with the left-wing parties when he became the party leader. In his heart, he remained a monarchist and hoped to amend the Weimar constitution to make it a more authoritarian system.

The significance of Brüning's career is almost completely concentrated into the two years of his chancellorship. He certainly did not sympathise with the Nazis, but his policies and decisions have been heavily criticised because:

- He called for the *Reichstag* election in September 1930 and misread the political consequences.
- He remained committed to the economic programme of balancing the budget, which resulted in enormous economic and political pressures.
- He relied on Hindenburg for the emergency decrees – and he failed to recognise his overdependence on the president.

In his defence, he was a man of integrity and a victim of exceptional circumstances. His historical reputation is perhaps overshadowed by the later development of the Nazi dictatorship.

Brüning's fall from power

In the spring of 1932 Hindenburg's first seven-year term of office as president came to an end. Brüning committed himself to securing Hindenburg's re-election and after frenetic campaigning Hindenburg was re-elected on the second ballot. He gained 19.3 million votes (53 per cent) compared with Hitler's 13.4 million (36.8 per cent). However, it was a negative victory. Hindenburg had been chosen only because he was the sole alternative between Hitler and the KPD candidate, **Ernst Thälmann**. Also, despite losing, Hitler had doubled the Nazi vote and had projected an even more powerful personal image. Moreover, Hindenburg showed no real gratitude to Brüning and, at the end of May 1932, the president forced his chancellor to resign because of the following factors:

- the banking crisis
- land reform
- intrigue.

Banking crisis

The collapse of the major bank, the Danat, and several others in June 1931 revived fears of financial crisis. By the end of the year unemployment was

 KEY FIGURE

Ernst Thälmann (1886–1944)

KPD leader 1925–33. *Reichstag* member 1924–33. Unquestioning supporter of the Soviet line. Held in concentration camp until his murder in 1944.

approaching 5 million people and there were demonstrations in the streets. In October 1931 the National Opposition (see page 120) was reborn as the Harzburg Front. It brought together a range of right-wing political, military and economic forces who demanded the resignation of Brüning and a new *Reichstag* election. The front arranged a massive rally to denounce Brüning, but in the winter of 1931–2 the chancellor still enjoyed the support of Hindenburg.

KEY TERM

Junkers The landowning aristocracy, especially from eastern Germany.

Land reform

Brüning aimed to issue an emergency decree to turn some **Junkers** estates in east Prussia into 600,000 allotments for unemployed workers. Landowners saw this as a threat to their property interests and dubbed it 'agrarian bolshevism'.

Intrigue

Brüning's unpopularity over land reform spurred on the group of right wingers, led by Kurt von Schleicher, who probably pushed for the resignation of the chancellor with the aim of creating a right-wing government (see Source B).

? Groener himself was forced to resign his own post just a few days before Brüning. How may this have affected Groener's explanation of Brüning's fall from power in Source B?

SOURCE B

From the memoirs of General Groener written in the 1930s, quoted in Geoff Layton, *From Bismarck to Hitler*, second edition, Hodder Arnold, 2002, p. 154.

I knew very well that the intention was to bring down the Chancellor. In the course of the winter, the Reich President had twice mentioned to me that Dr. Brüning did not quite represent his ideal as Reich Chancellor. He did not accept my comment that at the moment he would not find a better one. General Schleicher had also made no bones about the fact that he was thinking in terms of a change of Chancellor. In view of his connexions with the Reich President's entourage, it can be assumed that he took part in the removal of Dr. Brüning as Chancellor. During the absence of the Reich President in Neudeck, his country estate, where Brüning's fall was decided upon, General Schleicher was in continual contact by telephone with Hindenburg's son.

Brüning could be viewed as an innocent sacrifice who was removed by Hindenburg without consultation with the *Reichstag*. However, it should be borne in mind that he had only survived as chancellor because he enjoyed the personal backing of the president. Brüning had agreed to the creation of presidential government based on the powers granted by Article 48 of the constitution, but he was not astute enough to recognise the precarious nature of his own position. He depended solely on retaining the confidence of the president. This makes it harder to sympathise with him when he became the victim of the intrigue of the presidential court.

Assessment of Brüning

Brüning was an honest, hard-working and honourable man who failed. He was not really a committed democrat, but neither was he sympathetic to Nazism, an important point to remember. In many respects, Brüning was making good progress towards his aims, when he was dismissed:

- He succeeded in ending the payment of reparations.
- He sympathised with the reduction of the democratic powers of the *Reichstag*.

However:

- He was not astute enough to appreciate how dangerous and unstable the economic crisis had become in Germany by 1932.
- Neither did he realise how insecure was his own position. For as long as Brüning retained the confidence of Hindenburg, presidential government protected his position.

With no real hope of improvement in the economic crisis, it is not surprising that large sections of the population looked to the Nazis to save the situation. Brüning would have nothing to do with Hitler and the Nazis and he continued to uphold the **rule of law**. Sadly, presidential rule had made Germany become accustomed to rule by decree. In this way, democracy was undermined and the path was cleared for more extreme political parties to assume power. In the end, it is hard to escape the conclusion that Brüning's chancellorship was a dismal failure, and, in view of the Nazi tyranny that was soon to come, a tragic one.

 **KEY TERM**

Rule of law Governing a country according to its laws.

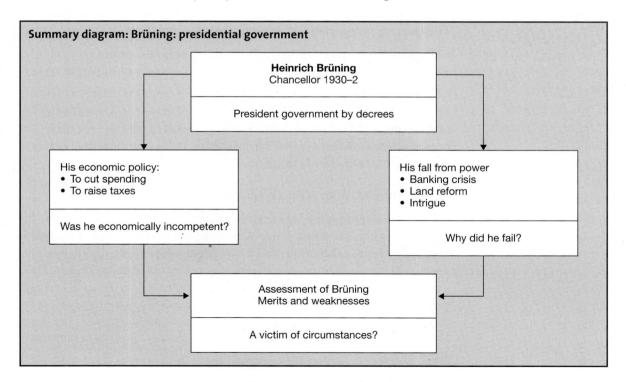

Summary diagram: Brüning: presidential government

Heinrich Brüning
Chancellor 1930–2

President government by decrees

His economic policy:
- To cut spending
- To raise taxes

Was he economically incompetent?

His fall from power
- Banking crisis
- Land reform
- Intrigue

Why did he fail?

Assessment of Brüning
Merits and weaknesses

A victim of circumstances?

Papen's 'Cabinet of Barons'

> ▶ *What was Papen's political aim in 1932?*
> ▶ *Why was the* Reichstag *election of July 1932 so politically significant?*

Schleicher now sought to use his influence with Hindenburg by recommending Franz von Papen as the new chancellor. If many greeted the choice of Papen with disbelief, it was his very lack of ability which appealed to Schleicher, who saw the opportunity to influence events more directly through him. As an aristocrat, Papen had good connections with high society; as a Catholic, he was a member of the ZP, although his political views mirrored those of the nationalists. His outlook quickly formed the basis for a close friendship with Hindenburg.

Papen was politically ambitious, but his understanding and experience of politics were limited (he did not even hold a seat in the *Reichstag*). The new cabinet was called a non-party government of 'national concentration', although it was soon nicknamed the 'Cabinet of Barons'. It was a presidential government dominated by aristocratic landowners and industrialists – like Papen, many were not even members of the *Reichstag*. In order to strengthen the government, Papen and Schleicher wanted to secure political support from the Nazis. Hitler agreed not to oppose the new government in return for two concessions:

- the dissolution of the *Reichstag* and the calling of fresh elections
- the end of a government ban on the SA and SS, introduced after violence during the presidential campaign.

Papen and Schleicher hoped that this agreement with the Nazis would result in the creation of a right-wing authoritarian government with some popular support in the form of the Nazis. The *Reichstag* was therefore dissolved and an election was arranged for 31 July 1932.

Reichstag election: July 1932

The election campaign was brutal, as street violence once again took hold in the large cities. In the month of July alone 86 people died as a result of political fights. Yet, such bloodshed provided Schleicher and Papen with the excuse to abolish the most powerful regional state government in Germany: Prussia. This government of Prussia had long been a coalition of the SPD and the ZP and had been the focus of right-wing resentment since the creation of the republic. So, on 20 July 1932, it was simply removed by Papen, who declared a state of emergency and appointed himself as *Reich* Commissioner of Prussia. This was of immense significance:

- It was an arbitrary and unconstitutional act.
- It replaced a parliamentary system with a presidential authoritarian government.

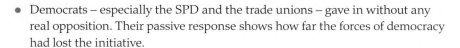

Franz von Papen

1879	Born into a Catholic aristocratic family
1913–18	Cavalry officer and diplomat
1932	In May he was appointed chancellor to head his 'Cabinet of Barons'
	Dissolved the *Reichstag*, with serious consequences
	Removed the Prussian state government in July
	Defeated by a vote of no confidence in the *Reichstag* in September
1933	Appointed as vice-chancellor in Hitler's coalition
1934	Resigned after the Night of the Long Knives

| 1946 | Found not guilty of war crimes in the Nuremberg trials |
| 1969 | Died |

Papen had limited political experience and was really out of his depth. His advance was mainly due to his connections with the aristocracy, the Catholic Church and big business. He was always a monarchist and a nationalist (although nominally a member of ZP). As chancellor, he aspired to undo the Weimar constitution and was quite happy to rule by presidential decrees and to denounce the state government of Prussia. Despite pursuing his personal ambitions he was quickly outmanoeuvred by Hitler.

- Democrats – especially the SPD and the trade unions – gave in without any real opposition. Their passive response shows how far the forces of democracy had lost the initiative.

Many on the right wing congratulated Papen on the Prussian coup. However, it did not win him any additional electoral support. When the election results came in (see Table 5.4, page 130), it was again the Nazis who had cause to celebrate, which raised serious implications for the country, as reported by a Reich minister in Source C.

SOURCE C

From a report by ex-Reich minister Dr Külz in a memorandum, quoted in J.W. Hiden, *The Weimar Republic*, Longman, 1974, pp. 101–2.

Looked at politically, objectively, the result of the election is so fearful because it seems that the present election will be the last normal Reichstag election for a long time to come … The elected Reichstag is totally incapable of functioning …

If things are faced squarely and soberly the situation is such that more than half the German people have declared themselves against the present state, but have not said what sort of state they would accept. Thus, any organic development is for the moment impossible. As the lesser of many evils to be feared, I think, would be the open assumption of dictatorship by the present government.

Explain why the author in Source C states that the 'Reichstag is totally incapable of functioning'. Refer also to the details in Table 5.4.

It is worth bearing in mind the following key features about the performance of the political parties:

- Nazis: with 230 seats and 37.3 per cent of the vote the NSDAP became the largest political party in Germany.

- Nationalists: the vote of the DNVP fell further to 5.9 per cent.
- Middle-class democratic parties: the DDP and the DVP collapsed disastrously. They polled only 2.2 per cent of the vote and gained just eleven seats between them.
- Left-wing parties: the vote of the SPD declined further to 21.6 per cent, although in contrast the vote of the KPD increased to 14.3 per cent.

In electoral terms the gains of the Nazis could be explained by:

- the collapse of the DDP and DVP vote
- the decline of the DNVP
- a small percentage of disgruntled workers changing from SPD to NSDAP
- the support for the 'other parties' falling from 13.8 to 2.9 per cent, which suggests that their loyalty transferred to the Nazis
- the turnout increasing to 84 per cent, which indicated the same trend as in September 1930 that the party was attracting even more 'new voters'.

Table 5.4 *Reichstag* election results 1928–32. (See also major political parties on page 16.)

	Turnout	NSDAP	DNVP	DVP	ZP/BVP	DDP	SPD	KPD	Others
May 1928									
Seats	491	12	73	45	78	25	153	54	51
%	75.6	2.6	14.2	8.7	15.2	4.9	29.8	10.8	14.0
September 1930									
Seats	577	107	41	30	87	20	143	77	72
%	82.0	18.3	7.0	4.5	14.8	3.8	24.5	13.1	13.8
July 1932									
Seats	608	230	37	7	97	4	133	89	11
%	84.1	37.3	5.9	1.2	15.7	1.0	21.6	14.3	2.9

Table 5.5 Germany's governments 1928–33

Chancellor	Dates in office	Type of government
Hermann Müller (SPD)	May 1928–March 1930	Parliamentary government. A coalition cabinet of SPD, ZP, DDP and DVP. (See pages 119–21)
Heinrich Brüning (ZP)	March 1930–May 1932	Presidential government dependent on emergency decrees. A coalition cabinet from political centre and right. (See pages 121–7)
Franz von Papen (ZP, but very right wing)	May 1932–December 1932	Presidential government dependent on emergency decrees. Many non-party cabinet members. (See pages 128–32)
General Kurt von Schleicher (Non-party)	December 1932–January 1933	Presidential government dependent on emergency decrees. Many non-party cabinet members. (See pages 146–7)
Adolf Hitler (NSDAP)	1933–45	Coalition cabinet of NSDAP and DNVP, but gave way to Nazi dictatorship. (See pages 147–8)

Two further points are worth remembering about the *Reichstag* election of July 1932. First, only 39.5 per cent voted for the pro-democratic parties; and secondly, added together, the percentage of votes for the KPD and NSDAP combined to 51.6 per cent. These two political facts are telling indeed. The German people had voted to reject democracy.

German Communist Party 1919–33 (*Kommunistische Partei Deutschlands*, KPD)

It is easy to forget during the Nazi rise to power that the communist movement remained a powerful alternative ideology until 1933. Indeed, the KPD was the largest communist party in Europe, with over 300,000 members in 1932.

The KPD had been formed in 1919 by the Spartacists. It was involved in most of the left-wing revolutionary disturbances of 1919–23 (see pages 39–42) and as a result these failures meant that it had lost its real militant potency. On the other hand, in the mid-1920s the new KPD leadership under Thälmann abandoned the goal of immediate revolution and committed itself to contesting *Reichstag* elections with some success, winning nine to twelve per cent of the national vote.

Ideologically, the leadership committed itself as loyal to the USSR under Stalin. More significantly, the KPD used these years to create a clear party identity with organisations which advanced the communist cause:

- The Red Front Fighters' League: the self-proclaimed military organisation which served to show its physical strength in the brawls with the SA.
- *The Red Flag* and *The Workers' Newspaper*: the two most significant instruments for propaganda and agitation.
- The Youth Communist League: recreational activities especially for working-class young people; set up for political indoctrination.
- The Alliance of Red Women and Girls.

In these ways, the KPD created an active party which was able to exploit the depression but only to a limited extent. For many of the long rows of unemployed people, communism gave them their last hope and its vote dramatically increased (see Table 5.6).

The KPD remained an opposition party with no commitment to the republic and no sympathy for democracy. Its uncompromising line was to blame the ruling bourgeoisie for the crisis of capitalism that would give way to a socialist revolution. Even more controversially, its theory of 'social fascism' saw the SPD as the main enemy. This scuppered any possibility of a united front with the SPD against the rising power of the Nazis.

Within a few months the KPD felt the full forces of the Nazi terror. It was blamed for the *Reichstag* fire; there were mass arrests and offices were closed down (see page 150). From that time, brave communists could only function as an underground opposition.

Table 5.6 KPD *Reichstag* election results in seats and percentage of vote 1924–32

Dec. 1924	45 (9%)
May 1928	54 (11%)
Sept. 1930	77 (13%)
July 1932	89 (14%)
Nov. 1932	100 (17%)

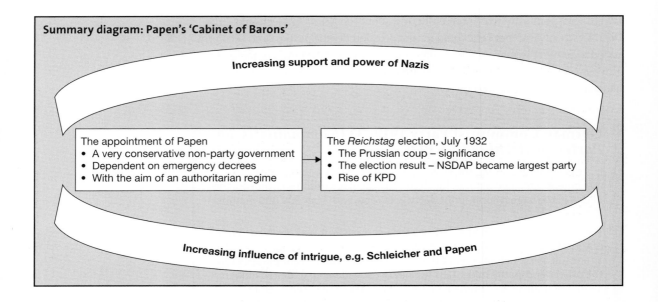

Summary diagram: Papen's 'Cabinet of Barons'

Increasing support and power of Nazis

The appointment of Papen
- A very conservative non-party government
- Dependent on emergency decrees
- With the aim of an authoritarian regime

The *Reichstag* election, July 1932
- The Prussian coup – significance
- The election result – NSDAP became largest party
- Rise of KPD

Increasing influence of intrigue, e.g. Schleicher and Papen

5 The death of Weimar democracy

▶ *When and why did democracy die?*

It is now clear that Weimar democracy was almost dead well before the establishment of the Nazi dictatorship (see pages 148–53). The problem for the historian is trying to determine when the Weimar Republic expired and why. Three fundamental weaknesses of the Weimar Republic stand out.

The hostility of Germany's vested interests

From the very start, the Weimar Republic faced the hostility of Germany's established elites. Following military defeat and the threat of revolution, this opposition was at first limited. However, the fact that so many key figures in German society and business rejected the idea of a democratic republic was a major problem for Weimar. They worked against the interests of Weimar and hoped for a return to the pre-war situation. This was a powerful handicap to the successful development of the republic in the 1920s and, in the 1930s, it was to become a decisive factor in its final collapse.

Ongoing economic problems

The republic was also troubled by an almost continuous economic crisis that affected all levels of society. It inherited the enormous costs of the First World War followed by the burden of post-war reconstruction, Allied reparations and the heavy expense of the new welfare benefits. So, even though the inflation crisis of 1923 was overcome, problems in the economy were disguised and remained unresolved. These were to have dramatic consequences with the onset of the world economic crisis in 1929.

Limited base of popular support

Weimar democracy never enjoyed widespread political support. There was never total acceptance of, and confidence in, its system and its values. From the republic's birth its narrow base of popular support was caught between the extremes of left and right. But, as time went by, Weimar's claims to be the legitimate government became increasingly open to question. Sadly, Weimar democracy was associated with defeat and the humiliation of the Treaty of Versailles and reparations. Its reputation was further damaged by the crisis of 1922–3. Significantly, even the mainstays of the Weimar Republic had weaknesses:

- The main parties of German liberalism, DDP and DVP, were losing support from 1924.
- The ZP and DNVP were both moving to the political right.
- Even the loyalty and the commitment of the SPD to democracy has to be balanced against its failure to join the coalitions in the mid-1920s and its conflict with its left-wing partner, the KPD.

In short, a sizeable proportion of the German population never had faith in the existing constitutional arrangements and, as the years passed, more were looking for change.

The changing phases of the Weimar Republic

These unrelenting pressures meant that Weimar democracy went through a number of phases:

- The difficult circumstances of its birth in 1918–19 left it impaired. It was in many respects, therefore, a major achievement that it survived the problems of the period 1919–23.
- The years of relative stability from 1924 to 1929, however, amounted to only a short breathing space and did not result in any strengthening of the Weimar system. On the eve of the world economic crisis it seemed that Weimar's long-term chances of survival were already far from good.
- In the end, the impact of the world depression, 1929–33, intensified the pressures that brought about Weimar's final crisis.

In the view of some historians, Weimar had been a gamble with no chance of success. For others, the republic continued to offer the hope of democratic survival right until mid-1932, when the Nazis became the largest party in the July *Reichstag* election. However, the manner of Brüning's appointment and his decision to rule by emergency decree created a particular system of presidential government. This fundamentally undermined the Weimar system and was soon followed by the electoral breakthrough of the Nazis. From this time, democracy's chance of surviving was very slim indeed. Democracy lived on with ever increasing weakness before it reached its demise in July 1932. However, in truth, democratic rule in Weimar Germany was terminal from the summer of 1930.

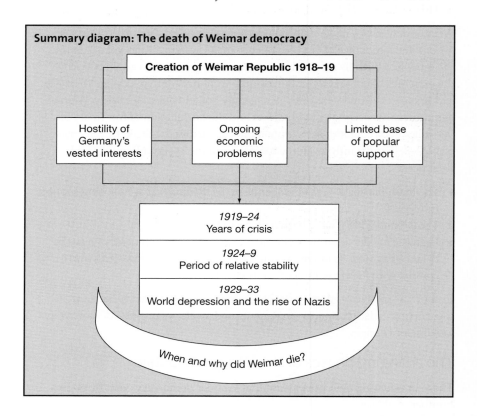

Summary diagram: The death of Weimar democracy

Creation of Weimar Republic 1918–19

Hostility of Germany's vested interests

Ongoing economic problems

Limited base of popular support

1919–24
Years of crisis

1924–9
Period of relative stability

1929–33
World depression and the rise of Nazis

When and why did Weimar die?

6 The Nazi mass movement

▶ *Who voted for the Nazis and why?*

The point is often made that Hitler and the Nazis never gained an overall majority in *Reichstag* elections. However, such an occurrence was very unlikely because of the number of political parties in Weimar Germany and the operation of the proportional representation system. Considering this, Nazi electoral achievements by July 1932 were very impressive. Only one other party on one other occasion had polled more: the SPD in the revolutionary atmosphere of January 1919 (see page 17). Nazism had become a mass movement with which millions identified and, as such, it laid the foundations for Hitler's coming to power in January 1933. Who were these Nazi voters and why were they attracted to the Nazi cause?

The results of the elections in 1928–32 show the changing balance of the political parties (see pages 122 and 130), although really these figures on their own are limited in what they show us about the nature of Nazi support. The graph and table in Figure 5.2 reveal a number of significant points about the kind of people who actually voted for the Nazis. From this, it seems fairly clear that the Nazis made extensive gains from those parties with a middle-class and/or a Protestant identity. By contrast, it is apparent that the Catholic parties, the Communist Party and, to a large extent, the Social Democrats were able to withstand the Nazi electoral gains.

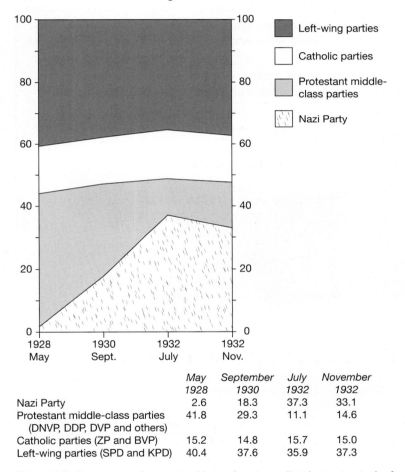

	May 1928	September 1930	July 1932	November 1932
Nazi Party	2.6	18.3	37.3	33.1
Protestant middle-class parties (DNVP, DDP, DVP and others)	41.8	29.3	11.1	14.6
Catholic parties (ZP and BVP)	15.2	14.8	15.7	15.0
Left-wing parties (SPD and KPD)	40.4	37.6	35.9	37.3

Figure 5.2 Percentage of vote gained by each major political grouping in the four *Reichstag* elections 1928–32.

Geography and denomination

These political trends are reflected in the geographical base of Nazi support, which was generally higher in the north and east of the country and lower in the south and west. Across the North German Plain, from East Prussia to

Schleswig-Holstein, the Nazis gained their best results and this seems to reflect the significance of two important factors: religion and urbanisation.

In the predominantly Catholic areas (see Figure 5.3) the Nazi breakthrough was less marked, whereas the more Protestant regions were more likely to vote Nazi. Likewise, the Nazis fared less well in the large industrial cities, but gained greater support in the more rural communities and in residential suburbs.

The Nazi vote was at its lowest in the Catholic cities of the west, such as Cologne and Düsseldorf. It was at its highest in the Protestant countryside of the north and north-east, such as Schleswig-Holstein and Pomerania. Therefore, Bavaria, a strongly Catholic region and the birthplace of Nazism, had one of the lowest Nazi votes. Such a picture does not, of course, take into account the exceptions created by local circumstances. For instance, parts of the province of Silesia, although mainly Catholic and urbanised, still recorded a very high Nazi vote. This was probably the result of nationalist passions generated in a border province, which had lost half its land to Poland.

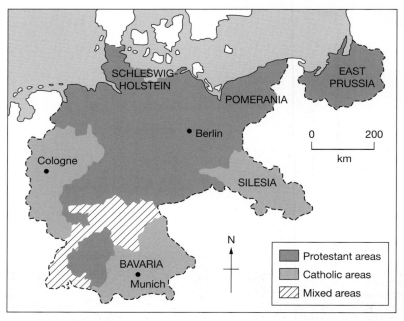

Figure 5.3 Electoral split by religion.

Class

Nazi voters also reflected the rural/urban division in terms of their social groupings. It therefore seems that the Nazis tended to win a higher proportion of support from:

- the peasants and farmers
- the *Mittelstand* (the lower-middle classes, such as artisans, craftsmen and shopkeepers)

- the established middle classes, such as teachers, **white-collar workers** and public employees.

Also, actual Nazi membership lists (see Figure 5.4 and Table 5.7) reveal clearly that a significantly higher proportion of the middle-class subsections (government officials/employees, self-employed and white-collar workers) tended to join the Nazi Party than the other classes. However, it is worth bearing in mind two other points. First, although the working class did join the Nazi Party in smaller proportions, it was still the largest section in the NSDAP. Secondly, although it seems that the peasantry tended to vote for the Nazis, the figures show they did not join the NSDAP in the same proportion.

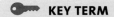

KEY TERM

White-collar workers
Workers not involved in manual labour.

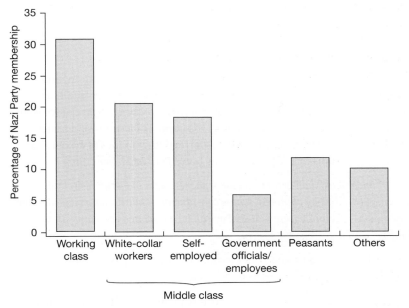

Figure 5.4 Nazi Party members in 1932.

Table 5.7 German society as a whole in 1933 (percentage)

	Middle class				
Working class	White-collar workers	Self-employed	Government officials/ employees	Peasants	Others
46.3	12.4	9.6	4.8	20.7	6.2

The appeal of Nazism

It is clear that more of the Protestants and the middle classes voted for Nazism in proportion to their percentage in German society. The real question is: why were Catholics or socialists not so readily drawn to voting for the Nazis?

- First, both Catholicism and socialism represented well-established ideologies in their own right and both opposed Nazism on an intellectual level.
- Secondly, the organisational strength of each movement provided an effective counter to Nazi propaganda. For socialism, there was the trade union structure: for Catholicism, there was the Church hierarchy, extending right down to the local parish priest.
- Thirdly, both movements had suffered under the Imperial German regime. As so often happens, persecution strengthened commitment. It was, therefore, much harder for the Nazis to break down the established loyalties of working-class and Catholic communities, and their traditional **associationism**, or identity, remained strong. In contrast, the Protestants, the farmers and the middle classes had no such loyalties. They were therefore more likely to accept the Nazi message.

KEY TERM

Associationism Having a strong identity or affiliation with a particular group.

The 'politics of anxiety'

What was common among many Nazi voters was their lack of faith in, and lack of identity with, the Weimar system. They believed that their traditional role and status in society was under threat. For many of the middle classes (see Figure 5.4) the crisis of 1929–33 was merely the climax of a series of disasters since 1918. Hitler was able to exploit what is termed 'the politics of anxiety', as expressed by the historian T. Childers in his book *The Nazi Voter* (1983):

> [By 1930] the NSDAP had become a unique phenomenon in German electoral politics, a catch-all party of protest, whose constituents, while drawn primarily from the middle class electorate were united above all by a profound contempt for the existing political and economic system.

In this way Hitler seemed able to offer to many Germans an escape from overwhelming crisis and a return to former days.

The observations of individuals reinforce this explanation. For example, in a letter in Source D a school headmaster gives an account of his thoughts at the time.

SOURCE D

According to Source D, what were the main motives for supporting the Nazis?

From a letter by the headmaster of a school written after the war in 1967, quoted in John Laver, *Nazi Germany 1933–45*, Hodder & Stoughton, 1991, p. 6.

I observed many things in Berlin which could not be noticed – or only to a degree – in small towns. I saw the Communist danger, the Communist terror, their gangs breaking up bourgeois meetings, the bourgeois parties being utterly helpless, the Nazis being the only party that broke terror by anti terror. I saw the complete failure of the bourgeois parties to deal with the economic crisis … Only National Socialism offered any hope. Anti-Semitism had another aspect in Berlin: Nazis mostly did not hate Jews individually, many had Jewish friends, but they were concerned about the Jewish problem … Nobody knew of any way to deal with it, but they hoped the Nazis would know.

Young people

Another clearly identifiable group of Nazi supporters was the youth of Germany. The depression hit at the moment when young adults from the pre-war baby-boom came of age and, however good their qualifications were, many had little chance of finding work. In a study of Nazi Party membership, 41.3 per cent of those who joined before 1933 had been born between 1904 and 1913, despite this age group representing only 25.3 per cent of the total population. Equally striking, of the young adults aged 20–30 who became members of political parties, 61 per cent joined the Nazis. Thus, it was the young who filled the ranks of the SA – often unemployed, disillusioned with traditional politics and without hope for the future. They saw Nazism as a movement for change, not a source of respectability. Equally, the SA activities gave them something to do. All ages were prepared to vote for the Nazis, but the younger members of society were actually more likely to become involved by joining the party.

Nazism: the people's party

The previous analysis should not obscure the fact that the Nazis still boasted a broader cross-section of supporters than any other political party. Unlike most of the other parties, the Nazis were not limited by regional, religious or class ties. So, by 1932 it is fair to say that the NSDAP had become Germany's first genuine *Volkspartei* or broad-based people's party. This point was made in a recent study of voting habits that suggests the Nazis became a mass party only by making inroads into the working-class vote. Hitler, therefore, succeeded in appealing to *all* sections of German society; it is simply that those from Protestant, rural and middle-class backgrounds supported the party in much greater numbers.

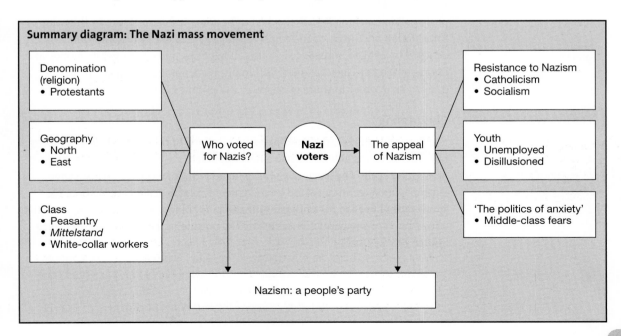

Summary diagram: The Nazi mass movement

7 Nazi political methods

▶ *In what ways did Goebbels develop propaganda?*

▶ *Did Nazi violence advance the rise of Nazism?*

It would be wrong to assume that voters for the Nazi Party were simply won over by the appeal of a radical political ideology at a time of economic crisis. There were still various fringe parties on the extreme right, which publicised similar messages. What made the Nazis stand out for the voters was their revolutionary political style. Or, to use present-day idiom, it was the presentation and packaging of the party and its programme.

Propaganda

From his earliest days in politics, Hitler had shown an uncanny, but cynical, awareness of the power of propaganda. In 1924 in *Mein Kampf* he had written:

> *The receptive powers of the masses are very restricted, and their understanding is feeble. On the other hand, they quickly forget. Such being the case, all-effective propaganda must be confined to a few bare essentials and those must be expressed as far as possible in stereotyped formulas.*

Such thinking was to remain the basis of Nazi propaganda, and there can be little doubt that its implementation in the years 1929–33 played a vital part in Nazi success.

The whole process of Nazi propaganda was highly organised. From April 1930 Joseph Goebbels was promoted and put in complete charge of the party's propaganda machine, which reached right down to branch level. In this way, information and instructions could be sent out from party headquarters and adapted to local circumstances. It also allowed the party to target its money and efforts in the key electoral districts. Finally, it encouraged feedback from the grassroots in order to share good ideas and put them into practice.

Canvassing

Posters and leaflets had always played an important role in Nazi electioneering, but Goebbels was able to initiate a new approach. He practised mass politics on a grand scale. The electorate was deluged with material that had a range of propaganda techniques and an increasingly sophisticated application. He showed a subtlety in his understanding of psychology, as shown by the directive issued by his propaganda office during the presidential campaign of 1932 (see Source E).

SOURCE E

From the Nazi *Reich* Propaganda Department to all regional departments, quoted in J. Noakes and G. Pridham, editors, *Nazism 1919–45*, volume 1, University of Liverpool Press, 1988, p. 73.

... Hitler poster. The Hitler poster depicts a fascinating Hitler head on a completely black background. Subtitle: white on black – 'Hitler'. In accordance with the Führer's wish this poster is to be put up only during the final days (of the campaign). Since experience shows that during the final days there is a variety of coloured posters, this poster with its completely black background will contrast with all the others and will produce a tremendous effect on the masses ...

SOURCE F

'Our Last Hope.' A Nazi poster of the 1932 presidential election.

According to Sources E and F, in what ways does Goebbels expect the poster to have an impact?

Goebbels correctly recognised the need to direct propaganda according to people's social and economic interests. Specific leaflets were produced for different social groups, and Nazi speakers paid particular attention to the concerns of the individual clubs and societies they addressed. In this way, the Nazi propaganda message was tailored to fit a whole range of people. For example:

- To appeal to farmers and peasants by offering special benefits to offset the collapse of agricultural prices.
- To appeal to the unemployed and the industrial workers by aiming to overcome the depression and offering 'bread' and 'work'.
- To appeal to the *Mittelstand*, for example, by limiting the control of large department stores.
- To appease the industrialists by playing down the fear of nationalisation and the state control of the economy.

Technology

Modern technology was also exploited. Loudspeakers, radio, film and records were all used. Expensive cars and aeroplanes were hired, not only for the practical purpose of transporting Hitler quickly to as many places as possible, but also to project a statesman-like image. In 1932 three major speaking programmes were organised for Hitler, called the 'Flight over Germany'. At a local level the political message was projected by the party arranging social events and entertainments such as sports, concerts and fairs.

Mass suggestion

It was in the organisation of the mass rallies that the Nazis showed their mastery of propaganda. The intention was to create an atmosphere so emotional that all members of the crowd would succumb to the collective will. This is the idea of **mass suggestion** and every kind of device was used to heighten the effect: uniforms, torches, music, salutes, flags, songs and anthems, and speeches from leading personalities. Many people have since described how they were converted as a result of such meetings.

Unifying themes and scapegoats

In order to project itself as a mass people's party, Nazism tried to embrace and bring together many of the disparate elements in Germany. This was partly achieved by Goebbels, who showed an astute ability to play on social and psychological factors to influence people (see Figure 5.5). Three key unifying themes dominated Nazi propaganda:

- The *Führer* cult. Hitler was portrayed as a messiah-type figure, who could offer strong authoritarian leadership and a vision for Nazi Germany's future.
- The *Volksgemeinschaft* (national community). To appeal to the people for the development of a unifying idea, regardless of class.

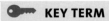
KEY TERM

Mass suggestion
A psychological term suggesting that large groups of people can be unified simply by the atmosphere of the occasion. Hitler and Goebbels used their speeches and large rallies to particularly good effect.

- German nationalism. To play on German nationalism and to exploit the discontent since the First World War. To make Germany great again.

Through these themes, Nazi propaganda successfully portrayed itself as both revolutionary and reactionary. The party aimed to destroy the republic, while at the same time promising a return to a glorious bygone age.

In addition, Nazism cynically played on the idea of 'scapegoats'. It focused on several identifiable groups, which were denounced and blamed for Germany's suffering:

- The 'November criminals'. The politicians responsible for the Armistice and the creation of the republic became representative of all aspects associated with Weimar democracy.
- Communists. By playing on the fears of communism – the KPD was a sizeable party of thirteen to seventeen per cent of the vote in 1930–2 – and the increasing threat of communist USSR.
- Jews. It was easy to exploit the long-established history of anti-Semitism in Europe as a whole, and in Germany in particular (although Jewish people only made up less than one per cent of the German population).

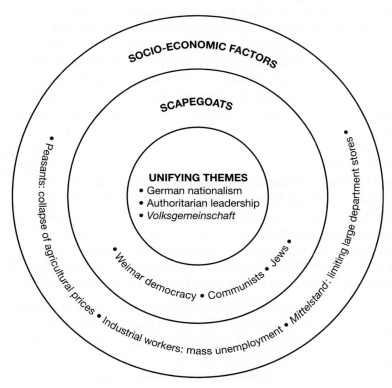

Figure 5.5 Nazi propaganda.

Violence

There was one other strand to the political style of this Nazi revolution: the systematic encouragement and use of violence. Weimar politics had been a bloody affair from the start, but the growth of the SA and SS unleashed an unprecedented wave of violence, persecution and intimidation.

The growth of unemployment resulted in a phenomenal expansion of the SA, led by Röhm, in 1921–3 and 1930–4. Understandably, many people joined as members of the SA out of desperation, for food and accommodation, although much of it was just thuggery. The SA mainly was responsible for the violence against the opposition, especially the Communists. All this helped to destabilise the already difficult situation in Germany and, in the wake of the presidential election (see page 125), the SA was actually banned for three months. However, it was restored by the new chancellor, Papen, in June 1932. So, during the campaign of July 1932, there were 461 political riots in Prussia alone: battles between Communists and Nazis on 10 July left ten people dead; a week later, nineteen died after the Nazis marched through a working-class suburb of Hamburg.

Such violent activities were encouraged by the Nazi leadership as control of the streets was seen as essential to the expansion of Nazi power. The ballot box of democracy remained merely a means to an end, and, therefore, other non-democratic tactics were considered legitimate in the quest for power. The Nazis poured scorn on rational discussion and fair play. For them, the end did justify the means. For their democratic opponents, there was the dilemma of how to resist those who exploited the freedoms of a democratic society merely to undermine it.

The Stennes' revolt

Despite the Nazi violence, Hitler became increasingly keen to maintain the policy of legality. He felt that it was important to keep discipline, so he could maintain the image of a party that could offer firm and ordered government. The SA had generally supported the radical socialist aspects of Nazism, and yet Hitler was concerned increasingly with appealing to the middle-class conservative Nazi voters. The most serious disagreement between the SA and the party leadership has become known as the Stennes' revolt, in February 1931.

Walther Stennes, the leader of the Berlin SA, rebelled against the orders of Hitler and Goebbels to act legally and to limit the violence. Hitler defeated the revolt with a small purge, but it underlined the fact that the relationship between the party leadership and the SA was at times very difficult. These differences were not really resolved until the infamous **Night of the Long Knives** in 1934 (see pages 165–71).

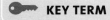 **KEY TERM**

Night of the Long Knives
A crucial turning point when Hitler arranged for the SS to purge the SA leadership. About 200 victims were murdered, including Röhm, Strasser and Schleicher.

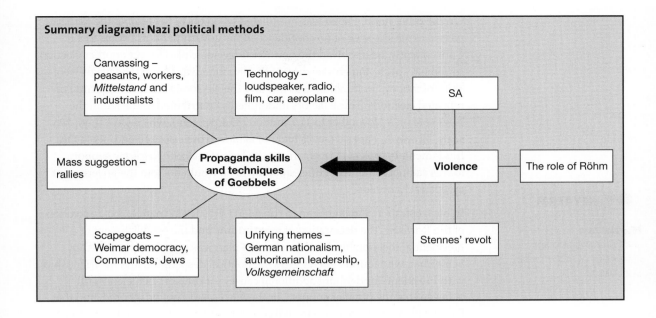

Summary diagram: Nazi political methods

8 · Political intrigue and the appointment of Hitler

▶ *Why did Papen and Schleicher fail?*

▶ *Why did President Hindenburg eventually appoint Hitler as chancellor?*

The political strength of the Nazi Party following the July 1932 *Reichstag* elections was beyond doubt (see pages 129–30). However, there still remained the problem for Hitler of how to translate this popular following into real power. He was determined to take nothing less than the post of chancellor for himself. This was unacceptable to both Schleicher and Papen, who were keen to have Nazis in the cabinet, but only in positions of limited power. Therefore, the meeting between Hitler, Papen and Hindenburg on 13 August ended in deadlock.

Papen's failure

As long as Papen retained the sympathy of Hindenburg, Hitler's ambitions would remain frustrated. Indeed, a leading modern historian, Jeremy Noakes, describes the period from August to December 1932 as 'the months of crisis' for the Nazis, since 'it appeared the policy of legality had led to a cul-de-sac'. Party morale declined and some of the wilder SA members again became increasingly restless.

On the other hand, Papen was humiliated when on 12 September the *Reichstag* passed a massive vote of no confidence in his government (512 votes to 42). Consequently, he dissolved the new *Reichstag* and called for yet another election. In some respects, Papen's reading of the situation was sound. The Nazis were short of money, their morale was low and the electorate was growing tired of repeated elections. These factors undoubtedly contributed to the fall in the Nazi vote on 6 November to 11.7 million (33.1 per cent), which gave them 196 seats. However, Papen's tactics had not achieved their desired end, since the fundamental problem of overcoming the lack of majority *Reichstag* support for his cabinet remained. Hitler stood firm: he would not join the government except as chancellor.

In his frustration, Papen began to consider a drastic alternative; the dissolution of the *Reichstag*, the declaration of **martial law** and the establishment of a presidential dictatorship. However, such a plan was completely opposed by Schleicher, who found Papen's growing political desperation and his friendship with President Hindenburg additional causes for concern. Schleicher still believed that the popular support for the Nazis could not be ignored, and that Papen's plan would give rise to civil commotion and perhaps civil war. When he informed Hindenburg of the army's lack of confidence in Papen, the president was forced, unwillingly, to demand the resignation of his friendly chancellor.

Schleicher's failure

Schleicher at last came out into the open. Over the previous two years he had been happy to play his role behind the scenes, but he now decided to become the dominant player, when he gained the favour of Hindenburg and was appointed chancellor on 2 December.

Schleicher's aims, rather ambitiously, were to achieve political stability and restore national confidence by creating a more broadly based government. He had a two-pronged strategy:

- First, to gain some support from elements of the political left, especially the trade unions, by suggesting a programme of public works.
- Second, to split the Nazis and attract the more socialist wing of the Nazi Party, under Gregor Strasser, by offering him the position of vice-chancellor.

With these objectives, Schleicher, therefore, intended to project himself as the chancellor of national reconciliation. However, his political manoeuvres came to nothing.

First, the trade unions remained deeply suspicious of his motives and, encouraged by their political masters from the SPD, they broke off negotiations. Moreover, the idea of public works alienated some of the landowners and businessmen. Secondly, although Schleicher's strategy of offering Strasser the post of vice-chancellor was a very clever one, in the end it did not work. Strasser himself responded positively to Schleicher's overtures and he was keen to accept

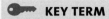

KEY TERM

Martial law Government and control by military authorities over the civilian population.

the post, but the appointment exacerbated the fundamental differences between Hitler and Strasser and led to a massive row. Hitler retained the loyalty of the party's leadership and Strasser was left isolated and promptly forced to resign from the party; which also marked a major defeat to its socialist elements.

Nevertheless, the incident had been a major blow to party morale, and tensions remained high in the last few weeks of 1932 as the prospect of achieving power seemed to drift away.

Hitler's success

Hitler's fortunes did not begin to take a more favourable turn until the first week of 1933. Papen had never forgiven Schleicher for dropping him. Papen was determined to regain political office and he recognised that he could achieve this only by convincing Hindenburg that he could muster majority support in the *Reichstag*. Consequently, secret contacts were made with Nazi leaders, which culminated in a meeting on 4 January 1933 between Papen and Hitler. Here, it was agreed in essence that Hitler should head a Nazi–Nationalist coalition government with Papen as vice-chancellor.

Backstairs intrigue to unseat Schleicher now took over. Papen looked for support for his plan from major landowners, leaders of industry and the army. It was only now that the conservative establishment thought that they had identified an escape from the threat of communism and the dangerous intrigues of Schleicher. But, above all, Papen had to convince the president

SOURCE G

What image of Nazism is projected in the photo of Source G?

Nazi parade celebrating Hitler's appointment as chancellor near the Brandenburg Gate in Berlin during the evening of 30 January 1933.

himself. Hindenburg, undoubtedly encouraged by his son, Oskar, and his state secretary, Meissner, eventually gave in. Schleicher had failed in his attempt to bring stability. In fact, he had only succeeded in frightening the powerful vested interests with his ambitious plans.

It was only in this situation that Hindenburg finally agreed, on the advice of Papen, to withdraw his support for Schleicher and to appoint Hitler as chancellor in the mistaken conviction that Hitler could be controlled and used in the interests of the conservative establishment. Papen believed that Hitler would be a chancellor in chains and so two days later, on 30 January 1933, Hindenburg agreed to sanction the creation of a Nazi–Nationalist coalition.

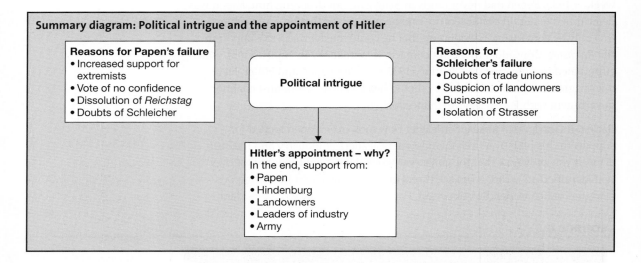

Summary diagram: Political intrigue and the appointment of Hitler

Reasons for Papen's failure
- Increased support for extremists
- Vote of no confidence
- Dissolution of *Reichstag*
- Doubts of Schleicher

Political intrigue

Reasons for Schleicher's failure
- Doubts of trade unions
- Suspicion of landowners
- Businessmen
- Isolation of Strasser

Hitler's appointment – why?
In the end, support from:
- Papen
- Hindenburg
- Landowners
- Leaders of industry
- Army

⑨ The Nazi 'legal revolution'

▶ *What were the political strengths and weaknesses of Hitler?*

▶ *How did Hitler create a dictatorship in two months?*

Although Hitler had been appointed chancellor, his power was by no means absolute. Hindenburg had not been prepared to support Hitler's appointment until he had been satisfied that the chancellor's power would remain limited. Such was Papen's confidence about Hitler's restricted room for manoeuvre that he boasted to a friend, 'In two months we'll have pushed Hitler into a corner so hard that he'll be squeaking.'

Hitler's limitations as chancellor

At first sight, the confidence of the conservatives seemed to be justified, since Hitler's position was weak in purely constitutional terms:

- There were only two other Nazis in the cabinet of twelve: **Wilhelm Frick** as minister of the interior and Hermann Göring (see page 196) as a minister, but with no specific responsibility. There were, therefore, nine other non-Nazi members of the cabinet, all from conservative-nationalist backgrounds, such as the army, industry and landowners.
- Hitler's coalition government did not have a majority in the *Reichstag*, suggesting that it would be difficult for the Nazis to introduce any dramatic legislation.
- The chancellor's post, as the previous twelve months had clearly shown, was dependent on the whim of President Hindenburg, and he openly resented Hitler. Hindenburg had made Hitler chancellor, but he could as easily sack him.

Hitler was very much aware of the potential power of the army and the trade unions. He could not alienate these forces, which could break his government. The army could arrange a military coup or the trade unions could organise a general strike, as they had done in 1920 (see page 46).

Hitler's strengths as chancellor

Within two months the above restraints were overcome by Hitler. Moreover, power was to be achieved by carrying on with the policy of legality, which the party had pursued since 1925. Hitler already possessed several key strengths when he became chancellor:

- He was the leader of the largest political party in Germany, which was why the policy of ignoring him had not worked. During 1932 it had led only to the ineffectual governments of Papen and Schleicher. Therefore, political realism forced the conservatives to work with him. They probably needed him more than he needed them. The alternative to Hitler was civil war or a communist coup – or so it seemed to many people at the time.
- More importantly, the Nazi Party had now gained access to the resources of the state. For example, Göring not only had a place in the cabinet but was also minister of the interior in Prussia, with responsibility for the police. It was a responsibility that he used blatantly to harass opponents, while ignoring Nazi crimes. Goebbels (see page 218), likewise, exploited the propaganda opportunities on behalf of the Nazis. 'The struggle is a light one now,' he confided in his diary, '… since we are able to employ all the means of the state. Radio and press are at our disposal.'
- Above all, however, Hitler was a masterly political tactician. He was determined to achieve absolute power for himself whereas Papen was really politically naïve. It soon became clear that 'Papen's political puppet' was too clever to be strung along by a motley collection of ageing conservatives.

 KEY FIGURE

Wilhelm Frick (1877–1946)

Trained as a lawyer and an early member of NSDAP. Minister of the interior 1933–43, but lost influence after his dismissal. Executed in the Nuremburg trials.

The *Reichstag* election, 5 March 1933

Hitler lost no time in removing his strings. Within 24 hours of his appointment as chancellor, new *Reichstag* elections had been called. He felt that new elections would not only increase the Nazi vote, but also enhance his own status.

The campaign for the final *Reichstag* elections held according to the Weimar constitution had few of the characteristics expected of a democracy: violence and terror dominated, with meetings of the socialists and communists being regularly broken up by the Nazis. In Prussia, Göring used his authority to enrol an extra 50,000 into the police; nearly all were members of the SA and SS. Altogether 69 people died in street fights during the five-week campaign.

The Nazis also used the atmosphere of hate and fear to great effect in their election propaganda. Hitler set the tone in his 'Appeal to the German People' of 31 January 1933. He blamed the prevailing poor economic conditions on democratic government and the terrorist activities of the communists. He cultivated the idea of the government as a peaceful 'national uprising' determined to restore Germany's pride and unity. In this way, he played on the deepest desires of many Germans, but never committed himself to the details of a political and economic programme.

Another key factor was the improved Nazi financial situation. At a meeting on 20 February with twenty leading industrialists, Hitler was promised 3 million marks. With such financial backing and Goebbels' exploitation of the media, the Nazis were confident of securing a parliamentary majority.

The *Reichstag* fire

As the campaign moved towards its climax, one further bizarre episode strengthened the Nazi hand. On 27 February the *Reichstag* building was set on fire, and a young Dutch communist, Marinus van der Lubbe, was arrested in incriminating circumstances. At the time, it was believed by many that the incident was a Nazi plot to support the claims of a communist coup, and thereby to justify Nazi repression. However, to this day the episode has defied satisfactory explanation. A major investigation in 1962 concluded that van der Lubbe had acted alone; a further eighteen years later Berlin authorities posthumously acquitted him; whereas in his recent biography of Hitler, Ian Kershaw remains convinced that van der Lubbe acted on his own in a series of three attempted arsons within a few weeks. So, it is probable that the true explanation will never be known. The real significance of the *Reichstag* fire is the cynical way it was exploited by the Nazis to their advantage.

On the next day, 28 February, Frick drew up, and Hindenburg signed, the 'Decree for the Protection of People and State'. In a few short clauses, most civil and political liberties were suspended and the power of central government was strengthened. The justification for the decree was the threat posed by

SOURCE H

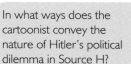

In what ways does the cartoonist convey the nature of Hitler's political dilemma in Source H?

'Not the most comfortable seat.'
A US cartoon drawn soon after Hitler's appointment as chancellor in 1933.

the communists. Following this, in the final week of the election campaign, hundreds of anti-Nazis were arrested and the violence reached new heights.

Election result

In this atmosphere of fear, Germany went to the polls on 5 March. The election had a very high turnout of 88 per cent – a figure this high suggests the influence and intimidation of the SA, corruption by officials and increased government control of the radio.

Somewhat surprisingly, the Nazis increased their vote from 33.1 per cent to only 43.9 per cent, thereby securing 288 seats. Hitler could claim a majority in the new *Reichstag* only with the help of the 52 seats won by the Nationalists. It was not only disappointing; it was also a political blow, since any change in the existing Weimar constitution required a two-thirds majority in the *Reichstag*.

The Enabling Law, March 1933

Despite this constitutional hurdle, Hitler decided to propose to the new *Reichstag* an Enabling Law that would effectively do away with parliamentary procedure and legislation and instead transfer full powers to the chancellor and his government for four years. In this way, the dictatorship would be grounded in legality. However, the successful passing of the law needed a two-thirds majority, which depended on gaining the support or abstention of some of the other major political parties.

A further problem was that the momentum built up within the lower ranks of the Nazi Party was proving increasingly difficult for Hitler to contain in the regional areas. Members were impatiently taking the law into their own hands and this gave the impression of a '**revolution from below**', as was highlighted by Rudolf Diels, the first head of the *Gestapo*, in his memoirs (see Source I).

SOURCE I

From Rudolf Diels, *Lucifer Ante Portas*, 1950, p. 200, quoted in J. Noakes and G. Pridham, editors, *Nazism 1919–45*, volume 1, University of Liverpool Press, 1988, p. 147.

The uprising of the Berlin SA electrified the remotest parts of the country … In Silesia, the Rhineland, Westphalia and the Ruhr area unauthorised arrests, insubordination to the police, forcible entry into public buildings, disturbances of the work of the authorities, the smashing up of dwellings and night raids had begun before the Reichstag fire at the end of February.

It was no longer possible to tell which public or private spheres had been penetrated by the SA, and scarcely possible to guess the purposes for which it allowed itself to be hired, and employed. There was hardly a single business undertaking which had not employed an 'old fighter' of the SA for protection against the dangers of coordination, denunciation, and threats. They were present everywhere as self-appointed directors, special commissars and SA delegates.

The 'revolution from below' threatened to destroy Hitler's image of legality, and antagonise the conservative vested interests and his DNVP coalition partners. Such was his concern that a grandiose act of reassurance was arranged. On 21 March, at the Potsdam garrison church, Goebbels orchestrated the ceremony to celebrate the opening of the *Reichstag*. In the presence of Hindenburg, the crown prince (the son of Kaiser Wilhelm II) and many of the army's leading generals, Hitler symbolically aligned National Socialism with the forces of the old Germany.

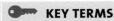

KEY TERMS

Revolution from below
The radical elements in the party that wanted to direct the Nazi revolution from a more local level rather than from the leadership in Berlin.

Gestapo *Geheime Staatspolizei*. Secret state police. A key policing organisation for surveillance and repression.

How does Diels in Source I challenge the Nazi claim of the peaceful national uprising?

Two days later the new *Reichstag* met in the Kroll Opera House to consider the Enabling Law, and on this occasion the Nazis revealed a very different image. The Communists (those not already in prison) were refused admittance, while the deputies in attendance faced a barrage of intimidation from the ranks of the SA who surrounded the building.

The Nazis still required a two-thirds majority to pass the law and, on the assumption that the SPD would vote against, they needed the backing of the ZP. Hitler thus promised in his speech of 23 March to respect the rights of the Catholic Church and to uphold religious and moral values. These were false promises, which the ZP deputies deceived themselves into believing. In the end, only the Social Democrats voted against, and the Enabling Law was passed by 444 to 94 votes.

Germany had succumbed to what K.D. Bracher later in the 1950s has called 'legal revolution'. Within the space of a few weeks Hitler had legally dismantled the Weimar constitution. The way was now open for him to create a one-party dictatorship.

Conclusion: why was Weimar replaced by Hitler and the Nazis?

The Great Depression transformed the Nazis into a mass movement. Admittedly, 63 per cent of Germans never voted for them, but 37 per cent of the electorate did, so that the Nazis became by far the strongest party in a multi-party democracy. The Great Depression had led to such profound social and economic hardship that it created an environment of discontent, which was easily exploited by the Nazis' style of political activity. Indeed, it must be questionable whether Hitler would have become a national political figure without the severity of that economic downturn. However, his mixture of racist, nationalist and anti-democratic ideas was readily received by a broad spectrum of German people, and especially by the disgruntled middle classes.

Yet, other extreme right-wing groups with similar ideas and conditions did not enjoy similar success. This is partially explained by the impressive manner in which the Nazi message was communicated: the use of modern propaganda techniques, the violent exploitation of scapegoats – especially Jews and communists – and the well-organised structure of the party apparatus. All these factors undoubtedly helped but, in terms of electoral appeal, it is impossible to ignore the powerful impact of Hitler himself as a charismatic leader with a cult following. Furthermore, he exhibited a quite extraordinary political acumen and ruthlessness when he was involved in the detail of political infighting.

Nevertheless, the huge popular following of the Nazis, which helped to undermine the continued operation of democracy, was insufficient on its own to give Hitler power. In the final analysis, it was the mutual recognition by Hitler and the representatives of the traditional leaders of the army, the landowners and heavy industry that they needed each other, which led to

Hitler's appointment as chancellor of a coalition government on 30 January 1933. Ever since September 1930 every government had been forced to resort almost continuously to the use of presidential emergency decrees because they lacked a popular mandate.

In the chaos of 1932 the only other realistic alternative to including the Nazis in the government was some kind of military regime – a presidential dictatorship backed by the army, perhaps. However, that, too, would have faced similar difficulties. Indeed, by failing to satisfy the extreme left and the extreme right there would have been a very real possibility of civil war. A coalition with Hitler's Nazis, therefore, provided the conservative elites with both mass support and some alluring promises: a vigorous attack on Germany's political left wing; and rearmament as a precursor to economic and political expansion abroad. For Hitler, the inclusion of Papen and Hugenberg (see page 149) gave his cabinet an air of conservative respectability.

In the end, Hitler became chancellor because the political forces of the left and centre were too divided and too weak, and because the conservative right wing was prepared to accept him as a partner in government in the mistaken belief that he could be tamed. With hindsight, it can be seen that 30 January 1933 was decisive. The dictatorship did not start technically until the completion of the 'legal revolution' in February–March 1933 (see pages 148–53), but Hitler was already entrenched in power and, as one historian has claimed, now he 'could only be removed by an earthquake'.

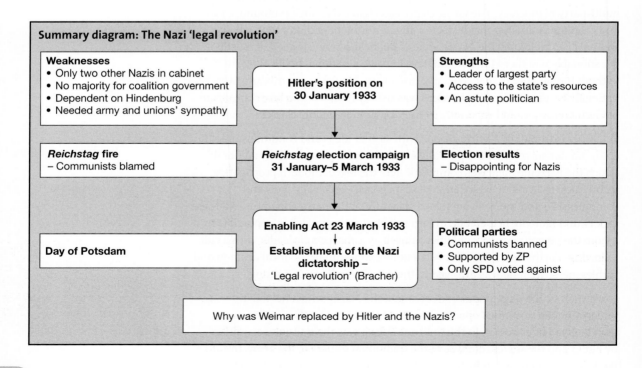

Summary diagram: The Nazi 'legal revolution'

Weaknesses
- Only two other Nazis in cabinet
- No majority for coalition government
- Dependent on Hindenburg
- Needed army and unions' sympathy

Hitler's position on 30 January 1933

Strengths
- Leader of largest party
- Access to the state's resources
- An astute politician

Reichstag fire
– Communists blamed

Reichstag election campaign 31 January–5 March 1933

Election results
– Disappointing for Nazis

Day of Potsdam

Enabling Act 23 March 1933
↓
Establishment of the Nazi dictatorship –
'Legal revolution' (Bracher)

Political parties
- Communists banned
- Supported by ZP
- Only SPD voted against

Why was Weimar replaced by Hitler and the Nazis?

10 Key debate

▶ *Was the creation of the Nazi dictatorship an inevitable product of German history?*

From the very outset, the establishment of the Nazi dictatorship presented observers not only with profound political and economic questions, but also with serious moral ones. Even many years later, objective historians cannot help but bring a small degree of subjectivity to their interpretations.

Left-wing Marxists: Nazism, the result of crisis capitalism

In the 1930s many left-wing analysts sought to explain the unexpected rise of Nazism (and the rise of fascism in Italy). They came to believe that there was a close connection between the advance of Nazism and the crisis of capitalism faced by Germany in 1929–33. Consequently, big business lost faith in the Weimar Republic and supported the Nazis, who were seen as mere 'agents' for the controlling capitalists who sought to satisfy their desire for profits.

Anti-German determinists: Hitler, the result of German history

Left-wing arguments were matched by some equally strong views from critics of Germany. Clearly, anti-German feelings can be put down to the impact of wartime propaganda in Britain. Nevertheless, some academic historians after the Second World War portrayed Nazism as the natural product of German history. The renowned English historian A.J.P. Taylor wrote in *The Course of German History* in 1945: 'It was no more a mistake for the German people to end up with Hitler than it is an accident when a river flows into the sea.'

The culmination of this kind of anti-German determinist view was probably reached with the publication in 1959 of William Shirer's *Rise and Fall of the Third Reich*. This monumental work, written by a US journalist who had worked as a correspondent in Germany between 1926 and 1941, had a profound impact on the general public. He argued that Germany's political evolution, its cultural and intellectual heritage, and the people's national character all contributed to the inevitable success of Hitler.

EXTRACT I

From W.H. Shirer, *The Rise and Fall of the Third Reich*, Secker & Warburg, 1960, pp. 122–3.

Acceptance of autocracy, of blind obedience, to the petty tyrants who ruled as princes, became ingrained in the German mind. The idea of democracy, or rule by parliament ... did not sprout in Germany. This political backwardness of Germany ... set Germany apart from and behind the other countries of the West. There was no natural growth of a nation. This has to be borne in mind if

In Shirer's view in Extract I, what were the main reasons for the failure of Weimar democracy?

one is to comprehend the disastrous road this people subsequently took and the warped state of mind which settled over it …

There thus arose quite artificially a state born of no popular force nor even an idea except that of conquest, and held together by the absolute power of the ruler, by narrow-minded bureaucracy which did his bidding and by a ruthless disciplined Army … The state, which was run with the efficiency and soullessness of a factory, became all; the people were little more than cogs in the machinery …

Gerhard Ritter: Nazism, the result of a 'moral crisis' in Europe

Not surprisingly, the implicit anti-German sentiments were not kindly received in Germany. As a consequence, there emerged in the post-war decade in West Germany a school of thought that emphasised the 'moral crisis of European society' epitomised by Ritter, who focused on the European circumstances in which Nazism had emerged. In his view, it was hard to believe that Germany's traditions, such as the power of the Prussian state, or its rich cultural history could have contributed to the emergence of Hitler. Instead, Ritter emphasised the events and developments since 1914 in Europe as a whole. It was the shock given to the traditional European order by the First World War that created the environment for the emergence of Nazism. The decline in religion and standards of morality, a tendency towards corruption and materialism, and the emergence of mass democracy were all exploited by Hitler to satisfy his desire for power.

Structuralists: Nazism, a response to Germany's social and economic 'structures'

The 1960s witnessed a phenomenal growth in research on the Third Reich, partly due to the release of the German archives by the Western Allies. By the late 1960s and early 1970s historians, such as Martin Broszat and Hans Mommsen, had started to exert a major influence on our understanding of the rise of Hitler and the Third Reich and they have been dubbed as **structuralists**.

In essence, the structuralist interpretation has emphasised Germany's continuities from the 1850s to 1945. It argues that Germany's society and economy had remained dominated by authoritarian forces, such as the armed services and the bureaucracy, and had not really developed democratic institutions. As a result, the power and influence of such conservative vested interests continued to rule Germany – even after the creation of the Weimar Republic – and therefore, these conservatives sympathised with the Nazi movement, which provided the means to uphold a right-wing authoritarian regime.

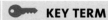 **KEY TERM**

Structuralists Historians who interpret history by analysing the role of social and economic forces and structures. They tend to place less emphasis on the role of the individual in shaping history.

EXTRACT 2

From Hans-Ulrich Wehler, *The German Empire, 1871–1918*, Berg, 1985, pp. 230–1.

No judgement on Weimar's chances of survival can skirt round the problem that after a little more than a dozen years the downward spiral to Brüning's authoritarian regime began only to be followed by the successful National Socialist 'seizure of power' in 1933. The latter undoubtedly represented a convergence of certain trends in German history …

Since continuity in the imperial bureaucracy and the Army, in the educational system and the political parties, in the economy and its pressure groups, and so on, were largely preserved, one thing at least was assured: the traditional power elites were able to depute the stirrup holders for Hitler … In the concrete circumstances which prevailed, however, the Führer could never, at any rate, have climbed into the saddle without the stirrups to help him. Viewed in this light, the costs of the decision taken in 1918–19 began in 1933, to assume undreamt-of dimensions which were eventually to involve the whole world.

> According to Wehler in Extract 2 which institutions made it possible for Hitler to gain power?

Intentionalists: Nazism, a result of Hitler's ideology and his evil genius

Some historians have continued to argue that there is no escape from the central importance of Hitler the individual in the Nazi seizure of power. Indeed, **intentionalists**, such as Klaus Hildebrand and Eberhard Jäckel, believe that the personality and ideology of Hitler remain so essential that Nazism can be equated with the term 'Hitlerism'. This is because, although the intentionalists accept the special circumstances created by Germany's history, they emphasise the pivotal role of Hitler, who was a brilliant **demagogue** with masterly political skills which enabled him to outmanoeuvre the other elites.

Ian Kershaw: Hitler's coming to power, the result of miscalculation

The latest interpretation of Kershaw, arguably the leading British historian of Nazi Germany, goes well beyond the framework of mere biography. He deliberately tries to balance structuralist and intentionalist views. Kershaw recognises the circumstances of the time, such as the xenophobic nationalism, the defeat of the war and Weimar's difficult condition which allowed the 'Austrian drifter' to emerge. Yet, most significantly, he emphasises that the appointment of Hitler was not inevitable, but the result of multiple miscalculations. Even until the very last moment at 11 o'clock on 30 January 1933, there was a possibility that a Hitler chancellorship might not materialise.

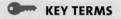

KEY TERMS

Intentionalists Historians who interpret history by emphasising the role (intentions) of people who shape history.

Demagogue A leader who plays on the prejudices of the masses with populist emotions.

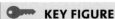

? How and why does
Kershaw argue in
Extract 3 that there was
no inevitability in Hitler's
rise to power?

KEY FIGURE

**Otto von Bismarck
(1815–98)**

Chancellor of Prussia from
1862 and then of Germany
1871–90.

EXTRACT 3

From Ian Kershaw, *Hitler*, Longman, 1991, p. 38.

*There was no inevitability about Hitler's triumph in January 1933. Five years earlier, the Nazi Party had been a fringe irritant in German politics, but no more … External events, the Young Plan to adjust German reparations payments, the Wall Street Crash and Brüning's entirely unnecessary decision to have an election in summer 1930 – put the Nazis on the political map. Though democracy had by that time an unpromising future, a Nazi dictatorship seemed far less likely than some other form of authoritarian dictatorship or even a reversion to a **Bismarckian** style of government, possibly under a restored monarchy. In bringing Hitler to power, chances and conservative miscalculation played a larger role than any actions of the Nazi leader himself.*

Chapter summary

Hitler and Nazism had made a limited impression in the 1920s, yet the world depression destabilised the fragile Weimar Republic. The socio-economic impact was very severe in Germany, which resulted in increasingly desperate political measures. Brüning's resorting to the use of presidential decrees marked a crucial turning point in the breakdown of German democracy. But the political crisis was exacerbated markedly by the electoral success of the Nazis in becoming the largest party. Therefore, when the governments of Papen and Schleicher collapsed, Hitler was appointed as chancellor by Hindenburg in the mistaken belief that Hitler could be controlled and used in the interests of the conservative establishment. It then took the Nazis just two months to impose the dictatorship.

Refresher questions

Use these questions to remind yourself of the key material covered in this chapter.

1 How did the economic crisis affect the lives of the German people?

2 Why did the economic crisis turn into a political one?

3 Why was Brüning's decision to call the 1930 *Reichstag* election so significant?

4 Was Brüning a failure?

5 Which social groups tended to vote Nazi? And why?

6 Why has Nazism been described as a 'people's party'?

7 In what ways did Goebbels develop Nazi propaganda?

8 How did violence help to advance the rise of Nazism?

9 Why did Papen's and Scheicher's governments fail to achieve political stability?

10 Why did President Hindenburg eventually appoint Hitler as chancellor?

11 Why was Weimar replaced by Hitler and the Nazis?

Question practice

ESSAY QUESTIONS

1 'Hitler could only come to power ten years after the failed Munich *putsch* of 1923.' Explain why you agree or disagree with this view.
2 'The Weimar Republic was swept away in an economic blizzard.' Assess the validity of this view.
3 How important was the role of Goebbels and propaganda in the rise of Nazism?
4 To what extent was Hitler's accession to power in 1933 the result of backstairs intrigue rather than popular support?

SOURCE ANALYSIS QUESTIONS

1 With reference to Sources 1 and 2 (below and on page 160), and your understanding of the historical context, which of these two sources is more valuable in explaining why the political intrigue led to the appointment of Hitler?
2 With reference to Sources 1, 2 and 3 (below and on page 160), and your understanding of the historical context, assess the value of these sources to a historian studying the events leading to the appointment of Hitler as chancellor.

SOURCE 1

From a letter of industrialists to President Hindenburg in November 1932, quoted in C. Hinton and J. Hite, *Weimar and Nazi Germany*, John Murray, 2000, p. 143.

The outcome of the Reichstag had demonstrated that the present cabinet … has failed to find sufficient support among the German people for its actual policies.

… It is quite apparent that another dissolution of parliament leading to yet another general election with its inevitable frenzied party-political struggles would be harmful to political as well as economic peace and stability. But it is also apparent that any constitutional change that does not have widespread popular support would have even greater negative economic, political and moral effects.

We therefore consider it to be our duty, Your Excellency, to humbly beg you to consider reconstituting the cabinet in a manner which would guarantee it with the greatest possible popular support.

We demand ourselves to be free from any specific party-political interests. But we recognise in the nationalist movement, which is sweeping through our people, the auspicious beginnings of an era of rebirth for the German economy which can only be achieved by surmounting class conflict.

We greet Your Excellency with the greatest respect

Bosch, Schacht, Thyssen, Krupp (and 20 other industrialists).

SOURCE 2

Otto Meissner, the state secretary to the president, giving evidence to the Nuremberg trials in 1946, quoted in J. Noakes and G. Pridham, editors, *Nazism 1919–45*, volume 1, University of Liverpool Press, 1988, pp. 117–18.

Schleicher came to Hindenburg with a demand for emergency powers as a prerequisite of action against the Nazis. Furthermore, he believed it necessary to dissolve, and even temporarily eliminate, the Reichstag, and this was to be done by presidential decrees on the basis of Article 48 – the transformation of his government into a military dictatorship … Schleicher first made these suggestions to Hindenburg in the middle of January 1933, but Hindenburg at once evinced grave doubts as to its constitutionality. In the meantime von Papen had returned to Berlin, and by arrangement with Hindenburg's son had had several interviews with the President.

SOURCE 3

A Rhineland newspaper reports on the growing political crisis, 28 January 1933, quoted in S. Lee, *The Weimar Republic*, Routledge, 1998, p. 110.

Reich Chancellor von Schleicher today informed the Reich President … that the present national government would be unable to defend itself vis à vis *[in relation to] the Reichstag if it did not obtain in advance the power to dissolve parliament. Reich President Hindenburg stated that he could not grant this proposal because of current conditions. Reich Chancellor Schleicher then announced the resignation of the government … Reich President Hindenburg summoned former Chancellor Papen and requested him to clarify the political situation and to suggest possible procedures.*

CHAPTER 6

The Nazi dictatorship

It is all too easy to assume, in the wake of the 'legal revolution', that Nazi Germany became a tightly structured, well-organised dictatorship. Yet, in reality, it became a very complex system of political forces which changed over time. Therefore, the following main areas need to be considered:

★ Co-ordination: *Gleichschaltung*

★ A 'second revolution?'

★ The role of Hitler

★ The Nazi Party and the state

★ The 'police state'

★ The German Army

★ The economic recovery

★ The Four-Year Plan and the industrial elites

★ Conclusion: the nature of the Nazi dictatorship

The key debate on *page 202* of this chapter asks the question: Was Nazi Germany an all-powerful dictatorship?

Key dates

1933	March	Appointment of Schacht as president of the *Reichsbank*	1935		Mass arrests by *Gestapo* of socialists and communists
	July 14	All political opposition to NSDAP declared illegal	1936	June	Appointment of Himmler as chief of police
1934	June 30	Night of the Long Knives; purge of SA		Oct.	Four-Year Plan established under Göring
	July	Appointment of Schacht as minister of economics	1937	Nov.	Resignation of Schacht as minister of economics
	Aug. 2	Death of Hindenburg: Hitler merged posts of chancellor and president to become *Führer*	1938	Feb.	Forced resignation of Field Marshal Blomberg and General Fritsch. Purge of army leadership
	Aug. 20	Oath of loyalty taken by the army	1939	Sept.	Creation of RSHA (Reich Security Office)
	Sept.	The New Plan introduced			

Co-ordination: *Gleichschaltung*

▶ *What was* Gleichschaltung?

▶ *In what ways did Nazism achieve co-ordination?*

The Enabling Law was the constitutional foundation stone of the Third Reich. In purely legal terms the Weimar constitution was not dissolved until 1945, and the Enabling Law provided a legal basis for the dictatorship, which evolved from 1933 (see page 152). The intolerance and violence used by the Nazis to gain power could now be used as tools within government by Hitler and the party.

The degeneration of Weimar's democracy into the Nazi system is usually referred to as *Gleichschaltung* or co-ordination. It applied to the Nazifying of German society and structures and specifically to the establishment of the dictatorship, 1933–4. To some extent it was generated by the power and freedom exploited by the SA at the local level – a 'revolution from below'. But it was also directed by the Nazi leadership from the political centre in Berlin – a 'revolution from above'. These two political forces attempted to 'co-ordinate' as many aspects of German life as possible along Nazi lines. However, differences over the exact long-term goals of National Socialism laid the foundations for future conflict within the party.

Co-ordination has been viewed rather neatly as the 'merging' of German society with party associations and institutions in an attempt to Nazify life in Germany. At first, many of these Nazi organisations had to live alongside existing bodies, but they gradually replaced them. In this way, much of Germany's educational and social life became increasingly controlled (see also pages 210–55).

Primarily, in 1933, the priority of the Nazi leadership was to secure its *political* supremacy through the process of 'co-ordination'. It therefore had to deal with agencies at odds with Nazi political aspirations, such as the regional states, the political parties and the independent trade unions.

The regional states (*Länder*)

The regions had a very strong tradition in German history (see page 19). This obstructed Nazi desires to create a fully unified country. Nazi activists had already exploited the climate of February–March 1933 to intimidate opponents and to infiltrate regional state governments. Indeed, their 'political success' rapidly degenerated into terror and violence that seemed even beyond the control of Hitler, who called for restraint because he was afraid of losing the support of the conservatives. The situation was resolved in three legal stages:

● First, a law of 31 March 1933 dissolved regional parliaments (*Landtage*) and reformed them with acceptable majorities, allowing the Nazis to dominate them.

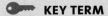

KEY TERM

Gleichschaltung 'Bringing into line' or 'co-ordination'.

- Secondly, a law of 7 April 1933 created Reich governors (*Reichstatthalter*) who more often than not were the local party *Gauleiters* with full powers.
- Finally, in January 1934 regional parliaments were abolished. The governments of all the states were subordinated to the Ministry of the Interior in Berlin central government.

By early 1934 the federal principle of government was as good as dead. Even the Nazi Reich governors existed simply 'to execute the will of the supreme leadership of the Reich'.

The trade unions

Germany's trade union movement was powerful because of its mass membership and its strong connections with socialism and Catholicism. In 1920 it had clearly shown its industrial muscle when a general strike defeated the Kapp *putsch* (see page 46). German organised labour was hostile to Nazism so posed a major threat to the stability of the Nazi state.

Yet, by May 1933 it was a spent force. The depression had already severely weakened it by reducing membership and lessening the will to resist. However, the trade union leaders deluded themselves that they could work with the Nazis and thereby preserve a degree of independence and at least the structure of trade unionism. Their hope was that:

- in the short term, trade unionism would continue to serve its social role to help members
- in the long term, it could provide the framework for development in the post-Nazi era.

However, the labour movement was deceived by the Nazis.

The Nazis surprisingly declared 1 May (the traditional day of celebration for international socialist labour) a national holiday, which gave the impression to the trade unions that perhaps there was some scope for co-operation. This proved to be the briefest of illusions. On the following day, trade union premises were occupied by the SA and SS, union funds were confiscated and many of the leaders were arrested and sent to the early concentration camps such as Dachau.

Independent trade unions were then banned and in their place all German workers' organisations were absorbed into the German Labour Front (*Deutscher Arbeitsfront*, DAF), led by Robert Ley. DAF became the largest organisation in Nazi Germany with 22 million members, but it acted more as an instrument of control than as a genuine representative body of workers' interests and concerns (see pages 220–1). Also, it lacked the most fundamental right to negotiate wages and conditions of work. So, by the end of 1933, the power of the German labour movement had been decisively broken.

Political parties

The process of *Gleichschaltung* could never allow the existence of other political parties. Nazism openly rejected democracy and any concessions to alternative opinions. Instead, it aspired to establish authoritarian rule within a one-party state. This was not difficult to achieve:

- The Communists had been outlawed since the *Reichstag* fire (see pages 150–1).
- Soon after the destruction of the trade unions the assets of the Social Democrats were seized and they were then officially banned on 22 June.
- Most of the major remaining parties willingly agreed to dissolve themselves in the course of late June 1933 – even the Nationalists (previously coalition partners to the Nazis) obligingly accepted.
- Finally, the Catholic Centre Party decided to give up the struggle and followed suit on 5 July 1933.

Thus, there was no opposition to the decree of 14 July that formally proclaimed the Nazi Party as the only legal political party in Germany.

SOURCE A

The Law against the Establishment of Parties, 14 July 1933, quoted in J. Noakes and G. Pridham, editors, *Nazism 1919–45*, volume 1, Liverpool University Press, 1988, p. 167.

Art 1. The Nationalist Socialist German Workers' Party constitutes the only political party in Germany.

Art 2. Whoever undertakes to maintain the organisation of another political party or to form a new political party shall be punished with penal servitude of up to three years or with imprisonment of between six months and three years, unless the act is subject to a heavier penalty under other regulations.

? How important was the measure outlined in Source A in the consolidation of Nazi power?

The success of *Gleichschaltung*

By the end of 1933 the process of *Gleichschaltung* was well advanced in many areas of public life in Germany, although far from complete. In particular, it had made limited impression on the role and influence of the army, big business and the Churches (although an agreement was made with the papacy in July 1933, see page 220). Also, the civil service and education had only been partially co-ordinated. This was mainly due to Hitler's determination to shape events through the 'revolution from above' and to avoid antagonising such powerful vested interests. Yet, there were many in the lower ranks of the party who had contributed to the 'revolution from below' and who now wanted to extend the process of *Gleichschaltung*. It was this internal party conflict which laid the basis for the bloody events of June 1934.

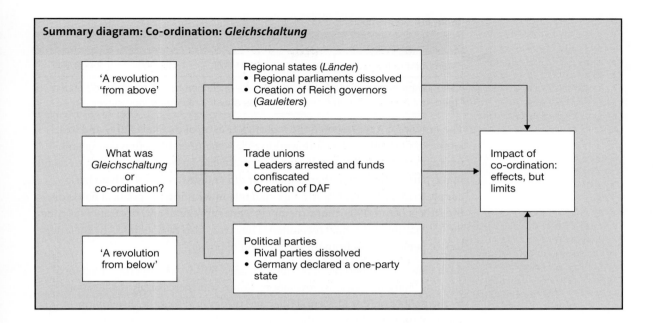

Summary diagram: Co-ordination: *Gleichschaltung*

'A revolution 'from above'

What was *Gleichschaltung* or co-ordination?

'A revolution from below'

Regional states (*Länder*)
- Regional parliaments dissolved
- Creation of Reich governors (*Gauleiters*)

Trade unions
- Leaders arrested and funds confiscated
- Creation of DAF

Political parties
- Rival parties dissolved
- Germany declared a one-party state

Impact of co-ordination: effects, but limits

2   A 'second revolution?'

▶ *What was the nature of Hitler's political dilemma in 1933–4?*

▶ *Did Germany undergo a political revolution in the years 1933–4?*

Within six months of coming to power Hitler had indeed turned Germany into a one-party dictatorship. However, in a speech on 6 July 1933 to the Reich governors, Hitler warned of the dangers of a permanent state of revolution. He therefore formally declared an end to the revolution and demanded that 'the stream of revolution must be guided into the safe channel of evolution'.

Hitler was caught in a political dilemma. He was increasingly concerned that the behaviour of party activists was beyond his control. This was likely to create embarrassment in his relations with the more conservative forces whose support he still depended on, for example big business, civil service and, above all, the army. Hitler's speech amounted to a clear-cut demand for the party to accept the realities of political compromise and the necessity of change from above.

The position of the SA

Hitler's appeal failed to have the desired effect. If anything, it reinforced the fears of many party members that the Nazi leadership was prepared to dilute National Socialist ideology. Such concerns came in particular from within the ranks of the SA giving rise to calls for a **'second revolution'**.

 KEY TERM

'Second revolution' The aims of Röhm and the SA were for social and economic reforms and the creation of a 'people's army' which would merge the army and the SA. These aims were more attractive to 'left-wing socialist Nazis' or 'radical Nazis'.

Table 6.1 SA membership 1931–4

	1931	1932	1933	1934
Membership figures	100,000	291,000	425,000	3,000,000
SA membership grew at first because of the large number of unemployed young men, but from 1933 many joined simply as a way to advance themselves.				

The growing SA represented the radical, left wing of the Nazi Party and to a large extent it reflected a more working-class membership, often young and unemployed (see Table 6.1). It placed far more emphasis on the socialist elements of the party programme than Hitler ever did and saw no need to hold back simply to satisfy the elites. After its vital role in winning the political battle on the streets before 1933, many members were embittered and frustrated over the limited nature of the Nazi revolution. They were also disappointed by their own lack of personal gain from this acquisition of power.

Such views were epitomised by the SA leader, Röhm, who openly called for a genuine 'National Socialist revolution'. Röhm was increasingly disillusioned by the politics of his old friend Hitler and recognised that the developing confrontation would decide the future role of the SA in the Nazi state. In a private interview in early 1934 with a local party boss, Rauschning, Röhm gave vent to his feelings and his ideas: 'Adolf is a swine. He will give us all away. He only associates with the reactionaries now … Getting matey with the East Prussian generals. They're his cronies now.'

Ernst Röhm

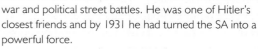

1887	Born in Munich
1914–18	Served in the First World War and reached the rank of captain
1919	Joined the *Freikorps* and the Nazi Party
1921	Helped to form the SA and was leader in 1921–3
1923	Participated in the Beer Hall *putsch* and jailed
1925–30	Released from prison and left for Bolivia as a military adviser
1930–4	Returned to Germany at Hitler's request and took over SA again
1933	Invited to join the cabinet
1934	Arrested and murdered in the Night of the Long Knives

Röhm was always a controversial character. He was a homosexual and a heavy drinker, and enjoyed the blood and violence of war and political street battles. He was one of Hitler's closest friends and by 1931 he had turned the SA into a powerful force.

Conflict between the party and the SA grew increasingly serious and after the Nazi consolidation of power, Röhm was committed to pursuing a 'second revolution' which would reflect the reforms of the 'left-wing socialist Nazis', or 'radical Nazis'. He did not sympathise with the conservative forces in Germany and aimed to create a 'people's army' by merging the army with the SA. These fundamental differences culminated in the Night of the Long Knives and his own murder.

Röhm did not want SA marches and rallies to degenerate into mere propaganda shows now that the street-fighting was over. He wanted a more political role for the SA, amalgamating it with the army into a people's militia – of which he would be the commander. He also had hopes for more fundamental social and economic reforms.

The power struggle between the SA and the army

Röhm's plan was anathema to the German Army, which saw its traditional role and status directly threatened. Hitler was therefore caught between two powerful, but rival, forces. Both could create considerable political difficulties for him. The SA consisted of 3 million committed Nazis (see Table 6.1) with his oldest political friend leading it. It had fought for Hitler in the 1923 Munich *putsch* and in the battle of the streets, 1930–3. The SA was far larger than the army, but the army was the one organisation that could unseat Hitler. The officer class was suspicious of Hitler and had close social ties with many of the powerful interests, for example the civil service and *Junkers*. Moreover, the army alone possessed the military skills vital to the success of his foreign policy aims. However large, the SA could never match the discipline and professional expertise of the army.

Political realities dictated that Hitler had to retain the backing of the army but, in the winter of 1933–4, he was still loath to engineer a showdown with his old friend, Röhm. He tried to conciliate Röhm by bringing him into the cabinet. He also called a meeting in February between the leaders of the army, the SA and the SS to seek an agreement about the role of each within the Nazi state. However, the tension did not ease. Röhm and the SA resented Hitler's apparent acceptance of the privileged position of the army, while the unrestrained actions and ill-discipline of the SA increased dissatisfaction among the generals.

The Night of the Long Knives

The developing crisis came to a head in April 1934 when it became apparent that President Hindenburg did not have much longer to live. The implications of this were profound, as Hitler wanted to assume the presidency without opposition. He certainly did not want a contested election, and had no sympathy for those who wanted to restore the monarchy. Hitler's hand was forced by the need to secure the army's backing for his succession to Hindenburg.

The support of the army had become the key to the survival of Hitler's regime in the short term, while in the long term it offered the means to fulfil his ambitions in foreign affairs. Any personal loyalty Hitler felt for Röhm and the SA was finally put to one side. The army desired their elimination and an end to the talk of a 'second revolution' and a 'people's army'. By agreeing to this, Hitler could gain the favour of the army generals, secure his personal position and remove an increasingly embarrassing millstone from around his neck.

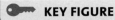

KEY FIGURE

Werner von Blomberg (1878–1946)

Member of the General Staff. Appointed as minister of defence in 1933 and later war minister and commander-in-chief of armed forces 1935–8. Forced to resign in 1938.

Without primary written evidence it is difficult to establish the exact details of the events in June 1934. However, it seems highly probable that, at a meeting on the battleship *Deutschland* in April 1934, Hitler and the two leading generals, **Blomberg** and Fritsch, came to an agreed position against Röhm and the SA. Furthermore, influential figures within the Nazi Party, in particular Göring and Himmler, were also manoeuvring behind the scenes. They were aiming for a similar outcome in order to further their own ambitions by removing a powerful rival. Given all that, Hitler probably did not decide to make his crucial move to solve the problem of the SA until mid-June when Papen gave a speech calling for an end to SA excesses and criticised the policy of co-ordination. Not surprisingly, these words caused a real stir and were seen as a clear challenge. Hitler now recognised that he had to satisfy the conservative forces – and that meant destroying the power of the SA immediately.

On 30 June 1934, the Night of the Long Knives, Hitler eliminated the SA as a political and military force once and for all. Röhm and the main leaders of the SA were shot by members of the SS, although the weapons and transport were actually provided by the army. There was no resistance of any substance. In addition, various old scores were settled: Schleicher, the former chancellor, and Strasser, the leader of the radical socialist wing of the Nazi Party, were both killed. Altogether it is estimated that 200 people were murdered.

From a very different perspective, the *Völkischer Beobachter* (*People's Observer*), the Nazi newspaper, reported on the cabinet meeting held two days earlier (see Source B).

? Using your historical knowledge, is there any evidence supporting the claim in Source B that there was a 'high treason plot'? What is the significance of the law approved on 3 July?

SOURCE B

From the *Völkischer Beobachter* (*People's Observer*), 5 July 1934, quoted in J. Noakes and G. Pridham, editors, *Nazism 1919–45*, volume 1, Liverpool University Press, 1988, p. 182.

… The Reich Chancellor began by giving a detailed account of the origin and suppression of the high treason plot. The Reich Chancellor stressed that lightning action had been necessary otherwise many thousands of people would have been in danger of being wiped out.

Defence Minister General von Blomberg thanked the Führer in the name of the Cabinet and the Army for his determined and courageous action, by which he had saved the German people from civil war. The Führer had shown greatness as a statesman and a soldier. This had aroused in the hearts of the members of the cabinet and of the whole German people a vow of service, devotion and loyalty in this grave hour.

The Reich Cabinet then approved a law on measures for the self-defence of the state. Its single paragraph reads: 'The measures taken on 30 June and 1–2 July to suppress the acts of high treason are legal, being necessary for the self-defence of the state.'

The significance of the Night of the Long Knives

It would be difficult to overestimate the significance of the Night of the Long Knives. In one bloody action, Hitler overcame the radical left in his own party, and neutralised the conservative right of traditional Germany. By the summer of 1934, the effects of the purge could be seen clearly:

- The army had endorsed the Nazi regime, as shown by Blomberg's public vote of thanks to Hitler on 1 July. German soldiers agreed to take a personal oath of loyalty to Hitler rather than to the state.
- The SA was virtually disarmed and played no further political role in the Nazi state. Just as Röhm had feared, its major role was to attend propaganda rallies as a showpiece force.
- More significantly for the future, the incident marked the emergence of the SS. German generals had feared the SA, but they failed to recognise the SS as the party's elite institution of terror.
- Above all, Hitler had secured his own personal political supremacy. His decisions and actions were accepted, so in effect he had managed to legalise murder. He told the *Reichstag* that 'in this hour, I was responsible for the fate of the German nation and thereby the supreme judge'. From that moment, it was clear that the Nazi regime was not a traditional authoritarian one, like Imperial Germany 1871–1918; it was a personal dictatorship with frightening power.

When Hindenburg died on 2 August there was no political crisis. Hitler merged the offices of chancellor and president, and took the new official title of *Führer*. The Nazi regime had been stabilised and the threat of a 'second revolution' had been completely removed.

The Nazi revolution?

Between 1933 and 1934 Hitler and the Nazis effectively established a dictatorship. This was achieved through a range of key factors:

- *Terror.* The Nazis used violence, increasingly without legal restriction, for example, the arrest of the communists and the Night of the Long Knives. Nazi organisations also employed violence at a local level to intimidate opposition.
- *Legality.* The use of law by the Nazis gave a legal justification for the development of the regime, for example the Emergency Decree of 28 February 1933, the Enabling Law and the dissolution of the parties.
- *Deception.* Hitler misled powerful groups in order to destroy them, for example the trade unions and the SA.
- *Propaganda.* The Nazis successfully cultivated powerful images – especially when Goebbels took on responsibility for propaganda. Myths were developed about Hitler as a respectable statesman, for example the Day of Potsdam (see page 152).

- *Weaknesses of the opposition.* In the early Weimar years, the left had considerable potential power, but it became divided between the Social Democrats and the Communists – and was marred by the economic problems of the depression.
- *Sympathy of the conservative right.* Many of the traditional vested interests, for example the army and the civil service, were not wholly committed to Weimar and they really sympathised with a more right-wing authoritarian regime. They accepted the Night of the Long Knives.

Having said this, the term revolution should be used with caution. It means a fundamental change – an overturning of existing conditions. If Germany had undergone a 'political revolution' in the course of 1933–4, the evidence must support the idea that there was a decisive break in the country's political development.

Arguments for

At first sight, the regime created by the Nazis by the end of 1934 seems the very opposite of the Weimar Republic. However, Weimar democracy had ceased to function effectively well before Hitler became chancellor. The strength of the anti-democratic forces had threatened the young democracy from the very start, so that it was never able to establish strong roots. Yet, even by comparison with pre-1918 Germany, the Nazi regime had wrought fundamental changes:

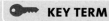

KEY TERM

Autonomy The right of self-government.

- the destruction of the **autonomy** of the federal states
- the intolerance shown towards any kind of political opposition
- the reduction of the *Reichstag* to complete impotence.

Clearly, *Gleichschaltung* decisively affected political traditions which had been key features of Imperial Germany 1871–1918. Thus, it is reasonable to view the events of 1933–4 as a 'political revolution', since the Nazis had turned their backs quite categorically on the federal and constitutional values which had even influenced an authoritarian regime like Imperial Germany.

Arguments against

There were elements of continuity, however. At the time of Hindenburg's death, major forces within Germany were still independent of the Nazi regime; namely, the army, big business and the civil service. One might even include the Christian Churches, although they did not carry the same degree of political weight.

Hitler's willingness to enter into political partnership with these representatives of the old Germany had encouraged Röhm and the SA to demand a 'second revolution'. The elimination of the power of the SA in the Night of the Long Knives suggests that Hitler's claim for a 'national revolution' had just been an attractive slogan. In reality, this 'revolution' was strictly limited in scope. It involved political compromise and had not introduced any fundamental social or economic change. In this sense, one could suggest that the early years of the Nazi regime were merely a continuation of the socio-economic forces which had dominated Germany since 1871.

Certainly, this would seem to be a fair assessment of the situation until late 1934. However, the true revolutionary extent of the regime can only be fully assessed by considering the developments in Germany throughout the entire period of the Third Reich. These will be the key points of the next few chapters.

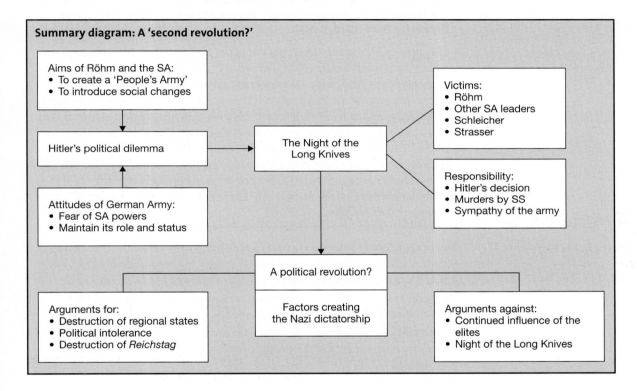

Summary diagram: A 'second revolution?'

Aims of Röhm and the SA:
• To create a 'People's Army'
• To introduce social changes

Hitler's political dilemma

Attitudes of German Army:
• Fear of SA powers
• Maintain its role and status

The Night of the Long Knives

Victims:
• Röhm
• Other SA leaders
• Schleicher
• Strasser

Responsibility:
• Hitler's decision
• Murders by SS
• Sympathy of the army

A political revolution?

Factors creating the Nazi dictatorship

Arguments for:
• Destruction of regional states
• Political intolerance
• Destruction of *Reichstag*

Arguments against:
• Continued influence of the elites
• Night of the Long Knives

3 The role of Hitler

▶ *What was the role of Hitler in Nazi Germany?*

In theory, Hitler's power was unlimited. Nazi Germany was a one-party state and Hitler was undisputed leader of that party. In addition, after the death of Hindenburg in August 1934, the 'Law Concerning the Head of State of the German *Reich*' combined the posts of president and chancellor. Constitutionally, Hitler was also commander-in-chief of all the armed services. (This image of Hitler was very much presented in the poster on page 173: 'Adolf Hitler is Victory'.

'Führer power'

If one studies contemporary documents, such as the extract (Source C) from a leading Nazi theorist, E. Huber, it is clear that Hitler's personal dictatorship was portrayed in more than purely legal terms.

SOURCE C

From E. Huber, *Verfassungsrecht des Grossdeutschen Reiches* (*Constitutional Law of the Greater German Reich*), Hanseatische Verlagsanstalt, 1939, p. 142, quoted in J. Noakes and G. Pridham, editors, *Nazism 1919–45*, volume 1, Liverpool University Press, 1988, p. 198.

The office of Führer has developed out of the National Socialist movement. In its origins it is not a state office. The office of Führer has grown out of the movement into the Reich … The position of Führer combines in itself all sovereign power of the Reich: all public power in the state as in the movement is derived from the Führer's power. If we wish to define political power in the völkisch Reich correctly, we must not speak of 'state power' but of 'Führer power'. For it is not the state as an impersonal entity which is the source of political power, but rather political power is given to the Führer as the executor of the nation's common will. 'Führer power' is comprehensive and total: it unites within itself all means of creative political activity: it embraces all spheres of national life.

? What was the nature and theory of Hitler's power as described in Source C? What do you think was the purpose of this statement?

Huber's grandiose theoretical claims for '*Führer* power' could not mask basic practical problems. First, there was no all-embracing constitution in the Third Reich. The government and law of Nazi Germany emerged over time in a haphazard fashion. Secondly, there was no way one individual could ever be in control of all aspects of government. Thus, Hitler was still dependent on sympathetic subordinates to put policy decisions into effect. And thirdly, Hitler's own personality and attitude towards government were mixed and not conducive to strong and effective leadership.

Hitler's character

Hitler certainly appeared as the charismatic and dynamic leader. His magnetic command of an audience enabled him to play on mass suggestion; he portrayed himself as the ordinary man with the vision, willpower and determination to transform the country. However, this was an image perpetuated by the propaganda machine and, once in government, Hitler's true character revealed itself, as is shown in the memoirs of one of his retinue (see Source D, page 173).

Hitler liked to cultivate the image of himself as an artist, but really he was quite lazy. This was accentuated further by Hitler's lifestyle: his unusual sleeping hours; his long periods of absence from Berlin when he stayed in the Bavarian Alps; his tendency to become immersed in pet projects such as architectural plans. Furthermore, as he got older he became neurotic and moody, as was demonstrated in his obsession with his health and medical symptoms, both real and imagined.

SOURCE D

From F. Wiedemann, *Der Mann der Feldherr werden wollte* (*The Man Wanted to be Commander*), Blick + Bild Verlag, 1965, p. 69, quoted in J. Noakes and G. Pridham, editors, *Nazism 1919–45*, volume 2, Liverpool University Press, 1988, p. 207.

Hitler normally appeared shortly before lunch … When Hitler stayed at Obersalzberg it was even worse. There he never left his room before 2.00p.m. He spent most afternoons taking a walk, in the evening straight after dinner, there were films … He disliked the study of documents. I have sometimes secured decisions from him without his ever asking to see the relevant files. He took the view that many things sorted themselves out on their own if one did not interfere … He let people tell him the things he wanted to hear, everything else he rejected. One still sometimes hears the view that Hitler would have done the right thing if people surrounding him had not kept him wrongly informed. Hitler refused to let himself be informed … How can one tell someone the truth who immediately gets angry when the facts do not suit him?

According to Source D, in what ways does Hitler appear to be a 'poor leader'?

SOURCE E

'Adolf Hitler is Victory!' A 1943 poster of Adolf Hitler.

What kind of image of Hitler is portrayed in Source E?

Hitler was not well educated and had no experience that prepared him for any role in government or administration. As cynics say, Hitler's first real job was his appointment as chancellor. He followed no real working routine; he loathed paperwork and disliked the formality of committees in which issues were discussed. He casually believed that mere willpower was the solution to most problems.

Hitler's leadership

Surprisingly, Hitler was not even very decisive when it came to making a choice. Although he was presented to the world as the all-powerful dictator, he seldom showed any inclination to co-ordinate the government of Nazi Germany. For example, the role of the cabinet declined quite markedly after 1934. In 1933 the cabinet met 72 times, but only four times in 1936, and the last official cabinet meeting was held in February 1938. Consequently, rivalry between the various factions of the party and state was rife and decision-making became, more often than not, the result of the *Führer*'s whim or an informal conversation rather than rational clear-cut chains of command.

Despite everything, Hitler still played a decisive role in the development of the Third Reich, as will be further discussed on pages 202–5. In his own research, Ian Kershaw (1998) has outlined an interpretation of Hitler's style of rule as one of 'charismatic domination' and suggests that:

- Hitler was crucial because he was still responsible for the overall Nazi dream.
- He had no real effective opposition to his aims.
- Although the government structure was chaotic, Hitler did not get lost in the detail of the day-to-day government.
- He generated an environment in which his followers carried out his presumed intentions. In this way, others willingly took the responsibility 'to work towards the *Führer*'.

SOURCE F

In Source F, what insight does Willikens give into Hitler's style of government?

From a speech by Werner Willikens, state secretary in the Prussian Agricultural Ministry, in February 1934, quoted in Ian Kershaw, *Hitler, 1889–36: Hubris*, Allen Lane, 1998, p. 529.

Everyone with opportunity to observe it knows that the Führer *can only with great difficulty order from above everything that he intends to carry out sooner or later. On the contrary, up till now everyone with a post in the new Germany has worked best when he has, so to speak, worked towards the* Führer. *Very often and in many spheres it has been the case – in previous years as well – that individuals have simply waited for orders and instructions. Unfortunately, the same will be true in the future; but in fact it is the duty of everyone to try to work towards the* Führer *along the lines he would wish.*

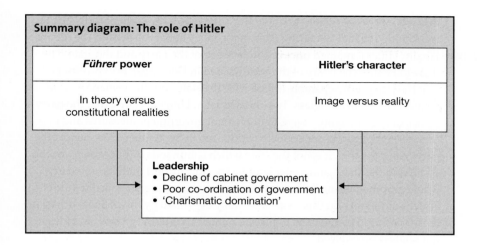

Summary diagram: The role of Hitler

Führer power

In theory versus constitutional realities

Hitler's character

Image versus reality

Leadership
- Decline of cabinet government
- Poor co-ordination of government
- 'Charismatic domination'

④ The Nazi Party and the state

▶ *Why was the relationship between the Nazi Party and the state so unclear?*

▶ *Who lost out: the Nazis or the state?*

By July 1933 Germany had become a one-party state, in which the Nazi Party claimed sole political authority. Nazi **totalitarian** claims, reinforced by a powerful propaganda machine, deceived many people at the time into thinking that Nazism was a clear and well-ordered system of government. The reality was very different. Fundamentally, this was because the exact relationship between the structure of the party on the one hand and the apparatus of the German state on the other was never clarified satisfactorily. It meant that there was much confusion between the two forces in Nazi government, and this clash has been given the term **dualism**.

The revolutionary elements within the party wanted party control of the civil service in order to smash the traditional organs of government and to create a new kind of Germany. However, there seem to have been three reasons why the Nazi leadership did not do this:

- Many recognised that the bureaucracy of the German state was well established and staffed by educated and effective people. Initially, therefore, there was no drastic purge of the state apparatus. The 'Law for the Restoration of the Professional Civil Service' of April 1933 only called for the removal of Jews and well-recognised opponents of the regime (see page 243).
- Another factor which emerged during 1933 after the Nazi consolidation of power was a vast increase in party membership. It increased three-fold from 1933 to 1935 as people jumped on the bandwagon. The so-called

 KEY TERMS

Totalitarian A system of government in which all power is centralised and does not allow any rival authorities.

Dualism A government system in which two forces coexist, for example the Nazi Party and the German state.

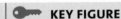
'**March converts**' tended to dilute the influence of the earlier Nazis, further weakening the radical cutting edge of the party apparatus within the regime.

- Finally, Hitler remained unclear on the issue of the party and the state. The 'Law to Ensure the Unity of the State' issued in December 1933 proclaimed that the party 'is inseparably linked with the state', but the explanation was so vague as to be meaningless. Two months later, Hitler declared that the party's principal responsibilities were to implement government measures and to organise propaganda and indoctrination. Yet, in September 1934, he told the party congress that 'it is not the state which commands us but rather we who command the state', and a year later he specifically declared that the party would assume responsibility for those tasks which the state failed to fulfil. Hitler's ambiguity on this issue is partially explained by the political unrest of these years and by the need to placate numerous interest groups, and it was not really ever resolved.

Dualism: state institutions

In Germany the term 'civil servant' was a very broad one; it ranged from officials in the ministries to judges and even teachers. Generally, the state bureaucracy was unsympathetic to Weimar democracy, but was loyal to the institutions of the state. However, in 1934 civil servants, the same as the army, were forced to make a new oath of loyalty to Hitler. Only five per cent of the civil servants dissented and were purged and, as time passed, more and more joined the party until it became compulsory in 1939 (see Figure 6.1, page 177).

Reich Chancellery

The Reich Chancellery was responsible for co-ordinating government and, as the role of the cabinet declined from 1934, the Chancellery became increasingly important. Its head was **Hans-Heinrich Lammers** and he played a pivotal role because he:

- drew up all government legislation
- became the vital link between Hitler and all other organisations, so he in effect controlled all the flow of information.

But even as a very efficient bureaucrat Lammers found it impossible to co-ordinate effectively the growing number of organisations.

Government ministries

Ministries, such as Transport, Education and Economics, were run by leading civil servants. They were generally very conservative, most notably the foreign office. They were under pressure in the late 1930s from growing Nazi institutions: for example, the Economics Ministry was affected by the Four-Year Plan (see pages 194–8) and the foreign office lost its position of supreme control to the so-called **Ribbentrop Bureau**. Very significantly, the aristocrat Neurath was replaced as foreign minister in 1938 by the Nazi Joachim von Ribbentrop. More Nazi officials were then brought in.

Judiciary

In the 1920s the judiciary was hostile to the Weimar Republic. It had been ultra-conservative and in notorious cases it had been biased against the left and in favour of the right (see page 50). So, on one level the judiciary was reasonably content to work with the regime. Still, like the rest of the civil service, judges and lawyers were 'co-ordinated' and obliged to join the Nazi Lawyers' Association and make the oath. Yet, very few were replaced – and more surprisingly, the justice minister until 1941, Franz Gürtner, was not a Nazi.

The judiciary was not immune from Nazi interference, however, and over the years it felt the ever-increasing power of the Nazi organisations. First of all, the structure of new courts enabled the Nazis to get round the established system of justice:

- In 1933 special courts were set up to try political offences without a jury.
- In 1934 the people's court was established to try cases of **high treason** with a jury composed specifically of Nazi Party members (7000 out of the 16,000 cases resulted in a death sentence in 1934–45).

Secondly, all legal authorities became subordinated to the arbitrary power of the SS-Police system, which increasingly behaved above the law (see pages 182–4). The 1941 decree ***Nacht und Nebel*** gave the SS-Police system the right to imprison without question any person thought to be dangerous. In that way, although the traditional role of the judiciary in the state continued to function, it was severely subverted.

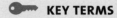

KEY TERMS

High treason The crime of betraying one's country, especially by attempting to overthrow the leader or government.

Nacht und Nebel 'Night and fog.' Name given to a decree by Hitler in December 1941 to seize any person thought to be dangerous. They should vanish into *Nacht und Nebel*.

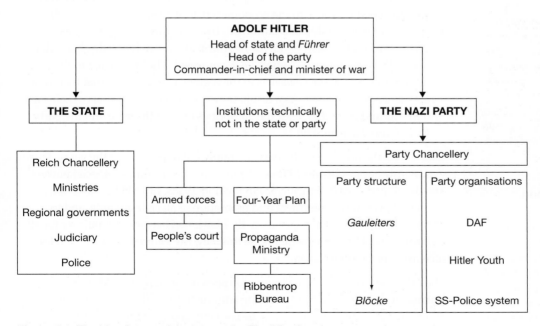

Figure 6.1 The Nazi Party and the state in the Third Reich.

Regional state governments

By early 1934 *Gleichschaltung* had destroyed the federal principle of government (see pages 162–3). The Nazi Reich governors existed only 'to execute the will of the supreme leadership of the *Reich'*, who more often than not were the local party *Gauleiters* with full powers (although their role within the party structure was certainly not clear, see pages 177 and 179).

Dualism: party institutions

The role and shape of the Nazi Party was determined by its background and composition. Its organisation had been created and had evolved in order to *gain* political power and it had proved remarkably well designed for this purpose. However, the party had to find a new role from 1933 and yet it was by no means a unified structure and not really geared to the task of government. The party's problems were caused by the following:

- Up to 1933 it had developed out of the need to attract support from different sections of society and it consisted of a mass of specialist organisations, such as the Hitler Youth (see pages 226–7), the SA and the National Socialist Teachers' League. Once in power, such groups were keen to uphold and advance their own particular interests.
- The party became increasingly splintered. Various other organisations of dubious political position were created and some institutions were caught between the state and the party. For example, Goebbels' propaganda machine was a newly formed ministry (see page 211) and the Four-Year Plan Office was an added response to the economic crisis of 1936 (see pages 194–8).
- The actual membership and administrative structure of the party was established on the basis of the *Führerprinzip* in a major hierarchy, but it did not really work in terms of effective government. The system led to the dominating role of the *Gauleiters* in the regions who believed that their only allegiance was to Hitler. As a result, they endeavoured to preserve their own interests and tended to resist the authorities of both the state and the party (see Figure 6.2, page 179).

In one way, the position of the party certainly did improve over the years. This was mainly because **Rudolf Hess**, Deputy *Führer*, was granted special powers and developed a party bureaucracy in the mid-1930s. In 1935 he was given the right to vet the appointment and promotion of all civil servants, and to oversee the drafting of all legislation. By 1939 it had become compulsory for all civil servants to be party members. In this way, the foundations were laid for increasing party supervision.

The other key figure in the changing fortunes of the party was **Martin Bormann**, a skilled and hard-working administrator with great personal ambition. Working alongside Hess, he correctly analysed the problems confronting the party and created two new departments with the deliberate aim of strengthening the party's position (and thereby his own):

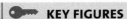

KEY FIGURES

**Rudolph Hess
(1894–1987)**

Early party member and long-standing secretary to Hitler. Deputy leader of the party 1933–41. Absolutely loyal to Hitler. Had limited real power but helped with Bormann to develop a more influential party bureaucracy. His growing mental instability was even noticed by fellow Nazis. He flew to Scotland on his own initiative to negotiate peace in 1941. Interned and sentenced to life at Nuremberg trials.

**Martin Bormann
(1900–45)**

Gauleiter of Thuringia and chief-of-staff to Hess. Improved the influence of the party's bureaucracy. Head of the party chancellery from 1941 and Hitler's secretary from 1943. Died in the ruins of Berlin in 1945.

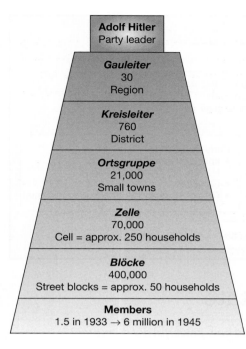

Figure 6.2 Nazi Party structure and leadership.

Adolf Hitler
Party leader

Gauleiter
30
Region

Kreisleiter
760
District

Ortsgruppe
21,000
Small towns

Zelle
70,000
Cell = approx. 250 households

Blöcke
400,000
Street blocks = approx. 50 households

Members
1.5 in 1933 → 6 million in 1945

- The Department for Internal Party Affairs, which had the task of exerting discipline within the party structure.
- The Department for Affairs of State, which aimed to secure party supremacy over the state.

The trend to strengthening the party continued in the war years and Bormann was then put in charge of the party chancellery. Thereafter, by constant meddling, by sheer perseverance and by maintaining good personal relations with Hitler, Bormann effectively advanced the party's fortunes. By 1943, when he officially became Hitler's secretary, and thus secured direct access to the *Führer*, Bormann had constructed an immensely strong power-base for himself.

Conclusion

The Nazi Party became more than merely an organisation geared to seizing power. It strengthened its position in relation to the traditional apparatus of the state. Undoubtedly, it was one of the key power blocs within Nazi Germany, and its influence continued to be felt until the very end. However:

- The party bureaucracy had to compete strenuously for influence over the established state institutions, and the latter were never destroyed, even if they were significantly constrained.
- The internal divisions and rivalries within the party itself were never overcome.
- The independence of the *Gauleiters* was one of the main obstacles to control.

Consequently, the Nazi Party never became an all-pervasive dominating instrument. The next section examines a number of other power blocs.

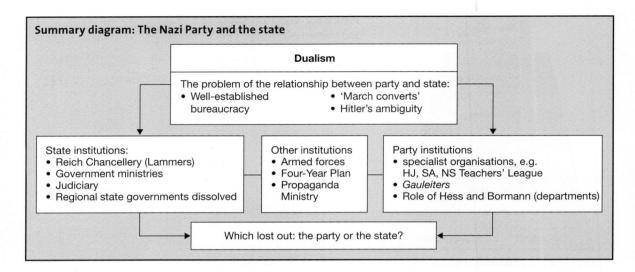

Summary diagram: The Nazi Party and the state

Dualism

The problem of the relationship between party and state:
- Well-established bureaucracy
- 'March converts'
- Hitler's ambiguity

State institutions:
- Reich Chancellery (Lammers)
- Government ministries
- Judiciary
- Regional state governments dissolved

Other institutions
- Armed forces
- Four-Year Plan
- Propaganda Ministry

Party institutions
- specialist organisations, e.g. HJ, SA, NS Teachers' League
- *Gauleiters*
- Role of Hess and Bormann (departments)

Which lost out: the party or the state?

5 The 'police state'

▶ *How did the SS emerge and how powerful did it become?*

▶ *Did the* Gestapo *really control the people?*

Amid all the confusion of the state and party structure an organisation emerged which became the mainstay of the Third Reich: the SS. The SS developed an identity and structure of its own which kept it separate from the state and yet, through its dominance of police matters, linked it with the state.

The emergence of Himmler and the SS

The SS had been formed in 1925 as an elite bodyguard for Hitler, but it remained a relatively minor section of the SA, with only 250 members, until Himmler became its leader in 1929 (see his profile on page 275). By 1933 the SS numbered 52,000, and it had established a reputation for blind obedience and total commitment to the Nazi cause.

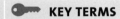

KEY TERMS

SD *Sicherheitsdienst*. Security service.

RSHA Reich Security Office, which amalgamated all police and security organisations.

Himmler had also created in 1931 a special security service, **SD** (*Sicherheitsdienst*), to act as the party's own internal security police. In 1933–4 he assumed control of all the police in the *Länder*, including the *Gestapo* in Prussia. Thus, Hitler turned to Himmler's SS to carry out the purge of June 1934 (see page 168). The loyalty and brutal efficiency of the SS on the Night of the Long Knives had its rewards, for it now became an independent organisation within the party. In 1936 all police powers were unified under Himmler's control as '*Reichsführer* SS and Chief of all German Police', including the *Gestapo*. In 1939 all party and state police organisations involving police and security matters were amalgamated into the **RSHA**, overseen by Himmler, but actually co-ordinated by his deputy, Heydrich (see page 247).

The SS-Police system which had been created, therefore, served four main functions:

- Intelligence gathering by the SD. It was responsible for all intelligence and security and was controlled by its leader, Heydrich (see page 247), but still part of the SS. All its responsibilities grew as occupied lands spread.
- Policing by the *Gestapo* and the **Kripo**. The *Kripo* was responsible for the maintenance of general law and order, for example dealing with **asocials** and thieves. In 1936 the *Kripo* was linked with the *Gestapo*. The *Gestapo* was the key policing organisation for upholding the regime by using surveillance and repression. It had a reputation for brutality and it could arrest and detain anyone without trial, for instance the mass arrests of socialists and communists, although its thoroughness and effectiveness have been questioned (see pages 183–4).
- Disciplining the opposition. Torture chambers and concentration camps were created early in 1933 to deal with political opponents, mainly socialists and communists. In 1936 the number of inmates was still limited to about 6000. Thereafter, this increased dramatically when, using Dachau as the model, the Nazis began to formalise their system of concentration camps. They then started to round up anyone who did not conform – asocials, beggars, gypsies – and the numbers grew to 21,000 by 1939.
- Military action by the first units of the **Waffen SS**. Up to 1938 it consisted of about 14,000 soldiers in three units, but it was racially pure, fanatically loyal and committed to Nazi ideology. Its influence grew rapidly. This was affected by the weakening of the army in the Blomberg–Fritsch crisis (see pages 185–6) and also by the more anti-Semitic policies (see pages 242–7).

KEY TERMS

Kripo *Kriminalpolizei.* Criminal police responsible for the maintenance of general law and order.

Asocials The Nazi '*Volksgemeinschaft*' excluded those who were 'socially unfit', as they deviated from the norms of society. The term 'asocial' was applied in an elastic manner to vagabonds, prostitutes, alcoholics, homosexuals, criminals, 'idlers', even grumblers.

***Waffen* SS** The armed SS: a paramilitary organisation of elite troops.

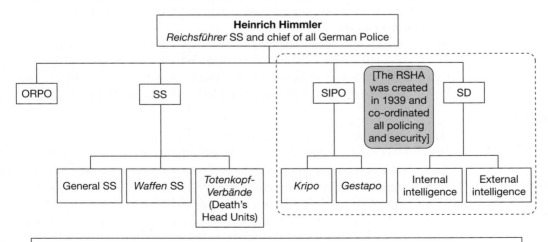

Figure 6.3
The SS-Police system in 1939.

The SS state

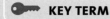 **KEY TERM**

New Order A phrase given by the Nazis to the economic, political and racial integration of Europe under the Third Reich.

It is important to keep in perspective the extent of the influence of the SS in its early years. Yet, the takeover of territories from 1938 to 1941 and the creation of the '**New Order**' marked the start of a significant expansion of the power of the SS.

As *Reichsführer* SS, Himmler controlled a massive police apparatus answerable only to Hitler. The SS system grew into a key power bloc in the Third Reich. It became, in the words of E. Kogon in the 1950s, a 'state within a state'. It was a huge organisation, which numbered 250,000 in 1939 and had begun to eclipse other interest groups in terms of influence. As German troops gained control over more and more areas of Europe, the power of the SS was inevitably enhanced:

- *Security.* All responsibilities of policing and intelligence expanded as occupied lands spread. The job of internal security became much greater and SS officers were granted the authority to crush opposition.
- *Military.* The *Waffen* SS increased from three divisions in 1939 to 35 in 1945, which developed into a 'second army': committed, brutal and militarily highly rated. By 1944 the *Waffen* SS was so powerful it rivalled the position of the German Army.
- *Economy.* The SS became responsible for the creation of the 'New Order' in the occupied lands of eastern Europe. Such a scheme provided opportunities for plunder and economic exploitation on a massive scale, which members of the SS exploited to the full. By the end of the war, the SS had created a massive commercial organisation of over 150 firms, which exploited slave labour to extract raw materials and to manufacture textiles, armaments and household goods.
- *Ideology and race.* The racial policy of extermination and resettlement was pursued with vigour and the system of concentration camps was widely established and run by the SS Death's Head Units (see also pages 270–7). The various 'inferior' races were even used for their economic value such as slave labour.

The SS was not immune to the rivalries and arguments which typified government in Nazi Germany. Disagreements often arose, particularly with local *Gauleiters* and the governors of the occupied territories. However, the SS state under Himmler not only preserved the Nazi regime through its brutal, repressive and often arbitrary policies of law enforcement, but gradually extended its influence. In this way, it evolved over time to become the key power group in the Third Reich.

Tensions with the SS were illustrated in a memorandum written by Wilhelm Frick, the minister of the interior (see Source G).

SOURCE G

From a memorandum written by Wilhelm Frick to Lammers and Hitler in December 1935, quoted in J. Noakes and G. Pridham, editors, *Nazism 1919–45*, volume 2, Liverpool University Press, 1988, p. 510.

I have noticed recently an increase in tension in domestic politics which clearly requires, as a matter of urgency, the clarification of authority both as regards the general police and, more especially, the political police …

There has been of late a marked increase in cases of protective study. The decree on protective study issued by the Reich Minister of the Interior has long been rendered invalid by the actions of the political police … In particular, civil servants have long been taken into custody or have been subjected to Gestapo investigations without the previous knowledge of their superiors.

Abductions by officers of the political police on foreign territory have lately created serious incidents in the sphere of foreign affairs and the Reich Ministry of Economics has pointed out the disturbing effect on the economy which must result from the various political incidents caused by the police, the atmosphere of insecurity caused by cases of protective custody and the latest case of a boycott of the Jews.

Either responsibility rests with the Reich Minister of the Interior or with Reichsführer SS who is already claiming the control of the political in the Reich.

> According to Source G, **?** what were the concerns raised by Frick? Why do you think Frick wrote this memorandum?

The power of the *Gestapo*

Although it has been generally accepted that the SS developed into the key power in the Third Reich, its influence over people's everyday lives has been questioned. Traditionally, the *Gestapo* was seen as representing the all-knowing police state.

This view was actually cultivated by the *Gestapo* itself, by the Allied propagandists during the war and by many post-war films. This interpretation was largely upheld in academic circles, most notably in the standard work *The History of the Gestapo* by Jacques Delarue in 1962. He entitled one chapter 'The *Gestapo* is Everywhere' and then wrote: 'Never before, in no other land and at no other time, had an organisation attained such a comprehensive penetration [of society], possessed such power and reached such a degree of "completeness" in its ability to arouse terror and horror, as well as in its actual effectiveness.'

Many local studies of Germany have led to an influential reinterpretation. The German historians K.M. Mallman and G. Paul, and the US historian R. Gellately, have drawn attention to the limits of the *Gestapo*'s policing by revealing that:

- The manpower of the *Gestapo* was limited: only 40,000 agents for the whole of Germany. Large cities, like Frankfurt or Hamburg, with about half a million people, were policed by just about 40–50 agents.

- Most *Gestapo* work was actually prompted by public informers: between 50 and 80 per cent in different areas. Much information and many denunciations were mere gossip, which generated enormous paperwork for limited return.
- The *Gestapo* had relatively few 'top agents', so it coped by over-relying on the work of the *Kripo*.

Perhaps, it should be noted that the police apparatus of the **GDR** from 1949 was much more extensive than the *Gestapo*.

More recently, the US historian Eric Johnson has tried to put the latest **revisionist** views into perspective through his case study of the Rhineland. He accepts the limitations of the *Gestapo*, and argues that it did not impose a climate of terror on ordinary Germans. Instead, it concentrated on surveillance and repression of specific enemies: the political left, Jews and, to a lesser extent, religious groups and asocials. Controversially, he claims that the Nazis and the German population formed a grim 'pact': the population turned a blind eye to the *Gestapo*'s persecution and, in return, the Nazis overlooked minor transgressions of the law by ordinary Germans.

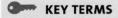

KEY TERMS

GDR German Democratic Republic. Communist East Germany, 1949–90.

Revisionism In general terms it is the aim to modify or change something. In this context, it refers specifically to a historian who challenges a well-established interpretation.

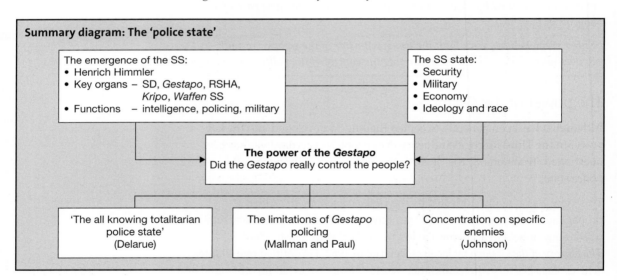

Summary diagram: The 'police state'

The emergence of the SS:
- Henrich Himmler
- Key organs – SD, *Gestapo*, RSHA, *Kripo*, *Waffen* SS
- Functions – intelligence, policing, military

The SS state:
- Security
- Military
- Economy
- Ideology and race

The power of the *Gestapo*
Did the *Gestapo* really control the people?

'The all knowing totalitarian police state'
(Delarue)

The limitations of *Gestapo* policing
(Mallman and Paul)

Concentration on specific enemies
(Johnson)

6 The German Army

▶ *To what extent did the army co-operate with the Nazi regime?*

Despite its suspicion of Nazism, the army accepted the Nazi accession to power and co-operated in the manoeuvrings which led to the Night of the Long Knives (see page 152). Moreover, the generals were confident that they had gained the upper hand when Hitler agreed to the destruction of his own SA. Ironically, they believed that now the radical element within Nazism had been removed they could make the Nazi state work for them.

Co-operation

The army succeeded only in preserving its influence in the short term by a compromise which was fatal in the long term. This is most clearly shown by the new oath of loyalty demanded by Hitler of all soldiers, and accepted by Field Marshal von Blomberg, the defence minister, and General von Fritsch, the commander-in-chief of the army:

> *I swear by God this sacred oath: that I will render unconditional obedience to the* Führer *of the German Reich and people, Adolf Hitler, the Supreme Commander of the Armed Forces, and will be ready as a brave soldier to risk my life at any time for this oath.*

For a German soldier, bound by discipline and obedience, such words marked a commitment which made any future resistance an act of the most serious treachery.

In the years 1934–7 the relationship between the Nazi state and the army remained cordial. The generals were encouraged by:

- the expansion of the rearmament programme from 1935
- Hitler's reintroduction of conscription in March 1935, thereby increasing the size of the army to 550,000
- the diplomatic successes over the Saar (1935) and the Rhineland (1936) (see page 259).

Blomberg even issued a number of military decrees in an attempt to adjust army training according to Nazi ideology and to elevate the *Führer*. Yet, Blomberg and the army leaders deceived themselves into believing that its independent position was being preserved. In fact, the power of the SS was growing fast, while Hitler had little respect for the conservative attitudes held by many army officers. It was merely political realism which held him back from involvement in army affairs until 1938.

The Blomberg–Fritsch crisis 1937–8

The balance between the army and Hitler changed in the winter of 1937–8 after the so-called Hossbach conference meeting on 5 November 1937. In this meeting Hitler outlined to Germany's chiefs of the armed forces his foreign policy aims for military expansion. Blomberg and **Fritsch**, in particular, were both seriously concerned by Hitler's talk of war and conquest, especially bearing in mind Germany's state of military unpreparedness. Their doubts further convinced Hitler that the army leadership was spineless, and in February 1938 both men were forced out of office after revelations about their private lives. Blomberg had just married for the second time, with Hitler as principal witness, but it subsequently became known that his wife had a criminal record for theft and prostitution. Fritsch was accused of homosexual offences on evidence conveniently produced by Himmler.

 KEY FIGURE

Werner von Fritsch (1880–1939)

Commander-in-chief of the army 1934–8, but hostile to the growing power of the SS. Forced to resign in 1938, yet acquitted of homosexual accusations. Killed in the Battle of Warsaw in September 1939.

? According to Source H,
what was the conflict
between Fritsch and the
party? How reliable is
Fritsch's account?

SOURCE H

**From an account written by Fritsch two days before his enforced resignation,
quoted in John Laver, *Nazi Germany 1933–45*, Hodder & Stoughton, 1991,
p. 60.**

*On 3 January 1934 I was appointed Commander-in-Chief with effect from
1 February against the Führer's wishes, against Blomberg's wishes, but under
the strongest pressure from Field Marshal von Hindenburg … the party's
struggle against me began on the day of my appointment, in so far as it had not
already begun … The party sees in me not only the man who opposed the
ambitions of the SA but also tried to block the influx of party political maxims
into the Army.*

*Finally, the SS military wing, which is continually being expanded, must create
conflict with the Army through its very existence. It is the living proof of
mistrust towards the Army and its leadership.*

This infamous episode provided Hitler with the perfect opportunity to
subordinate the army. He abolished the post of defence minister and took the
title commander-in-chief and minister of war himself. Day-to-day leadership
of all armed forces was given to the High Command (*Oberkommando der
Wehrmacht*), headed by a loyal and subservient General Keitel. The new
commander-in-chief of the army was General Brauchitsch, another willing
supporter of the regime. Also, a further sixteen generals were retired and
44 transferred from office. At the same time, Foreign Minister Neurath was
replaced by the Nazi Ribbentrop. In the words of E. Feuchtwanger (1995): 'It was
a crisis of the regime not unlike the Night of the Long Knives in 1934, although
this time there was no bloodshed. Again Hitler was the undisputed winner and
the national-conservative elites who had helped him into the saddle, suffered a
further loss of influence' (see Figure 6.4).

From 1938 the army's ability to shape political developments in Germany was
drastically reduced. At first Hitler had correctly recognised the need to work
with the army leadership, but by early 1938 he was strong enough to mould it
more closely to his requirements. The army was not without power, but it had
been tamed to serve its new master. It still remained the one institution with
the technical means of striking successfully at the regime. For example, in the
summer of 1938 a plan was drawn up by General **Beck** and other generals to
arrest Hitler if a full-scale European war broke out over the Czech crisis (see
page 259). It came to nothing because the peaceful surrender by Anglo-French
appeasers in September cut the ground from beneath the plotters' feet.

 **KEY TERM**

Wehrmacht The name of
the combined armed forces
1935–45. From 1921 to
1935 the term *Reichswehr*
had referred simply to the
German Army. In 1935 the
German armed forces were
reorganised and given the
term *Wehrmacht*. It consisted
of the army, the navy and the
air force.

KEY FIGURE

**Ludwig Beck
(1880–1944)**

Chief of staff of the army
1935–8. Tried to organise
joint action against Hitler's
war plans in 1938, but failed.
Resigned and became
increasingly involved in the
resistance. Shot in the July
Bomb Plot.

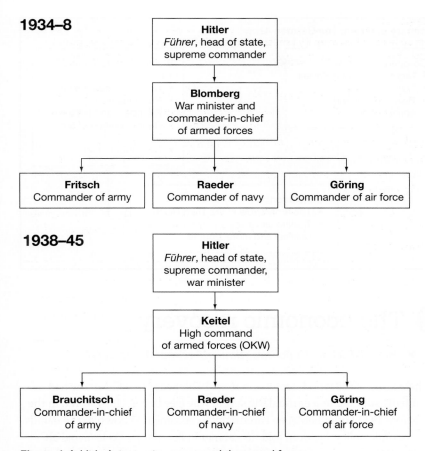

Figure 6.4 Hitler's increasing power and the armed forces.

Conclusion

Generally, historians have not been sympathetic to the role played by the German Army. It is difficult to avoid the conclusion that the army leadership played a naïve and inept political game. Conditioned by its traditions of obedience, loyalty and patriotism, and encouraged by the authoritarian position of the Third Reich, the army became a vital pillar of the Nazi regime in the early years. Even when its own power to influence events had been drastically reduced in 1938 and the full implications of Nazi rule became apparent during the war, the army's leaders could not escape from their political and moral dilemma. From 1938 to 1942 Nazi diplomatic and military policy was so successful that it effectively ruined the plans of any doubting officers.

Even before the war began in 1939, resistance was not only unpatriotic, but actually treasonable. However, by early 1943, when the military situation had changed dramatically, a growing number of generals come to believe that the war could not be won and opposition started to grow.

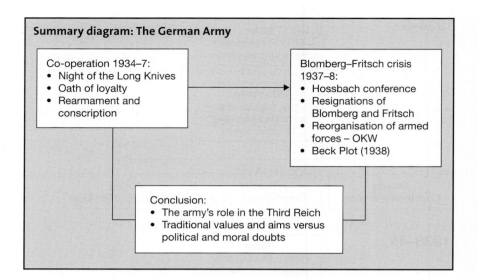

Summary diagram: The German Army

Co-operation 1934–7:
- Night of the Long Knives
- Oath of loyalty
- Rearmament and conscription

Blomberg–Fritsch crisis 1937–8:
- Hossbach conference
- Resignations of Blomberg and Fritsch
- Reorganisation of armed forces – OKW
- Beck Plot (1938)

Conclusion:
- The army's role in the Third Reich
- Traditional values and aims versus political and moral doubts

 # The economic recovery

▶ *How did Schacht's policies stimulate economic recovery?*

The sheer scale of the world depression from 1929 meant that Germany had undoubtedly suffered in a particularly severe way (see pages 116–19). Yet, in the years before 1933 Hitler had been careful not to become tied down to the details of an economic policy. He even told his cabinet in February 1933 to 'avoid all detailed statements concerning an economic programme of the government'. Nevertheless, Hitler was also politically astute enough to realise that the survival and stability of the dictatorship depended on bringing Germany out of depression.

Schacht's economic strategy

In the early years, Nazi economic policy was under the control of Hjalmar Schacht, president of the *Reichsbank* (1933–9) and minister of economics (1934–7). This showed the need of the Nazi leadership to work with the powerful forces of the economic elites. Schacht was already a respected international financier because of his leading role in the creation of the new currency in the wake of the 1923 hyperinflation.

It is certainly true that the economic depression reached its low-point in the winter of 1932–3 and that afterwards the trade cycle began to improve. This undoubtedly worked to the political and economic advantage of the Nazis. Nevertheless, there was no single, easy 'quick fix' solution. The heart of economic recovery lay in the major revival of public investment led, for the most part, by the state itself, which embarked on a large-scale increase in its own spending in an effort to stimulate demand and raise national income. So, under

Schacht's guidance and influence, deficit financing was adopted through a range of economic measures.

Banking and the control of capital

Initially, because the German banking system had been so fundamentally weakened, the state increasingly assumed greater responsibility for the control of capital within the economy. It then proceeded to set interest rates at a lower level and to reschedule the large-scale debts of local authorities.

Assistance for farming and small businesses

Particular financial benefits were given to groups, such as farmers and small businesses. This not only stimulated economic growth, but also rewarded some of the most sympathetic supporters of the Nazis in the 1930–3 elections. Some of the measures included:

- tariffs on imported produce being maintained in order to protect German farmers
- subsidies given by the Reich Food Estate, as part of a nationally planned agricultural system
- the Reich Entailed Farm Law, which tried to offer more security of land ownership to small farmers: debts were reduced by tax concessions and lower interest rates
- allowances to encourage the rehiring of domestic servants
- the allocation of grants for house repairs.

State investment: public works

Of the greatest significance was the direct spending by the state on a range of investment projects. In June 1933 the 'Law to Reduce Unemployment' was renewed and expanded (from a scheme which had originally been started by Papen in 1932) and the RAD (*Reicharbeitsdienst*, Reich Labour Service) was extended to employ 19–25-year-olds. For a long time most historians assumed that rearmament was the main focus of investment, but the figures for public expenditure show that this was initially spread among rearmament, construction and transportation. The investment in the first three years was directed towards work creation schemes such as:

- reforestation
- land reclamation
- motorisation: the policy of developing the vehicle industry and the building of improved roads, for example the *Autobahnen* (motorways)
- building: especially the expansion of the housing sector and public buildings.

The cumulative effect of these policies was to triple public investment between 1933 and 1936 and to increase government expenditure by nearly 70 per cent over the same period (see Tables 6.2 and 6.3, page 190). By early 1936 the economic recovery was well advanced and then emphasis began to turn even more towards rearmament.

Table 6.2 Public investment and expenditure in billions of *Reichsmark* 1928–36

	1928	1932	1933	1934	1935	1936
Total public investment	6.6	2.2	2.5	4.6	6.4	8.1
Total government expenditure	11.7	8.6	9.4	12.8	13.9	15.8

Table 6.3 Public expenditure by category in billions of *Reichsmark* 1928–36

Category	1928	1932	1933	1934	1935	1936
Construction	2.7	0.9	1.7	3.5	4.9	5.4
Rearmament	0.7	0.7	1.8	3.0	5.4	10.2
Transportation	2.6	0.8	1.3	1.8	2.1	2.4

As a result of these strategies, there was a dramatic growth in jobs. From the registered peak of 6 million unemployed in January 1932, the official figure for 1936 showed it had declined to 2.1 million (see Table 6.4 below). For those many Germans who had been desperately out of work, the Nazi economic policy was to be welcomed. Even in other democratic countries scarred by mass unemployment, observers abroad admired Germany's achievement of job creation. As Hitler proudly claimed in his speech in 1935:

SOURCE I

From Hitler's speech to the *Reichstag* on 21 May 1935, quoted in N. Baynes, translator and editor, *The Speeches of Adolf Hitler 1922–39*, volume 1, Oxford University Press, 1942, pp. 910–11.

What we have achieved in two and half years in the way of a planned provision of labour, a planned regulation of the market, a planned control of prices and wages, was considered a few years ago to be absolutely impossible … In order to guarantee the functioning of the national economy it was necessary first of all to put a stop to the everlasting fluctuations of wages and prices. It was further necessary to remove the conditions giving rise to interference, which did not spring further from higher national economic necessities i.e. to destroy the class organisations of both camps which lived on the politics of wages and prices. The destruction of the trade unions both of employers and employees, which were based on the class struggle demanded a similar removal of the political parties which were maintained by these groups of interest, which interest in return supported them. Here arose the necessity for a new conservative and vital constitution and a new organisation of the Reich and the state.

? According to Hitler in Source I, what were the measures taken for Germany's recovery?

Table 6.4 Unemployment and production in Germany 1928–36

	1928	1929	1930	1931	1932	1933	1934	1935	1936
Unemployment (millions)	1.4	1.8	3.1	4.5	5.6	4.8	2.7	2.2	1.6
Industrial production (1928 = 100)	100	100	87	70	58	66	83	96	107

Yet, even in 1936, the government public deficit certainly did not run out of control, since Schacht maintained taxes at a relatively high level and encouraged private savings in state savings banks. Of course, it must be remembered that all this took place as the world economy began to recover, and Schacht was aided by the natural upturn in the business cycle after its low-point in winter 1932. Nevertheless, it is difficult to believe that such a marked turnaround in investment and employment could have been achieved without Nazi economic policy.

The balance of payments problem

Germany made an impressive economic recovery between 1933 and 1936, but two underlying worries remained:

- the fear that a rapid increase in demand would rekindle inflation
- the fear that a rapid increase in demand would lead to the emergence of a balance of trade deficit.

In fact, the problem of inflation never actually materialised, partly because there was a lack of demand in the economy, but also because the regime established strict controls over prices and wages. This had been helped by the abolition of the trade unions in May 1933 (see page 163). On the other hand, what was to be a recurring balance of payments problem emerged for the first time in the summer of 1934. This was a consequence of Germany's importing more raw materials while failing to increase its exports. Its gold and foreign currency reserves were also low.

The balance of payments problem was not merely an economic issue, for it carried with it large-scale political implications. If Germany was so short of foreign currency (essential to buy foreign goods), which sector of the economy was to have priority in spending the money? The early economics minister, Schmitt, wanted to try to reduce unemployment further by manufacturing more consumer goods for public consumption, for example textiles. However, powerful voices in the armed forces and big business were already demanding more resources for major programmes, for example rearmament.

Hitler could not ignore such pressure, especially as this economic problem coincided with the political dilemma over the SA (see pages 165–9). Consequently, Schmitt's policy was rejected and he was removed, thereby allowing Schacht to combine the offices of minister of economics and president of the *Reichsbank*.

Schacht's 'New Plan'

By the law of 3 July, Schacht was given dictatorial powers over the economy, which he then used to introduce the 'New Plan' of September 1934. This provided for a comprehensive control by the government of all aspects of trade, tariffs, capital and currency exchange in an attempt to prevent excessive imports.

SOURCE J

In what ways do you think that the photograph in Source J could be seen as propaganda?

The first *autobahn* was prompted by the mayor of Cologne, Konrad Adenauer; the stretch from Cologne to Bonn was opened in 1932. A further 3000 km of motorway roads were developed in 1930s. They served as an economic stimulus, but were also politically used as a propagandist tool. Their military value has been doubted.

From that time, the government decided which imports were to be allowed or prohibited. For example, imports of raw cotton and wool were substantially cut, whereas metals were permitted in order to satisfy the demands of heavy industry.

The economic priorities were set by a series of measures:

- *Trade treaties.* Schacht tried to promote trade and save foreign exchange by signing **bilateral trade treaties**, especially with the countries of south-east Europe, for example Romania and Yugoslavia. These often took the form of straightforward barter agreements (thus avoiding the necessity of formal currency exchange). In this way, Germany began to exert a powerful economic influence over the Balkans long before it obtained military and political control.
- *The* Reichsmark *currency.* Germany agreed to purchase raw materials from all countries it traded with on the condition that *Reichsmarks* could only be used to buy back German goods (at one time it is estimated that the German *Reichsmark* had 237 different values depending on the country and the circumstances).

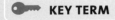 **KEY TERM**

Bilateral trade treaty
A trade agreement between two countries or parties.

Hjalmar Schacht

1877	Born in North Schleswig, Germany
1923	Set up the new currency, *Rentenmark* (see page 65), and made president of the *Reichsbank* 1923–30
1933	Reappointed as president of the *Reichsbank*
1934	Appointed as minister of economics. Drew up and oversaw the 'New Plan' to control all capital and trade
1937	Increasingly lost influence and resigned as minster of economics
1939	Resigned as president of the *Reichsbank*
1944–5	Arrested after the 20 July Bomb Plot (see page 287) and held in Ravensbrück concentration camp
1945–6	Charged at the Nuremberg trials, but acquitted
1950–63	Private financial consultant to the governments of many countries
1970	Died

Schacht was an economic genius. He built his reputation on the way he stabilised the German economy through the creation of the new currency, the *Rentenmark*, in 1923. He served as president of the *Reichsbank* to all the Weimar governments 1923–30, but he was a strong nationalist and eventually resigned over the Young Plan (see page 120).

Schacht was increasingly persuaded by Hitler's political programme. From 1930 his influence went through three clear stages:

- He played a vital role in encouraging big business to finance the rise of the Nazis and he backed Hitler's appointment.
- In the years 1933–6 Schacht dominated the Nazi economy and it was he who shaped Germany's recovery by deficit financing and the 'New Plan' of 1934.
- However, he disagreed with the emphasis on rearmament in the Four-Year Plan crisis and his power waned.

Schacht resigned his major economic posts before the end of the war and became increasingly disaffected with the Nazi regime. He made connections with the anti-Nazi resistance, yet he survived a concentration camp and Allied war trials. Even in his eighties he remained a well-respected financial advisor to many developing countries.

- *Mefo bills.* Mefo were special government money bills (like a credit note) designed by Schacht. They were issued by the *Reichsbank* and guaranteed by the government as payment for goods and were then held for up to five years earning four per cent interest per annum. The main purpose of Mefo bills was that they successfully disguised government spending.

Schacht was never a member of the Nazi Party, but he was drawn into the Nazi movement and the regime. His proven economic skills earned him respect both in and outside the party and it was he who laid the foundations for economic recovery. By mid-1936:

- unemployment had fallen to 1.5 million
- industrial production had increased by 60 per cent since 1933
- GNP had grown over the same period by 40 per cent.

However, such successes disguised fundamental structural weaknesses, which came to a head in the second half of 1936 over the future direction of the German economy.

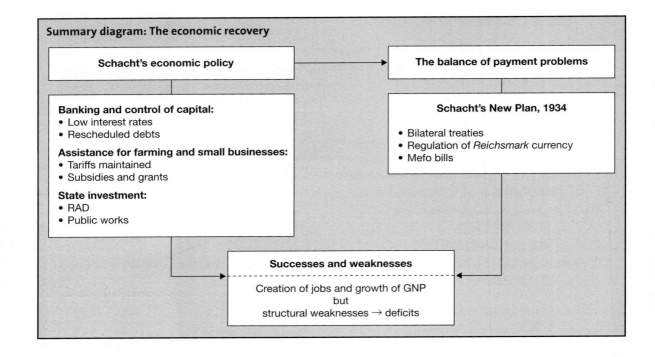

Summary diagram: The economic recovery

Schacht's economic policy

The balance of payment problems

Banking and control of capital:
- Low interest rates
- Rescheduled debts

Assistance for farming and small businesses:
- Tariffs maintained
- Subsidies and grants

State investment:
- RAD
- Public works

Schacht's New Plan, 1934
- Bilateral treaties
- Regulation of *Reichsmark* currency
- Mefo bills

Successes and weaknesses

Creation of jobs and growth of GNP
but
structural weaknesses → deficits

8 The Four-Year Plan and the industrial elites

▶ *What was the purpose of the Four-Year Plan and why was its implementation so significant for Nazi Germany?*

In many respects, as Schacht himself was only too aware, he had merely hidden the balance of payments problem by a series of clever financial tricks. Despite his sympathy for deficit financing, Schacht believed that a combination of a budget deficit and a balance of payments deficit could not be maintained indefinitely. In early 1936 it became clear to him that, as the import demands for rearmament and consumption of goods increased, the German balance of payments would go deeply into the red. He therefore suggested a reduction in arms expenditure in order to increase the production of industrial goods which at least could be exported so as to earn foreign exchange. Such a solution had its commercial supporters, especially among those with interests in exporting, for example textiles, coal, iron and steel, and tool-making machines. However, it was unacceptable to the armed forces and to the Nazi leadership, as it implied that it would be at the expense of rearmament. By the mid-1930s, then, this debate was popularly summed up by the question: should the economy concentrate on producing **guns or butter?**

KEY TERM

Guns or butter? A question used to highlight the controversial economic choice between rearmament and consumer goods.

The aims and objectives of the plan

Most significantly, Hitler himself expressed his position in a secret memorandum presented to Göring in August 1936. This has been seen as one of the most significant documents of Nazi history, as it provides a clear insight into Hitler's war aims and the development of the Nazi economy. He concluded by writing:

> There has been time enough in four years to find out what we cannot do. Now we have to carry out what we can do. I thus set the following tasks.
> (i) The German armed forces must be operational within four years
> (ii) The German economy must be fit for war within four years.

The politico-economic crisis of 1936 was resolved by the introduction of the Four-Year Plan – essentially the implementation of the August memorandum – under the control of Hermann Göring who, in October of that year, was appointed 'Director of the Four-Year Plan'. Its aims were clearly to expand rearmament and **autarky** to make Germany as self-sufficient as possible in

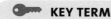

KEY TERM

Autarky The aim for self-sufficiency in the production of food and raw materials, especially when at war.

Hermann Göring

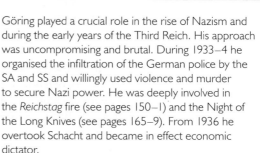

1893	Born in Bavaria, the son of the German South West Africa governor
1923	Took part in the Munich *putsch* and injured
1933	Joined Hitler's cabinet as minister without portfolio
	Used the *Reichstag* fire to discredit the communists. Exploited the terror to impose the dictatorship
1934	Helped to organise the Night of the Long Knives
1935	Commander-in-chief of the new *Luftwaffe* (air force)
1936	Appointed director of the Four-Year Plan
1940–5	Retained most of his offices. Increasingly isolated within the Nazi leadership
1946	Killed himself an hour before his execution at the Nuremberg trials

Göring came from a well-to-do family and with this status and the contacts provided by his aristocratic first wife, he was able to give Nazism a more respectable image in high society. He was popular because of his witty and charming conversation.

Göring played a crucial role in the rise of Nazism and during the early years of the Third Reich. His approach was uncompromising and brutal. During 1933–4 he organised the infiltration of the German police by the SA and SS and willingly used violence and murder to secure Nazi power. He was deeply involved in the *Reichstag* fire (see pages 150–1) and the Night of the Long Knives (see pages 165–9). From 1936 he overtook Schacht and became in effect economic dictator.

Göring acquired a host of titles and posts, and in 1939 he was officially named as Hitler's successor. However, he became increasingly resented by other leading Nazis for his ambition and greed. After the failure of the *Luftwaffe* to win the Battle of Britain (1940) he was more isolated within the leadership and his influence declined.

food and industrial production. In order to achieve this, the plan highlighted a number of objectives:

- To regulate imports and exports, so as to prioritise strategic sectors, for example chemicals and metals, at the expense of agricultural imports.
- To control the key sectors of the labour force, so as to prevent price inflation, for example the creation of a Reich Price Commissioner and increased work direction by DAF (see pages 219–21).
- To increase the production of raw materials, so as to reduce the financial cost of importing vital goods, for example steel, iron and aluminium.
- To develop *ersatz* (substitute) products, for example oil (from coal) and artificial rubber (buna).
- To increase agricultural production, so as to avoid imported foodstuffs, for example grants for fertilisers and machinery.

The effects of the Four-Year Plan

The decision to implement the Four-Year Plan marked an important turning point in the Nazi regime. Nazi control over the German economy became much tighter, as Schacht described in his own book written in 1949:

SOURCE K

From H. Schacht, *Account Settled*, Weidenfeld & Nicolson, 1949, pp. 98–9.

Göring set out, with all the folly and incompetence of the amateur, to carry out the programme of economic self-sufficiency, or autarky, envisaged in the Four Year Plan. He exploited the plenary powers Hitler had given him as chief of the Four Year Plan operations in order to extend his own influence over economic policy, which he did not find difficult, since he was now, of course, in a position to place really large contracts … On December 17th 1936, Göring informed a meeting of big industrialists that it was no longer a question of producing economically, but simply of producing. And as far as getting hold of foreign exchange was concerned it was quite immaterial whether the provisions of the law were complied with or not … Göring's policy of recklessly exploiting Germany's economic substance necessarily brought me into more and more acute conflict with him, and for his part he exploited his powers, with Hitler and the party behind him, to counter my activity as Minister of Economics to an ever-increasing extent.

In what ways does Schacht criticise the Four Year Plan in Source K?

Schacht had no real respect for Göring, who had no economic expertise and who deliberately and increasingly ignored Schacht's advice. Schacht recognised that his influence was on the wane and eventually in November 1937 he resigned. He was replaced by the weak Walther Funk, although from this time Göring himself became the real economic dictator.

The success of the plan was mixed over the years (see Table 6.5 on page 197). On the one hand, production of a number of key materials, such as aluminium and explosives, had expanded greatly, or at least at a reasonable rate. On the other hand, it fell a long way short of the targets in the vital commodities of rubber and oil, while arms production never reached the levels desired by the armed forces and Hitler. All in all, the Four-Year Plan had succeeded in the sense that Germany's reliance on imports had not increased. However, this still meant that when war did break out Germany was dependent on foreign supplies for one-third of its raw materials.

Table 6.5 The Four-Year Plan launched in 1936

Commodity (in thousands of tons)	Four-Year Plan target	Actual output for 1936	Actual output for 1938	Actual output for 1942
Oil	13,830	1,790	2,340	6,260
Aluminium	273	98	166	260
Rubber (buna)	120	0.7	5	96
Explosives	223	18	45	300
Steel	24,000	19,216	22,656	20,480
Hard coal	213,000	158,400	186,186	166,059

The power and influence of the industrial elites

The position of the business community began to improve form 1933. However, it would be wrong to see business as a uniform interest group; different sectors were affected in different ways. Small business was squeezed out by the power of the industrial elites, whose support was more crucial in the creation of new jobs. The building and the giant coal and steel industries initially prospered most, while consumer goods' production remained relatively depressed. So, in the first few years of Nazi rule, big business was able to exert a strong influence – particularly through the leadership of Schacht. It maintained a privileged position in its own sphere, just as the army generals did in the military field (see also pages 184–5).

The Four-Year Plan in 1936 marked an important development. Schacht and the leaders of traditional heavy industry had urged for a reduction of rearmament and an increased emphasis on consumer goods and exports. However, this was a fatal error of political judgement which weakened Schacht's influence and brought an end to the supremacy of heavy industry. Instead, Göring was now in control and the only groups with real influence were in the electrical and chemical sectors because of their crucial role in rearmament:

- In the chemical industry IG Farben led the way with its development of synthetic substitutes for products such as rubber and oil.
- In the armaments and transport sector Daimler-Benz was crucial for the production of trucks and aircraft.
- The electrical industry was dominated by Siemens.

Most telling of all was the less influential position of the so-called 'Ruhr barons' of coal and iron and steel. When they refused to co-operate, Göring nationalised the iron-ore deposits and created a new state firm, the Reichswerke Hermann Göring, to exploit them.

From 1936 the divisions in big business meant that the needs of the economy were determined by political decisions, especially those in foreign and military policy. Private property always remained in private hands, but the free market and business independence gave way to state regulation. On the whole, the industrial elites accepted the controls of the political leadership, fearing that resistance to state interference would weaken their situation further. This was because the material benefits were on the whole just too attractive. Profits generally continued to grow until the last phase of the war, so this was reason enough to work with the regime, although they were never directly in charge of policy. From 1936 this was clearly determined by the Nazi leadership. In a mocking simile R. Grunberger (1971) writes: 'German business can be likened to the conductor of a runaway bus, who has no control over the actions of the driver, but keeps collecting the passengers' fares right up to the final crash.'

A war economy in peacetime?

Not surprisingly, the nature of the Nazi economy in the 1930s has been the focus of controversy because it was closely linked with the regime's leadership and the onset of war in 1939.

B.H. Klein: limited war preparations

Klein in the 1950s argued that Germany's economic mobilisation for war was initially 'quite modest'. He claimed that Nazi economic policy was deliberately connected with the military strategy of **Blitzkrieg**. In his view, Hitler and the armed forces recognised Germany's precarious position over the production of raw materials, and consequently developed the strategy of short wars. This would avoid the economic strain of 'total war' and also had the political advantage of not reducing the production of consumer goods excessively. In that way, Germany seemed to have both 'guns and butter'. Klein argued that pre-1939 civilian consumption remained comfortable. Indeed, he claimed, it was not until after the defeat at Stalingrad in 1943 (see page 262) that a 'total war economy' began in earnest.

Tim Mason: overheating pressures

In contrast, the Marxist historian Tim Mason in the 1970s has argued that the Nazi economy was in fact under increasing strain from 1937. He believes that Hitler's war aims were clearly driving the pace of rearmament to such an extent that the economy was put under tremendous pressures and it was in danger of expanding too quickly and overheating. He particularly points out economic indicators that:

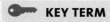 **KEY TERM**

Blitzkrieg Literally, 'lightning war'. The name of the military strategy developed to avoid static war. It was based on the use of dive-bombers, paratroopers and motorised infantry.

- There were growing shortages of raw materials, food and consumer goods.
- There were labour shortages, especially the skilled, which increased wages.
- The balance of trade was going further into the red and becoming difficult to finance.
- The government expenditure and deficit were expanding.

Most significantly, Mason argues that all these pressures were contributing to significant social discontent among the working class. He goes so far as to suggest that by 1939 the situation was so serious that Hitler embarked on the war as the only way out of Germany's domestic economic dilemma.

Richard Overy: a massive economic mobilisation

However, Richard Overy, writing in the 1990s, has rejected the traditional opinions. This is because, although an economic historian, he has been influenced by the work of diplomatic historians, who see Hitler stumbling unintentionally into a major European war in September 1939. Overy has argued that Hitler had always envisaged a great conflict for world power and that this necessitated the transformation of the economy to meet the demands of total war. However, his preparations for this kind of war were not intended to be finished until 1943. The war with Poland in 1939 was meant to be a local war which Hitler wrongly believed would not involve Britain and France. The premature outbreak of continental conflict inevitably found the German economy only partially mobilised.

Overy, therefore, believes that the underlying principles of Nazi economic policy were abundantly clear from 1936. The German economy had been unashamedly directed towards war preparation, so that two-thirds of all German investment went into war-related projects:

- Full employment was achieved, but over a quarter of the workforce was involved in rearmament.
- Levels of government expenditure more than doubled in the same period, with the result that the government debt increased accordingly.
- In the last full year of peace seventeen per cent of Germany's GNP went on military expenditure (compared to eight per cent in Britain and one per cent in the USA).

According to such a view, the German economy by 1939 was already dominated by the preparations for war, though not reaching the full-scale mobilisation required of total war, since that was not envisaged until about 1943. In a thought-provoking conclusion Overy suggested: 'If war had been postponed until 1943–5 as Hitler had hoped, then Germany would have been much better prepared … The German economy in 1939 was still a long way short of being fully mobilised, but it was certainly on more of a war footing than Britain or France.'

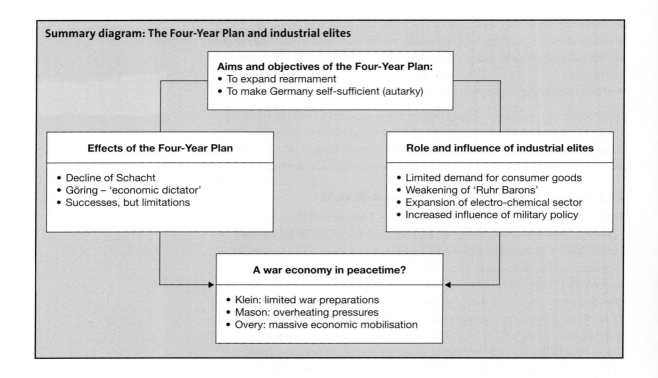

Summary diagram: The Four-Year Plan and industrial elites

Aims and objectives of the Four-Year Plan:
- To expand rearmament
- To make Germany self-sufficient (autarky)

Effects of the Four-Year Plan
- Decline of Schacht
- Göring – 'economic dictator'
- Successes, but limitations

Role and influence of industrial elites
- Limited demand for consumer goods
- Weakening of 'Ruhr Barons'
- Expansion of electro-chemical sector
- Increased influence of military policy

A war economy in peacetime?
- Klein: limited war preparations
- Mason: overheating pressures
- Overy: massive economic mobilisation

9 Conclusion: the nature of the Nazi dictatorship

▶ *Where did the power really lie in 1939?*

The changing balance of power

In the early years, Hitler and the Nazis were heavily dependent on the sympathy of the army and the industrial elites; consequently, they did not attempt to control them directly as they feared alienating them. Indeed, the destruction of the SA in 1934 was driven by the need to satisfy those traditional vested interests, and was a blow to radical Nazis. At this stage the SS-Police system was relatively limited. The rearmament programme and the early moves in foreign policy acted as a powerful focus of common interest: profits for industry and the restoration of prestige for the army.

All this changed during 1936–8. Hitler's personal political position became stronger and was supported by the emerging power of Himmler's SS-Police system. Hitler was therefore less restricted by the need for political compromise and he could pursue his aims more vigorously. Moreover, the economic crisis of 1936 led to the introduction of the Four-Year Plan under Göring and the decline of Schacht. This development represented a major shift in the balance of political power away from big business as a whole, although the regime was strongly supported by the electrochemical sector because of its links with arms production. Although the army had sided with the Nazi leadership in 1936, it was severely weakened two years later by the purge of major generals after Blomberg and Fritsch (see pages 185–6) had expressed their doubts about the direction of Hitler's foreign policy.

By 1938, therefore, big business, the army and the traditional elites within the state bureaucracy had been reduced to the role of junior partners in the Third Reich's power structure. The weakening of their positions was to continue in subsequent years, although at first the army gained great kudos from military victories. In contrast, the power and influence of the SS-Police system was to grow to make it the dominant power bloc – so much so that some historians have spoken of the emergence of the 'SS state'.

Internal Nazi tensions

Of course, there was a lack of planning and organisation on Hitler's part, which led to internal tensions, and it is now generally appreciated that divisions and rivalries were rife in the government of the Third Reich. The leading Nazis headed their own institutional empires and their aims and interests often brought them into conflict with each other. For example, the economy from 1936 was in the hands of major wrangling leaders and their offices:

- Göring as the director of the Four-Year Plan
- Schacht as president of the *Reichsbank*
- Funk as minister of economics
- Ley in charge of DAF.

On top of this, there were personality clashes which led to personal rivalries and ambitions at the expense of efficient government. Most notably, Bormann and Himmler despised each other, and Göring and Goebbels were barely on speaking terms. In a telling phrase, the historian J. Noakes writes (1984): 'Perhaps, the most outstanding characteristic of the political system of the Third Reich was its lack of formal structure.'

Yet, despite all this talk of individual and institutional confrontation, it is difficult to ignore the importance of Hitler. He created the party and headed a regime built on the principle of authoritarian leadership. It is impossible to pinpoint any major domestic development which was contrary to Hitler's wishes; it was mainly his personality and ideology which led to a dramatic radicalisation of policy in key spheres, such as:

- politically, by the creation of a one-party state brutally upheld by the SS-Police system
- socially, by an increasingly radical racial policy to reshape society
- in foreign policy, by the drive towards a German world **hegemony**.

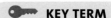 **KEY TERM**

Hegemony Political leadership and dominance.

It is hard to envisage all these developments without Hitler at the helm. It is also surely telling that the SS-Police system eventually emerged as the dominant power bloc – and its guiding principle from the start had been unquestioning obedience to the will of the *Führer*.

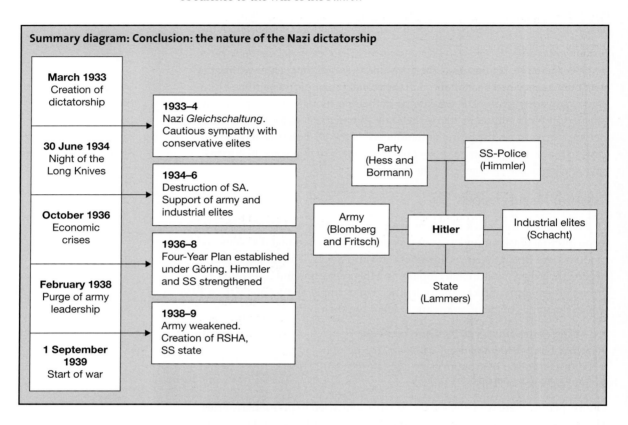

Summary diagram: Conclusion: the nature of the Nazi dictatorship

March 1933
Creation of dictatorship

30 June 1934
Night of the Long Knives

October 1936
Economic crises

February 1938
Purge of army leadership

1 September 1939
Start of war

1933–4
Nazi *Gleichschaltung*. Cautious sympathy with conservative elites

1934–6
Destruction of SA. Support of army and industrial elites

1936–8
Four-Year Plan established under Göring. Himmler and SS strengthened

1938–9
Army weakened. Creation of RSHA, SS state

Party (Hess and Bormann) — SS-Police (Himmler)

Army (Blomberg and Fritsch) — **Hitler** — Industrial elites (Schacht)

State (Lammers)

10 Key debate

▶ *Was Nazi Germany an all-powerful dictatorship?*

The debate about the political structure of the Third Reich stands at the heart of nearly all aspects of understanding Nazi Germany. It has raised important issues about the role and power of Hitler and all the other institutions – and by extension the efficiency of the regime. Historians have advanced different interpretations of the nature of the Nazi dictatorship.

Nazism: a model of totalitarianism

The concept of totalitarianism was explored by George Orwell in the late 1940s, in the aftermath of Nazism and the shadow of the new Cold War with Stalin's

USSR. In his futuristic novel *Nineteen Eighty-Four* he portrayed a political system and a society which became a 'model' of totalitarianism. There was no place for the individual. Every aspect of life was controlled by the party, which in turn was dominated by the all-pervasive personality of 'Big Brother'.

In the 1950s historians began to interpret the Nazi regime as an example of the totalitarian model. According to such interpretations, there were no fundamental differences between the regimes of Fascist Italy, Nazi Germany and Soviet Russia. Indeed, Carl Friedrich's analysis went so far as to identify six major features common to totalitarian dictatorships:

- an official ideology
- a single mass party
- terroristic control by the police
- monopolistic control over the media
- a monopoly of arms
- central control of the economy.

The idea of Nazism as a form of totalitarianism held great weight in the 1950s, but this thinking was a product of the Cold War, when liberal Western historians rather too readily assumed close similarities between Hitler's Germany and Stalin's Russia. So although the term is still used to describe Nazi Germany, it is somewhat misleading, as it did not follow the single, all-powerful structure on two main counts. First, although Germany was a one-party state, the Nazi Party did not have the same degree of organisation and unity as the communists in the USSR. Secondly, the Nazis never established a centralised control over the economy, again in direct contrast to the situation in the USSR.

Hitlerism: the strong dictator

Not surprisingly, the so-called 'intentionalist' approach has maintained that Hitler himself played the vital role in the directing of the Third Reich. In a telling phrase, N. Rich wrote (1973): 'The point cannot be stressed too strongly. Hitler was master in the Third Reich.' Many continue to concur.

The concept of the strong dictator has been most overtly outlined by the work of Hildebrand and Jäckel in the 1970s and 1980s. In their view, Hitler took the responsibility for taking the 'big' decisions, which shaped the direction of Nazi Germany in foreign and race policy. Moreover, although there were other power bases within the party, Hitler preserved his own authority by tolerating only key Nazis, who were personally loyal, for example Himmler. Finally, he hired and fired both Nazis and non-Nazis whom he could use. For example, Schacht had considerable freedom of manoeuvre for a time, but was removed when he no longer conformed. In that sense, Nazism was in essence Hitlerism and all the vital developments of the Third Reich grew from Hitler and his 'blueprint for power'.

Interestingly, although the historian K.D. Bracher (1969) remains in the same camp, he differs in focus of emphasis. He recognises that there was division and confusion in Hitler's regime. However, he believes that it was the result of a deliberate policy of 'divide and rule' on the part of Hitler. Moreover, he claimed that this strategy was successful in maintaining the *Führer*'s own political authority.

EXTRACT I

From Sebastian Haffner, *The Meaning of Hitler*, Macmillan, 1979, pp. 43–4.

Hitler deliberately destroyed the state's ability to function in favour of his personal omnipotence and irreplaceability, and he did so from the start ... [He] brought about a state of affairs in which the most various autonomous authorities were ranged alongside and against each other, without defined boundaries, in competition and overlapping – and only he was at the head of them ... absolute rule was not possible in an intact state organism but only amid chaos. That was why, from the outset, he replaced the state by chaos – and one has to hand it to him that, while he was alive, he knew how to control it.

? According to Haffner in Extract 1, how did Hitler set out from the start to establish total authority?

A polycracy: a chaotic power structure

In marked contrast, structuralist historians, such as Broszat and Mommsen, writing in the 1970s, have focused their analysis on the structure of the Third Reich. They believe that the Nazi regime really just evolved from the pressure of the circumstances and not from Hitler's dominant role. In fact, Hitler's personal weaknesses and limitations led to poor leadership. He was considered incapable of making effective decisions and, as a result, the government lacked clear direction. He was not able to keep the tensions in the economy and the state under control. Moreover, he was never able to manage the other powerful institutions, for example, the army and the civil service. Finally, the leading Nazis exerted their own influence for their own objectives and frequently Hitler did not intervene. Indeed, Mommsen even goes as far as to describe Hitler as 'unwilling to take decisions, frequently uncertain, exclusively concerned with upholding his prestige and personal authority, influenced in the strongest fashion by his current entourage, in some respects a weak dictator'.

This is why structuralists have seen the Third Reich in its power system as a 'polycracy', which became an alliance of different overlapping power groups. Although they did not always agree, they were dependent on each other and prepared to work together as partners in power. The most important of these blocs would seem to have been the Nazi Party itself, the SS-Police system and the army, big business and the higher levels of the state bureaucracy.

EXTRACT 2

M. Broszat, *The Hitler State*, Longman, 1981, p. xi.

In various ways my work offers a corrective to the oversimplified picture of a monolithic system and a well-oiled super state ... Hitler practised no direct and systematic leadership, but from time to time jolted the government or the party into action, supported one or another initiative of party functionaries or department heads and thwarted others, ignored them or left them to carry on without a decision ...

The characteristic conflict between rival forces in the Third Reich can by no means be understood merely in terms of a Machiavellian [politically expedient] policy of 'divide and rule' deliberately instituted by Hitler to make himself indispensable. On the contrary, it was a largely unavoidable corollary of the Führer's absolutism, and in practice was not conducive to the long-term survival of the regime.

According to Broszat in Extract 2, how did Hitler's poor leadership skills weaken the regime?

Charismatic domination: working towards the *Führer*

Kershaw (1998) provides a synthesis of structuralist and intentionalist interpretations. In many ways, his methodology may well be defined as structuralist, and yet he underlines that the extent and centrality of Hitler's authority is placed in the wider context, particularly the German elites and the complicity of German society.

Kershaw certainly does not portray Hitler as the weak dictator. This was because Hitler succeeded in generating an environment in which his followers carried out his presumed intentions and willingly took the responsibility 'to work towards the *Führer*' (see page 174).

EXTRACT 3

Ian Kershaw, *Hitler, 1889–36: Hubris*, Allen Lane, 1998, p. 530.

These three tendencies – erosion of collective government, emergence of clearer ideological goals, and Führer *absolutism – were closely interrelated. Hitler's personal actions, particularly in the field of foreign policy, were certainly vital to the development. But the decisive component was that unwittingly singled out in his speeches by Willikens. Hitler's personalised form of rule invited initiatives from below and offered such initiatives backing, so long as they were in line with his broadly defined goals. This promoted ferocious competition at all levels of the regime amongst competing agencies, and most individuals within these agencies.*

According to Extract 3, what effect did Hitler's personalised form of rule have on decision making in the regime?

Chapter summary

Despite his limited political expertise, Hitler effectively extended his dictatorial powers in 1933–4 by 'co-ordinating' many aspects of German life. By the end of 1933 the trade unions, all other political parties and the federal states were brought under Nazi control, although, in the short-term, key forces such as the military, bureaucratic and economic elites initially escaped from the process. Even so, the ongoing clash of the army leadership and the SA could have led to a civil war. In the end, Hitler's order to destroy his own storm troopers secured his own personal leadership and stabilised the dictatorship.

Yet, despite the image of the Nazi regime as an all-powerful dictatorship, the reality was rather more complex. It was not effectively organised; instead, it continued to be a range of overlapping competing powers. The traditional elites were moulded over time to satisfy Nazi political objectives. But in the institutions of the party and the state, an unstable dualism prevailed, so rivalries and divisions persisted – although it is true that eventually the party strengthened its position in relation to the traditional apparatus of the state. The SS-Police system extended its influence and became the key power group in the Third Reich. As for Hitler, his position was unique and through his personal leadership style he was able to direct events by ensuring that others were 'working towards the *Führer*'.

Refresher questions

Use these questions to remind yourself of the key material covered in this chapter.

1 What was *Gleichschaltung* and how successful was the process of co-ordination by the end of 1933?

2 When and why did the political conflict between the SA and the army come to a head?

3 How significant was the Night of the Long Knives?

4 In what ways did the Nazis successfully consolidate their power between 1933 and 1934?

5 What was the role of Hitler in Nazi Germany?

6 Why was the relationship between the party and the state unclear?

7 How did the institutions of the Nazi Party and the state develop in the Third Reich?

8 Who lost out: the party or the state?

9 How did the SS-Police system emerge to become so powerful in the Third Reich?

10 Did the *Gestapo* really control the people?

11 To what extent did the German Army co-operate with the Nazi regime?

12 Why was the Blomberg–Fritsch crisis so significant?

13 How did Schacht's policies stimulate Germany's economic recovery?

14 How did Schacht try to resolve the balance of payments problem?

15 What were the main aims of the Four-Year Plan and why was it so significant politically and economically?

16 Where did the power really lie in the Third Reich by 1939?

Question practice

ESSAY QUESTIONS

1 To what extent did the Nazi regime rely on terror and violence to consolidate its hold on power in the years 1933–4?

2 How successful was Germany's economic recovery in the years 1933–9?

3 To what extent would you agree with the description of the Third Reich as 'a police state'?

4 'The government of the Nazi regime was chaotic and lacked coherence in the years 1933–9.' Assess the validity of this statement.

SOURCE ANALYSIS QUESTION

1 With reference to the Sources 1, 2 and 3 (below and page 208), and your understanding of the historical context, assess the value of these sources to a historian studying the relationship between the party and the state in the years 1933–9.

SOURCE I

From a report by an SPD agent to the headquarters in exile (SOPADE) in June 1935, quoted in J. Noakes and G. Pridham, editors, *Nazism 1919–45*, volume 2, Liverpool University Press, 1988, p. 238.

The NSDAP is no longer a united whole. Nobody really talks of the party any more but rather of the Labour Front, the Air Defence League, the Hitler Youth etc. The party is the basis for job advancement and in many jobs one has only got prospects if one is in the party. Otherwise it plays no role. It is torn apart internally by a plethora of intrigues among the public and is pushed out of the spotlight by other organisations which arouse more interest among the public.

At the Gau rally in Hessen ... the conference itself was composed of sessions for the specialist organisations such as the NS Doctors' League, the NS Teachers' League. There can be no question of the party's having a unified political line. Everywhere the old fighters complain that the new members are given precedence over them.

SOURCE 2

From a speech by Adolf Hitler at the Nuremberg rally, 15 September 1935, quoted in N. Rothnie, *National Socialism in Germany*, Macmillan, 1987, pp. 70–1.

The function of the state is the continuance of the administration. The function of the party is:

1. the building up of its own internal organisations so as to create a stable, self-renewing, permanent cell of National Socialism teaching

2. the education of the entire people in the meaning of this idea

3. the introduction of those who have been so trained into the state to serve either as leaders or as followers.

At present, the old party–state conflicts are still taking place, and thus during this transient period it may happen that the party finds itself compelled to intervene by way of warning … when the leaders of the state are contravening National Socialist principles. But this can only be effected through the agency of the relevant state institutions which are already occupied by National Socialists. The final goal must be to win over all Germans to National Socialism so that in the future only National Socialists shall be admitted to either party or state posts.

SOURCE 3

From a report by a state official of Kreuznach in the Rhineland, December 1935, quoted in J. Noakes and G. Pridham, editors, *Nazism 1919–45*, volume 2, Liverpool University Press, 1988, pp. 256–7.

It is true that I was told by the mayor and police officers that co-operation had improved between the officers of the party and the local administration. But against this is the statement from a reliable source that the party itself does not find co-operation with the administration satisfactory because the state officials are not obedient enough.

After nearly three years' service in the district, I feel obliged to say again clearly that the duplication in the work of the party and of the authorities in administrative matters has become intolerable and jeopardises constructive work … I get the impression that the main cause of all this is the personal ambition of the political leaders. They seek to claim success for administrative work and exploit it with the public and in the press, while their failures are blamed on the authorities which in any case have to bear the responsibility.

The endeavour of the political leaders to fill civil servants' posts solely on the grounds of length of party membership has meant that non-party members, and even those who have joined since 30 January 1933, have been excluded from promotion even if they have far more skill and higher moral qualities.

CHAPTER 7

The racial state: Nazi society 1933–9

This chapter will introduce the concept of the *Volksgemeinschaft* and examine the Nazi use of propaganda and censorship as a means of indoctrinating the German people. It then considers Nazi aims and policies and their impact on different aspects of German society. It finishes by raising the difficult question of assessing the popularity of the regime. The main points are considered through the following sections:

★ The Nazi *Volksgemeinschaft*

★ Propaganda and censorship

★ Social groups

★ Education and youth

★ Religion

★ Women and the family

★ Outsiders

★ Anti-Semitism

★ Opposition and consent: the popularity of the Nazi regime

Key dates

1933	March	Creation of the Ministry of Popular Enlightenment and Propaganda under Goebbels	1934		Creation of the Confessional Church
	April 1	First official boycott of Jewish shops and professions	1935	Sept. 15	Nuremberg Race Laws introduced
	May	The burning of the books	1937		Papal encyclical *Mit Brennender Sorge* issued
		Creation of DAF (German Labour Front)			
	July	Concordat signed with the papacy	1938	Nov. 9–10	*Kristallnacht*: anti-Jewish pogrom
1934	May	Reich Ministry of Education created; control of education taken away from *Länder*	1939		Creation of the Reich Central Office for Jewish Emigration

1 The Nazi *Volksgemeinschaft*

▶ *What purpose did the Nazis have in promoting the idea of the Volksgemeinschaft?*

When Nazi ideology developed in the 1920s it was based on three key elements: racism, nationalism and authoritarianism (see pages 104–8). However, Hitler always claimed that National Socialism was more than just a political ideology; it aimed to transform German society. It rejected the values of communism, liberal democracy and Christianity and in their place upheld the concept of *Volksgemeinschaft*.

Volksgemeinschaft was probably the vaguest element of Nazi ideology, so it is difficult to define precisely. Historians are divided between those who see it as a 'pseudo-ideology' built on image alone, and those who see it as a more concrete movement with genuine support. The essential purpose of the *Volksgemeinschaft* was to overcome the old German divisions of class, religion and politics and to bring about a new collective national identity by encouraging people to work together.

This new social mentality aimed to bring together the disparate elements and to create a German society built on the Nazi ideas of race and struggle. It aimed to unite traditional German values with the new ideology, although there were some clear ideological, biological and asocial groups who were 'outsiders' and did not conform to the Nazis' dream (see pages 239–40). The ideal German image was that of the classic peasant working on the soil in the rural community; this was exemplified in the Nazi concept of **Blut und Boden** and by upholding the traditional roles of the two sexes.

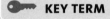

KEY TERM

Blut und Boden 'Blood and soil.' Nationalist and racist romanticism which glorified the rural role of the peasantry.

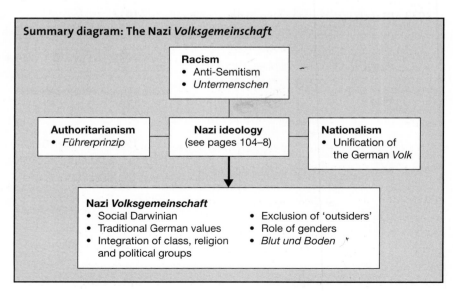

Summary diagram: The Nazi *Volksgemeinschaft*

Racism
- Anti-Semitism
- *Untermenschen*

Authoritarianism
- *Führerprinzip*

Nazi ideology
(see pages 104–8)

Nationalism
- Unification of the German *Volk*

Nazi *Volksgemeinschaft*
- Social Darwinian
- Traditional German values
- Integration of class, religion and political groups
- Exclusion of 'outsiders'
- Role of genders
- *Blut und Boden*

Propaganda and censorship

▶ *In what ways did Nazi propaganda use the media and German culture?*

▶ *How effective was Nazi propaganda and censorship?*

Goebbels gave a speech at his very first press conference on the creation of the Ministry of Popular Enlightenment and Propaganda (see Source A).

SOURCE A

Speech by Goebbels on 15 March 1933, quoted in J. Noakes and G. Pridham, editors, *Nazism 1919–45*, volume 2, Liverpool University Press, 1988, p. 381.

The most important tasks of this Ministry must be the following: first, all propaganda ventures and all institutions of public information belonging to the Reich and the states must be centralized in one hand. Furthermore, it must be our task to instil into these propaganda facilities a modern feeling and bring them up to date. We must not allow technology to run ahead of the Reich but rather the Reich must keep pace with technology. Only the latest thing is good enough. We are living in an age when policies must have mass support … the leaders of today must be modern princes of the people, they must be able to understand the people but need not follow them slavishly. It is their duty to tell the masses what they want and put it across to the masses in such a way that they understand it too.

According to Goebbels in Source A, how did he intend to use and shape propaganda?

Considerable resources were directed towards the development of the propaganda machine in order to achieve the following aims:

- to glorify the regime
- to spread the Nazi ideology and values (and by implication to censor the unacceptable)
- to win over the people and to integrate the nation's diverse elements into the *Volksgemeinschaft*.

All the means of public communication were brought under state control.

Radio

Goebbels (and Hitler) had always recognised the effectiveness of the spoken word over the written and they had already begun to use new technology during the election campaigns of 1932–3. Up until this time, German broadcasting had been organised by regional states. Once in power, Goebbels efficiently brought all broadcasting under Nazi control by the creation of the Reich Radio Company. Furthermore, he arranged the dismissal of thirteen per cent of the staff on political and racial grounds, and replaced them with his own men. He told his broadcasters: 'I am placing a major responsibility in your hands, for you have in your hands the most modern instrument in existence for influencing the masses. By this instrument you are the creators of public opinion.'

Yet, control of broadcasting was of little propaganda value unless the people had the means to receive it. In 1932 fewer than 25 per cent of German households owned a wireless (radio), although that was quite a high figure compared to the rest of the world. Consequently, the Nazi government arranged the production of a cheap set, the People's Receiver (*Volksempfänger*). Radio was a new and dynamic medium and access increased markedly. By 1939, 70 per cent of German homes had a radio – the highest national figure in the world – and it became a medium of mass communication controlled completely by the regime.

Broadcasting was also directed at public places. The installation of loudspeakers in restaurants and cafés, factories and offices made them all into venues for collective listening. 'Radio wardens' were even appointed, whose duty it was to co-ordinate the listening process.

Press

Control of the press was not so easily achieved by Goebbels. Germany had over 4700 daily newspapers in 1933; a result of the strong regional identities which still existed in a state that had only been unified in 1871. All were papers owned privately, and traditionally owed no loyalty to central government; their loyalty was to their regional publishing company.

Various measures were taken to achieve Nazi control:

- The Nazi publishing house, Eher Verlag, bought up numerous newspapers, so that by 1939 it controlled two-thirds of the German press.
- The various news agencies were merged into one, the state-controlled Deutsches Nachrichtenbüro, which vetted news material before it got to journalists.
- Goebbels introduced a daily press conference at the Propaganda Ministry to provide guidance on editorial policy.
- The so-called Editors' Law of October 1933 made newspaper content the sole responsibility of the editor, who had to satisfy the requirements of the Propaganda Ministry or face the appropriate consequences. As a cynic implied, 'There was no need for censorship because the editor's most important function was that of censor.'

To a large extent, the Nazis succeeded in muzzling the press so that even the internationally renowned *Frankfurter Zeitung* was forced to close in 1943, whereas the circulation of the party's official newspaper, *Völkisher Beobachter*, continued to grow after 1933, reaching 1.7 million by 1944. However, the price of that success was the evolution of bland and sterile journalism, which undoubtedly contributed to a ten per cent decline in newspaper circulation before 1939.

The Berlin Olympics

The 1936 Olympic Games were awarded to Berlin in 1931, well before Hitler and the Nazis had come to power. Yet, despite Hitler's initial doubts, Goebbels was determined to exploit them as a propaganda 'goldmine'. Initially, he saw the games as a means to present Nazi propaganda aims, but with several important caveats:

- They were to glorify the regime not only for the German people, but also for millions of people across the world, who would see Germany as the centre of attention.
- They were trying to spread Nazi ideological themes, without causing international upset. So, for example, many anti-Jewish posters were removed and newspapers were made to play down their virulent messages.

Everything was done to present a positive image of the 'new Germany'. Over 42 million *Reichsmarks* were spent on the 130-hectare (325-acre) Olympics sports complex and the gigantic Olympic stadium was built of natural stone in the classical style, the original modernist plan having been rejected. It could seat 110,000 spectators and at the time it was the world's largest stadium. The new Berlin Olympic Village was also a prototype for future games with excellent facilities.

Not surprisingly, the Nazi government was meticulous in overseeing all the media preparations:

- *Radio.* Twenty transmitting vans were put at the disposal of the foreign media along with 300 microphones. Radio broadcasts at the Olympics were given in 28 different languages.
- *Film.* The Nazis promoted and financed filming by the director Leni Riefenstahl. She brought 33 camera operators to the Olympics and shot over a million feet of film. It took her 18 months to edit the material into a four-hour film, *Olympia*, which was released in two parts beginning in April 1938.
- *Television.* Television was in its early stages, but the games prompted a significant technical development. Broadcasts of the games were made and seen by 150,000 people in 28 public television rooms in Berlin, although the image quality was variable.

The Nazi ideal of the tall, athletic, blue-eyed Aryan race was further emphasised through the image of the athlete Siegfried Eifrig lighting the torch at the start of the games in the Olympic stadium.

On the sports front, Germany successfully finished top of the medal table, gaining 89 medals with the Americans coming in second with 56. However, the Nazi dream was marred by the success of the black American athlete Jesse Owens, who won four gold medals in the 100m, 200m, long jump and the four by four 100m relay.

In what ways could the photograph in Source B be seen as effective propaganda for the Nazis?

SOURCE B

Siegfried Eifrig lights the Olympic flame to mark the start of the 1936 Olympic Games.

Overall, the Berlin Olympics were a major success for the Nazis, who gained praise for their excellent management and impressive spectacle, as was recognised by the US correspondent William Shirer: "I'm afraid the Nazis have succeeded with their propaganda. First, the Nazis have run the games on a lavish scale never before experienced, and this has appealed to the athletes. Second, the Nazis have put up a very good front for the general visitors, especially the big businessmen.'

Nazi ritual

One final aspect of the Goebbels propaganda machine was the deliberate attempt to create a new kind of social ritual. The *Heil Hitler* greeting, the Nazi salute, the **Horst Wessel** anthem and the preponderance of militaristic uniforms were all intended to strengthen the individual's identity with the regime. This was further encouraged by the establishment of a series of public festivals to commemorate historic days in the Nazi calendar (see Table 7.1).

Culture

Nazi culture was no longer to be promoted merely as 'art for art's sake'. Rather, it was to serve the purpose of moulding public opinion, and, with this in mind, the Reich Chamber of Culture was supervised by the Propaganda Ministry. Germany's cultural life during the Third Reich was simply to be another means

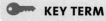 **KEY TERM**

Horst Wessel A young Nazi brownshirt killed in a fight with communists in 1930. The song he wrote became a Nazi marching song and later virtually became an alternative national anthem.

Table 7.1 Significant days in the Nazi calendar

Date	Event
30 January	The seizure of power (1933)
24 February	Party Foundation Day (1925)
16 March	Heroes' Remembrance Day (war dead)
20 April	Hitler's birthday
1 May	National Day of Labour
Second Sunday in May	Mothering Sunday
21 June	Summer solstice
Second Sunday of July	German culture
September	Nuremberg party rally
October	Harvest festival
9 November	The Munich *putsch* (1923)
Winter solstice	Pagan festival to counter Christmas

of achieving censorship and indoctrination, although Goebbels expressed it in more pompous language: 'What we are aiming for is more than a revolt. Our historic mission is to transform the very spirit itself to the extent that people and things are brought into a new relationship with one another.'

Culture was therefore 'co-ordinated' by means of the Reich Chamber of Culture, established in 1933, which made provision for seven sub-chambers: fine arts, music, the theatre, the press, radio, literature and films. In this way, just as anyone in the media had no option but to toe the party line, so all those involved in cultural activities had to be accountable for their creativity. Nazi culture was dominated by a number of key themes reflecting the usual ideological prejudices:

- anti-Semitism
- militarism and the glorification of war
- nationalism and the supremacy of the Aryan race
- the cult of the *Führer* and the power of absolutism
- **anti-modernism** and the theme of 'Blood and Soil'
- neo-paganism and a rejection of traditional Christian values.

Music

The world of music managed to cope reasonably well in the Nazi environment, partly because of its less obvious political overtones. Also, Germany's rich classical tradition from the works of Bach to Beethoven was proudly exploited by the regime. However, Mahler and Mendelssohn, both great Jewish composers, were banned, as were most modern musical trends. The new wave of modern classical composers, Schoenberg and Hindemith, were disparaged for their atonal music. Also, the new 'genres' of jazz and dance-band were respectively labelled 'negroid' and 'decadent'.

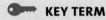

KEY TERM

Anti-modernism Strand of opinion which rejects, objects to or is highly critical of changes to society and culture brought about by technological advancement.

Literature

Over 2500 of Germany's writers left their homeland during the years 1933–45. This fact alone is a reflection of how sadly German writers and dramatists viewed the new cultural atmosphere. Among those who left were:

- Thomas Mann, the author and Nobel Prize winner, who was a democrat and an old-fashioned liberal
- Bertolt Brecht, the prestigious modern playwright, who was a communist
- Erich Maria Remarque, the author of *All Quiet on the Western Front*, who was a pacifist.

Their place was taken by a lesser literary group, who either sympathised with the regime or accepted the limitations. It is difficult to identify a single book, play or poem written during the Third Reich, and officially blessed by the regime, which has stood the test of time.

Actors, like the musicians, tended to content themselves with productions of the classics – Schiller, Goethe (and Shakespeare) – in the knowledge that such plays were politically acceptable and in the best traditions of German theatre.

Visual arts

The visual arts were also effectively limited by the Nazi constraints. Modern schools of art were held in total contempt and Weimar's rich cultural awakening was rejected as degenerate and symbolic of the moral and political decline of Germany under a system of parliamentary democracy. Thus, the following were severely censored:

- 'new functionalist' artists, like Georg Grosz and Ernst Kirchner, as their paintings had strong political and social messages (see pages 89–90)
- the Bauhaus style started by Walter Gropius with its emphasis on the close relationship between art and technology (see pages 89–90).

The modern styles of art were resented by Nazism so much that in July 1937 two contrasting art exhibitions were launched entitled 'Degenerate Art' and 'Great German Art'. The first one was deliberately held up to be mocked and many of the pieces were destroyed; the second one glorified all the major Nazi themes of *Volksgemeinschaft* and celebrated classic styles and traditional nineteenth-century **German romanticism**. Most admired were:

- the sculptor Arno Breker
- the architect Albert Speer, who drew up many of the great plans for rebuilding the German cities and oversaw the 1936 Berlin Olympics stadium
- the artists Adolf Ziegler and Hermann Hoyer.

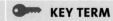

KEY TERM

German romanticism
German classicism in art, literature and music.

Cinema

Only in the field of film can it be said that the Nazi regime made a genuine cultural contribution. Germany's cinematic reputation had been established in the 1920s and a degree of continuity was maintained, as many of the major film studios were in the hands of nationalist sympathisers. However, Jewish film actors and directors such as Fritz Lang were removed and then decided to leave Germany. Perhaps the most famous German *émigrée* was the actress Marlene Dietrich, who swiftly established a new career in Hollywood.

Goebbels recognised the importance of expanding the film industry, not only as a means of propaganda, but also as an entertainment form; this explains why, out of 1097 feature films produced between 1933 and 1945, only 96 were specifically at the request of the Propaganda Ministry. The films can be divided into three types:

- Overt propaganda, for example *The Eternal Jew* (*Der Ewige Jude*), a tasteless, racist film that portrayed Jews as rats, and *Hitlerjunge Queux*, based on the story of a Nazi murdered by communists.
- Pure escapism, for example *The Adventures of Baron von Münchhausen*, a comedy based on an old German legend which gives the baron the powers of immortality.
- Emotive nationalism, for example *Olympia*, Leni Riefenstahl's docu-drama of the Berlin Olympics, *Triumph of the Will*, her film about the 1934 Nuremberg rally, and *Kolberg*, an epic produced in the final year of the Second World War, which played on the national opposition to Napoleon. These last two films are still held in high regard by film buffs for their use of subtle cinematic techniques despite the clear underlying political messages.

Conclusion

Control of the press and radio was Goebbels' prime objective, and he gradually also took control of film, music, literature and art. However, despite this, it is difficult for historians to assess the real effectiveness of Nazi propaganda. This clearly has implications for evaluating true public opinion at the time, which is considered on pages 248–54.

Historians initially assumed rather too readily that Nazi propaganda was successful because it was possible to highlight the way Goebbels exploited all the means for propaganda: photographs, party rallies, sport, festivals. This view was underlined by R. Herzstein's book in the 1960s, *The War that Hitler Won*. However, more recent research from local studies of oral history has raised serious doubts about its effectiveness and tended to show that the degree of success of propaganda varied according to different purposes. Very generally, it is felt that propaganda succeeded in the sense that it:

- cultivated the 'Hitler myth' of him as an all-powerful leader
- strengthened the Nazi regime after Germany's political crisis, 1929–33
- appealed effectively to reinforce established family values and German nationalism.

Josef Goebbels

1897	Born in the Rhineland and slightly disabled
1926	Sided with Hitler against Strasser in the party conflict
	Appointed by Hitler as *Gauleiter* of Berlin
1930	Put in charge of Nazi propaganda
1933–45	Minister of public enlightenment and propaganda
1938	An affair with the actress Lída Baarová undermined his position
	Issued the orders for the anti-Semitic attacks of *Kristallnacht*
1943	Called for 'total war' to rouse the nation after the defeat at Stalingrad
1945	Died in a suicide pact with his wife after poisoning their children

Goebbels was a man from a humble background with many talents who became one of the few intellectuals in the Nazi leadership. He gained a doctorate from Heidelberg University in German and linguistics. However, he suffered from a strong inferiority complex over his physical limitations and he became an embittered and committed anti-Semite.

As propaganda chief of the party, Goebbels played a crucial role in exploiting every possible method to sell the Nazi image in the 1930–3 elections. He developed public relations techniques that were ahead of their time. Unscrupulous and amoral in his methods, he was mainly responsible for advancing the idea of Nazi totalitarianism, censoring all non-Nazi culture and media, and promoting all the main ideological ideas of Nazism. Goebbels was also a skilled, hypnotic orator, second only to Hitler.

Goebbels remained a central figure until the collapse of the regime, although other leading Nazis, such as Göring and Ribbentrop, distrusted him. His rivals exploited his many love affairs to undermine his position and he became politically isolated in the years 1938–42. But with his personal leadership and his organisational skills he played an important part in the final two years of the Second World War in making the nation ready for 'total war' by:

- organising help for people in the bombed cities
- giving the orders to put down the July Bomb Plot (see page 287)
- maintaining civilian morale, for example by visiting bombed cities (unlike Hitler)
- taking the responsibility to mobilise the last efforts to resist the Allied advance.

On the other hand, propaganda failed more markedly in its attempt:

- to denounce the Christian Churches
- to seduce the working classes away from their established identity through the ideal of *Volksgemeinschaft*
- to develop a distinctive Nazi culture.

Such points give backing to the view that the propaganda machine was of secondary importance compared to the power and influence of the SS-Police system in upholding the Third Reich.

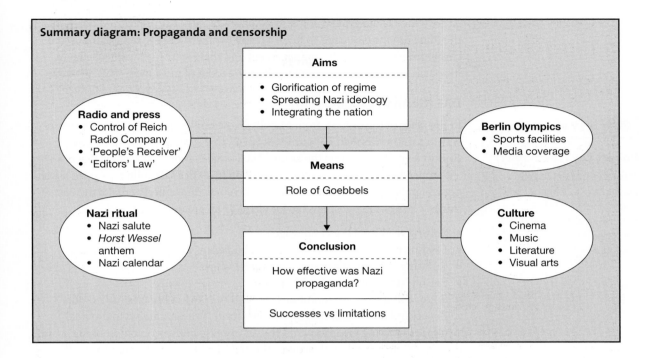

Summary diagram: Propaganda and censorship

Aims
- Glorification of regime
- Spreading Nazi ideology
- Integrating the nation

Radio and press
- Control of Reich Radio Company
- 'People's Receiver'
- 'Editors' Law'

Berlin Olympics
- Sports facilities
- Media coverage

Means

Role of Goebbels

Nazi ritual
- Nazi salute
- *Horst Wessel* anthem
- Nazi calendar

Culture
- Cinema
- Music
- Literature
- Visual arts

Conclusion

How effective was Nazi propaganda?

Successes vs limitations

③ Social groups

▶ *Which classes lost out and which gained?*

Before the onset of war in 1939 it seemed to many Germans as if the revival of the economy had pulled their country out of the quagmire. However, in material terms the effects varied considerably from one class to another.

Industrial workers

The working class was by far the largest social group in German society (see Table 7.2). The Nazi regime could not assume that the workers would be won over to the promised ideas of the *Volksgemeinschaft*. Under Weimar, many workers had belonged to independent trade unions and had generally voted for the SPD and KPD.

Table 7.2 German society

	Working class	Middle classes			Peasants	Others
		White-collar workers	Self-employed	Government officials/ employees		
German society as a whole in 1933 (%)	46.3	12.4	9.6	4.8	20.7	6.2

At first, the Nazi regime wanted to establish its authority and closed down all the trade unions (see page 163). As a result, workers lost the right of industrial bargaining. Consequently, management and the government controlled pay increases and were able to limit workers' freedom of movement.

DAF (German Labour Front)

In the place of the unions, from May 1933, the only available option to workers was to join the German Labour Front (DAF, *Deutsche Arbeitsfront*). Led by **Robert Ley**, DAF became the largest Nazi organisation in the Third Reich with a membership that increased from 5 million in 1933 to 22 million in 1939. It was not compulsory to join, but advisable to do so if you wanted to make the best of things. DAF became responsible for virtually all areas of work, such as:

- Setting working hours and wages.
- Dealing harshly with any sign of disobedience, strikes or absenteeism.
- Running training schemes for apprenticeships.
- Setting stable rents for housing.
- Supervising working conditions through the DAF subsection called the Beauty of Labour (SdA, *Schönheit der Arbeit*). The SdA aimed to provide cleaner working environments, meals, exercise and even non-smoking rooms.
- Organising recreational facilities through the Strength through Joy (KdF, *Kraft durch Freude*). It provided very real opportunities to millions of workers: cultural visits, education, sports facilities and holiday travel. By 1939 it had over 7000 paid employees and 135,000 voluntary workers, organised in every factory and workshop employing more than twenty people. Official statistics showed that the number of people in KdF holidays had grown from 2.3 million in 1934 to 10.3 million in 1938.

Wages and conditions

Assessing the material effects of the Nazi regime on the workers is a highly complicated issue, mainly because there are so many variables, such as age, occupation and geographical location. The obvious and most significant benefit for industrial workers was the creation of employment. For the many millions who had suffered from the distress of mass unemployment, the creation of jobs was accepted gratefully. Indeed, by the late 1930s Germany had achieved full employment and there was a growing shortage of workers.

Yet, to put that major benefit into context, it is important to bear in mind a number of key factors:

- Average workers' real wages only rose above 1929 levels in 1938. Also, workers were forced to pay extensive contributions for DAF and insurance/tax.
- The generalised picture disguises the fact that the biggest gains were clearly made by the workers associated with the boom in the rearmament industries, whereas those in consumer goods struggled to maintain their real incomes.

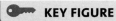
KEY FIGURE

Robert Ley (1890–1945)

Trained as a chemist and worked for IG Farben. Made leader of DAF 1933–45, but became an alcoholic and lost the support of other leading Nazis during the war.

- Working hours increased over time. The average working week was officially increased from 43 hours in 1933 to 47 hours in 1939. As military demands grew, there was pressure on many workers to do more overtime.
- The fall in unemployment figures from the statistics owed much to the removal of women and Jewish workers (albeit only one per cent of the overall population) and the introduction of male conscription to the army and RAD, Reich Labour Service (see page 189).

Although there is considerable evidence suggesting that workers' discontent was increasing, there was little willingness for industrial action (see Source C).

SOURCE C

From an SPD report in Bavaria in September 1938, quoted in J. Noakes and G. Pridham, editors, *Nazism 1919-45*, volume 2, Liverpool University Press, 1988, p. 372.

The incredible increase in the work rate has not generally strengthened the will to resist amongst the workers. The development of solidarity in the plants [factories] is very weak. The low purchase of real wages, their continual reduction through all manner of contributions etc., which do not appear in any statistics, are for the present not favourable to strengthen our resistance …

Relations between the workers suffer from the increasingly tight controls and supervision within the plants. The system of informers is continually being expanded within the plants. The result is that workers only establish personal relations with those whom they know well.

> According to Source C, what were the pressures faced by the workers in the factories? Why was worker resistance still so weak?

Peasants and small farmers

The farming community had been attracted to the Nazis by the promise of financial aid, as it had suffered from a series of economic problems from the mid-1920s. Moreover, peasants felt increasingly that they were losing out to the growing urban society of industrial Germany (see page 73).

The Nazi ideology of 'Blood and Soil' portrayed the peasantry as racially the purest element of the *Volk*; the providers of Germany's food and symbols of traditional German values. In promoting **Richard Darré**, Hitler and Himmler found a leader, who advanced two key aims:

- to restore the role and values of the countryside and to reverse the drive towards urbanisation by promoting the concept of 'Blood and Soil'
- to support the expansionist policy of *Lebensraum* (see page 106) and to create a German racial aristocracy based on selective breeding.

The Nazi regime certainly took initiatives on agriculture:

- Many farm debts and mortgages were written off and small farmers were given low interest rates and a range of tax allowances.
- The government maintained extensive tariffs to reduce imports.

> **KEY FIGURE**
>
> **Richard Darré (1895–1953)**
>
> Influential adviser on racial and agricultural ideas. In 1933 he became Reich peasant leader, minister of agriculture and food, and leader of the Central Office for Race and Settlement (RuSHA). But his vision of a rural utopia conflicted with the economic demands of war production and in 1942 he was forced to resign all offices.

- The Reich Entailed Farm Law of 1933 gave security of tenure to the occupiers of medium-sized farms between 7.5 and 125 hectares, and forbade the division of farms, in order to promote efficient agriculture.
- The Reich Food Estate, established in 1933, supervised every aspect of agricultural production and distribution, especially food prices and working wages (although its bureaucratic meddling became the focus of resentment, when, for example, it stipulated that each hen had to lay 65 eggs per year).

Impact

The economic realities meant that in practice the impact of Nazi agricultural policy was rather mixed. At first, all farmers benefited from an increase in prices between 1933 and 1936 and so farmers' incomes did improve markedly, although they only recovered to 1928 levels in 1938. However, it seems that by 1936–7 any benefits were giving way to growing peasant disillusionment. This was for several reasons:

- Agricultural production increased by twenty per cent from 1928 to 1938, but a significant drift of people to the towns continued – three per cent of the population. Wages were higher there, and agriculture just did not have the economic power to compete with other sectors of the economy.
- The positive aspects of the Reich Food Estate were accepted, but the regulations became increasingly resented by the peasantry.
- The Reich Entailed Farm Law also caused resentment and family discontent. In trying to solve the problem of excessive subdivision by passing on farms to just one child, farmers faced the very real dilemma of not being able to provide a future for their remaining children.

With the onset of the war in 1939 pressures on the peasantry developed in many ways. Men were increasingly conscripted to the military fronts, so increasing the shortage of agricultural labour.

Landowners

The landed classes had been initially suspicious of radical social change. They resented the political interference of the party, but above all they feared that the Nazis would redistribute the large landed estates. However, they soon learned to live quite comfortably with the Nazi regime and in the years before 1939 their economic interests were not really threatened. Indeed, German victories in the early years of the war offered the chance of acquiring more cheap land. The real blow for the landowners actually came in 1945 when the occupation of eastern Germany by the USSR resulted in the nationalisation of land. The traditional social and economic supremacy of the German landowners was broken.

Mittelstand

Another social class that expected to benefit from the Nazi regime was the *Mittelstand* (see page 60). Its problems were in many ways comparable to those of the peasantry. It had suffered from the decline in commerce in Germany since the First World War and it struggled to compete with the increasing power of big business and trade unions.

Research has shown that in the elections 1930–3 the *Mittelstand* had voted for Nazism in greater proportion than the rest of German society and the Nazi regime was keen to take sympathetic measures to maintain that support:

- Money from the confiscation of Jewish businesses was used to offer low interest rate loans.
- The Law to Protect Retail Trade (1933) banned the opening of new department stores and taxed the existing ones, many of which were owned by Jews.
- Many new trading regulations were imposed to protect small craftsmen.

However, despite the Nazis' attempt to implement electoral promises made before 1933 and the economic recovery, the *Mittelstand* continued the decline that had started with Germany's industrialisation. The costs of small businesses meant that they could not compete with the lower costs of the large department stores. The problem was made worse because the Nazis needed big business to bring about rearmament.

The average age of the *Mittelstand* was rising. In 1933, 20 per cent of the owners of small businesses were under 30 years old and fourteen per cent over 60. By 1939 the corresponding figures were ten per cent under 30 and nineteen per cent over 60. In addition, from 1936–9 it is reckoned that the number of traditional skilled craftsmen declined by ten per cent; the *Mittelstand* was just being squeezed out.

Business

With the commercial recovery came general benefits for business (this is also considered on pages 197–8). From 1933 the position of the business community was helped by the upturn in world trade, Schacht's economic stimulus and then by the Nazi destruction of the free trade unions. As a result, despite an increasing range of government controls, the financial gains were impressive. The value of German industry steadily increased, as shown by the following:

- The share price index (the list of the prices of shares) increased from 41 points in 1932 to 106 in 1940.
- Annual dividends (profits returned to investors) grew from an average 2.83 per cent to 6.6 per cent over the same period.
- Average management salaries increased from RM3700 in 1934 to RM5420 in 1938.
- The annexations of lands from 1938 provided enormous opportunities for taking over foreign property, land and companies.

However, it would be wrong to see business as a uniform interest group; different sectors were affected in different ways. Small business was squeezed out more by the power of big business; and consumer goods' production remained relatively depressed.

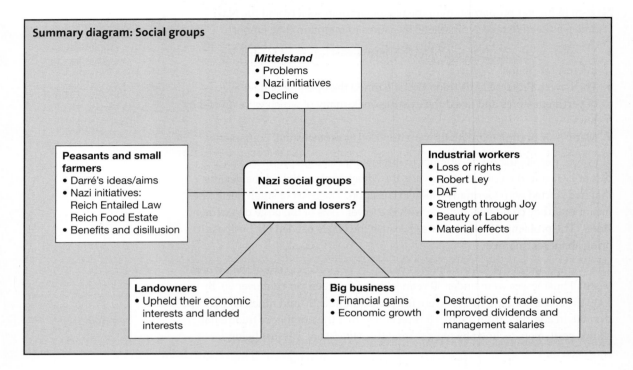

Summary diagram: Social groups

Mittelstand
- Problems
- Nazi initiatives
- Decline

Peasants and small farmers
- Darré's ideas/aims
- Nazi initiatives:
  Reich Entailed Law
  Reich Food Estate
- Benefits and disillusion

Nazi social groups
- - - - - - - - - - -
Winners and losers?

Industrial workers
- Loss of rights
- Robert Ley
- DAF
- Strength through Joy
- Beauty of Labour
- Material effects

Landowners
- Upheld their economic interests and landed interests

Big business
- Financial gains
- Economic growth
- Destruction of trade unions
- Improved dividends and management salaries

4 Education and youth

▶ *In what ways did the Nazis try to indoctrinate young people?*
▶ *How successful were the aims of Nazi education?*

In Nazi Germany, education became merely a tool for the consolidation of the Nazi system. Hitler expressed his views chillingly in 1933:

> *When an opponent declares, 'I will not come over to your side', I calmly say, 'Your child belongs to us already … What are you? You will pass on. Your descendants, however, now stand in the new camp. In a short time they will know nothing else but this new community.'*

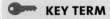 **KEY TERM**

Indoctrination Inculcating and imposing a set of ideas.

Education in the Third Reich was therefore intended to **indoctrinate** its youth so completely in the principles and ethos of National Socialism that the long-term survival of the 'New Order' would never be brought into question. A National Socialist Teachers' League official wrote pompously in 1937:

German youth must no longer – as in the Liberal era in the cause of so-called objectivity – be confronted with the choice of whether it wishes to grow up in a spirit of materialism or idealism, of racism or internationalism, of religion or godlessness, but it must be consciously shaped according to the principles which are recognised as correct and which have shown themselves to be correct: according to the principles of the ideology of National Socialism.

This was to be achieved not only through the traditional structure of the educational system, but also by the development of various Nazi youth movements.

Schools

The actual organisation of the state educational system was not fundamentally altered, although by a law of 1934 control was taken from the regional states and centralised under the Reich Ministry of Education, Culture and Science, led by Reich Minister Bernhard Rust. The ministry was then able to adapt the existing system to suit Nazi purposes.

First, the teaching profession was 'reconditioned'. Politically unreliable individuals were removed and Jewish teachers were banned, and many women were encouraged to conform to Nazi values by returning to the home (see pages 233–7). Special training courses were arranged for those teachers who remained unconvinced by the new requirements. The National Socialist Teachers' League (NSLB, *Nationalsozialistische Lehrerbund*) was established and its influence and interference continued to grow. By 1937 it included 97 per cent of all teachers and two-thirds of the profession had been on special month-long courses on Nazi ideology and the changes to the curriculum.

Secondly, the curricula and syllabuses were adapted. To fit the Nazi Aryan ideal, much greater emphasis was placed on physical education. Fifteen per cent of school time was given over to it, and games teachers assumed an increased status and importance in the school hierarchy. On the academic front, Religious Studies was dropped to downgrade the importance of Christianity, whereas German, Biology and History became the focus of special attention:

- German language and literature were studied to create 'a consciousness of being German', and to inculcate a martial and nationalistic spirit. Among the list of suggested reading for fourteen-year-old pupils was *The Battle of Tannenberg*, which included the following extract: 'A Russian soldier tried to bar the infiltrator's way, but Otto's bayonet slid gratingly between the Russian's ribs, so that he collapsed groaning. There it lay before him, simple and distinguished, his dream's desire, the Iron Cross.'
- Biology became the means by which to deliver Nazi racial theory: ethnic classification, **population policy** and racial genetics were all integrated into the syllabus.

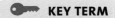 **KEY TERM**

Population policy In 1933–45 the Nazi government aimed to increase the birth rate.

- History, not surprisingly, was also given a special place in the Nazi curriculum, so that the glories of German nationalism could be emphasised.

One final innovation was the creation of various types of elite schools. They were intended to prepare the best of Germany's youth for future political leadership, were modelled on the principles of the Hitler Youth, and focused on physical training, paramilitary activities and political education. The 21 *Napolas* (National Political Educational Institutions) and the ten Adolf Hitler Schools were both for boys of secondary school age, and the three *Ordensburgen* for boys of college age.

Hitler Youth

The responsibility for developing a new outlook lay with the youth movements. There was already a long and well-established tradition of youth organisation in Germany before 1933, but at that time the Hitler Youth (HJ, *Hitler Jugend*) represented only one per cent of the total.

SOURCE D

? In what ways could the poster in Source D be seen as effective propaganda for the Nazis?

'Youth serve the *Führer*! All ten-year-olds join the Hitler Youth!' A Nazi propaganda poster of 1940.

The term 'Hitler Youth' in fact embraced a range of youth groups under the control of its leader **Baldur von Schirach**, and in the next six years the structure and membership of the HJ grew remarkably (see Table 7.3), although this was partly because parents were pressured to enrol their children and by 1939 membership became compulsory. By then all other youth organisations had been abolished.

Table 7.3 Hitler Youth movements. The percentages indicate the percentage of the total youth population aged ten to eighteen years who were members

Year	Number	Percentages
1932	200,000	1.5
1934	3,500,000	46.5
1936	5,400,000	62.8
1938	7,100,000	77.2

There was a great stress on political indoctrination, emphasising the life and achievements of the *Führer*, German patriotism, athletics and camping for all children (see Table 7.4). In addition, the sexes were moulded for their future roles in Nazi society. Boys engaged in endless physical and military-type activities, for example target shooting, and girls were prepared for their domestic and maternal tasks, for example cooking.

Table 7.4 Youth groups

Youth group	Organisation
Boys 10–14 years old	German Young People (DJ, *Deutsche Jungvolk*)
Boys 14–18 years old	Hitler Youth (HJ, *Hitler Jugend*)
Girls 10–14 years old	League of Young Girls (JM, *Jungmädel*)
Girls 14–18 years old	League of German Girls (BDM, *Bund Deutscher Mädel*)

Successes and failures

It is difficult to assess the 'success' of any educational system. It depends on the criteria chosen and the 'evidence' is open to conflicting interpretations. Therefore, conclusions must be tentative.

Teaching

The teaching profession certainly felt its status to be under threat, despite its initial sympathy for the regime. Thirty-two per cent were members of the party in 1936: a figure markedly higher than the figure of seventeen per cent of the Reich Civil Service as a whole. The anti-academic ethos and the crude indoctrination alienated many, while the party's backing of the HJ and its activities caused much resentment. Not surprisingly, standards in traditional academic subjects had fallen by the early years of the war. This was particularly the case in the various elite schools, where physical development dominated. By 1938 recruitment of teachers had declined and there were 8000 vacancies, and only 2500 were graduating from teacher training colleges. In higher education, the number of students had halved even before the war.

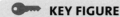

KEY FIGURE

Baldur von Schirach (1907–74)

Youth leader of the German Reich 1933–9 and *Gauleiter* of Vienna 1940–5. His loyalty and charm allowed him to remain influential with Hitler; he even wrote poetry to the *Führer*! But his effeminate nature alienated other leading Nazis.

Youth conformity

The impact of the HJ seems to have been very mixed. In some respects, the emphasis on teamwork and extracurricular activities was welcomed by many youngsters, especially when compared to the limited provision available in many European countries. The provision for sports, camping and music genuinely excited many of the youth, and for those from poorer backgrounds the HJ really offered opportunities. Most significantly, the HJ successfully conveyed to many youngsters an atmosphere of fun and a sense of belonging to the new Germany, as expressed by a young member of the Hitler Youth, Heinrich Metelmann, in Source E.

SOURCE E

From Heinrich Metelmann, 'Life in the Third Reich', in *New Perspective*, volume 2, number 3, March 1998.

The structural system of that youth organisation was based on the military. Our group consisted of about 150–200 boys, subdivided into three troops – just like a company of soldiers. We met together, marched and played together in close comradeship until the age of 18 … Every company had a Heim *[home; often a barn or cellar] which we decorated in a nationalist/militarist style. Swastika flags, and other Nazi emblems had places of honour, as well as decorated pictures of our* Führer *… But when we had our close togetherness there, we felt happy on our own. We were sure and proud that we were the future of Germany, come what may.*

However, the HJ suffered from its rapid overexpansion and the leadership was inadequate. By the late 1930s it became more difficult to run the movement effectively and, as a result, the increasing Nazi emphasis on military drill and discipline was certainly resented by many adolescents who saw it as too regimented. Moreover, recent research suggests that sizeable pockets of the adolescent population had not been won over by 1939 and that alienation and dissent increased quite markedly. The regime even established a special youth section of the secret police and a youth concentration camp was set up at Neuwied.

A number of youth groups developed that deliberately exhibited codes of behaviour at odds with the expected social values of Nazism. 'Swing Youth' was one such craze among mainly middle-class youngsters who took up the music and imagery associated with the dance-bands of Britain and the USA. The ***Edelweiss Piraten*** was a general name given to a host of working-class youths who formed gangs, such as the 'Roving Dudes' and 'Navajos'. Their members had been alienated by the military emphasis and discipline of the Hitler Youth. They met up and organised their own hikes and camps which then came into conflict with the official ones. In several instances during the war, 'Pirates' became involved in more active resistance.

> ? In what ways does Metelmann in Source E help to explain the appeal of the Hitler Youth?

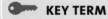

KEY TERM

Edelweiss Piraten Edelweiss Pirates. The name given to a loose collection of youth groups who did not conform. Edelweiss is a white alpine flower which served as a symbol of opposition.

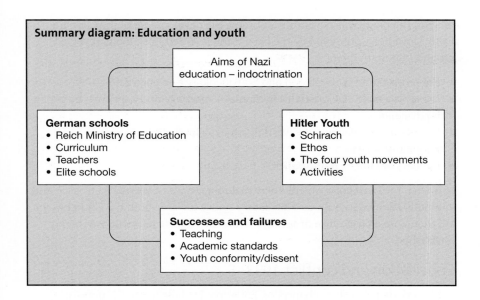

Summary diagram: Education and youth

Aims of Nazi education – indoctrination

German schools
- Reich Ministry of Education
- Curriculum
- Teachers
- Elite schools

Hitler Youth
- Schirach
- Ethos
- The four youth movements
- Activities

Successes and failures
- Teaching
- Academic standards
- Youth conformity/dissent

5 Religion

▶ *Did Nazi religious policy succeed in its aims?*

The rise of Nazism posed fundamental political and ethical problems for the Christian Churches, while Nazism could not ignore these well-established and powerful institutions.

In his rise to power Hitler avoided direct attacks on the Churches, and number 24 of the party's 25-points programme spoke in favour of 'positive Christianity' which was closely linked to racial and national views. However, there can be little doubt that Nazism was a fundamentally anti-Christian philosophy. Where Christianity taught love, forgiveness and neighbourly respect, Nazism glorified strength, violence and war. Moreover, Christianity was regarded as the product of an inferior race – Jesus was a Hebrew – and therefore, it could not be reconciled with Nazi ***völkisch*** thought. Some leading Nazis, such as Himmler and his deputy, Heydrich, openly revealed their contempt for Christianity. Hitler himself was more cautious, although what were probably his true feelings were revealed in a private conversation in 1933:

> *Neither of the denominations – Catholic or Protestant, they are both the same – has any future left … That won't stop me stamping out Christianity in Germany root and branch. One is either a Christian or a German. You can't be both.*

The German Faith Movement

In place of Christianity, the Nazis aimed to cultivate a **teutonic paganism**, which became known as the German Faith Movement. Although a clear Nazi

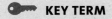

KEY TERM

Teutonic paganism The pre-Christian beliefs of the Germans.

religious ideology was never fully outlined, the development of the German Faith Movement, promoted by the Nazi thinker Alfred Rosenberg, revolved around four main themes:

- the propagation of the 'Blood and Soil' ideology (see page 210)
- the replacement of Christian ceremonies – marriage and baptism – by pagan equivalents
- the wholesale rejection of Christian ethics – closely linked to racial and nationalist views
- the **cult of** Hitler's **personality**.

However, the Nazi government knew that religion was a very delicate issue and it initially adopted a cautious conciliatory stance towards both the Churches to lull them into a false sense of security while the Nazi dictatorship was being established.

Conciliation and conflict 1933–5

In his very first speech as chancellor, Hitler paid tribute to the Churches as being integral to the well-being of the nation. Members of the SA were even encouraged to attend Protestant Church services. This was done to give weight to the idea that the Nazi state could accommodate Protestantism. The 'Day of Potsdam' (see page 152) further gave the impression of a unity between the Protestant Church and the state.

Likewise, the Catholic Church responded sympathetically to the overtures of the Nazis. Catholic bishops, in particular, were frightened of the possibility of a repeat of the so-called *Kulturkampf* in the late nineteenth century. Catholic bishops were concerned to safeguard the position of the Church under the Nazis so in July 1933 a **Concordat** was signed between the papacy and the regime (represented by Vice-Chancellor Papen, who was a Catholic). In the agreement it was decided that:

- the Nazis would guarantee the Catholic Church religious freedom
- the Nazis would not interfere with the Catholic Church's property and legal rights
- the Nazis would accept the Catholic Church's control over its own education
- in return, the Catholic Church would not interfere in politics and would give diplomatic recognition to the Nazi government.

In the short term, the Concordat seemed to be a significant success. However, the courting of both of the Churches by the Nazis was insincere and by the end of 1933 Nazi interference in religious affairs was already causing resentment and disillusionment in both Catholic and Protestant Churches.

The Nazi regime hoped that the Protestant Churches would gradually be 'co-ordinated' through the influence of the group known as the German Christians (*Deutsche Christen*). This group hoped to reconcile their Protestant

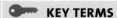

KEY TERMS

Cult of personality Using the power and charisma of a political leader to dominate the nation.

Kulturkampf A struggle for culture or civilisation. Bismarck's anti-Catholic policy of the 1870s aimed at reducing the role and power of the Catholic Church in Germany.

Concordat An agreement between Church and state. A concordat was signed by the papacy and the Nazi government in July 1933.

ideas with Nazi nationalist and racial thinking by finding common ground. So, a new Church constitution was formulated in July 1933 with the Nazi sympathiser Ludwig Müller as the first Reich Bishop – an interesting application of the *Führerprinzip*.

Such Nazi policies alienated many Protestant pastors, and there soon developed an opposition group, the Confessional Church (*Bekennende Kirche*), which upheld orthodox Protestantism and rejected Nazi distortions. Led by **Pastor Niemöller**, by 1934 the Confessional Church gained the support of about 7000 pastors out of 17,000. They claimed to represent the true Protestant Churches of Germany.

Churches and the state

By 1935 it was clear that the Nazi leadership had achieved only limited success in controlling the Churches. It was torn between a policy of total suppression, which would alienate large numbers of Germans, and a policy of limited persecution, which would allow the Churches too much independence. In fact, although the ultimate objective was never in doubt, Nazi tactics degenerated into a kind of war of attrition against the Churches.

In order to destabilise the Churches, the Ministry of Church Affairs, led by **Hanns Kerrl**, was established. He adopted a policy of undermining both the Protestant and Catholic Churches by a series of anti-religious measures, including:

- closure of Church schools
- undermining of Catholic youth groups
- personal campaigns to discredit and harass the clergy, for example monasteries were accused of sexual and financial malpractices
- confiscation of Church funds
- campaign to remove crucifixes from schools
- arrest of more and more pastors and priests.

The Churches were undoubtedly weakened by the approach, but it also stimulated individual declarations of opposition from both Protestants and Catholics:

- Niemöller delivered a sermon in which he said that 'we must obey God rather than man'; he was interned from 1937 and was held until the end of the war.
- **Pope Pius XI** eventually criticised the Nazi system but did not go so far as condemning Nazism in his encyclical, or public letter, of 1937 entitled *With Burning Concern* (*Mit Brennender Sorge*).

Clearly, the conflict between the Churches and the state was set to continue.

The outbreak of war initially brought about a more cautious policy, as the regime wished to avoid unnecessary tensions. However, following the military victories of 1939–40 the persecution intensified, as a result of pressure applied by anti-Christian enthusiasts, such as Bormann and Heydrich and the SS hierarchy.

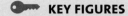

KEY FIGURES

Martin Niemöller (1892–1984)

A nationalist and conservative, a former U-boat commander, who became a Protestant pastor. He soon had doubts about the Nazi regime and was a co-founder of the Confessional Church in 1934. His critical sermons led to his arrest in 1937 and he was held in Sachsenhausen and Dachau concentration camps until the end of the war.

Hanns Kerrl (1887–1941)

Minister of church affairs 1935–41. Increasingly marginalised by the more extreme Nazis. Died of natural causes in 1941 and not replaced.

Pope Pius XI (1857–1939)

Accepted the dissolution of the Catholic ZP and agreed to the Concordat of July 1933. Yet, increasingly disillusioned with the Nazi regime, he issued a critical encyclical in 1937. He was also preparing a further encyclical condemning anti-Semitism just before he died.

Monasteries were closed, Church property was attacked and Church activities were severely restricted. Even so, religion was such a politically sensitive issue that Hitler did not allow subordination of the Churches to give way to wholesale suppression within Germany.

Conclusions

The Nazis achieved only limited success in their religious policy. The German Faith Movement was clearly a failure. Neo-paganism never achieved support on any large scale. The 1939 official census recorded only five per cent of the population as members, although it shows the direction that might have been taken, if the likes of Himmler had won the war.

Many individual Christians made brave stands against the Nazis. This made the dictatorship wary of launching a fundamental assault on religion, so German loyalty to Christianity survived in the long term despite Nazism. In 1974 the historian J.R.C. Wright said: 'The Churches were severely handicapped but not destroyed. Hitler's programme needed time: he was himself destroyed before it had taken root.'

Both the Catholic and Protestant Churches failed to provide effective opposition to Nazism. Neither was 'co-ordinated' so both enjoyed a measure of independence. Both could have provided the focus for active resistance. Instead, they preferred, as institutions, to adopt a pragmatic policy towards Nazism. They stood up for their own religious practices and traditions with shows of dissent, but generally denunciations of the regime were left to individuals.

The reasons for the Churches' reluctance to show opposition to the regime lay in their conservatism:

- They distrusted the politics of the left, which seemed to threaten the existing order of society. The most extreme form of communism rejected the existence of religion itself and the Catholic Church saw Nazism as a bulwark against 'Godless Communism'.
- There was a nationalist sympathy for Nazism, especially after the problems of 1918–33. For many Church leaders it was too easy to believe that Hitler's 'national renewal' was simply a return to the glorious days before 1914. This was particularly true of the Lutheran Protestant Church, which had been the state Church in Prussia under Imperial Germany.
- Both Churches rightly feared the power of the Nazi state. They believed that any gestures of heroic resistance were more than likely to have bloody consequences. In such a situation, their emphasis on pastoral and spiritual comfort was perhaps the most practical and realistic policy for them.

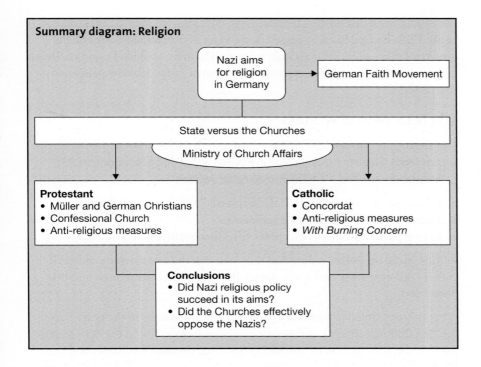

Summary diagram: Religion

Nazi aims for religion in Germany → German Faith Movement

State versus the Churches

Ministry of Church Affairs

Protestant
- Müller and German Christians
- Confessional Church
- Anti-religious measures

Catholic
- Concordat
- Anti-religious measures
- *With Burning Concern*

Conclusions
- Did Nazi religious policy succeed in its aims?
- Did the Churches effectively oppose the Nazis?

6 Women and the family

▶ *What was the ideal role of women in Nazi society?*

▶ *How successful was Nazi policy on women and the family?*

The first quarter of the twentieth century witnessed two important social changes in German family life:

- Germany's population growth had decelerated markedly, which is *not* to say that the actual population had declined. In 1900 there had been over 2 million live births per annum, whereas by 1933 the figure was below a million.
- Over the same period female employment expanded by at least a third, far outstripping the percentage increase in population.

Both of these trends had been partially brought about by long-term changes in social behaviour common to many industrialised countries. It was recognised that the use of contraception to limit family size would improve the standard of living and give better-educated women the opportunity to have a vocation as well as children. However, Germany's recent past history exaggerated these developments. Economic mobilisation during the First World War had driven women into the factories, while the post-war difficulties caused by the inflation had encouraged them to stay on working out of economic necessity. In addition, the war had left a surplus of 1.8 million marriageable women, as well as many wives with invalided husbands. Finally, the changing balance of the economy in the 1920s had led to an increased demand for non-manual labour and the growth of mass-production techniques requiring more unskilled workers. These factors tended to favour the employment of women, who could be paid less than men.

The Nazi view of women

The ideology of National Socialism was in stark contrast to the above social trends. Nazism fundamentally opposed social and economic female emancipation and had the following aims for women:

- To have more children and to take responsibility for bringing them up.
- To care for the house and their husbands.
- To stop paid employment except for specialist vocations, such as midwifery.

In the view of the Nazis, nature had ordained that the two sexes should fulfil entirely different roles, and it was simply the task of the state to maintain this distinction.

What this amounted to was that 'a woman's place was to be in the home' (see the 'Ten Commandments' for choosing a spouse below). Or, as the Nazi slogan presented it, they were to be devoted to the three German Ks: '*Kinder, Küche, Kirche*' ('Children, Kitchen and Church'). Such dogma was upheld by the party, even before 1933 – there was not a single female Nazi deputy in the *Reichstag*, and a party regulation of 1921 excluded women from all senior positions within its structure.

Nazi views on women tied in with their concern about the demographic trends. A growing population was viewed as a sign of national strength and status – a reflection of Germany's aspiration to the status of an international power. How could they demand nationalist expansionism in eastern Europe if the number of Germans was in fact levelling out? It was therefore considered essential to increase the population substantially and, to this end, women were portrayed as primarily the mothers of the next generation – an image that suited Nazi anti-feminism.

Nazi Ten Commandments for the choice of a spouse

1 Remember that you are German!

2 If you are genetically healthy, do not stay single.

3 Keep your body pure.

4 Keep your mind and spirit pure.

5 Marry only for love.

6 As a German, choose only a spouse of similar or related blood.

7 In choosing a spouse, ask about his forebears.

8 Health is essential to physical beauty.

9 Don't look for a playmate but for a companion in marriage.

10 You should want to have as many children as possible.

Female employment

Initially, attempts to reduce the number of women in work seem to have been quite successful. Between 1933 and 1936 married women were in turn debarred from jobs in medicine, law and the higher ranks of the civil service. Moreover, the number of female teachers and university students was reduced considerably – only ten per cent of university students could be female. Such laws had a profound effect on professional middle-class women, although their actual number was small.

Nazi incentives

In other sectors of the economy, a mixture of party pressure and financial inducements was employed to cajole women out of the workplace and back into the home. From June 1933 interest-free loans of RM600 were made available to young women who withdrew from the labour market in order to get married. The effects of the Great Depression also worked in favour of Nazi objectives. They not only drastically reduced the number of female workers (although proportionately far less than male workers), but also enabled the government to justify its campaign for women to give up work for the benefit of unemployed men. On these grounds, **labour exchanges** and employers were advised to discriminate positively in favour of men. As a result of all this, the percentage of women in employment fell from 37 to 31 per cent of the total from 1932 to 1937, although the policy was not entirely effective as the actual *number* of women employed in this period rose because employment overall was growing.

Nazi women's organisations

Women were quite specifically excluded from the Nazi machinery of government. The only employment opportunities available to them were within the various Nazi women's organisations, such as the National Socialist Womanhood (NSF, *National Sozialistische Frauenschaft*) and the German Women's Enterprise (DFW, *Deutsches Frauenwerk*), led by **Gertrud Scholtz-Klink**. Yet, the NSF and DFW were regarded by the party as mere tools for the propagation of the **anti-feminist** ideology by means of cultural, educational and social programmes. And so, when a campaign started in the NSF for enhanced opportunities for women within the party, its organisers were officially discredited.

Effects

By 1937 Nazi ideological convictions were already threatened by the pressures of economic necessity. The introduction of conscription and the rearmament boom from the mid-1930s soon led to an increasing shortage of labour, as the Nazi economy continued to grow. The anti-feminist ideology could only be upheld if economic growth was slowed down and that, in turn, would restrict the rearmament programme. Of course, Hitler was not prepared to sanction this.

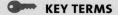

KEY TERMS

Labour exchanges Local offices created by the state for finding employment. Many were created in countries to counter mass unemployment.

Anti-feminist Opposing female advancement.

KEY FIGURE

Gertrud Scholtz-Klink (1902–99)

A nurse in Berlin who joined the NSDAP in 1929. Leader of the DFW 1934–45. Visited Britain in 1939 and portrayed as 'The perfect Nazi woman'. Remained committed to Nazism after the war and felt the benefits outweighed the bad.

Consequently, market forces inevitably began to exploit this readily available pool of labour, and the relative decline in female employment was reversed. Between 1937 and 1939 it rose from 5.7 million to 7.1 million, and the percentage of women increased from 31 to 33 per cent of the total workforce (see Table 7.5). At this point, the government decided to end the marriage loan scheme (see below) for women who withdrew from the labour market.

Table 7.5 Women in regular manual and non-manual employment

	1932	1937	1939
Millions of women	4.8	5.7	7.1
Women as a percentage of the total	37	31	33

Note: the comparative figure for 1928 was 7.4 million.

The contradictions between theory and practice of female employment were exacerbated further with the onset of war. So, although the trend of female employment continued to increase, the Nazi regime did not fully exploit the valuable resource of women as munitions workers. Whereas British women were required to play a major role on the home front, German women remained underemployed right to the end of the war (see page 279). This was due to:

- Germany's poor economic mobilisation
- the unconvincing appeal for women to do war work in arms factories
- women's farming responsibilities.

Marriage and family

The Nazi state was obsessed not only with a desire to increase Germany's population (quantitative), but also with a 'qualitative' improvement.

SOURCE F

From a Nazi pamphlet of October 1934, quoted in J. Noakes and G. Pridham, editors, *Nazism 1919–45*, volume 2, Liverpool University Press, 1988, p. 455.

To be a mother means giving life to healthy children, bringing to fruition all the physical, mental and spiritual faculties of these children and creating a home for them which represents a place where nationalist and racialist culture is nurtured. It means realising in the community of the family a part of the ideal Volksgemeinschaft and giving to the nation, in the form of grown-up children, people who are physically and mentally developed to the fullest extent, who are aware of their responsibility to the nation and race who will lead their nation onwards and upwards.

According to Source F, what was the Nazi view of a woman's role in the *Volksgemeinschaft*?

The Nazi regime therefore promptly introduced a series of measures:

- Marriage loans. The loan was worth just over half a year's earnings and a quarter of it was converted into a straight gift for each child that was born. (The scheme was introduced in June 1933, but progressively reduced from 1937.)

- Family allowances were improved dramatically, particularly for low-income families.
- Income tax was reduced in proportion to the number of children, and those families with six or more children did not pay any.
- Maternity benefits were improved.
- The anti-abortion law introduced under the Weimar Republic was enforced much more strictly.
- Contraceptive advice and facilities were restricted.

Inevitably, these incentives and laws were backed up by an extensive propaganda campaign, which glorified motherhood and the large family. There were also rewards: the Honour Cross of the German Mother in bronze, silver and gold, awarded for four, six and eight children, respectively. Such glorification reached its climax in the coining of the Nazi slogan 'I have donated a child to the *Führer*' (as contemporary humorists soon pointed out, this was presumably because of Hitler's personal unwillingness or inability to father children of his own).

Table 7.6 Social trends in Nazi Germany 1933–9

Year	Marriages per 1000 inhabitants	Divorces per 10,000 existing marriages	Births per 1000 inhabitants
1933	9.7	29.7	14.7
1936	9.1	32.6	19.0
1939	11.1	38.3	20.3

The statistics in Table 7.6 show several trends:

- From 1933 the birth rate increased significantly, reaching a peak in 1939 (although thereafter it again slowly declined).
- The divorce rate continued to increase.
- The figure of marriages was fairly consistent (apart from the blip in 1939 – probably connected to the onset of the Second World War).

The real problem for the historian is deciding whether Nazi population policy was actually *responsible* for the demographic trends. Interpreting population statistics is difficult because it involves so many different factors: social, economic and even psychological. Also, it is extremely hard to assess the *relative* significance of Nazi population policy over such a short period, when its background was the effects of the depression.

Lebensborn

In connection with the aim of improving 'racial standards', the Nazis established an extraordinary organisation of social engineering called **Lebensborn**. Initially set up by Himmler and the SS in 1935, the programme provided homes for the increasing number of unmarried mothers as long as their illegitimate children met Nazi racial criteria. Eventually, ten 'homes' were created (and a further 25 abroad from 1939), all with very good maternity facilities. Later, the institution

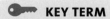

KEY TERM

Lebensborn Literally, the 'spring' or 'fountain of life'. Founded by Himmler and overseen by the SS to promote doctrines of racial purity.

also made the necessary arrangements for girls to be impregnated by members of the SS in organised brothels. It is reckoned that by the end of the regime about 11,000 children were born under these circumstances.

Conclusion

Feminist historians have been highly critical of Nazi population and family policies that reduced the status of women. One historian, Gisela Bock, in the 1980s viewed Nazi thinking on women as a kind of secondary racism in which they were the victims of a sexist–racist male regime that reduced them to the status of mere objects. Such an interpretation would have been denied by the Nazis, who viewed women as 'different', rather than inferior. Interestingly, some modern-day non-feminist historians have tried to explain the positive features of Nazi policy for women. Improved welfare services made life easier for women in many ways, especially in more isolated rural areas. Also, with husbands away during the Second World War, they were protected from having to combine paid work with bringing up a family and running the household.

Yet, despite these different perspectives, Nazi policy objectives for women and the family could not be squared with the social realities of twentieth-century Germany. With the changing population trend (see page 233) and the increasing employment of women, Nazi views on women and the family were idealistic but impractical. Consequently, Nazi policy towards women and the family was contradictory and incoherent.

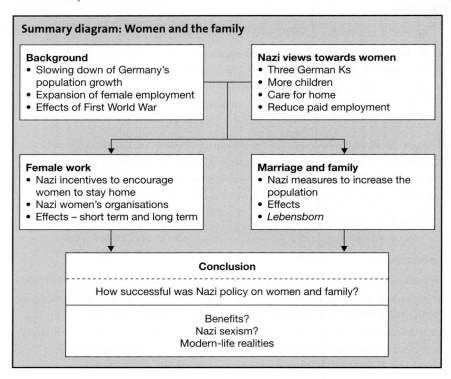

Summary diagram: Women and the family

Background
- Slowing down of Germany's population growth
- Expansion of female employment
- Effects of First World War

Nazi views towards women
- Three German Ks
- More children
- Care for home
- Reduce paid employment

Female work
- Nazi incentives to encourage women to stay home
- Nazi women's organisations
- Effects – short term and long term

Marriage and family
- Nazi measures to increase the population
- Effects
- *Lebensborn*

Conclusion

How successful was Nazi policy on women and family?

Benefits?
Nazi sexism?
Modern-life realities

7 Outsiders

▶ *Who were the outsiders in the* Volksgemeinschaft?

Despite the Nazi vision of an all-embracing society, certain people were not allowed to be part of the *Volksgemeinschaft* in the Third Reich. Those who did not conform to the expected criteria were to be discriminated against – and persecuted. They were definitely treated as 'outsiders'.

Ideological opponents

This term could most obviously be applied to the socialists and communists. Their leaders were sent to early concentration camps in 1933 and more were arrested by the *Gestapo* in the purge of 1935 (see page 254). However, increasingly it became a broader term to cover anyone who did not 'ideologically conform' to the regime. As the years went on, a broader range of political, religious and ethical opponents was identified and more were imprisoned, for example Pastor Niemöller (see page 231).

The 'biologically inferior' (*Untermenschen*)

The term **Untermenschen** covered all the races who, according to the Nazis, were seen as 'inferior' or subhuman, such as Gypsies, Slavs and Jews (see below). It also included mentally and physically disabled people.

The Nazis were strong supporters of **eugenics**, which had evolved from nineteenth-century Social Darwinism (see page 105) and had gained support from some scientists. Nazi ideology aspired to a pure Aryan race in which any 'inferior blood' – as found in other races and the mentally and physically unsound – should be removed.

As early as July 1933 the Nazis proclaimed 'The Law for the Prevention of Hereditarily Diseased Offspring', which allowed for the compulsory sterilisation of those with hereditary conditions like schizophrenia, Huntington's chorea, hereditary blindness or deafness. It also targeted those with existing conditions such as epilepsy or severe physical deformity which made them mentally or physically unfit.

In a twelve-year period 350,000 people were sterilised under this law, either voluntarily or as the result of judgements from one of the 220 hereditary health courts.

In addition, the 'Law for the Protection of the Hereditary Health of the German Nation' was passed in October 1935, which forbade the marriage of anyone suffering from mental disability or with a hereditary disease.

 KEY TERMS

Untermenschen 'Sub-humans.' Covered all races who, according to the Nazis, were 'inferior', or subhuman. Included Jews, Slavs and Gypsies (Sinti and Roma).

Eugenics The scientific programme for the genetic improvement of the race.

According to Source G, what were the Nazi reasons for the sterilisation law?

SOURCE G

From 'The Law for the Prevention of Hereditary Diseased Offspring', 14 July 1933, quoted in J. Noakes and G. Pridham, editors, *Nazism 1919–45*, volume 2, Liverpool University Press, 1988, p. 457.

Anyone who has a hereditary illness can be rendered sterile by a surgical operation, if according to the experience of medical science, there is a strong probability that his/her offspring will suffer from serious hereditary defects of a physical or mental nature …

It is not only the decline in population but also the deteriorating genetic make-up of our people which are causes of serious concern. Whereas the hereditary healthy families have for the most part adopted a policy of having only one or two children, countless numbers of inferiors and those suffering from hereditary ailments are reproducing unrestrainedly while their sick and asocial offspring are a burden on the community.

KEY TERMS

Euthanasia Ending the lives of people suffering from incurable illnesses.

Operation T-4 The collation of information about mentally and physically ill patients in offices in Tiergartenstrasse 4 in Berlin as part of the euthanasia programme.

These policies went much further from 1938, when Hitler himself initiated the idea of using **euthanasia** for children with severe disabilities (such as Down's syndrome and cerebral palsy) by presenting it as a 'mercy death'. In order to counter any public outrage at their plans, the government launched a propaganda campaign which focused on the cost of caring for psychiatric patients at the expense of ordinary German citizens. The question in Source H from a Maths textbook illustrates this.

SOURCE H

From a Nazi Maths textbook, quoted in Helen Brocklehurst, *Who's Afraid of Children? Children, Conflict and International Relations*, Ashgate Publishing, 2006, p. 72.

Question 97: To keep a mentally ill person costs approx. 4RM per day, a cripple 5.5RM, a criminal 3.50RM. Many civil servants receive only 4RM per day, white-collar employees barely 3.50RM, unskilled workers not even 2RM per head for their families. a) Illustrate these figures with a diagram. According to conservative estimates, there are 300,000 mentally ill, epileptics etc. in care. b) How much do these people cost to keep in total at a cost of 4RM a head? c) How many marriage loans at 1000RM each could be granted from this money?

According to Source H, how does this maths question show Nazi attitudes towards the physically and mentally ill?

No specific law permitted the euthanasia of such patients, but many were killed in asylums under the name of **Operation T-4**. From September 1939 all public, private or religious institutions caring for mental patients had to submit details of their inmates' conditions to the T-4 offices in Berlin, where a panel of doctors selected those who should die. Initially, the patients were transferred to 'killing wards' where they were killed through drug overdose or gradual starvation, but, given the large numbers of victims, it soon became clear that carbon monoxide gassing would be more efficient. About 70,000 were gassed in 1940–1, but, following public rumours and Catholic opposition, the operation was stopped (see page 252). Nevertheless, child euthanasia and the killing of mentally and physically handicapped patients by other methods still continued until 1945.

Asocials

The term was used very broadly to cover anyone whose behaviour was not viewed as acceptable. These social outcasts included alcoholics, prostitutes, criminals, tramps and the workshy: indeed, anyone who did not, could not or would not perform their duties to the national community.

Those asocials who were 'orderly' but avoided work were rounded up and organised into a compulsory labour force; and those who were judged as 'disorderly' were imprisoned and sometimes sterilised or experimented on.

Homosexual men were also classed as asocials. They were seen as breaking the laws of nature and undermining traditional Nazi family values. In 1936 the Reich Central Office for the Combating of Homosexuality and Abortion was established. Between 10,000 and 15,000 homosexuals were imprisoned and those sent to camps were forced to wear pink triangles. Provided they were discreet, lesbians were not persecuted as badly as men, as they were not seen as a threat to society in the same way.

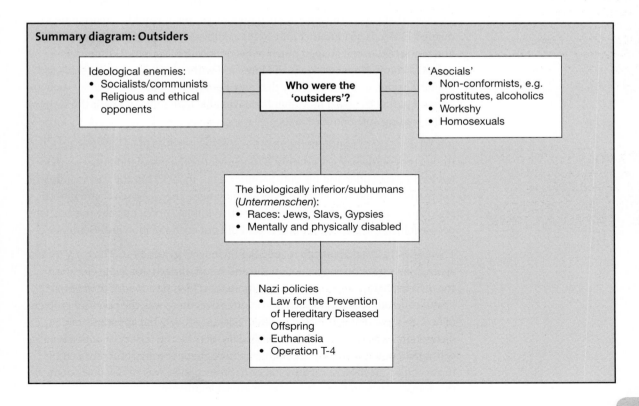

Summary diagram: Outsiders

Ideological enemies:
- Socialists/communists
- Religious and ethical opponents

Who were the 'outsiders'?

'Asocials'
- Non-conformists, e.g. prostitutes, alcoholics
- Workshy
- Homosexuals

The biologically inferior/subhumans (*Untermenschen*):
- Races: Jews, Slavs, Gypsies
- Mentally and physically disabled

Nazi policies
- Law for the Prevention of Hereditary Diseased Offspring
- Euthanasia
- Operation T-4

Anti-Semitism

▶ *How and why did Nazi anti-Semitism change over time?*

At the very centre of Nazi social policy was the issue of race and, specifically, anti-Semitism. Hitler's obsessive hatred of the Jews was perhaps the most dominant and consistent theme of his political career. The translation of such ideas into actual policy was to lead to racial laws, government-inspired violence and the execution of the **genocide** policy that culminated in what became known as the **Holocaust**. For historians, such questions pose immense problems.

The context

The emergence of right-wing racist *völkisch* nationalism was clearly apparent before 1914 (see pages 43–4). Its attractions expanded in the aftermath of the First World War: the self-deception of the 'stab in the back' myth; the humiliation of the Versailles Treaty; and the political and economic weaknesses of the Weimar Republic. So, by the early 1920s, there were about 70 relatively small right-wing racist parties, such as the Nazi Party.

In that environment Hitler was able to exploit hostility towards the Jews and turn it into a radical ideology of hatred. He was the product, not the creator, of a society that was permeated by such prejudices. Yet, it would be inaccurate to dismiss Hitler as just another anti-Semite. Hitler's hatred of Jews was obsessive and vindictive, and it shaped much of his political philosophy. Without his personal commitment to attack the Jews and without his charismatic skills as a political leader, it seems unlikely that anti-Semitism could have become such an integral part of the Nazi movement. He was able to mobilise and stir the support of the leading anti-Semitic Nazis.

It is all too easy to highlight the rhetoric of Nazi anti-Semitism as the reason for the success of the party. Certainly, 37.3 per cent of the population may seem to have voted for Hitler and his anti-Semitic stance in 1932, but the vast majority of Germans were motivated more by unemployment, the collapse of agricultural prices and the fear of communism. Indeed, in a 1934 survey into the reasons why people joined the Nazis, over 60 per cent did not even mention anti-Semitism.

Therefore, the Nazi approach to anti-Semitism was **gradualist**. The early moves against Jews gave no suggestion of the end result. Indeed, for some Germans the discriminatory legislation was no more than Jews deserved. For the more liberal minded, who found such action offensive, there was the practical problem of how to show opposition and to offer resistance. Once the apparatus of dictatorship was well established by the end of 1934, the futility of opposition was apparent to most people. Feelings of hopelessness were soon replaced by those of fear. To show sympathy for, or to protect Jews, was to risk one's own freedom or one's own life. It was an unenviable dilemma.

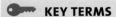

KEY TERMS

Genocide
The extermination of a whole race.

Holocaust Term to describe mass slaughter – in this context it refers to the extermination of the Jews.

Gradualism Changing by degrees; progressing slowly.

Legal discrimination

Many radical Nazis were keen to take immediate measures against Jewish people and their businesses, but the party's leadership was worried that these could get out of hand. Those concerns were confirmed when a one-day national boycott was organised for 1 April 1933. Jewish-owned shops, cafés and businesses were picketed by the SA, who stood outside urging people not to enter. However, the boycott was not universally accepted by the German people and it caused bad publicity abroad.

The Nazi leaders developed their anti-Semitism in a more subtle way. Once the Nazi regime had established the legal basis for its dictatorship, it was legally possible to initiate an anti-Jewish policy, most significantly by the creation of the Nuremberg Laws in September 1935. This clearly stood in contrast to the extensive civil rights that Jews had enjoyed in Weimar Germany. The discrimination against Jewish people got worse as an ongoing range of laws was introduced (see Table 7.7). In this way; all the rights of Jews were gradually removed even before the onset of the war.

Interestingly, an SPD agent wrote a report about the Nuremberg Laws in September 1935 (see Source I, page 244).

Table 7.7 Major Nazi anti-Jewish laws 1933–9

	Date	Law
1933	7 April	Law for the Restoration of the Professional Civil Service. Jews excluded from the government's civil service
	4 October	Law for the exclusion of Jewish journalists
1935	15 September	The Nuremberg Race Laws: 1 Reich Citizenship Act. 'A citizen of the Reich is a subject who is only of German or kindred blood.' Jews lost their citizenship in Germany. 2 Law for the Protection of German Blood and German Honour. Marriages and extramarital relations between Jews and German citizens forbidden
1938	26 April	Decree for the registration of Jewish Property
	5 July	Decree prohibiting Jewish doctors practising medicine
	28 October	Decree to expel 17,000 Polish Jews resident in Germany
	12 November	Decree to exclude Jews from German Economic Life (arising from inter-ministerial meeting chaired by Göring)
	15 November	Law excluding Jewish pupils from schools and universities
	28 November	Law restricting the freedom of movement of Jews, for example public swimming pools, theatres
	3 December	Law for the compulsory closure and sale of all Jewish businesses
1939	1 September	Decree for the introduction of curfew for Jews

? What are the different attitudes towards the Jews described in Source I? How useful is this source?

SOURCE I

From an SPD agent report in Saxony in 1935, quoted in J. Noakes and G. Pridham, editors, *Nazism 1919–45*, volume 2, Liverpool University Press, 1988, p. 545.

The Jewish are not taken very seriously because the population has other problems on its mind and is mostly of the opinion that the fuss about the Jews is only being made to divert people's attention from other things and give the SA something to do. But one must not imagine that the anti-Jewish agitation does not have the desired effect on many people. On the contrary, there are enough people who are influenced by the defamation of the Jews and regard the Jews as the originators of many bad things. They have become fanatical opponents of the Jews. This enmity often finds expression in the form of spying on people and denouncing them for having dealings with the Jews, probably in the hope of winning recognition and advantage from the Party. But the vast majority of the population ignore the defamation of the Jews; they even demonstratively prefer to buy in Jewish departments …

Propaganda and indoctrination

Nazism also set out to cultivate the message of anti-Semitism; in effect to change people's attitudes so that they hated the Jews. Goebbels himself was a particularly committed anti-Semite and he used his propagandist skills to indoctrinate the German people. All aspects of culture associated with the Jews were censored. Even more forceful was the full range of propaganda methods used to advance the anti-Semitic message, such as:

- posters and signs, for example 'Jews are not wanted here'
- newspapers, for example *Der Angriff*, which was founded by Goebbels; *Der Stürmer*, edited by the *Gauleiter* Julius Streicher, which was overtly anti-Semitic with a seedy range of articles devoted to pornography and violence
- cinema, for example *The Eternal Jew; Süss the Jew.*

A particular aspect of anti-Semitic indoctrination was the emphasis placed on influencing German youth. The message was obviously put across by the Hitler Youth, but all schools also conformed to the new revised curriculum, which focused on reinforcing Nazi racism, for example through studying negative portrayals of Jews in literature and history and even presenting anti-Semitic mathematical problems such as '… calculate the number of Jews in Germany'.

Terror and violence

In the early years of the regime, the SA, as the radical left wing of the Nazis, took advantage of their power at local level to use violence against Jews, for example through damage to property, intimidation and physical attacks. However, after the Night of the Long Knives in June 1934 (see pages 165–9), anti-Semitic violence became more sporadic for two probable reasons. First, in

SOURCE J

According to Source J, how were the Jews portrayed in Nazi Germany?

Poster for the anti-Semitic film *The Eternal Jew*. The caption reads: 'A Documentary about World Jewry'.

1936 the anti-Semitic campaign was suspended because of the Berlin Olympics and the need to avoid international alienation. Secondly, conservative forces still had a restraining influence: for example, Schacht had continued to express worries about the implications of anti-Semitic action for the economy. However, with his dismissal in September 1937, along with other conservatives (see pages 185–6), this cleared the way for the development of a more extreme anti-Semitic policy. In 1938–9 the violence and intimidation of two major events showed that there was a more radicalising pressure against the Jews even before the start of the Second World War.

The *Anschluss*

The takeover of Austria (the *Anschluss*) in March 1938 (see page 259) was received with euphoric support by the vast majority in both countries, but it resulted in violence and humiliation for the 190,000 Austrian Jewish population, on a scale not seen in Germany.

At first, Jewish properties and businesses were looted, particularly in Vienna, and some Jews were made to publicly wash buildings and pavements. Thousands were also arrested. More systematically, later that summer, Jewish houses and businesses were sold off at low prices and officially '**Aryanised**'.

The events in Austria encouraged Göring to believe that there were benefits to adopting a similar, though more orderly, approach throughout Germany. On 26 April 1938 he issued a 'Decree for the Registration of Jewish Property', which demanded that all Jewish property worth more than RM5000 be valued and registered with the state. This was a step towards confiscating all Jewish property and excluding the Jews from German economic life.

Kristallnacht

On 9–10 November 1938 there was a sudden violent pogrom against the Jews, which became known as the 'Night of Crystal Glass' (*Kristallnacht*) because of all the windows which were smashed in the process. The pogrom was prompted by an unforeseen incident: the assassination, of Ernst von Rath, a German diplomat, by Herschel Grünspan, a Polish Jew on 7 November in Paris. *Kristallnacht* started in Berlin and spread throughout Germany with dramatic effects: the destruction of numerous Jewish homes, with 100 deaths; attacks on 10,000 Jewish shops and businesses; the burning down of 200 synagogues; and the deportation of 20,000 Jewish people to concentration camps.

Nevertheless, even leading Nazis were surprised and shocked by the extent of the damage in the pogrom and concerned about international criticism. It was officially portrayed as a 'spontaneous demonstration' of popular outrage, but in fact it was very much fuelled by local Nazis and co-ordinated by Goebbels. He had hoped that the anti-Semitic actions might also win Hitler's favour, and compensate for his disreputable affair with a Czech actress.

Significantly, Göring exploited *Kristallnacht* to chair an inter-ministerial meeting on Jewish policy which agreed on the decree to exclude Jews from German Economic Life. This resulted in various laws (see Table 7.7 on page 243) which formally extended the Aryanisation of Jewish-owned property and laid the basis for the segregation of Germans and Jews in every aspect of day-to-day living.

Forced emigration

From the start of the Nazi dictatorship some Jews had decided to leave Germany voluntarily. Many Jews with influence, high reputation or sufficient wealth could find the means to leave. The most popular destinations were Palestine, Britain

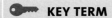

KEY TERM

Aryanise To remove all non-Aryans from office, business and property.

and the USA, and among the most renowned *emigrés* were Albert Einstein, the scientist, and Kurt Weill, the composer.

From 1938 a new dimension to anti-Semitism developed: forced emigration. As a result of the events in Austria in 1938, the Central Office for Jewish Emigration was established in Vienna, overseen by **Adolf Eichmann**. Jewish property was confiscated to finance the emigration of poor Jews. Within six months Eichmann had forced the emigration of 45,000 and the scheme was seen as such a success that, in January 1939, Göring was prompted to create the Reich Central Office for Jewish Emigration, run by **Heydrich** and Eichmann (see Table 7.8).

Table 7.8 The Jewish community in Germany 1933–45

Year	Total number	*Emigrés* each year
1933	503,000	38,000
1939 (May)	234,000	78,000*
1945	20,000	–

* The cumulative figure of Jewish *emigrés* between 1933 and 1939 was 257,000.

It is therefore estimated that the Nazi persecution led to about half of the Jewish population leaving before the war. Technically, the Jews had voluntarily emigrated but they were forced to leave behind all their belongings. Faced with that prospect, the other half stayed. Some assumed that this was just another phase in the history of European pogroms, and would pass. Others felt they were so rooted in Germany that they could not comprehend living elsewhere. Whatever the reason, the remainder decided to take their chances, rather than lose their homes and all their possessions.

Conclusion

Despite the number of anti-Semitic measures of 1933–9, it is difficult to claim that the Nazis had pursued a planned overall policy to deal with the 'Jewish question'. In many respects the measures were at first haphazard. However, on one point it is very clear – the year 1938 marked an undoubted **'radicalisation'** of Nazi anti-Semitism. The laws, the violence connected with *Kristallnacht* and the forced emigration came together, suggesting that the regime had reached a pivotal year, a fact confirmed by the tone of the speech in the *Reichstag* by Hitler on 30 January 1939: 'If the international Jewish financiers in and outside Europe should succeed in plunging the nations once more into a world war, then the result will not be the Bolshevising [making communist] of the earth, and thus the victory of Jewry, but the annihilation of the Jewish race in Europe'.

It is difficult to truly assess how popular the anti-Semitic policies of 1933–9 were with non-Jewish Germans. Certainly there was much anti-Semitism, and it is likely that the initial commercial and social discrimination was generally well received. But attitudes in the aftermath of *Kristallnacht* are another matter. By then, open opposition from non-Jewish Germans would have been dangerous and there would have been serious consequences for any dissenters.

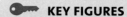

KEY FIGURES

Adolf Eichmann (1906–62)
A NSDAP member who was quickly chosen to join the SD of the SS in 1932. A central figure who was responsible for the deportation of millions of Jews to ghettos and camps. He took the notes at the infamous Wannsee Conference, 1942. Arrested and executed by Israel in 1962.

Reinhard Heydrich (1904–42)
Undoubtedly talented, but his skills were marred by traits of selfishness, ambition and brutality. Made chief of secret police at the age of 32 and in 1939 appointed head of RSHA and the leader of the Central Office for Jewish Emigration. As Reich protector of Bohemia, he was assassinated in May 1942 by Czech resistance in Prague.

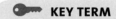

KEY TERM

Radicalisation A policy of increasing severity.

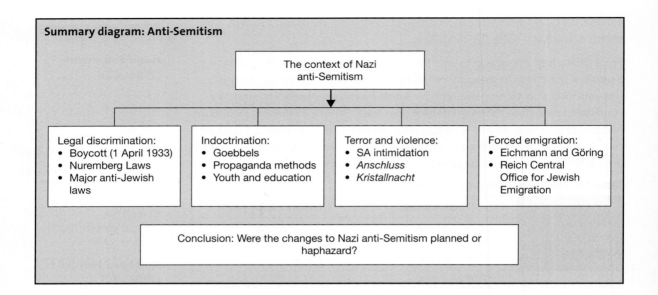

Summary diagram: Anti-Semitism

The context of Nazi anti-Semitism

Legal discrimination:
• Boycott (1 April 1933)
• Nuremberg Laws
• Major anti-Jewish laws

Indoctrination:
• Goebbels
• Propaganda methods
• Youth and education

Terror and violence:
• SA intimidation
• *Anschluss*
• *Kristallnacht*

Forced emigration:
• Eichmann and Göring
• Reich Central Office for Jewish Emigration

Conclusion: Were the changes to Nazi anti-Semitism planned or haphazard?

⑨ Opposition and consent: the popularity of the Nazi regime

▶ *How popular was the Nazi regime in the years of peacetime 1933–9?*

Assessing the popularity of a regime is far from easy. It is hard enough in a modern-day democracy, like Britain or Germany, even when we have access to sophisticated methods of analysis. Yet, trying to gauge the degree of consent and opposition to a totalitarian dictatorship is even more difficult. There was not a black-and-white distinction between them, as is shown by the spectrum in Figure 7.1. Moreover, shades of opinion were not static – they changed over time. So can historians really agree on this one crucial question: how popular was the Nazi regime 1933–9?

The historical sources

Historians face serious problems in trying to assess public opinion on the popularity of the a regime. Significantly, Kershaw, in his book *The Hitler Myth: Image and Reality*, states: 'We cannot quantify Hitler's popularity at any given time during the Third Reich.' The elections and plebiscites of the 1930s – although the only formal measure of popularity – were rigged and the media were effectively controlled (see pages 211–12). Nevertheless, two important sources have been used to understand the nature of public opinion in Nazi Germany.

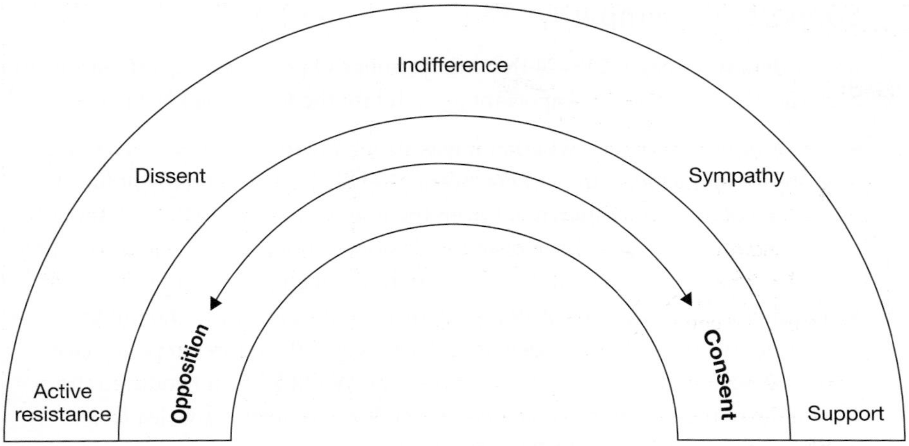

Figure 7.1 A suggested spectrum of public attitudes to the Nazi regime.

First, records of the *Gestapo* and the SD. By the start of the war, 3000 full-time officials co-ordinated information from a broad range of contacts across the whole country and produced analytical reports, such as the one in Source K.

SOURCE K

From a *Gestapo* report of 1937 in the Düsseldorf area, quoted in C. Hinton and J. Hite, *Weimar and Nazi Germany*, John Murray, 2000, p. 327.

… the illegal activity of the SPD is the same as that outlined in the newly published guidelines for the conspiratorial work of the KPD; the setting up of cells in factories, sports clubs and other organisations. Since the former SPD members carry on propaganda only by word of mouth, it is very difficult to get hold of proof of their illegal activities which would be used in court.

How useful and reliable are Sources K and L for historians?

Secondly, the records of SOPADE (the SPD in exile). They included monthly reports from the SPD's contacts travelling or working secretly underground, such as the one in Source L.

SOURCE L

From a SOPADE report of 1937, quoted in C. Hinton and J. Hite, *Weimar and Nazi Germany*, John Murray, 2000, p. 326.

It becomes increasingly evident that the majority of the people have two faces; one which they show to their good and reliable acquaintances; and the other for the authorities, the party officers, keen Nazis, for strangers. The private face shows the sharpest criticism of everything that is going on now; the official one beams with optimism and contentment.

Such material is very enlightening, yet it remains contentious and needs careful evaluation, as the sources are subjective.

Support and sympathy

It is evident from pages 219–24 that many groups of people had good reasons to back the Nazi regime. It is important to highlight the following key factors:

- The economic recovery, whether it was strong or weak, represented concrete gains for many German workers. Schacht's policies substantially reduced the scar of mass unemployment from the human crisis of 1930–3. Although industrial workers may have resented the longer hours and the relatively low wages, they benefited from the restoration of full employment by 1939.
- The diplomatic successes of 1935–9 (which soon gave way to the military victories of 1939–41) were seen as real achievements in foreign policy (see page 259). For a nation that had lost the First World War and endured the 'shame' of the Versailles Treaty, Hitler was seen as an effective leader in contrast to the failings of Weimar.
- The restoration of political and economic stability was well received by many people, especially the middle classes, who were afraid of the threat of communism.
- Despite Nazi ideological objectives, many youngsters did enjoy the social and physical aspects of the Hitler Youth.
- The social benefits introduced through the Nazi welfare organisations, such as the KdF and SdA, had a broadly positive effect. Somehow the Nazi regime government did succeed with its practical changes in making the people feel that the government recognised their problems and anxieties.
- Traditional family values – at the expense of women's rights – were not so unpopular, particularly in the rural areas.

These factors contributed greatly, at the very least, to the German people's acceptance or, even, support of the regime (see Table 7.9).

Table 7.9 The results of public opinion polls taken in democratic West Germany 1948–55.

Question: Do you think National Socialism was a good idea only badly carried out? (October 1948)	
Yes:	57%
No:	28%
I don't know:	15%

Question: Everything that was built up between 1933 and 1939 was destroyed by the war. Would you say that without the war Hitler would have been one of the greatest ever statesmen? (May 1955)			
	Total	Male	Female
Yes, he would have been	48%	51%	45%
No, he would not have been	36%	38%	35%
I don't know	14%	9%	18%
Other answers	2%	2%	2%

Shaped consent

Nevertheless, popular consent was also deliberately 'shaped' by the Nazi regime. Nazi control of all means of communication effectively enabled them to have power over all propaganda and censorship. As shown on pages 217–20, there were limitations to this control, but in the years before the war the propaganda machine was successful in the sense that:

- It cultivated the Hitler myth of him as an effective leader – of almost messianic qualities which glorified him as a 'saviour'.
- It portrayed the Nazi regime and its *Volksgemeinschaft* model as a stabilising force which promised harmony and security after the civil strife and conflicts of the Weimar years.
- It played on frustrated German nationalism.

For many, it was perhaps easier to believe the propaganda than to question it. Historians can question the true impact of the propaganda or marvel at the gullibility of those who were taken in. But to have lived in a society where only one point of view was disseminated must have blunted anyone's powers of judgement. Many people could push to one side their doubts about the regime because of its perceived successes and their memories of Weimar failures.

Terror and surveillance

Also, the Third Reich developed a regime built on terror and intimidation and backed by surveillance. Of course, the terror was not quite as pervasive as feared at the time (see pages 183–4); nevertheless, the brutality must not be underestimated. Civil rights and freedoms were lost and the courts were increasingly made to deliver judgements and sentences which upheld the regime. Any 'outsiders' were sent to camps or held in prison. Therefore, 'an atmosphere of fear' was created where people were coerced into submission. In this way, not only the potential opposition but also the non-committed and the indifferent were made aware of the dangers. Those individuals who were prepared to question must have known that their actions were futile gestures which would end in personal sacrifice.

As the leading historian in this area, P. Hüttenberger (1976), has written:

> *Whatever the perceptible reserve and discontent of the workers, sections of the middle class, and the peasantry, the fact cannot be ignored that the leadership of the Third Reich largely succeeded in producing such a degree of conformity, indeed readiness to collaborate, that its plans, especially preparation for war, were not endangered from within.*

Opposition: non-conformity, dissent and resistance

The Third Reich may have had Nazi totalitarian aspirations, yet it fell a long way short of winning the hearts and minds of the entire German population.

Nevertheless, the real threat posed by opponents was fairly limited. Active resistance to undermine the Nazi state could only have come from the elites, and the disillusioned elements did not act together until the late 1930s. Nor did the conservative opposition enjoy a sufficiently strong or broad base of support at any time.

In the years after the war historians tended to focus simply on those who 'actively' resisted the regime. Marxist historians from East Germany concentrated almost exclusively on the role of the internal communist opposition and portrayed it as the means to Germany's liberation from fascism by the USSR. On the other hand, in West Germany, the historical writings of Hans Rothfels, *The German Opposition* (1948), and G. Ritter, *The German Resistance* (1958), tended to highlight those famous individuals who valiantly fought for freedom and liberalism, and the focus of research was on the role of the traditional elites and conservatives.

A new generation of historians from the 1970s started to question the nature of the opposition by a completely new historical methodology. Mommsen adopted new research techniques to examine people's attitudes and beliefs at the grassroots of society through oral history. This was initiated by the so-called Bavaria Project led by Hüttenberger and then developed by English historians, Mason and Kershaw. The study of opposition to the Nazis has thus been broadened from the narrow area of active resistance to include anyone who did not conform to Nazi expectations.

Not surprisingly, such a methodology has its critics. Many see it as trying to play down active resistance and to exaggerate the importance of mere passive behaviour, which had little real effect on the regime. However, some historians, in an attempt to give clearer definition to the subtle differences of opposition, have proposed 'models' of resistance similar to the methods of social scientists. The models shown in Figure 7.2 are merely the suggestions of two historians who have tried to categorise opposition. None of them should be seen as providing all the answers to the problems raised. They are starting-points for discussion and analysis.

Much depends on the particular meanings applied to specific words. More significantly, there are dangers in the drawing of clear-cut boundary-lines; what emerges from all the research is that any individual's behaviour was rarely clear-cut. More often than not, most people exhibited a broad mixture of attitudes, variously shaped by religious, financial, moral or personal influences. For example, it was quite feasible for a Catholic priest to show opposition in the following ways:

- protest publicly over the Nazi euthanasia policy
- deliberately carry on traditional Catholic customs within the community.

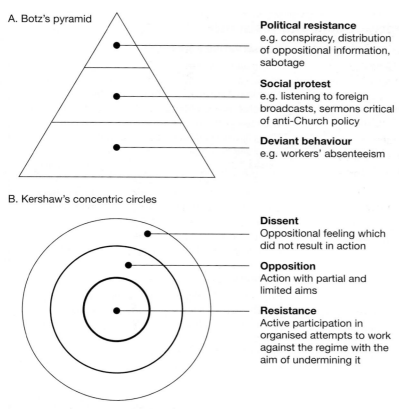

A. Botz's pyramid

Political resistance
e.g. conspiracy, distribution of oppositional information, sabotage

Social protest
e.g. listening to foreign broadcasts, sermons critical of anti-Church policy

Deviant behaviour
e.g. workers' absenteeism

B. Kershaw's concentric circles

Dissent
Oppositional feeling which did not result in action

Opposition
Action with partial and limited aims

Resistance
Active participation in organised attempts to work against the regime with the aim of undermining it

Figure 7.2 Models of resistance.

Yet, the priest could at the same time:

- still be generally supportive of Nazi foreign/military policy
- sympathise with the more authoritarian nature of Nazi government.

It should also be borne in mind that attitudes were rarely static; circumstances changed over time. Indeed, some of the most important figures in the **active resistance** among the conservative elites had initially supported the Nazi regime (see pages 282–8).

Conclusion

All the recent evidence suggests that the position of public opinion was a lot more 'fluid' than assumed previously. It is difficult to give a straight and clear answer to the question of how many people opposed or supported the regime. Nevertheless, a provisional assessment can be made of the state of play. It may now be possible to identify the range of dissent, but the underlying trend suggests that the regime enjoyed increasing popular support from its consolidation during the peace years – a position that was to be maintained until the winter of 1942–3. The regime enjoyed a trend of consensus that was not realistically threatened.

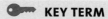 **KEY TERM**

Active resistance
Suggests opposition, by words or action, which tries to undermine or even overthrow the state.

Opposition: non-conformity, dissent and resistance

Army (see pages 184–7)

Conditioned by their traditions of obedience, loyalty and patriotism, many army officers initially worked with the Third Reich. However, the leading generals, Blomberg and Fritsch, who were critical of Hitler's ambitions, were removed in February 1938.

General Beck was particularly opposed to Hitler from the start. After his resignation in August 1938 he drew up plans to arrest Hitler over the Czech crisis, but these failed because of the peaceful surrender by Anglo-French appeasers in September. The following diplomatic successes and early military victories further allayed the doubts of many generals.

Churches (see pages 229–33)

The creation of the Confessing Church by Protestants was a significant gesture of resistance to the Nazi dictatorship; and by 1939 there were increasing concerns in the Catholic Church on ethical differences regarding sterilisation and euthanasia.

There were also brave individual Christian clerics, like Niemöller, who was openly critical in his sermons, and others did not conform. This made the dictatorship wary of launching a fundamental assault on religion in the years of peace. However, both the Catholic and Protestant Churches failed to provide effective opposition to Nazism and concentrated on protecting their own positions.

Youth (see pages 224–9)

Despite Nazi indoctrination, sizeable pockets of the adolescent population had not been won over. There were a number of youth subcultures exhibiting behaviour which challenged the expected social values of Nazism. Groups such as the 'Swing Youth' were born out of the popularity of American jazz, but were seen by the Nazis to be unpatriotic. Other groups such as the *Edelweiss Piraten* were more explicitly critical of Nazi society: particularly of the Hitler Youth, which they boycotted and ridiculed. However, in peacetime the alternative youth groups were merely non-conformist; it was not until the war that youth opposition turned into active resistance.

Conservative elites

There were critics in the government, the civil service and the judiciary. The conservative non-Nazi Konstantin von Neurath remained as foreign minister until 1938 and he maintained connections with the group of diplomats, like Ulrich von Hassell, who had reservations about the regime. Surprisingly, a crucial centre of opposition was *Abwehr*, the German Military Intelligence Office. The deputy leader, Hans Oster, established an extensive network of opponents, including Beck and even Schacht. The main problem confronting these conservatives was staging any kind of resistance in the face of Hitler's successes and his popularity with the ordinary German people.

Workers

All other political parties were banned in 1933, but those of the left wing were the focus of real persecution: in the wake of the *Reichstag* fire many communists were thrown into the early camps; and in 1935 there were mass arrests of socialists and communists by the *Gestapo*, who were becoming increasingly repressive.

Consequently, communists and social democrats went underground: the SPD was reformed in Prague and later Paris; while the KPD also established an office in Prague and maintained its connections with Moscow. Both groups arranged for the publication and distribution of newspapers and anti-Nazi pamphlets and they also established cells within Germany, especially in many of the large cities. As for ordinary workers, there were some strikes and other industrial action – such as work-to-rule – held in the early years, 1933–5. However, the key obstacle continued to be the lack of any co-ordinated opposition.

Assassination attempts

- Maurice Bavaud, a Catholic theological student, 9 November 1938 in Munich. Planned to shoot Hitler at a parade but abandoned this when he stood too far away. Later arrested and executed.
- Georg Elser, a socialist cabinet maker, 8 November 1939 in Munich. Planned to blow up Hitler at a speech. Bomb exploded and killed seven, but Hitler had left a few minutes before. Arrested and executed.

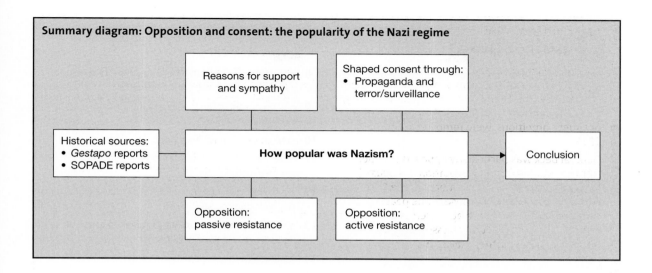

Summary diagram: Opposition and consent: the popularity of the Nazi regime

Chapter summary

In the *Volksgemeinschaft* the Nazis had an ambitious purpose to change German society. Yet, its actual impact over such a short period has been questioned.

Goebbels did successfully use propaganda and censorship to control all types of media and culture. As a result, Hitler and the regime were strengthened, and the evidence suggests that he enjoyed considerable support before the war – indeed, any opposition revealed itself as mere non-conformity, rather than active resistance. Yet, the *Volksgemeinschaft* failed to create an alternative new Nazi culture, or to challenge the Christian

Churches with the new religion of the German Faith Movement. Likewise, it is debatable whether Nazi ideology on the youth and the role of women had a real long-term impact on the people. In fact, those Nazi policies created real practical problems for the regime. Furthermore, even the initial benefits for the working class, peasantry and *Mittelstand* were offset by the increasing economic realities of the late 1930s.

If there was a revolutionary core to Nazi *Volksgemeinshaft*, it can be seen in the shift of Nazi racial policy from gradualism to radicalism in its treatment of 'outsiders', such as the *Untermenschen*, the asocials, the Jews and people with mental and physical disabilities. The consequences of these policies can be seen in Chapter 8.

Refresher questions

Use these questions to remind yourself of the key material covered in this chapter.

1 How did the Nazis aim to transform German society?

2 How did Goebbels intend to create mass support for the Nazis?

3 In what ways did the Nazis shape German culture?

4 How effective were Nazi propaganda and censorship?

5 What was the overall impact of full employment on the working classes?

6 How was education used to indoctrinate Nazi values?

7 To what extent did the Hitler Youth succeed in making youngsters conform?

8 How did the relationship between the Churches and the Nazi state change over time?

9 What were the main features of the German Faith Movement?

10 How successful was Nazi policy for women?

11 What was the impact of Nazi policy on population and the family?

12 Who were the outsiders in the *Volksgemeinschaft* (people's community)?

13 In what ways could Nazi anti-Semitism be seen as gradualist during the Third Reich?

14 Why was Nazi anti-Semitism radicalised in 1938?

15 To what extent did the German people support the regime?

 Question practice

ESSAY QUESTIONS

1 How successful were the Nazis in bringing about revolutionary social changes in the *Volksgemeinschaft*?

2 To what extent did the German people have more benefits than drawbacks from Nazi social and economic policies?

3 'Nazi propaganda and education won the heart and minds of Germany's young people.' Assess the validity of this view.

4 How successful was Hitler in being able to make his own anti-Semitism such a powerful feature of German society?

SOURCE ANALYSIS QUESTION

1 With reference to Sources 1, 2 and 3 (page 257), and your understanding of the historical context, assess the value of these sources to a historian studying the impact of Nazi policies on the young people in Germany 1933–9.

SOURCE 1

From a report of the Nazi Teachers' League Organisation in northern Bavaria, 1937, quoted in J. Noakes and G. Pridham, editors, *Nazism 1919–45*, volume 2, Liverpool University Press, 1988, p. 429.

The extraordinary attitude displayed by large numbers of our young people to school in general and to intellectual development in the grammar schools in particular gives rise to concern for the future. Many pupils believe that they can simply drift through for eight years and secure their school leaving certificate with minimal intellectual performance. The schools receive no support whatsoever from the Hitler Youth units; on the contrary, it is those pupils who are in positions of leadership there who often display unmannerly behaviour and laziness at school. School discipline has declined to an alarming extent.

SOURCE 2

From Ribbentrop speaking in 1938, quoted in N. Rothnie, *National Socialism in Germany*, Macmillan, 1987, p. 74.

The attainment of high intellectual standards will certainly continue to be urged upon the young people but they will be taught at the same time that their achievements must be of benefit to the Volksgemeinschaft to which they belong. Following the Nuremberg Laws, Jewish teachers and pupils have had to quit German schools … in this way, the natural race instincts of German boys and girls are preserved; the young people are made aware of their duty to maintain their racial purity and to bequeath it to succeeding generations. The teaching of such principles is not enough, it is constantly supplemented, in the National State, by opportunities for what may be called 'community life'. By this term we mean school journeys, school camps, school 'houses' in rural neighbourhoods, and similar applications of the local corporate principles to the life of schools and scholars.

SOURCE 3

From the memoirs of Melita Maschmann, a BDM leader, in her autobiography *Account Rendered*, 1964, quoted in J. Noakes and G. Pridham, editors, *Nazism 1919–45*, volume 2, Liverpool University Press, 1988, pp. 422–3.

Apart from its beginnings during the 'years of struggle', the Hitler Youth was not a youth movement at all: it became more and more the 'state youth organisation', that is to say, it became more and more institutionalised, and finally became the instrument used by the National Socialist regime to run its ideological training of young people and the war work for certain age groups.

And yet the Hitler Youth was a youth organisation. Its members may have allowed themselves to be dressed in uniforms and regimented, but they were still young people and they behaved like young people …

There was certainly a great deal of good and ambitious education in the Hitler Youth. There were groups who learned to act in a masterly way. People told stories, danced and practised handicrafts, and in these fields the regimentation was fortunately often less strict. But the idea of a competition (behind which lay the glorification of the fighter and the heroic) often enough banished the element of meditation even from musical activities, and the playful development of the creative imagination, free of any purpose, was sadly stunted.

CHAPTER 8

The impact of war 1939–45

Although there is a brief overview of military operations, the main aim of this chapter is to consider the impact of the war. This picks up and focuses on a range of issues raised from previous chapters: the direction of the economy, the actual effect on the people on the home front, racial policy and resistance. The main points are considered through the following sections:

★ The war

★ The Nazi war economy

★ The racial war

★ The 'home front'

★ Resistance and repression

★ 'Zero hour': Germany in 1945

The key debate on *page 292* of this chapter asks the question: Why did the Holocaust happen and who was responsible?

Key dates

1939	Sept. 1	Germany invaded Poland
	Dec.	Hitler's war economy decrees
1941	June 22	Germany invaded USSR: Operation Barbarossa
	Aug.	Bishop Galen's sermons against euthanasia
	Dec.	Rationalisation Decree
1942	Jan.	Wannsee Conference: Final Solution to exterminate the Jewish people
	Feb.	Appointment of Albert Speer as armaments minister
	Nov.	German defeat at El Alamein
1942–3		White Rose student group; distribution of anti-Nazi leaflets

1942–4		Transportation of Jews to death camps
1943	Jan.	German surrender at Stalingrad
	Feb. 18	Goebbels' speech rallied the people for a 'total war'
	July 24	Hamburg firestorm
1944	July 20	Stauffenberg Bomb Plot failed to overthrow the regime
	Nov.	Execution of twelve Edelweiss Pirates in Cologne
1945	May 7–8	German surrender: occupation and division of Germany

The war

▶ *Why was Germany so successful initially?*

▶ *When and why did the military balance turn against Germany?*

In *Mein Kampf* Hitler openly stated his ambitions for foreign policy (see page 106). Indeed, some historians believe that Hitler had a clearly defined set of objectives, which amounted to a stage-by-stage plan:

- The destruction of the Treaty of Versailles and the restoration of Germany's pre-1914 borders.
- The union of all German-speaking peoples such as Austria, western Poland, the borders of Czechoslovakia (the Sudetenland) and provinces in Hungary and Romania.
- The creation of *Lebensraum*: the establishment of a Nazi racial empire by expanding into eastern Europe at the expense of the Slavic peoples, particularly in Poland and Russia.

In the years 1935–8 Germany rapidly made some key gains which changed the continental balance of power:

- The Treaty of Versailles was challenged by the creation of an air force and by the introduction of a conscripted army of 555,000 (March 1935).
- The remilitarisation of the Rhineland (March 1936).
- The *Anschluss* ('union') with Austria (March 1938).
- The Munich Agreement ceded the German-speaking Sudetenland to Germany (September 1938).

However, once Nazi Germany had militarily occupied the non-German lands of Czechoslovakia in March 1939, Britain and France found it difficult to tolerate further German expansionism and immediately guaranteed to uphold the independence of Poland. Thus, when German armed forces attacked Poland on 1 September 1939 both Britain and France were obliged to declare war.

Although Germany found itself committed to a major war in the autumn of 1939, which Hitler had not expected to wage until the mid-1940s, Germany was not militarily destined to fail from the start. The string of victories from September 1939 to November 1941 bears witness to the military power exerted by the Nazi war-machine and suggests that Germany did not have to go down the road to total collapse. Although by early 1943 Germany faced serious military reverses, Germany's eventual defeat was not inevitable. It has to be explained, not merely assumed.

Initial victories

Without direct help from Britain or France, Poland was crushingly defeated by Germany's *Blitzkrieg* tactics within a few weeks. This gave the Germans access to valuable raw materials and labour as well as the aid received from the USSR under the terms of the **Nazi–Soviet Pact**. Hitler was therefore keen to maintain the military momentum and planned for an invasion of France to take place as early as November 1939. But the German attack was postponed several times, mainly because of the lukewarm attitude of senior army generals towards such an operation.

Phoney war

The German attack on the Western Front did not finally take place until May 1940, thus prolonging the Anglo-French **phoney war** for eight months. Hitler's thinking seems to have revolved around the idea of removing the threat posed by the Western democracies before turning east again. To that end, Germany needed to 'destroy France' and to make Britain accept German aspirations on the Continent. In this way, it was hoped to force Britain, under the pressure of military circumstances, into a 'deal' with Germany.

The Low Countries and France

The German defeat of the Low Countries (Belgium and the Netherlands) and France within six weeks was a dramatic triumph for both the armed forces and Hitler. Diffident generals could hardly fail to be impressed by the *Führer*'s military and political handling of events. German popular opinion was relieved and triumphant. Hitler ruled not only in Berlin but also in Paris, Oslo, Vienna, Prague and Warsaw, while the Third Reich was bordered by the three 'friendly' powers of Spain, Italy and the USSR. It was assumed by many that the war was as good as over.

The Battle of Britain

Britain could have settled with Germany; however, the new British prime minister, Winston Churchill, refused even to consider negotiations. The implications of this stubbornness for Germany were clear-cut: Germany needed to secure air superiority in order to invade Britain and to disable its military and strategic potential. Thus, Germany's failure to win the **Battle of Britain** in the autumn of 1940 was significant. Yet, even more so was Hitler's personal decision to switch the military focus, and to start preparing for the invasion of the USSR even before Britain had been neutralised.

Operation Barbarossa

On 18 December 1940 Hitler issued Directive No. 21 for Operation Barbarossa, stating that 'The German armed forces must be prepared to crush Soviet Russia in a quick campaign even before the end of the war against England.' This decision can only be explained by Hitler's belief that *Blitzkrieg* tactics could also succeed in bringing a quick victory against the USSR, as they had against Poland, France and the Low Countries.

The German invasion of the USSR eventually took place on 22 June 1941. It was delayed by the need to invade Yugoslavia and Greece in order to secure Germany's southern flank. At first all went well. Vast tracts of Russian territory were occupied and thousands of prisoners were taken, so by November 1941 German troops were only miles from Moscow and Leningrad.

Reasons for success

The German military advance was the high point of the war and in the years 1939–41 it was phenomenally successful for the following reasons:

- France and Britain failed to take the initiative and Poland was left to fight alone.
- Germany's *Blitzkrieg* strategy of rapid advances overwhelmed all of its enemies in the first two years.
- The French defensive strategy was based on the **Maginot Line** and it proved to be powerless in the face of German *Blitzkrieg* tactics. As a result, the French political and military leadership lost the will to resist.
- Germany's expansion (from 1938) allowed it to exploit all the labour and resources of those countries for its own purposes.
- The USSR was taken by surprise by the German attack and was not really prepared.

Despite Germany's successes, the military advance halted in December 1941. The Soviets had never lost the will to carry on fighting, while Anglo-American aid and the snows of Russia combined to consolidate the Eastern Front. Hitler's gamble to break the USSR by launching a *Blitzkrieg* invasion had failed and Germany was now faced with the prospect of a long war on two fronts.

The 'turn of the tide'

December 1941 was significant in another sense, too, as in that month the Japanese attack on the US naval base at **Pearl Harbor** in Hawaii 'globalised' the conflict. Although he was not obliged to do so, Hitler aligned Germany with Japan and declared war on the USA. This move was prompted by the USA's involvement in the **Battle of the Atlantic** even before Pearl Harbor. However, it did not fit easily with Germany's existing strategy and above all it turned the industrial capacity of the world's greatest power against it. It is tempting, therefore, to suggest that by the end of 1941 Hitler had lost the military and diplomatic grasp which had previously allowed him to shape international developments. Events were now starting to run out of the *Führer*'s control.

Yet, although it appears that the events of December 1941 were the vital turning point for German fortunes in the war, this was certainly not apparent at the time. Throughout 1942 German forces pushed deep into the Caucasian oilfields with the objective of capturing Stalingrad, while the Afrika Korps drove the British back across North Africa into Egypt. It was the eventual failure of these

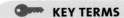
KEY TERMS

Maginot Line Extensive defence fortifications built on the Franco-German frontier by the French governments in the 1930s.

Pearl Harbor A US military base in the Pacific.

Battle of the Atlantic The naval struggle between the Allied convoys and the German U-boats in the northern Atlantic.

Turn of the tide The term used to describe the Allied military victories in the winter of 1942–3, when the British won at El Alamein in North Africa and the Russians forced the surrender of 300,000 German troops at Stalingrad.

Final Solution
A euphemism used by the Nazi leadership to describe the extermination of the Jews from 1941, although in the earlier years the term had been used more loosely before there was any real overall plan.

two offensives that enabled contemporaries to see the winter of 1942–3 as the **'turn of the tide'**. The British victory at El Alamein eventually led to the ejection of German forces from North Africa, and the encirclement and surrender of 300,000 troops at Stalingrad marked the beginning of the Soviet counter-offensive. These two defeats showed that the German armies were no longer invincible.

Defeat

From 1943 Germany's strategy was essentially defensive. Hitler was determined to protect 'Fortress Europe' from Allied invasion, but possibly his strategic and political thinking was losing touch with reality. Increasingly it became shaped by his belief in German invincibility and his own ideological prejudices about race and communism. For example, in spite of all the military difficulties, the creation of the new racial order continued: there was no postponement of the **Final Solution**. Hitler deluded himself into thinking that the alliance of the USSR and the Western Allies could not last and that this would then allow Germany to play off one against the other.

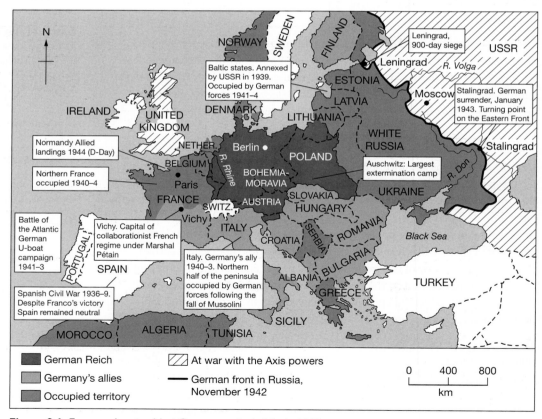

Figure 8.1 Europe, showing Nazi Germany at its height in 1942.

Allied military co-ordination continued to work reasonably well. By the end of 1943 Anglo-American forces had linked up in Africa and had then established a hold on southern Italy, while Soviet forces had reconquered much of Ukraine after the great tank victory at the Battle of Kursk in July 1943. The war had also begun to have an impact on Germany itself. The massive bombing raids caused destruction and dislocation, although their exact strategic value has been questioned over the years. It was becoming clear that the war could not be won by Germany and that it faced total devastation unless the Allied demand for **unconditional surrender** was accepted.

Such military failures triggered the attempted assassination of Hitler in July 1944 (see pages 287–8). His survival meant that the war would have to be fought to the bitter end. Thus, strong German resistance forced the Western Allies to fight extremely hard in order to break out of the beachhead established in Normandy, France, in 1944, while in the east the Soviet advance progressed through eastern Europe in the face of desperate defensive measures. Yet, even then, a blind optimism still prevailed in the minds of some Germans. It was not until 30 April 1945, when Soviet soldiers had advanced to within a mile of the Chancellery in Berlin, that Hitler killed himself. Only then was the German nation freed from the *Führer*'s command and Germany surrendered on 7–8 May 1945.

KEY TERM

Unconditional surrender
Roosevelt and Churchill's statement in 1943 that the Allies would not accept a negotiated peace.

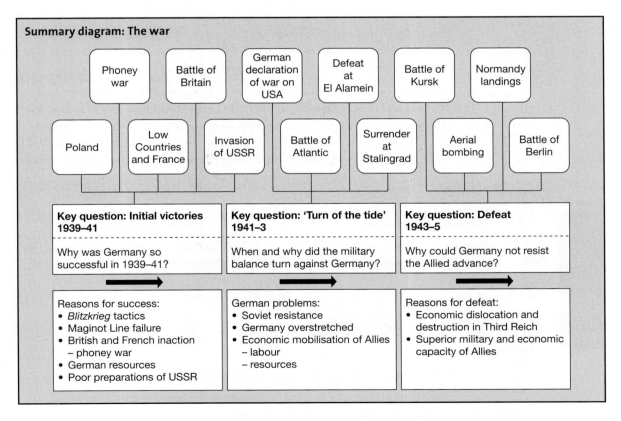

2 The Nazi war economy

▶ *How effectively did the Nazis mobilise the German economy to meet the demands of war?*

The string of military successes achieved by the German armed forces with their use of the *Blitzkrieg* strategy up to December 1941 won Hitler and the regime valuable popular support. Moreover, it gave the impression of an economy that had not been over-strained by the demands of war. Such a view, however attractive, does not actually square with either Nazi intentions or the economic statistics.

The expansion of the Nazi economy

First, Hitler was determined to avoid the problems faced by Germany in the First World War and to fight the coming war with an economy thoroughly prepared for a major and perhaps extended conflict. To this end, a series of war economy decrees was issued by Hitler in December 1939 outlining vast programmes for every possible aspect of war production, for example submarines and aircraft. These plans suggest that the Nazis went well beyond the demands of *Blitzkrieg* and a limited war.

Secondly, in real and percentage terms, German military expenditure doubled between 1939 and 1941, as shown by Table 8.1. It is worth noting, however, that Britain trebled its expenditure in the same period.

Thirdly, food rationing in certain items was introduced from the very start of the war and the German labour force was rapidly mobilised for war so that, by the summer of 1941, 55 per cent of the workforce was involved in war-related projects: a figure which then only crept up to a high-point of 61 per cent by 1944. In this light, it is hardly surprising that the first two years of war also witnessed a twenty per cent decline in civilian consumption.

Table 8.1 Military expenditure of Germany and Britain 1937–41

Year	Germany (RM billions)			Britain (£ billions)		
	GNP	Military expenditure	Military expenditure as a percentage of GNP	GNP	Military expenditure	Military expenditure as a percentage of GNP
1937	93	11.7	13	4.6	0.3	7
1938	105	17.2	17	4.8	0.4	8
1939	130	30.0	23	5.0	1.1	22
1940	141	53.0	38	6.0	3.2	53
1941	152	71.0	47	6.8	4.1	60

The limitations of economic mobilisation

Despite the intent of wholesale mobilisation, the actual results, in terms of armaments production, remained disappointingly low. Admittedly, there was a marked increase in the number of submarines, but surprisingly, Germany's air force had only increased from 8290 aircraft in 1939 to 10,780 in 1941 while in Britain over the same period the number of aircraft had trebled to 20,100. Likewise, Hitler was astonished to learn when drawing up plans for the invasion of the USSR that the Germans' armoured strength totalled only 3500 tanks, which was just 800 more than for the invasion of the West and fewer than the USSR put into the field.

It seems that despite the Nazi image of German order and purposefulness, the actual mobilisation of the German economy was marred by inefficiency and poor co-ordination. The pressures resulting from the premature outbreak of war created problems, since many of the major projects were not due to be ready until 1942–3. So, at first, there was undoubtedly confusion between the short-term needs and long-term plans of the Nazi leadership.

Nevertheless, this should not have been an impossible barrier if only a clear and authoritative central control had been established over the economy. Instead, a host of different agencies all continued to function in their own way and often in a fashion which put them at odds with each other. Although there was a Ministry of Armaments under **Fritz Todt**, it existed alongside three other competing governmental ministries: those of Economics, Finance and Labour. In addition, there was political infighting between the leading Nazi figures; for example, the *Gauleiters* tried to control their local areas at the expense of the overall plans of the state and the party – and also considerable financial corruption.

There were a number of groups responsible for armaments: the Office of the Four-Year Plan, the SS bodies and the different branches of the *Wehrmacht*. The armed forces, in particular, were determined to have their way over the development of munitions with the very best specifications possible and, as a result, the drive for quality was pursued at the expense of quantity. The consequence of all this was that after two years of war, and with the armed forces advancing into the USSR, Germany's economic mobilisation for total war had not achieved the expected levels of armaments production.

Total war 1942–5

By the end of 1941 Germany was at war with Britain, the USSR and the USA and yet its armaments production remained inferior to that of Britain. Preparations for a new approach had begun in the autumn of 1941 and Hitler had issued a 'Rationalisation Decree' to Todt in the December of that year which was intended to eliminate the waste of labour and materials.

The death of Todt and his replacement by **Albert Speer** as minister of armaments in February 1942 marked a real turning point. Speer had previously been the *Führer*'s personal architect and he enjoyed excellent relations with Hitler. He now used the *Führer*'s authority to cut through the mass of interests

 KEY FIGURES

Fritz Todt (1891–1942)

Although a Nazi, Todt was more of an engineer and technician than a politician. He was responsible for the construction of motorways from 1933 and in 1940 he was appointed minister of armaments, which caused increasing clashes with Göring and the *Wehrmacht*. He died in a plane crash.

Albert Speer (1905–81)

Close friend of Hitler who became the *Führer*'s personal architect. Appointed minister of armaments in 1942 and skilfully managed the war economy, with a significant increase in arms production 1942–4. Sentenced to 20 years at the Nuremberg trials.

and to implement his programme of 'industrial self-responsibility' to provide mass production. The controls and constraints previously placed on business, in order to fit in with Nazi wishes, were relaxed. In their place, a Central Planning Board was established in April 1942, which was in turn supported by a number of committees, each representing one vital sector of the economy. This gave the industrialists a considerable degree of freedom, while ensuring that Speer as the director of central planning was able to maintain overall control of the war economy. Speer also encouraged industrialists and engineers to join his ministerial team. At the same time, wherever possible, he excluded military personnel from the production process.

SOURCE A

From the 22 April 1942 decree to create the Central Planning Board, quoted in J. Noakes and G. Pridham, editors, *Nazism 1919–45*, volume 1, Liverpool University Press, 1988, p. 229.

A Central Planning Board shall be established with the framework of the Four Year Plan. Its sphere of activity embraces the whole economy and includes the power to decide whether existing schemes should be continued or new arrangements introduced, the apportionment of existing raw materials, the distribution of coal and energy to manufacture plants and the coordination of transport.

> ? According to Source A, what were the key powers of the Central Planning Board?

Speer was what would now be called a 'technocrat', in that he simply co-ordinated and rationalised the process of war production and more effectively exploited the potential of Germany's resources and labour force. Speer was able to exert influence because of his friendship with Hitler and he used his personal skills to charm or blackmail other authorities. In this way, he took a whole range of other personal initiatives to improve production, such as:

- employing more women in the arms factories
- making more effective use of forced labour
- preventing skilled workers from being lost to military conscription.

The successes and limitations of Speer's economic rationalisation

In a famous speech in February 1943, after the German Army surrender at Stalingrad, Goebbels invited the crowd to support 'total war'. However, the transformation of the Nazi economy really pre-dated Goebbels' propagandist appeal and was down to the work of Speer. As a result of Speer's first six months in power:

- ammunition production increased by 97 per cent
- tank production rose by 25 per cent
- total arms production increased by 59 per cent.

By the second half of 1944, when German war production peaked, there had been more than a three-fold increase since early 1942 (see Tables 8.2 and 8.3).

Table 8.2 Number of German, British, US and USSR tanks produced 1940–5

Year	Germany	Britain	USA	USSR
1940	1,600	1,400	300	2,800
1941	3,800	4,800	4,100	6,400
1942	6,300	8,600	25,000	24,700
1943	12,100	7,500	29,500	24,000
1944	19,000	4,600	17,600	29,000
1945	3,900	N/A	12,000	15,400

Table 8.3 Number of German, British, US and USSR aircraft produced 1940–5

Year	Germany	Britain	USA	USSR
1940	10,200	15,000	6,100	7,000
1941	11,000	20,100	19,400	12,500
1942	14,200	23,600	47,800	26,000
1943	25,200	26,200	85,900	37,000
1944	39,600	26,500	96,300	40,000
1945	N/A	12,100	46,000	35,000

Despite Speer's economic successes, Germany probably had the capacity to produce even more and could have achieved a level of output close to that of the USSR or the USA. He was not always able to counter the power of the party *Gauleiters* at a local level and the SS remained a law unto themselves, especially in the conquered lands. Indeed, although territories occupied by the Third Reich were well and truly plundered, they were not exploited with real economic efficiency.

Economic effects of Allied bombing

The question of whether bombing inhibited or undermined the Nazi economy is not a simple one. Certainly, at first in 1940–2, the effects of bombing were very limited, as Allied aircraft only had the technology to launch little more than nuisance raids.

With hindsight, the deliberate use of **blanket bombing** by the Allies in 1942–5 has been condemned by some on moral grounds and its effectiveness later questioned (see Table 8.4, page 268). It has been seen as a very blunt instrument, as bomb targeting was so inaccurate; indeed, critics have pointed to Speer's production figures as proof that the strategy failed to break the German war economy. However, it is probably more accurate to say that the effects of bombing prevented Germany from increasing its levels of arms production even further. The results of Allied bombing caused industrial destruction and breakdown in communications. Also, Germany was forced to divert significant available resources towards the construction of anti-aircraft installations and underground industrial sites.

 KEY TERM

Blanket bombing
The military policy of dropping large numbers of bombs so as to cause devastation of an area.

Table 8.4 Major Allied air raids

Date	Target
December 1940	First night raid on German city of Mannheim
May 1942	First 1000-bomber raid on Cologne
March 1943	Raids on Ruhr industrial area
May 1943	'Bouncing bomb' raid on German dams
July 1943	Massive raid on the seaport of Hamburg creating firestorm
November 1943	Sixteen raids on Berlin with 9000 bombers
March 1944	Raid on Nuremberg. Heavy British losses because of improved German air-defences
February 1945	Huge raid on the defenceless historic city of Dresden

KEY FIGURE

**Fritz Sauckel
(1894–1946)**

Gauleiter of Thuringia. General-plenipotentiary for mobilising labour 1942–5. He was responsible for the exploitation and death of millions of forced labour workers. Found guilty of war crimes at the Nuremberg trials and hanged.

From 1943 Speer could not reverse the detrimental effects of Anglo-American bombing; because of this, Germany was unable to achieve a total war economy. As it was, German arms production peaked in August 1944 at a level well below its full potential. And in the last nine months of the war the Allies had free rein to bomb Germany with limited resistance.

In the end, the Nazi economy had proved incapable of rising to the demands of total war and the cost of that failure was all too clearly to be seen in the ruins of 1945.

Foreign labour

It is important to note that foreign workers became a growing element of the labour force in the Nazi war economy. Indeed, by 1944, 6.5 million foreign workers made up nearly 25 per cent of the whole force. Some of them were volunteers in occupied territories, but the great majority were forced labour, including prisoners of war. They were mainly of the following nationalities:

- French: 1.1 million
- Poles: 1.4 million
- Russians: 2.1 million
- Czechs: 0.3 million.

There was a hierarchy of nationality and race, ranging from workers from France and Belgium at the top to the slave labourers from the so-called *Untermenschen* or Slavic countries. Racially, the Jews were the most exploited and seen as generally expendable.

Despite the Nazi racial contempt for the foreign workers, with the turning point of 1942 and the push for total mobilisation, they became key to the war effort. **Fritz Sauckel** was tasked with co-ordinating millions of forced labour workers, as able-bodied German workers were drafted to the fronts. Both large and small companies and even farmers exploited foreign labour, with the type of work ranging from mining to farming.

Living conditions for these workers varied: the worst were confined to forced labour camps sleeping in draughty wooden barracks with meagre food rations. They were defenceless against air raids as they were barred from the shelters. Women were particularly vulnerable, as they were often victims of sexual harassment.

The recruitment of foreign labour did not solve Germany's economic problems. Because of their appalling treatment and poor diet, it was not surprising that the foreign workers were not very productive.

SOURCE B

How does Source B show the impact of the Allied forces on Berlin?

?

Soviet troops in the ruins of Berlin in 1945.

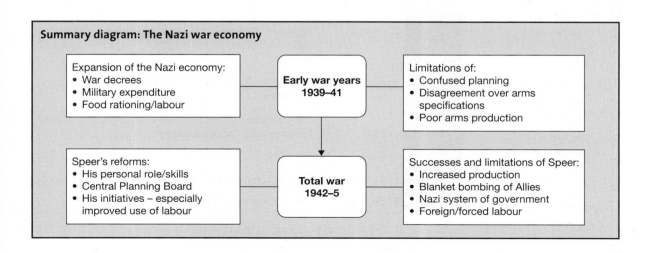

Summary diagram: The Nazi war economy

Expansion of the Nazi economy:
- War decrees
- Military expenditure
- Food rationing/labour

Early war years 1939–41

Limitations of:
- Confused planning
- Disagreement over arms specifications
- Poor arms production

Speer's reforms:
- His personal role/skills
- Central Planning Board
- His initiatives – especially improved use of labour

Total war 1942–5

Successes and limitations of Speer:
- Increased production
- Blanket bombing of Allies
- Nazi system of government
- Foreign/forced labour

3 The racial war

▶ *How did Nazi racism degenerate into genocide?*

It is clear that the year before the war marked an undoubted radicalisation in Nazi anti-Semitism (see pages 244–7 and Table 8.5). However, at the time it could have been hard to imagine that the Holocaust was possible. Who in 1939 could have predicted the scenario of the next six years? The suggestion that millions would be systematically exterminated would have been disbelieved. It is an event in modern European history which even now seems almost beyond comprehension. For those who lived in occupied Europe it was easier and more comfortable to dismiss the rumours as gross and macabre exaggerations – the result of wartime gossip and Allied propaganda. Yet, the unbelievable did happen and it required not only the actions of a 'criminal' minority but also the passive acceptance of the 'innocent' majority. For Germans the moral dimension has made this historical debate a particularly delicate one.

KEY TERM

SS *Einsatzgruppen*
SS Special Action Units. First used during the invasion of Poland. After the invasion of Russia four units were launched in eastern Europe. They were responsible for rounding up local Jews and murdering them in mass shootings.

Table 8.5 The Nazi racial war 1939–45

	Date	Action
1939	September	German invasion of Poland. **SS *Einsatzgruppen*** moved in
1940	April	First 'sealed' ghetto established in Łódź
1941	June	SS *Einsatzgruppen* moved into the USSR behind the advancing armies to round up and kill Jews
1941	1 September	All Jews forced to wear the Yellow Star of David
1941	October	First deportations of Jews from certain German provinces
1942	20 January	Wannsee Conference. Various government and party agencies agreed on the Final Solution to the 'Jewish problem'
	Spring	Extermination facilities set up at Auschwitz, Sobibór and Treblinka
1942–4		Transportation of Jews from all over German-occupied Europe to death camps began
1943	February	Destruction of Warsaw Ghetto
		The start of sending Germany's Gypsies to Auschwitz
1945	27 January	Liberation of Auschwitz by Soviet troops

Impact of Nazi racial policy in Poland

The onset of the continental war changed circumstances for Poland dramatically – and Germany's rapid victory in autumn 1939 left its citizens in a disastrous situation. Hitler was set on a 'harsh racial struggle' which had serious consequences for the Poles and the 3 million Polish Jews.

From the start of occupation, Nazi policies in Poland were brutal. In addition to the advancing German troops, special action groups called SS *Einsatzgruppen* were sent in to destroy all the elements of resistance and to 'render harmless' the Polish leadership. About 16,000 Poles were summarily executed in mass shootings in the autumn.

Politically, the country was divided into three areas, with draconian effects:

- Warthegau. These were the territories annexed and incorporated into the Reich. They were to be 'Germanised', with Poles arbitrarily deported and ethnic Germans imported into the area. Nazi legislation discriminated against all aspects of Polish life and schools and churches were closed.

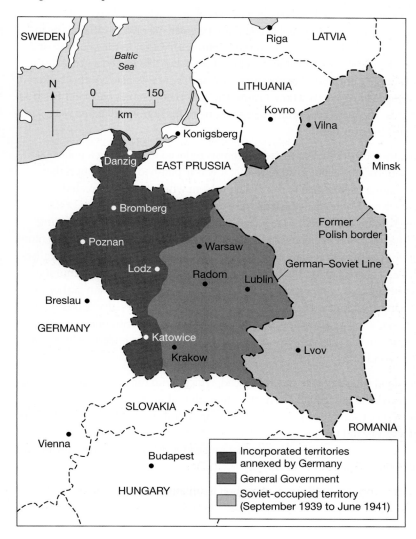

Figure 8.2 Occupied Poland.

- 'General Government'. This was the area not annexed by the Reich, but controlled by Germany. Its population was exploited and the Poles were reduced to a slave labour pool. Many were sent by force to work as labourers in Germany in factories and farms.
- The Occupied Soviet area. This was the area controlled by USSR in the period between the Nazi–Soviet Pact and the German invasion of Russia in 1939–41.

Polish Jews

Violent persecution of Polish Jews started immediately. The army encouraged its soldiers in the degrading, humiliating and arbitrary torturing of Jews and there were many cases of mass shootings. However, at this stage, this did not yet amount to their systematic murder.

It soon became clear to the Nazis that the problem of what to do with the estimated 3 million Jewish people could not be easily resolved. Initial plans to 'resettle' large numbers of people in the Lublin reservation in the south-west corner of the General Government were initiated, but this placed a great strain on food supplies and the transportation system. There was also conflict between some of the leading Nazis: **Hans Frank**, the governor general, particularly stood firm against the forced deportation of so many to his region. All plans were soon abandoned in early 1940.

In the years 1939–41 the Nazi leadership was reduced to pursuing a policy of 'ghettoisation'. This is not to suggest that it was a 'planned policy', but rather more a pragmatic approach to the racial problem which they had created for themselves. The Jewish **ghettos** were established in cities such as Łódź, Warsaw, Krakow and Lublin. They were initially set up as temporary holding bays while the Nazis decided what to do with the Jews but, because of the failure of the Lublin reservation plan, they lasted much longer. Jewish councils – called *Judenrat* – were created, on the pretext of maintaining 'an orderly community life', but in fact they were used as a means of control by the German authorities. From spring 1940, these ghettos became 'sealed', with the penalty of death for anyone caught trying to escape. Because of the heavy concentration of people, the situation in the ghettos deteriorated and the population ended up living in appalling conditions:

- *Food.* Food supplies were much reduced, which, with the limited contact with the outside world, resulted in deaths through malnutrition.
- *Disease.* Poor sanitation and cramped living conditions led to diseases such as tuberculosis and typhus.
- *Heating.* Limited access to heating fuel caused hardship and deaths during the cold Polish winters.

In the first two years of the war, about half a million Polish Jews died.

KEY FIGURE

Hans Frank (1900–46)

Trained as a lawyer and was one of the earliest members of the NSDAP. Became governor general of the General Government of Poland 1939–45 and oversaw the creation of many of the ghettos. He was found guilty of war crimes at the Nuremberg trials and hanged.

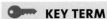

KEY TERM

Ghetto A term used to describe the historic area lived in by the Jews in a city.

> ## Plans for a Jewish resettlement in Madagascar?
>
> The beginning of a general European war made the emigration of Jews to independent countries more difficult. Because of this, during 1939–40, various plans for a 'resettlement' were considered by the Nazis. Most interesting was the suggestion of using Madagascar, a French colony, as a solution and this was met with much enthusiasm from Hitler and other leading Nazis. The plan could be seen as quite callous and calculating, since it was anticipated that many of the Jews would fail to survive the journey or the punishing living conditions on the island. In the end, the plans came to nothing because Germany failed to defeat Britain by the autumn of 1940 and to take control of the high seas.

The invasion of Russia

The invasion of Russia in June 1941 marked a decisive development in the racial war. As with the attack on Poland, SS *Einsatzgruppen* moved in behind the advancing armies. These four special 'Action Units', A, B, C and D, were responsible for rounding up local Jews and Communist Party officials, who were then murdered in their thousands in a series of mass shootings in the Baltic States, western Russia and Ukraine. Most infamously, 30,000 men, women and children were slaughtered in just two days in a ravine at Babi Yar near Kiev. It is estimated that by the end of 1941 some 600,000 Russian Jews had been killed. The massacring represented a major escalation of Nazi racial action. Yet, it is not entirely clear how this mass killing then progressed to the racial extermination in the gas chambers of the Holocaust.

The Final Solution

The actual decision-making process surrounding the Final Solution remains unclear. All the available evidence has been closely scrutinised and analysed, causing much controversy and debate among historians.

Written sources are hard to come by, either because they never existed or because they were destroyed in 1945 – either deliberately or by accident. Where there is written evidence, much of the language is deliberately euphemistic and open to interpretation.

Added to that, no written order for the killing of the Jews from Hitler has ever been found. However, among all this uncertainty there is also hard evidence. In January 1944 Himmler publicly stated in a speech to army officers that Hitler had given him 'a *Führer* order' to give priority to 'the total solution of the Jewish question'. This was further supported by the trial testimonies of Eichmann and R. Höss, the commandant of Auschwitz.

For some historians, like R. Hilberg and C. Browning, the initial rapid German military advance and the bloody massacre of the Russian Jews meant that July was the vital turning point. Indeed, Browning talks of the month's 'euphoria of victory' and he highlights Göring's memorandum of 31 July (see Source C).

SOURCE C

How significant is Source C as evidence of plans to proceed with the Final Solution?

From Göring's memorandum of 31 July 1941 to Heydrich, quoted in the Harry S. Truman Library, 'The War Crimes Trials at Nuremberg'.

As supplement to the task dated 24 January 1939, namely to solve the Jewish question by emigration and evacuation, in a way which is the most favorable in connection with the conditions prevailing at present, I herewith commission you with all preparations with regard to organization, the material side and financial viewpoints for bringing about a final solution of the Jewish question within the territories in Europe under German influence …

I furthermore commission you to submit to me as soon as possible a draft showing the administrative material and financial measures already taken for the execution of the intended final solution of the Jewish question.

There is still no further hard evidence of an overall genocide plan at that time. Rather, the majority of historians, like P. Burrin and Kershaw, view the crucial period as a little later – between mid-September and mid-October. This interpretation also fits in with the growing military concerns of not winning the war with Russia within four months combined with the increasing chaos of dealing with so many Jewish people in eastern Europe. Although the evidence is limited, it clearly supports this view:

- With the support of Hitler, Eichmann actually began the process of transportation to 'resettle' German Jews eastwards in October.
- Furthermore, Eichmann, in his testimony in 1960 in Israel, claimed to remember Heydrich telling him two or three months after the invasion of Russia that 'the *Führer* had ordered the physical extermination of the Jews'.
- There were also various local initiatives at that time to use vans to gas the Jews at Bełżec and Łódź.
- The first practice gassings of Zyklon B took place in Auschwitz in September.
- Heydrich was starting to make plans for the Wannsee Conference.

The Wannsee Conference

The Wannsee Conference, in west Berlin, on 20 January 1942 is often portrayed as the 'decisive' meeting for the Final Solution. But it should be borne in mind that the meeting was initially planned for early December, with the original invitations being sent out on 29 November; strongly suggesting that the decision for systematic extermination had been made in the previous month.

Moreover, the meeting, chaired by Heydrich and organised by Eichmann, did not discuss any fundamental new decisions on the Jewish question. It was more about co-ordinating the logistics, clarifying German law and securing the agreement of the various agencies of police, finance, labour and transport

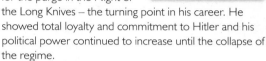

Heinrich Himmler

1900	Born in Munich and studied agriculture at technical college
1923	Joined the Nazi Party and took part in the Beer Hall *putsch*
1929	Appointed leader of the SS
1934	Arranged the purge of the SA on 30 June
1936	Given responsibility of '*Reichsführer* SS and Chief of all German Police'
1939	Made Commissar of the Strengthening of the German Nationhood
	Formed the RSHA
1943	Appointed minister of interior (replacing Frick)
1945	Arrested by British forces, but killed himself before trial

Himmler was in many respects a nondescript, unremarkable character who before 1929 achieved little in his work or in the party. Yet, with a reputation for an organised, obsessive, hard-working style, he quickly converted the small group of 250 SS troops into a major elite force.

Until 1934 Himmler and the SS were very much in the shade of Röhm and the SA. Himmler was responsible for the purge in the Night of the Long Knives – the turning point in his career. He showed total loyalty and commitment to Hitler and his political power continued to increase until the collapse of the regime.

Himmler became the leader of the brutally efficient SS machine, which really held the Third Reich together. He was responsible for:

- the development of surveillance, which created a system of control and repression
- the pursuit of the creation of a German master-race and the development of elite institutions like *Ordensburgen* and the *Lebensborn*
- the extermination of Jews and Gypsies in concentration camps
- the exploitation of all the occupied lands for slave labour and arms production
- the development of the *Waffen* SS as an elite military force that matched the might of the German Army by the end of the war.

(railways). All those who attended at Wannsee understood that the purpose of their gathering was to put Hitler's wishes into effect.

The meeting, which lasted a mere 90 minutes, outlined the grim details of the plan to gas to death Europe's 11 million Jews.

Extermination

In the course of 1942 a number of camps in Poland were developed into mass extermination centres, most notably Auschwitz, Sobibór and Treblinka. Most of the Polish Jews were cleared from their ghettos and then 'transported' by train in appalling conditions to their deaths in the gas chambers. It is believed that, of the original 3 million Polish Jews, only 4000 survived the war. In 1942–4 Jews from all over Europe were deported to face a similar fate – so that by 1945 it is estimated that 6 million European Jews had been murdered altogether in the Holocaust.

Conclusion

Hitler's authority was such that it encouraged initiatives from below as long as they were seen to be in line with his overall ideological vision, and clearly Hitler had often spoken in violent and vengeful terms about the Jews from an early stage in his political career. What is important to understand is how the Nazis' ideological hatred of the Jews developed into the systematic plan for the mass extermination of the race.

It now seems that the initial arrangements for the implementation of the Final Solution were haphazard and makeshift. Hitler and the Nazi leadership did not have any clear systematic programme for dealing with the Jewish question until 1941.

Probably around autumn 1941 it was decided by the top Nazi leadership to launch an extermination policy, and this was endorsed at the Wannsee Conference in January 1942 by a broad range of representatives of key agencies. If these points are accepted, then it might be that the Final Solution could be viewed as a pragmatic (practical) response to the confusion and chaos of war in 1941–2 rather than the culmination of long-term ideological intent.

SOURCE D

Jewish men are forced to work as labourers under the Nazi regime. They are guarded by German soldiers.

? How does the photo in Source D convey the treatment of the Jewish people in concentration camps?

Gypsies

In addition to Jews, Gypsies (Sinti and Roma) were also subject to racial persecution and became victims of Nazi genocide. Gypsies had been viewed as 'outsiders' throughout European history for several reasons:

- Their religion was indeterminate and they had their own Romany customs and dialect.

- They were non-white – because they had originated from India in the late medieval period.
- Their 'traveller' lifestyle, with no regular employment, was resented.

Even before the Nazi dictatorship and during Weimar's liberal years, there was official hostility towards Gypsies and, in 1929, 'The Central Office for the Fight against the Gypsies' was established.

By 1933 it is believed that the number of Gypsies in Germany was about 25,000–30,000 and they, too, were beginning to suffer from the gradualist policy of Nazi discrimination:

- Gypsies were defined exactly like the Jews as 'infallibly of alien blood' according to the Nuremberg Laws of 1935.
- Himmler issued, in 1938, a directive titled 'The Struggle Against the Gypsy Plague', which ordered the registration of Gypsies in racial terms.
- Straight after the outbreak of the war, Gypsies were deported from Germany to Poland – and their movements were severely controlled in working camps. Notoriously, in January 1940, the first case of mass murder through gassing was committed by the Nazis against Gypsy children at Buchenwald.

As with the Jews, the Gypsies during the war were the focus of ever-increasing repression and violence but there was no real, systematic Nazi policy of extermination until the end of 1942. In the first months of 1943 Germany's Gypsies were sent to Auschwitz camp and over 1943–4 a large proportion of Europe's Gypsy population from south-eastern Europe was exterminated: a figure between 225,000 and nearly 500,000.

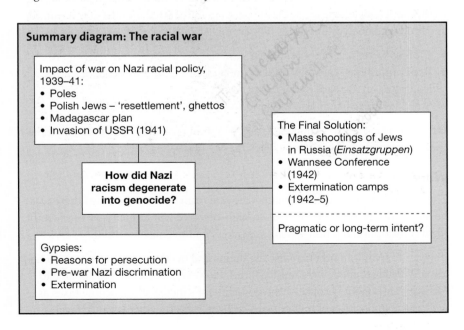

Summary diagram: The racial war

Impact of war on Nazi racial policy, 1939–41:
- Poles
- Polish Jews – 'resettlement', ghettos
- Madagascar plan
- Invasion of USSR (1941)

How did Nazi racism degenerate into genocide?

The Final Solution:
- Mass shootings of Jews in Russia (*Einsatzgruppen*)
- Wannsee Conference (1942)
- Extermination camps (1942–5)

Pragmatic or long-term intent?

Gypsies:
- Reasons for persecution
- Pre-war Nazi discrimination
- Extermination

The 'home front'

▶ *What was the impact of the war on the German people?*

The declaration of war in September 1939 was not met with the patriotic frenzy of August 1914. Rather, the mass of people seemed to be resigned and apprehensive. However, the German strategy of *Blitzkrieg* was incredibly successful and the victories of 1939–40 gave the impression of military and economic strength. Most of the people's doubts were, therefore, dispelled. On Hitler's return journey from France back to Berlin he was met by ecstatic crowds, the images of which were cleverly recorded in the newsreels.

Living standards

Despite the economic priorities for the military build-up, the Nazi economy was not really ready for a major war in 1939 (see pages 246–5). As a result, from the earliest days the Nazis had to prioritise and introduce the rationing of food, clothes and basics like soap and toilet paper. Still, the German population continued to be adequately fed – even up until early 1944 – with rations about ten per cent above the minimum calorific standard. However, the diet was very boring and restricted to such staples as bread and potatoes. In the last twelve months of the war food rationing led to real shortages (and real hunger by 1945).

Not surprisingly, the trade in consumer goods struggled from the very start. In the first two years furniture and clothing sales fell by 40 and 25 per cent, respectively. Coal was reserved for industrial production, which meant that there was less available for domestic heating. In the final months of the war, the situation worsened dramatically. For example:

- Clothes were in very short supply.
- Boots and shoes were also hard to find, because of the shortage of leather, leading to an increase in the use of wooden clogs.
- Small luxuries, like magazines and sweets, were also stopped.

Despite every attempt to make the ration system fair for all, the high demand for the above goods meant that the black market flourished.

Workers

The demand for labour had remained critical from the mid-1930s, so there was never a shortage of work. Workers in high-demand war industries were exempt from conscription but non-essential workers had to enlist for military service.

In order to maintain productivity, the bonus and overtime payments, which had initially been stopped, were reintroduced. However, workers were not able to feel any real benefit because of the government's increases in income taxes as well as the imposition of higher taxes on beer, tobacco, cinemas and travel.

From 1942 the demand for labour was extended when Speer directed the economy to focus on fighting a 'total war' (see pages 265–8). This created pressures:

- Working hours were increased from 52 hours in 1940 to 60 hours in 1944.
- Skilled labour became in serious shortage.
- Millions of foreign workers were mobilised to work (page 268).
- Non-essential businesses were closed in 1943 and all workers aged 16–65 had to register for vital work (which caused great resentment with the *Mittelstand*).

As circumstances from 1944 became more desperate there was a total ban on holidays, all bonuses were stopped and rewards were limited to just an increase in rations.

Peasantry

With the onset of the war in 1939 pressures on the peasantry developed in many ways. Young men were increasingly conscripted to the military fronts, which caused a growing shortage of agricultural labour. This necessitated the use of cheap forced labour from peasants from eastern Europe, for example Poles and Czechs, despite this conflicting with the Nazi view that these labourers were not racially acceptable. Although the rural communities complained of hardship because of the shortage of farm machinery and animal feed supplies, they were largely self-sufficient and did not suffer the same adversity and levels of bombing of those in the cities.

Women

In the early war years, the conscription of women to essential work was used sparingly. Indeed, because of the decline in consumer industries, the number of female workers actually decreased. Also, there was less incentive for women to work since families of conscripted soldiers received benefits.

Speer's aim to mobilise the economy for total war called for an increase in the conscription of women workers. However, Hitler himself wished to retain the traditional roles of women in order to maintain civilian morale. As a result, conscription for women aged 17–45 to work was introduced from 1943, but there were many exemptions, which limited the impact.

The Nazis were caught in the contradictions of their own ideology between the theory and practice of female employment. They were motivated by military expansionism which needed to employ women effectively, so, in the final two to three years of the Nazi state, more and more women ended up in work. Only in the last desperate twelve months of the war were women up to age of 50 conscripted, with many of them taking up auxiliary roles within the armed forces. By 1945 women comprised nearly 60 per cent of the workforce, but this only came about because of the decline in male workers.

With the unfolding of the war, greater pressure was put on women; with so many men away, they had to take on more responsibilities both in and out of the home. In the cities, long hours in arms factories made life very arduous, especially if women had to combine this with running a household and bringing up children. In the countryside, German women experienced considerable hardship meeting the continuous demands of running farms on their own. The shortage of agricultural labour had created major problems from the 1930s (see pages 221–2), but once the young men were sent away for military service, it got worse. Yet, the government could not bring itself to renounce fully its anti-feminist stance. As an official in the National Socialist Womanhood wrote, 'It has always been our chief article of faith that a woman's place is in the home – but since the whole of Germany is our home we must serve wherever we can best do so.'

Youth

The youth of Nazi Germany in the war was a very dislocated generation. The effects of evacuation, allied bombing and family losses all combined to take their toll on them emotionally and socially.

One main impact of the war on young people was the decline in education and academic standards – although this had already started in the late 1930s. Now, with the conscription of teachers to military service, there was a marked decline in the number and quality of teaching staff. Formal exams ceased in 1943 and by the end of 1944 any teaching in schools had all but petered out.

There was a general move in emphasis from learning to drill and discipline. With compulsory membership of the HJ in 1939 (see page 227), an even stronger focus on militarism was imposed on the youth. The age of military service was reduced to seventeen in 1943 and lowered again to sixteen in 1945. In addition, increasing numbers of teenagers were used for defence work such as manning anti-aircraft batteries. For young people there was no avoiding the increasing demands of war.

The German youth became increasingly polarised between those committed to the cause and the disaffected. Many of them were repelled by the regimentation and military training of the HJ and, as the war progressed, alienation set in. For a few, this disillusionment developed into the formation of counter-groups such as the Edelweiss Pirates (see page 228), but they remained a small minority.

Interestingly, a youth leader wrote in 1942 that 'the formation of cliques, i.e. groupings of young people outside the Hitler youth … has particularly increased during the war, to such a degree that a serious risk of the political, moral and criminal breakdown of youth must be said to exist'. The Nazi response became increasingly harsh. Various gangs were rounded up by the *Gestapo* and had their heads shaved. In some cases, young people were sent to camps – and most notoriously twelve Edelweiss Pirates were publicly hanged in Cologne.

SOURCE E

How does the photo in Source E portray mixed messages about the impact of the war on children?

By 1943 Allied bombing of German cities had increased to the level that children in cities were being encouraged to go to the countryside for safety. This photo shows a *Kinderlandverschickung* ('relocating children to the countryside') train leaving Berlin.

Morale and propaganda

The onset of the war underlined the totalitarian nature of the Nazi regime. Although the leadership no longer needed to show any regard for international approval, within Germany the Nazis remained very aware of public opinion and the importance of keeping up the nation's morale.

The early Nazi military victories were very easy to exploit as propaganda for the war. However, it became increasingly difficult for Nazi propaganda and censorship to disguise the reality of the situation from the winter of 1942–3. The German defeat at El Alamein was a significant loss, but the German surrender at Stalingrad was a strategic disaster and a damaging blow to the confidence of the German people.

An SD report highlighted the deepening cynicism in the nation about the political and military situation after Stalingrad: 'A large section of the nation cannot imagine how the war will end and the telling of vulgar jokes against the state, even about the *Führer* himself, has increased considerably since Stalingrad.'

Effects of bombing

The military defeats abroad, although demoralising, were at a distance for the people in Germany, but the Anglo-American bombing had a much more direct impact by bringing the war into their very homes. Certainly, one of the aims of the Allies in hitting the great urban centres day and night was to weaken morale.

In purely human terms, it is estimated that as a result of the air raids:

- 400,000 Germans were killed plus 60,000 foreign workers and prisoners of war
- 500,000 were disabled and severely injured
- 3.6 million homes were destroyed (twenty per cent of the total housing).

Most notably, on the night of 24 July 1943 a massive raid on Hamburg created a firestorm that killed 40,000 civilians. And more controversially, the bombing of Dresden on 13–15 February 1945, just twelve weeks before the end of the war, saw 1300 heavy bombers drop over 3900 tons of high-explosive bombs and incendiary devices, killing 35,000 and destroying 34 square kilometres (13 square miles) of the city.

The effects of the Allied bombing on German civilians (as opposed to the effects on industry, see pages 267–8) have been the subject of considerable discussion. Some historians have claimed that, despite the difficult circumstances faced by most Germans in the final two years of the war, there was no real sign of a decline in morale leading to the collapse of the regime itself. Indeed, in the face of Allied mass bombing many people came together against the enemy. H. Rumpf (1963) claims, 'Under the terrible blows of that terror from the skies the bonds grew closer and the spirit of solidarity stronger.' Nevertheless, morale was affected. Despite considerable efforts to counteract food shortages and repair the damage to housing, it became increasingly difficult for the government to withstand the cumulative effect of the sustained physical suffering and psychological trauma inflicted on the German people.

In response to these difficulties, Goebbels and his propaganda machine used all their skills. Hitler became more distant and instead Goebbels became the public face and voice of the Nazi regime. His famous speech on 18 February 1943 at the Berlin *Sportpalast* was in response to the surrender of Stalingrad – and a clear statement of defiance, which rallied the people for 'total war'. On the one hand, he used the multimedia approach of the Propaganda Ministry to appeal to all their emotions. The people were urged to:

- strive their very hardest
- resist all Germany's enemies
- endure all suffering.

On the other hand, Goebbels specifically used cinema to distract people from the realities of the war through fantasy action films such as *The Adventures of Baron Münchausen* and grand patriotic epics such as *Kolberg*, based on a historic German battle against Napoleon (see pages 216–17).

Despite Goebbels' efforts, from 1943 the reports from the SD began to show an escalation in grumbling and complaints, which illustrated the growing disaffection. People became increasingly resigned to the coming disaster. David Welch writes in his conclusion to *The Third Reich: Politics and Propaganda* (2002): 'The debacle of Stalingrad undoubtedly affected the morale of the German people. It forced them to question Nazi war aims and led to a crisis of confidence in the regime amongst broad sections of the population.' By autumn 1944 there had developed a growing atmosphere of doom because of the fear of the **Red Army** and the failure of special weapons like the **V-1 and V-2**. As a consequence, there was a significant loss of faith in the Nazi regime, but it was never really threatened from within.

KEY TERMS

Red Army The name given to the Soviet army created in 1917.

V-1 and V-2 The flying pilotless bombs and the long-range rocket developed by scientists in Germany. Used in air raids against Britain 1944–5.

SOURCE F

'One battle, one will, one goal: victory at any cost!' A propaganda poster from May 1942.

How does Goebbels' propaganda poster in Source F urge all German people to strive for total war?

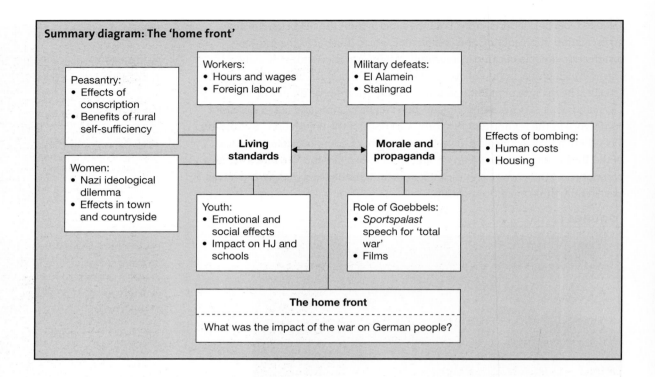

Summary diagram: The 'home front'

Peasantry:
• Effects of conscription
• Benefits of rural self-sufficiency

Women:
• Nazi ideological dilemma
• Effects in town and countryside

Workers:
• Hours and wages
• Foreign labour

Living standards

Youth:
• Emotional and social effects
• Impact on HJ and schools

Military defeats:
• El Alamein
• Stalingrad

Morale and propaganda

Effects of bombing:
• Human costs
• Housing

Role of Goebbels:
• *Sportspalast* speech for 'total war'
• Films

The home front

What was the impact of the war on German people?

(5) Resistance and repression

▶ *Who resisted the Nazi regime and why did they fail?*

'Active resistance' failed to topple Nazism and in the end the Third Reich was only destroyed when Germany was militarily defeated by the Allies. Those who set out to subvert the regime – however gloriously and heroically they have been portrayed – made enormous personal sacrifices without making any real impression on the Nazi stranglehold of power. The real question is: why did they fail?

Communists

Over half of KPD members were interned during the first year of Nazi rule and by 1935 the *Gestapo* had infiltrated the remains of the party, leading to a series of mass trials. Nevertheless, the communist movement was never entirely broken, but went underground. Small cells continued in many of the large German cities and they were particularly revived after the invasion of the USSR; examples of these were the Uhrig Group in Berlin and the Home Front in Hamburg. The most famous was the so-called ***Rote Kapelle***, a spy network which successfully infiltrated the government and military through Arvid Harnack and the aristocratic sympathiser Schulz-Boysen. The cell transmitted vital information back to Moscow and produced pamphlets attacking the Nazi government. However, the *Rote Kapelle,* along with many of the other cells, was destroyed by the *Gestapo* at the end of 1942.

The impact of the activities of German communists should not be overstated. They failed because:

- they took their orders from Moscow and were tainted by their association with Stalin and his purges of the 1930s
- they were seriously compromised by the period of co-operation between the Nazi government and the USSR as a result of the Nazi–Soviet Pact 1939–41
- even when the USSR and Germany did end up at war with each other in June 1941, the resistance groups remained very isolated.

Communist active resistance to the Nazi state was limited and in the end it really became more focused on self-preservation and preparation for the day when Nazism would be defeated and the Soviet 'liberation' could take place.

Christians

As Nazi persecution intensified from 1941, the evidence suggests that church attendance increased during the war and many individual churchmen put their own freedom and lives at risk in order to uphold their beliefs or to give pastoral assistance. It has been estimated that 40 per cent of the Catholic clergy and over 50 per cent of the Protestant pastors were harassed by the Nazis. The most damning opposition came from individual clerics rather than the religious institutions, and of these the most famous were:

- **Dietrich Bonhoeffer**. From the very start he was a consistent opponent of Nazism. However, by 1940 he had moved from religious dissent to political resistance, which brought him into direct contact with the conservative elites in the **Kreisau Circle** (see page 286). Over the next three years he helped Jews to emigrate and actively worked with the underground movement until he was picked up by the *Gestapo* in 1943.
- Bishop **von Galen of Münster**. He was a conservative, nationalist, aristocrat and a strong anti-communist, yet in the 1930s he began to have doubts about Nazi policy and the excesses of the *Gestapo*. He delivered three sermons in 1941, which condemned the Nazi euthanasia policy (see page 240). His attack proved so powerful with his congregations that the authorities recoiled from arresting him and actually stopped the programme.

Many individual Christians had doubts about Nazi ideology and their totalitarian aspirations. Indeed, a *Gauleiter* reported in June 1943:

> … *the war with all its sorrow and anguish has driven some families into the arms of the priests and the Church … in their weekly reports, the party regional organisations have repeatedly emphasised that the Churches of both confessions – but especially the Catholic Church – are in today's fateful struggle one of the main pillars of negative influence upon public morale.*

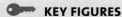

KEY FIGURES

Dietrich Bonhoeffer (1906–45)

Academic and pastor who joined the Confessional Church (see page 231). In 1940 he was banned from preaching and then made contact with the active resistance movement. Arrested by the *Gestapo* in 1943 and murdered in Flossenbürg concentration camp. An SS doctor wrote: 'in nearly 50 years as a doctor I never saw another man go to his death so possessed of the spirit of God'.

Clemens von Galen (1878–1946)

Bishop of Münster 1933–46 who became known as 'The Lion of Münster'. Made cardinal in 1945 and beatified in 2005.

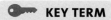

KEY TERM

Kreisau Circle Name given to the resistance group which met at the estates of Helmuth von Moltke.

But the Churches posed no real active threat to the strength of the regime. They were mainly concerned with self-preservation and maintaining their property and wealth and their power as institutions. There was no public condemnation of the Nazi genocide of the Jews.

Students: the White Rose group

The White Rose student resistance movement is probably the most famous of the youth groups because it went well beyond mere dissent. It was led by the brother and sister Hans and Sophie Scholl. *The White Rose* (the symbol of peace) was the title given to a series of leaflets printed in 1942–3; these were distributed initially among the students of Munich University but, in time, to many towns in central Germany. The content of the leaflets was highly political and openly condemned the moral and spiritual values of the Nazi regime. One of the early leaflets bore the headline: 'Isn't every decent German today ashamed of his government?'

The group represented a brave gesture of defiance and self-sacrifice. However, from the start the group's security was weak and it was only a matter of time before the *Gestapo* closed in. In February 1943 the six leaders were arrested, tortured and swiftly executed. Sophie Scholl openly said to the court: 'What we wrote and said is in the minds of you all. You just don't say it aloud.'

Conservative elites

It might seem surprising that the most influential active resistance emerged from the ranks of Germany's upper classes, who dominated the civil service and, most particularly, the officer corps. After all, these were the very same conservative nationalists who had initially given sympathetic backing to the Nazi dictatorship (see pages 162–71). The army as an institution was not fully 'co-ordinated' (until summer 1944) and therefore it enjoyed a degree of freedom from Nazi control. Moreover, with its access to arms, the military had the real capacity to resist. For these reasons, the development of the active resistance of the German elites formed around the army, although, like the other groups, it was to fail in its primary objective.

Kreisau Circle

There had been some opponents within the conservative elites from the late 1930s, for example, Beck (see page 254) and **Goerdeler**. In 1939–41 some army officers and foreign office officials became outraged by the criminality of the massacres and destruction on the Eastern Front. As a result, elements of an organised resistance began to emerge slowly from 1942 – and they were brought together by the military setbacks of winter 1942–3.

The so-called Kreisau Circle was a wide-ranging group of officers, aristocrats, academics and churchmen who met at the Kreisau estate of **Helmuth von Moltke**. The conferences discussed plans for a new Germany after Hitler and, in August 1943, a programme was drawn up in the 'Basic Principles for the New

KEY FIGURES

Carl Friedrich Goerdeler (1884–1945)

A conservative and monarchist member of the DNVP. He served as long-term mayor of Leipzig, but was forced to resign in 1937 and became a prominent opponent of Hitler. He was nominated by the Kreisau Circle to be the new chancellor if the Stauffenberg Plot succeeded.

Helmuth James Graf von Moltke (1907–45)

Great-nephew of Field Marshal Moltke, born at the family estates in Kreisau. A trained lawyer who refused to practise law in Nazi Germany, instead focused on international law. A leading member of the Kreisau Circle. Arrested, tortured and executed.

Order'. These principles were conservative and strongly influenced by Christian values, and called for:

- the principle of law
- the upholding of freedoms and civil rights
- the democratic integration of Germany into an interdependent Europe.

But behind these high principles there were many shades of opinion within the group about political constitution and the economy. Indeed, there were pacifist elements in the group who were even opposed to killing Hitler.

Stauffenberg Plot

By 1944 the *Gestapo* was aware of the existence of the circle and Moltke was arrested early in the year. Nevertheless, remaining members of the Kreisau Circle become supporters of the most daring act of resistance to Hitler's Germany: the Bomb Plot of 20 July 1944.

In this plot, a number of the civilian resistance figures approached dissident army officers, such as Beck and **Tresckow**, and schemed to assassinate Hitler and create a provisional government. Source G quotes the words of Tresckow just before the attempt.

SOURCE G

From a letter by Tresckow to Stauffenberg in July 1944, quoted in J. Fest, *Plotting Hitler's Death*, Weidenfeld & Nicolson, 1994, p. 236.

The assassination must take place, whatever the cost. Even if it should fail, the attempt to seize power in Berlin must take place. The practical consequences are immaterial. The German resistance must prove to the world and to posterity that it dares to take the decisive step.

The key figure in this plot was Colonel **von Stauffenberg**, who also came to believe that the assassination of Hitler was the only way to end the Nazi regime. He was an able and committed soldier who initially admired Hitler; however, his strong Catholic moral outlook raised increasing doubts about the regime by 1941. Initially, he was on the fringes of the Kreisau Circle, but he gave the resistance group a real purpose from early 1944 when he drew up the plan – codenamed Operation Valkyrie – to kill Hitler.

Stauffenberg took the personal responsibility to place the bomb in Hitler's briefing room at his headquarters in east Prussia on 20 July 1944. Unfortunately for the conspirators, the briefcase containing the bomb was moved a few metres away from the target just a minute before it exploded. Hitler consequently sustained only minor injuries. In the confused aftermath the generals in Berlin crucially hesitated, thus enabling a group of Hitler's loyal soldiers to arrest the conspirators and re-establish order. About 5000 supporters of the resistance were killed in the aftermath, including Stauffenberg, Beck, Tresckow, Rommel, Moltke and Goerdeler.

 KEY FIGURES

Henning von Tresckow (1901–44)

Army officer, but quickly disillusioned with Nazism and an opponent even before the war. Appalled by the atrocities on the Eastern Front and personally tried to kill Hitler with a bomb attempt on his plane. Killed himself the day after the failure of the Stauffenberg Plot.

Claus von Stauffenberg (1907–44)

Born in Bavaria of an aristocratic military family. Became lieutenant-colonel in the army and was badly injured in 1943. Drew up the plan to kill Hitler. After its failure on 20 July 1944 he was arrested and shot later the same evening.

 Why does Trescow claim in Source G that it was vital for the resistance to try to seize power?

Conclusion

The conservative elites proved incapable of fundamentally weakening the Nazi regime and in that sense their active resistance failed. Among the reasons for this are:

- They only recognised the need to resist the regime after the crucial developments of 1934 and 1938, by which time it was too well established.
- Because of the military oath the army was tied to the Nazi regime and its leader.
- Hitler's diplomatic and military successes in 1938–42 undoubtedly blinded the elites.
- Even after the 'turn of the tide' and the growing knowledge of brutal actions, the majority of army generals did not work with the resistance.
- Planning and organisation of effective resistance was always fraught with difficulties. The long-term political aims of the conservative elites lacked clarity. Their practical plans were inhibited by the environment of suspicion of the police state.

In the end, the bad luck and confusion of the Bomb Plot of 20 July became a symbol of the doomed nature of the resistance of the elites.

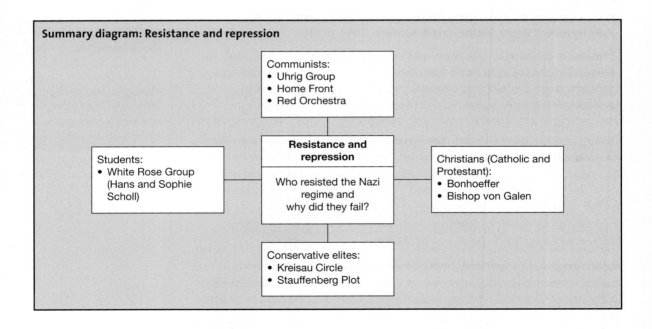

Summary diagram: Resistance and repression

Communists:
- Uhrig Group
- Home Front
- Red Orchestra

Students:
- White Rose Group (Hans and Sophie Scholl)

Resistance and repression

Who resisted the Nazi regime and why did they fail?

Christians (Catholic and Protestant):
- Bonhoeffer
- Bishop von Galen

Conservative elites:
- Kreisau Circle
- Stauffenberg Plot

6 'Zero hour': Germany in 1945

▶ *Why did Germany lose the war?*

▶ *How serious was Germany's condition in 1945?*

By May 1945 Germany lay in ruins. Nazi foreign policy had reached its destructive conclusion. Its ambitions had been extensive:

- To establish a 'Greater Germany', which went well beyond Germany's 1914 frontiers.
- To destroy Soviet Russia.
- To create a new order based on the concept of Aryan racial supremacy.

The means to these ends had involved the acceptance of violence and bloodshed on a massive scale.

On a superficial level, Hitler's final failure in his ambitions could be explained by his strategic bungling. It should be stressed that Hitler had always believed (along with most generals going back to Imperial Germany) that a war on two fronts had to be avoided. To this end, he needed an alliance with Britain and/ or France – or at least their neutrality – so that he could be free to launch an unrestrained attack in the east. Consequently, when Germany failed to secure either British neutrality or a British surrender in 1940–1, before attacking the USSR, the foundations for defeat were laid.

Germany had become engaged in a conflict for which it was not fully prepared. As has been seen on pages 198–9 and 264–8, at the start of the war Germany did not exploit fully the available resources and manpower. The alliance with Mussolini's Italy was also of little gain. Indeed, Italian military weakness in the Balkans and North Africa proved costly, since it diverted German forces away from the main European fronts. Yet, Hitler was driven on ideologically to launch an attack on the USSR with another *Blitzkrieg*.

The failure to defeat the USSR before the onset of winter in 1941, combined with the entry of the USA into the war, now tipped the balance. Britain was still free to act as a launch pad for a Western Front and also, in the meantime, could strike into the heart of Germany by means of aerial bombing. The USSR could maintain the Eastern Front by relying on its geography and sacrificing its huge manpower. As the Soviet leader Stalin recognised, the Allied victory could be summarised in his words: 'Britain gave the time; America the money; and Russia the blood.'

Hitler had militarily misjudged the antagonists, and now all the resources and the industrial capacity of the world's two political giants were directed towards the military defeat of Germany.

The following economic factors counted against Germany:

- The Four-Year Plan. In 1936 it was meant to make the country 'fit for war within four years', but the German economy was not really ready for a long war in 1939. Its capacity was only strong enough to sustain a couple of short campaigns.
- Anglo-American bombing. German industry peaked in the production of weapons in summer 1944, yet the German armed forces could not fully benefit from this because of the detrimental effects of Allied air raids.
- Shortage of labour. From the start Germany was short of labour. Millions of workers were required to keep up the industrial and agricultural production, and the gaps were only partially filled by forced labourers and an increase in female employment.
- Germany was deeply in debt. The reserves in gold and foreign currencies were almost completely used up by 1939 and the Nazi state had run up a debt of roughly 42 billion *Reichsmarks*.
- The power of the US economy. The USA was just too powerful. In 1944 the ratio of Germany's fuel supply compared to the supply of the Western Allies was one to three. The USA sent massive support to the Allies, especially to the USSR, which received 13,000 tanks and 15,000 planes.
- Soviet resources. The Soviet economy had undergone a ruthless industrialisation programme in the 1930s under Stalin and despite its limitations, Russia had vast resources of people and raw materials, for example oil, coal and iron.

These are all important contributory factors, but ultimately it was Hitler's strategic errors that led to Germany's defeat, not a lack of military preparedness or economic strains.

Such explanations might make historical analysis of Germany's defeat in the Second World War seem like a relatively straightforward exercise. However, before accepting such a simple view, it should be borne in mind that, even in 1942, Germany came very close indeed to capturing Stalingrad and to defeating Britain in Egypt. Such successes would have changed the course of the war and the final outcome might have been very different.

Germany in 1945

In the weeks before the capital fell to the Soviets, a typical Berliner's joke began to circulate: 'Enjoy the war while you can! The peace is going to be terrible.'

The German state had ceased to exist by May 1945. Hitler and Goebbels and a number of other Nazi leaders had killed themselves, while others had fled or been captured and arrested. Therefore, central government had broken down. Germany and Berlin had been divided by the Allies into four zones, each one with its own military commander giving orders and guidelines for the local economy and administration.

In the short term, the most telling problem facing Germany in that spring was the extent of the social and economic crisis.

Population displacement

At the end of the war it is estimated that one in two Germans were on the move:

- roughly 12 million German refugees fleeing from the east to the west
- 10 million of the so-called 'displaced persons', who had carried out forced labour or had been prisoners in the various Nazi camps
- over 11 million German soldiers, who had been taken as prisoners of war: 7.7 million in camps in the west were soon released, whereas the 3.3 million in the USSR were kept in captivity until the 1950s, of whom one-third did not survive.

All these people posed a serious problem to the British and the Americans because of the lack of food.

Urban destruction

Major German cities, especially Cologne, Hamburg and Berlin, had been reduced to rubble because of Anglo-American bombing and Soviet artillery firing (see the photograph on page 269). Twenty per cent of housing had been completely destroyed and a further 30 per cent badly damaged, which led many to take refuge in sheltered accommodation or to escape to the countryside.

Food and fuel shortages

Access to food was the immediate problem, and this was soon to be exacerbated with the onset of winter at the end of 1945. The average recommended daily calorie consumption of 2000 calories sank to 950–1150 and, if it had not been for emergency relief from the Western Allies and care parcels from charities, starvation would have been far worse. This level of malnourishment led to illnesses such as typhus, diphtheria and whooping cough.

Economic dislocation

Surprisingly, the economy had not completely collapsed, but it was very badly dislocated. Industrial capacity had obviously declined dramatically. Moreover, the infrastructure of bridges and railways and the utilities, like gas and water, had broken down during the end of the war. Also, the state had massive debts, so Germany was once again facing the problem of rising inflation causing a major black market in the supply of food and other goods.

The Third Reich had been destroyed in May 1945, but that left Germany in ruins. Violence, destruction and dislocation had brought it to **zero hour**.

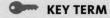 **KEY TERM**

Zero hour Used in German society to describe Germany's overall collapse at the end of the Second World War.

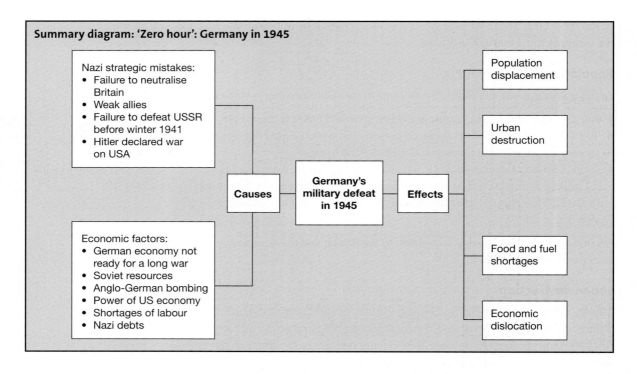

Summary diagram: 'Zero hour': Germany in 1945

Nazi strategic mistakes:
- Failure to neutralise Britain
- Weak allies
- Failure to defeat USSR before winter 1941
- Hitler declared war on USA

Economic factors:
- German economy not ready for a long war
- Soviet resources
- Anglo-German bombing
- Power of US economy
- Shortages of labour
- Nazi debts

Causes → Germany's military defeat in 1945 → Effects

Population displacement

Urban destruction

Food and fuel shortages

Economic dislocation

7 Key debate

▶ *Why did the Holocaust happen and who was responsible?*

The issue of the Holocaust remains one of the most fundamental controversies in history. The detached rational objectivity required of historical analysis is exceedingly difficult to achieve when the subject is so emotive, and in many respects so inexplicable.

Hitler's responsibility: his grand design

For intentionalist historians, Hitler is the key to our understanding of the Final Solution. Indeed, for those upholding the most extreme position, such as G. Fleming and L. Dawidowicz, Hitler is seen as having been committed to the extermination of the Jews at an early stage in his political career. This commitment was followed by a consistent gradualist policy which led systematically from the persecution of 1933 to the gates of Auschwitz. In the simplest explanation, they suggest that the Holocaust happened because Hitler willed it. Dawidowicz writes of Hitler's 'long-term plans to realise his ideological goals' with the destruction of the Jews. She concludes: 'Through a maze of time, Hitler's decision of November 1918 led to Operation Barbarossa. There never had been any ideological deviation or wavering. In the end only the question of opportunity mattered'.

There are more moderate intentionalists, who resist the idea of a long-term Hitlerian plan. They still believe that Hitler was the driving force behind Nazi anti-Semitic policy, but do question whether he had a strategy from the outset for a Final Solution. Saul Friedländer gives his view in Extract 1.

EXTRACT 1

From Saul Friedländer, *Nazi Germany and the Jews*, Harper Perennial, 1998, p. 3.

In all its major decisions the regime depended on Hitler. Especially, with regard to the Jews, Hitler was driven by ideological obsessions that were anything but the calculated devices of a demagogue; that is, he carried a very specific brand of racial anti-Semitism to its most extreme and radical limits. I call that distinctive aspect of his worldview 'redemptive anti-Semitism' … It was this redemptive dimension, this synthesis of a murderous rage and an 'idealistic' goal, shared by the Nazi leader and the hard core of the party, that led to Hitler's ultimate decision to exterminate the Jews.

> In what ways does Friedländer in Extract 1 claim that Hitler shaped the Nazi Final Solution of the Jews?

Additionally, P. Burrinin, writing in 1989, interestingly poses the question: 'If Hitler had died in the summer of 1941, would the Final Solution have taken place?' He concludes: 'Without him, the decisive thrust would probably have been absent.'

The pressure of circumstances: no master plan

On the other hand, historians of the structuralist school (also called functionalist) emphasise the unsystematic nature of Nazi policies as unclear responses to a disorderly government. According to the structuralist interpretation, the moral responsibility for the Final Solution extends beyond Hitler to include the whole apparatus of the regime.

Most notably, K. Schleunes, writing in 1970, has suggested that there was no direct path because of the existence of rival policies and the lack of clear objectives. He describes the road to Auschwitz as a 'twisted one' and concludes that 'the Final Solution as it emerged in 1941 and 1942 was not the product of a grand design.' Instead, from 1941 it came to be implemented as a result of the chaotic nature of government within the regime. Various institutions and individuals were responsible for developing the improvised policy which would deal with the military and human situation in eastern Europe by the end of 1941.

Obviously, that approach has led to claims of abnegating of individuals' responsibility. But nearly all structuralist historians have been keen to emphasise that this in no way reduces the guilt of Hitler himself, who was in total agreement with such a policy. For example, H. Mommsen concludes his analysis as follows (Extract 2, page 294).

How does Mommsen in
Extract 2 explain the
political process which led
to the Final Solution?

EXTRACT 2

From 'The Realization of the Unthinkable. The Final Solution of the Jewish Question in the Third Reich', in H. Mommsen, *From Weimar to Auschwitz*, Oxford University Press, 1991, p. 224.

It cannot be proved, for instance, that Hitler himself gave the order for the Final Solution, though this does not mean that he did not approve the policy. That the solution was put into effect is by no means to be ascribed to Hitler alone, but to the complexity of the decision-making process in the Third Reich, which brought about a progressive and cumulative radicalisation.

The Germans: ordinary people

Some historians have taken the structuralist interpretation a lot further and have adopted a more 'bottom-up' approach to explaining the Holocaust. They go as far as claiming that the Nazi leadership had little to do with starting the Holocaust and that the real initiative came from other groups. Götz Aly, writing in 1999, for example, has focused on the role of the German Army in instigating genocidal crimes (as opposed to the SS). He also highlighted the involvement of the broader government bureaucracy as 'a planning intelligentsia' and even the financial banking sector in driving anti-Semitic policy.

Even more controversially, the US historian Daniel Goldhagen has recently suggested in his book *Hitler's Willing Executioners* (1996) that the Holocaust was 'intended' by the ordinary German people because so many were prepared to participate in the Third Reich's darkest deed. This is explained, according to Goldhagen, by the fact that within German culture there had developed a violent variant of anti-Semitism in the Nazi years which was set on eliminating the Jews. Such a view has resurrected the old argument of 'collective national guilt and shame'.

How convincing is
Goldhagen's
interpretation in Extract 3?

EXTRACT 3

Daniel Goldhagen, *Hitler's Willing Executioners*, Little, Brown, 1996, pp. 416–18.

The study of the men and women who collectively gave life to the inert institutional forms, who peopled the institutions of genocidal killing must be set as the focus of scholarship on the Holocaust and become as central to the investigations of the genocide as they were to its commission.

These people were overwhelmingly and most importantly Germans. … this was above all a German enterprise; the decisions, plans, organisational resources, and the majority of its executors were German. Comprehension and explanation of the perpetration of the Holocaust therefore requires an explanation of the Germans' drive to kill Jews. Because what can be said about the German cannot be said about any other nationality or about all of the other nationalities – namely no German, no Holocaust – the focus here is appropriately on the German perpetrators.

In academic circles Goldhagen's ideas have not been generally well received. He has been condemned for:

- selecting his evidence to prove his thesis
- failing to recognise other overtly anti-Semitic cultures in pre-1933 Europe
- ignoring the role of many non-Germans in the murder of the Jews.

Structuralists have distanced themselves from Goldhagen's view because they cannot accept the anti-German generalisations. Christopher Browning explains that for the majority of the young men in the *Einsatzgruppen* and in the camps, their actions were motivated not by any kind of zealous anti-Semitism, but by much more mundane factors. In his chilling description 'One Day in Jozefow', in his book *The Path to Genocide: Essays on Launching the Final Solution* (1995), Browning detailed how one unit carried out its grim task. What emerges is that the perpetrators were influenced mainly by peer pressure, cowardice, careerism and alcohol – all exaggerated by the brutalising context which was entirely alien to their home environment.

In his very broad conceptual overview of Nazism, M. Burleigh has distanced himself from the structuralist interpretation of chaotic government. Although in his book *The Third Reich: A New History* (2001) he still portrays Hitler as a messianic leader who guided the movement, he also emphasises that the Holocaust was the direct result of the ideology of the *Volksgemeinschaft* utopia. In his interpretation he replaces the term 'class' with 'race' and shows how the Nazi policies on eugenics and euthanasia, the action against asocials and homosexuals, and the introduction of forced labour all combined to create an ideological justification for the Final Solution. By interpreting Nazism as a 'political religion', the Final Solution can be seen as a result of the 'moral force and consensual climate' of Germany.

Chapter summary

Despite the increasing military difficulties from 1942, the German resistance made no more impact than a few brave gestures. It was divided, with ineffective leadership. Still, there was a marked increase in dissent from 1943 in the wake of shortages and bombing, although the Nazi regime was never seriously threatened from within. In any case, all shades of opposition were dealt with brutally. It was only the Allies' military occupation that ultimately destroyed the Third Reich in 1945. The war economy was not effectively mobilised at first, and even Speer's reforms did not solve the fundamental problems of labour and resource shortages. The Nazi racial war was the result of ideology and 1930s' policies, but the Final Solution was not really premeditated: it was more a pragmatic response to the pressures and the desire of key forces to satisfy Hitler's vision.

Refresher questions

Use these questions to remind yourself of the key material covered in this chapter.

1 Why was Germany so militarily successful in 1939–41?

2 When and why did the military balance turn against Germany?

3 How effectively did the German economy expand in the early years of the war?

4 To what extent did the Nazis fail to mobilise the economy to the demands of 'total war'?

5 When and how did Nazi anti-Semitism degenerate into genocide?

6 Why were Gypsies persecuted?

7 How did the war affect people's living and working conditions?

8 Why did the war put particular pressure on German women?

9 How did the war change German people's attitudes?

10 Why was active communist resistance to the Nazi state so limited?

11 Did the resistance of Christians and the students achieve anything?

12 Why did 'active resistance' fail to undermine the Third Reich?

13 Why has Germany in 1945 been described as being at 'zero hour'?

 Question practice

ESSAY QUESTIONS

1 'The handling of the economy was poorly co-ordinated and this accounts for the weaknesses in German war production in the years 1939–45.' Assess the validity of this view.

2 'The systematic extermination of the Jews was the result of Hitler's personal obsessive anti-Semitism.' Assess the validity of this view.

3 How seriously did the German opposition threaten to destabilise the Nazi regime during the war?

4 To what extent was German civilian morale weakened on the 'home front'?

SOURCE ANALYSIS QUESTION

1 With reference to Sources 1, 2 and 3 (page 297), and your understanding of the historical context, assess the value of these sources to a historian studying the significance of the divisions between the opposition groups in Nazi Germany.

SOURCE 1

From part of a draft constitution drawn up by C. Goerdeler in September 1944 while in prison following the Bomb Plot, quoted in J.C.G. Röhl, *From Bismarck to Hitler*, Longman, 1970, p. 170.

It seems to me that a hereditary monarchy is the form of state for our people. Our fickle, unpolitical people needs ballast in the ship of state. The monarch shall not govern but shall watch over the constitution and represent the state. The House of Hohenzollern and the House of Wittelsbach could provide worthy monarchs … If it is not possible to put a monarchy in the saddle, then things have to remain with a Reichspresident *who must be eligible for unlimited re-election and who after his election for the third time can also be elected for life.*

SOURCE 2

From the programme of the Kreisau Circle in 1943, quoted in J.C.G. Röhl, *From Bismarck to Hitler*, Longman, 1970, p. 170.

The government of the German Reich sees in Christianity the basis for the ethical and religious revival of our people, for the conquest of hatred and lies, for the creation anew of the European community of people …

1. Justice, fallen and trampled, must be restored, and must be made supreme over all orders of human life. This justice, under the protection of conscientious, independent judges who are free from fear of men, will be the basis for the future moulding of peace.

2. Freedom of faith and conscience is guaranteed.

3. The right of work and property stands under public protection without regard to race, nationality or creed.

4. The basic unit of peaceful community life is the family.

5. Work must be arranged in such a way that it fosters rather than stunts the enjoyment of personal responsibility.

6. The personal political responsibility of everyone requires his co-determining participation in the self-administration of the small communities.

SOURCE 3

From a draft of an oath drawn up by Stauffenberg shortly before his death, quoted in J.C.G. Röhl, *From Bismarck to Hitler*, Longman, 1970, p. 165.

We desire a new order that makes all Germans the bearers of the state and guarantees to them law and justice; but we despise the lie of equality and bow before the ranks created by nature. We desire a people that, rooted in the soil of their homeland, remains close to the natural forces, that finds happiness and satisfaction in working within its given spheres … We desire leaders who, drawn from all ranks of the people, and linked with the divine powers, rise above all by their discipline and sacrifice.

AQA A-level History

Essay guidance

At both AS and A-level for AQA Component 2: Depth Study: Democracy and Nazism: Germany, 1918–1945, you will need to answer an essay question in the exam. Each essay question is marked out of 25:

- for the AS exam, Section B: answer one essay question from a choice of two
- for the A-level exam, Section B: answer two essay questions from a choice of three.

There are several question stems which all have the same basic requirement: to analyse and reach a conclusion, based on the evidence you provide.

The AS questions often give a quotation and then ask whether you agree or disagree with this view. Almost inevitably, your answer will be a mixture of both. It is the same task as for A-level – just phrased differently in the question. Detailed essays are more likely to do well than vague or generalised essays, especially in the Depth Studies of Paper 2.

The AQA mark scheme is essentially the same for AS and the full A-level (see the AQA website, www.aqa.org.uk). Both emphasise the need to analyse and evaluate the key features related to the periods studied. The key feature of the highest level is sustained analysis: analysis that unites the whole of the essay.

Writing an essay: general skills

- *Focus and structure.* Be sure what the question is asking and plan what the paragraphs should be about.
- *Focused introduction to the essay.* Be sure that the introductory sentence relates directly to the focus of the question and that each paragraph highlights the structure of the answer.
- *Use detail.* Make sure that you show detailed knowledge – but only as part of an explanation being made in relation to the question. No

knowledge should be standalone; it should be used in context.
- *Explanatory analysis and evaluation.* Consider what words and phrases to use in an answer to strengthen the explanation.
- *Argument and counter-argument.* Think of how arguments can be juxtaposed as part of a balancing act to give contrasting views.
- *Resolution.* Think how best to 'resolve' contradictory arguments.
- *Relative significance and evaluation.* Think how best to reach a judgement when trying to assess the relative importance of various factors, and their possible interrelationship.

Planning an essay

Practice question

To what extent did Hitler and the Nazi regime rely on terror to consolidate their hold on power in the years 1933–4?

This question requires you to analyse how and why the Nazi regime was able to consolidate its power. You must discuss:

- How the use of terror enabled the Nazis to strengthen their position of power (your primary focus).
- The other factors that allowed this to happen (your secondary focus).

A clear structure makes for a much more effective essay and is crucial for achieving the highest marks. You need three or four paragraphs to structure this question effectively. In each paragraph you will deal with one factor. One of these *must* be the factor in the question.

A very basic plan for this question might look like this:

- Paragraph 1: the impact of the use of terror.
- Paragraph 2: other factors used by the Nazis during 1933–4, such as propaganda and the legal system.

- Paragraph 3: the weakness of the opposition against the Nazis and the sympathy of other elements, such as the conservative elites.

It is a good idea to cover the factor named in the question first, so that you don't run out of time and forget to do it. Then cover the others in what you think is their order of importance, or in the order that appears logical in terms of the sequence of paragraphs.

The introduction

Maintaining focus is vital. One way to do this from the beginning of your essay is to use the words in the question to help write your argument. The first sentence of your answer to question 1, for example, could look like this:

The Nazis were successful in consolidating their power in 1933–4 partly because of the use of terror, but there were other factors as well to explain this.

This opening sentence provides a clear focus on the demands of the question, although it could, of course, be written in a more exciting style.

Focus throughout the essay

Structuring your essay well will help with keeping the focus of your essay on the question. To maintain a focus on the wording in question 1, you could begin your first main paragraph like this:

The use of terror by the Nazis was one very important factor which enabled the regime to consolidate its power.

- This sentence begins with a clear point that refers to the primary focus of the question (the Nazi consolidation of power) while linking it to a factor (the use of terror).
- You could then have a paragraph for each of your other factors.
- It will be important to make sure that each paragraph focuses on analysis and includes relevant details that are used as part of the argument.

- You may wish to number your factors. This helps to make your structure clear and helps you to maintain focus.

Deploying detail

As well as focus and structure, your essay will be judged on the extent to which it includes accurate detail. There are several different kinds of evidence you could use that might be described as detailed. These include correct dates, names of relevant people, statistics and events. For example, for sample question 1 you could use terms such as Potsdam Day (21 March 1933) and the Enabling Law (23 March 1933). You can also make your essays more detailed by using the correct technical vocabulary.

Analysis and explanation

'Analysis' covers a variety of high-level skills including explanation and evaluation; in essence, it means breaking down something complex into smaller parts. A clear structure which breaks down a complex question into a series of paragraphs is the first step towards writing an analytical essay. The purpose of explanation is to account for why something happened, or why something is true or false. An explanatory statement requires two parts: a *claim* and a *justification*.

For example, for question 1, you might want to argue that one important reason was that the Night of the Long Knives stabilised Hitler's position. Once you have made your point, and supported it with relevant detail, you can then explain how this answers the question. For example, you could conclude your paragraph like this:

So Hitler's decision to launch the purge on 30 June 1934 was important[1] because[2] it eliminated the SA as a political and military force. In addition, it meant that the army had aligned itself with the Nazi regime, and had accepted Hitler's personal supremacy.

1. The first part of this sentence is the claim while the second part justifies the claim.
2. 'Because' is a very important word to use when writing an explanation, as it shows the relationship between the claim and the justification.

Evaluation

Evaluation means considering the importance of two or more different factors, weighing them against each other, and reaching a judgement. This is a good skill to use at the end of an essay because the conclusion should reach a judgement which answers the question. Your conclusion to question 1 might read:

Clearly, the use of terror enabled Hitler and the Nazi leadership to weaken potential opponents, especially the left. However, they also resorted to the use of the law and propaganda. Moreover, they gained sympathy and support from the conservative elites, like the army. Therefore, although terror helped to consolidate the Nazi regime, its use was not enough to explain the creation of a one-party dictatorship.

Words like 'however' and 'therefore' are helpful to contrast the importance of the different factors.

Complex essay writing: argument and counter-argument

Essays that develop a good argument are more likely to reach the highest levels. This is because argumentative essays are much more likely to develop sustained analysis. As you know, your essays are judged on the extent to which they analyse.

After setting up an argument in your introduction, you should develop it throughout the essay. One way of doing this is to adopt an argument–counter-argument structure. A counter-argument is one that disagrees with the main argument of the essay. This is a good way of evaluating the importance of the different factors that you discuss. Essays of this type will develop an argument in one paragraph and then set out an opposing argument in another paragraph. Sometimes this will include juxtaposing the differing views of historians on a topic.

Good essays will analyse the key issues. They will probably have a clear piece of analysis at the end of each paragraph. While this analysis might be good, it will generally relate only to the issue discussed in that paragraph.

Excellent essays will be analytical throughout. As well as the analysis of each factor discussed above, there will be an overall analysis. This will run throughout the essay and can be achieved through developing a clear, relevant and coherent argument.

A good way of achieving sustained analysis is to consider which factor is most important.

Here is an example of an introduction that sets out an argument for question 1:

Although Hitler had been appointed as chancellor on 30 January 1933, his political position was not secure[1]. So the Nazis did use terror to weaken their opposition, however, this was not the only means by which they consolidated their power during 1933–4[2]. They also resorted to the media for propaganda and used the German legal system to change the constitution. But the most important reason for Nazi success was the way the conservative elites worked with Hitler[3].

1 The introduction begins with a claim.
2 The introduction continues with another reason.
3 Concludes with an outline argument of the most important reason.

- This introduction focuses on the question and sets out the key factors that the essay will develop.
- It introduces an argument about which factor was most significant.
- However, it also sets out an argument that can then be developed throughout each paragraph, and is rounded off with an overall judgement in the conclusion.

Complex essay writing: resolution and relative significance

Having written an essay that explains argument and counter-arguments, you should then resolve the tension between the argument and the counter-argument in your conclusion. It is important that the writing is precise and summarises the arguments made in the main body of the essay. You need to reach a supported overall judgement. One very appropriate way to do this is by evaluating the relative significance of different factors, in the light of valid criteria. Relative significance means how important one factor is compared to another.

The best essays will always make a judgement about which was most important based on valid criteria. These can be very simple, and will depend on the topic and the exact question.

The following criteria are often useful:

- Duration: which factor was important for the longest amount of time?
- Scope: which factor affected the most people?
- Effectiveness: which factor achieved most?
- Impact: which factor led to the most fundamental change?

As an example, you could compare the factors in terms of their duration and their impact. A conclusion that follows this advice should be capable of reaching a high level (if written, in full, with appropriate details) because it reaches an overall judgement that is supported through evaluating the relative significance of different factors in the light of valid criteria.

Having written an introduction and the main body of an essay for question 1, a concluding paragraph that aims to meet the exacting criteria for reaching a complex judgement could look like this:

Thus, the reasons for Nazi consolidation of power in 1933–4 were complex with several interrelated factors. Success was not guaranteed; indeed, a military coup against Hitler remained a possibility until the Night of the Long Knives. So, the Nazis did indeed blatantly exploit the use of terror to intimidate the opposition, especially the weak and divided left. Goebbels used his propaganda skills to improve the Nazi image to broaden national support. And, very effectively, the Nazi leadership exploited the German law to bring about a 'legal revolution' (Bracher). This combination of intimidation through terror, deception and legitimisation of Nazi actions succeeded in satisfying the conservative elites like the army and the civil service. In that way, on the death of Hindenburg, Hitler was formally created the Führer of a one-party state.

Sources guidance

Whether you are taking the AS exam or the full A-level exam for AQA Component 2: Depth Study: Democracy and Nazism: Germany, 1918–1945, Section A presents you with sources and a question which involves evaluation of their utility or value.

AS exam	A-level exam
Section A: answer question 1, based on two primary sources. (25 marks)	Section A: answer question 1, based on three primary sources. (30 marks)
Question focus: with reference to these sources, and your understanding of the historical context, which of these two sources is more valuable in explaining … ?	Question focus: with reference to these sources, and your understanding of the historical context, assess the value of these three sources to a historian studying …

Study the sources. They are all concerned with the events in 1932–3 leading up to the appointment of Hitler as chancellor on 30 January 1933.

SOURCE I

From a report by Dr Wilhelm Külz following the election of July 1932. He was a member of the DDP and had been minister of the interior in 1926. Quoted in J.W. Hiden, *The Weimar Republic*, Longman, 1974, pp. 101–2.

Looked at politically, objectively, the result of the election is so fearful because it seems that the present election will be the last normal Reichstag *election for a long time to come … The elected* Reichstag *is totally incapable of functioning …*

The one consolation could be the recognition that the National Socialists have passed their peak … but against this stands the fact that radicalism of the right has unleashed a strong radicalism on the left. The communists have made gains almost *everywhere and these internal political disturbances have become exceptionally bitter. If things are faced squarely and soberly the situation is such that more than half the German people have declared themselves against the present state, but have not said what sort of state they would accept. Thus, any organic development is for the moment impossible. As the lesser of many evils to be feared, I think, would be the open assumption of dictatorship by the present government.*

SOURCE 2

From a letter sent by industrialists to President Hindenburg in November 1932, quoted in C. Hinton and J. Hite, *Weimar and Nazi Germany*, John Murray, 2000, p. 143.

The outcome of the Reichstag *had demonstrated that the present cabinet … has failed to find sufficient support among the German people for its actual policies … It is quite apparent that another dissolution of parliament leading to yet another general election with its inevitable frenzied party-political struggles would be harmful to political as well as economic peace and stability. But it is also apparent that any constitutional change that does not have widespread popular support would have even greater negative economic, political and moral effects. We therefore* *consider it to be our duty, Your Excellency, to humbly beg you to consider reconstituting the cabinet in a manner which would guarantee it with the greatest possible popular support. We demand ourselves to be free from any specific party-political interests. But we recognise in the nationalist movement, which is sweeping through our people, the auspicious beginnings of an era of rebirth for the German economy which can only be achieved by surmounting class conflict. We greet Your Excellency with the greatest respect Bosch, Schacht, Thyssen, Krupp (and 20 other industrialists)*

SOURCE 3

From evidence to the Nuremberg trial in 1946 by Otto Meissner, state secretary to the president, quoted in J. Noakes and G. Pridham, editors, *Nazism 1919–45*, volume 1, Liverpool University Press, 1988, pp. 117–18.

Schleicher came to Hindenburg with a demand for emergency powers as a prerequisite of action against the Nazis. Furthermore, he believed it necessary to dissolve, and even temporarily eliminate, the Reichstag, and this was to be done by presidential decrees on the basis of Article 48 – the transformation of his government into a military dictatorship … Schleicher first made these suggestions to Hindenburg in the middle of January

1933, but Hindenburg at once evinced grave doubts as to its constitutionality. In the meantime von Papen had returned to Berlin, and by arrangement with Hindenburg's son had had several interviews with the President. When Schleicher renewed his demands for emergency powers, Hindenburg declared that he was unable to give him such a blank cheque and must reserve to himself decisions on every individual case.

AS style question

With reference to Sources 1 and 2, and your understanding of the historical context, which of these two sources is more valuable in explaining why Germany was politically unstable in 1932?

A-level style question

With reference to the Sources 1, 2 and 3, and your understanding of the historical context, assess the value of these sources to a historian studying the reasons for the intrigue leading to the appointment of Hitler as chancellor.

AS mark scheme

See the AQA website (www.aqa.org.uk) for the full mark schemes. This summary of the AS mark scheme shows how it rewards analysis and evaluation of the source material within the historical context.

Level 1	Describing the source content or offering generic phrases.
Level 2	Some relevant but limited comments on the value of one source or some limited comment on both.
Level 3	Some relevant comments on the value of the sources and some explicit reference to the issue identified in the question.
Level 4	Relevant well-supported comments on the value and a supported conclusion, but with limited judgement.
Level 5	Very good understanding of the value in relation to the issue identified. Sources evaluated thoroughly and with a well-substantiated conclusion related to which is more valuable.

A-level mark scheme

This summary of the A-level mark scheme shows how it is similar to the AS one, but covers three sources. Also the wording of the question means that there is no explicit requirement to decide which of the three sources is the most valuable. Concentrate instead on a very thorough analysis of the content and evaluation of the provenance of each source, using contextual knowledge.

Level 1	Some limited comment on the value of at least one source.
Level 2	Some limited comments on the value of the sources or on content or provenance or comments on all three sources but no reference to the value of the sources.
Level 3	Some understanding of all three sources in relation to both content and provenance, with some historical context; but analysis limited.
Level 4	Good understanding of all three sources in relation to content, provenance and historical context to give a balanced argument on their value for the purpose specified in the question.
Level 5	As Level 4, but with a substantiated judgement.

Working towards an answer

It is important that knowledge is used to show an understanding of the relationship between the sources and the issue raised in the question. Answers should be concerned with the following:

- provenance
- arguments used (and you can agree/disagree)
- tone and emphasis of the sources.

The sources

The two or three sources used each time will be contemporary – probably of varying types (for example, diaries, newspaper accounts, government reports). The sources will all be on the same broad topic area. Each source will have value and your task is to evaluate how much value in terms of its content and its provenance.

You will need to assess the *value of the content* by using your own knowledge. Is the information accurate? Is it giving only part of the evidence and ignoring other aspects? Is the tone of the writing significant?

You will need to evaluate the *provenance* of the source by considering who wrote it, and when, where and why. What was its purpose? Was it produced to express an opinion; to record facts; to influence the opinion of others? Even if it was intended to be accurate, the writer may have been biased – either deliberately or unconsciously. The writer, for example, might have only known part of the situation and reached a judgement solely based on that.

Here is a guide to analysing the provenance, content and tone for Sources 1, 2 and 3.

Analysing the sources

To answer the question effectively, you need to read the sources carefully and pull out the relevant points as well as add your own knowledge. You must remember to keep the focus on the question at all times.

Source 1 (page 302)

Provenance:

- The source is a contemporary report of the *Reichstag* elections of July 1932.
- The writer was a political observer and a democratic liberal member of the DDP.

Content and argument:

- The source provides a thoughtful analysis of the election results.
- It warns of the political implications of the rise of the NSDAP and KPD.
- It suggests that Weimar democracy had failed, but with no clear political alternative.

Tone and emphasis:

- The writer is informative and objective, but pessimistic of the way things are going because of the threat of the NSDAP and KPD.

Own knowledge:

- Use your own knowledge to agree/disagree with the source, for example: details of the political radicalisations from the election votes, but there is no reference to the political intrigue.

Source 2 (page 302)

Provenance:

- The source is from a letter by twenty leading industrialists. They have a particular view on how Germany should be governed bearing in mind the economic crisis.
- It is taken from a letter to President Hindenburg – it addresses him and advances the views of the big business sector.

Content and argument:

- The source argues that Papen's government is failing.
- The German economy has severe problems.
- The government has no power to rule effectively; it is doubtful whether another *Reichstag* election will solve the dilemma.
- A new government should be formed 'with the greatest possible popular support'.

Tone and emphasis:

- The tone is very polite and respectful to the president.
- But the industrialists are demanding that the president takes action, even though they are not actually political leaders.

Own knowledge:

- Use your own knowledge to agree/disagree with the source, for example: details about why Germany was economically suffering, or evidence relating to why the author thought that Papen's government was incapable of effective government, for example the *Reichstag* vote of no confidence.

Source 3 (page 303)

Provenance:

- The source is taken from evidence of the Nuremberg trials held in 1946.
- It provides a personal account presented in 1946 by Otto Meissner, the state secretary to the president, about events in the months leading up to Hitler's appointment in 1933.

Content and argument:

- The source reports that Schleicher wanted more powers to establish some sort of military dictatorship.
- But Hindenburg's refusal to support Schleicher led to a number of meetings between the president, his son and Papen.

Tone and emphasis:

- The tone is a very factual narrative of events.
- He comes over as a detached observer of events and distanced from involvement and responsibility.

Own knowledge:

- Use your own knowledge to agree/disagree with the source, for example: evidence about Schleicher's failure to form a new government by offering Strasser the job of vice-chancellor, and Papen's disappointment at being forced to resign in November 1932.

Answering AS questions

You have 45 minutes to answer the question. It is important that you spend at least one-quarter of the time reading and planning your answer. Generally, when writing an answer you need to check that you are remaining focused on the issue identified in the question and are relating this to the sources and your knowledge.

- You might decide to write a paragraph on each 'strand' (that is, provenance, content and tone), comparing the two sources, and then write a short concluding paragraph with an explained judgement on which source is more valuable.
- For writing about content, you may find it helpful to adopt a comparative approach, for example when the evidence in one source is contradicted or questioned by the evidence in another source.

At AS level you are asked to provide a judgement on which is more valuable. Make sure that this is based on clear arguments with strong evidence, and not on general assertions.

Planning and writing your answer

- Think how you can best plan an answer.
- Plan in terms of the headings above, perhaps combining 'provenance' with 'tone and emphasis', and compare the two sources.

As an example, here is a comparison of Sources 1 and 2 in terms of provenance, and tone and emphasis:

The two sources have different viewpoints. In terms of their provenance, Source 1 is a careful, astute analysis of Germany's political crisis; however, the author is a democratic liberal (a member of the DDP) and pessimistic about the rise of extremism. Source 2 also recognises the nature of the political and economic crisis, but clearly aims to advance the interests of big business by appealing to the president.

Then compare the *content and argument* of each source, by using your knowledge. For example:

Source 1 recognises the worrying implications of the rise of the NSDAP and KPD and that Weimar democracy had failed by July 1932; the violence in the streets between the SA and Communists; and the weakness of Papen and his 'cabinet of barons'.

Source 2 is clearly looking for a new government to stabilise Germany, as long as it works sympathetically with business (with some economic details of the depression). This source underlines the political and economic stability and implies it wants to work with 'nationalist' forces, but does not mention the Nazis.

Which is *more valuable*? This can be judged in terms of which is likely to be more valuable in terms of where the source came from; or in terms of the accuracy of its content. However, remember the focus of the question – in this case, why Germany was so politically unstable.

With these sources, you could argue that Source 1 is the more valuable because it was a relatively balanced view, and it portrays an astute assessment of Germany's situation – the Weimar Republic had been democratically 'outvoted' and there was no

clear alternative solution. Whereas although Source 2 is still very helpful, it is more limited to the letter of one interest group trying to advance its own position with less focus on the overall political dilemma.

Then check the following:

- Have you covered the 'provenance' and 'content' strands?
- Have you included sufficient knowledge to show understanding of the historical context?

Answering A-level questions

The same general points for answering AS questions (see 'Answering AS questions') apply to A-level questions, although of course here there are three sources and you need to assess the value of each of the three, rather than choose which is most valuable. Make sure that you remain focused on the question and that when you use your knowledge it is used to substantiate (add to) an argument relating to the content or provenance of the source.

If you are answering the A-level question with Sources 1, 2 and 3 above:

- Keep the different 'strands' explained above in your mind when working out how best to plan an answer.
- Follow the guidance about 'provenance' and 'content' (see the first two points of the AS guidance).
- Here you are *not* asked to explain which is the most valuable of the three sources. You can deal with each of the three sources in turn if you wish.
- However, you can build in comparisons if it is helpful, but it is not essential. It will depend to some extent on the three sources.
- You need to include sufficient knowledge to show understanding of the historical context. This might encourage cross-referencing of the content of the three sources, mixed with your own knowledge.
- Each paragraph needs to show clarity of argument in terms of the issue identified by the question.

Glossary of terms

Active resistance   Suggests opposition, by words or action, which tries to undermine or even overthrow the state.

Alliance   An agreement where members promise to support the other(s), if one or more of them is attacked.

Allies   The nations who were allied against Germany and Austria-Hungary during the First World War. They were Russia, France, Great Britain and later others, including the USA.

Annexation   Taking over of another country against its will.

Anschluss   Usually translated as 'union'. Although the population of Austria was wholly German the Versailles Treaty outlawed any political union between Germany and Austria.

Anti-capitalism   Rejects an economic system based on private property and profit.

Anti-feminist   Opposing female advancement.

Anti-Marxism   Opposition to the ideology of Karl Marx.

Anti-modernism   Strand of opinion which rejects, objects to or is highly critical of changes to society and culture brought about by technological advancement.

Anti-Semitism   Hatred of Jews. It became the most significant part of Nazi racist thinking. For Hitler, the 'master-race' was the pure Aryan (the people of northern Europe).

Arbitration treaty   An agreement to accept the decision by a third party to settle a conflict.

Armistice   A suspension of fighting pending a final peace settlement.

Article 48   Gave the Weimar president the power to rule by decree in an emergency.

Aryan   Defined by the Nazis as the non-Jewish people of northern Europe. Technically, refers to people whose language has an Indian/European root.

Aryanise   To remove all non-Aryans from office, business and property.

Asocials   The Nazi *Volksgemeinschaft* excluded those who were 'socially unfit', as they deviated from the norms of society. The term 'asocial' was applied in an elastic manner to vagabonds, prostitutes, alcoholics, homosexuals, criminals, 'idlers', even grumblers.

Associationism   Having a strong identity or affiliation with a particular group.

Autarky   The aim for self-sufficiency in the production of food and raw materials, especially when at war.

Authoritarianism   A broad term meaning government by strong non-democratic leadership.

Autocracy   A system where one person (usually a hereditary sovereign) has absolute rule.

Autonomy   The right of self-government.

Avant garde   A general term suggesting new ideas and styles in art.

Balance of trade   The difference in value between exports and imports. If the value of the imports is above that of exports, the balance of the payments has a deficit that is often said to be 'in the red'.

Balanced budget   A financial programme in which a government does not spend more than it raises in revenue.

Battle of Britain   Name given to the air battle fought over the skies of southern England in July to October 1940.

Battle of the Atlantic   The naval struggle between the Allied convoys and the German U-boats in the northern Atlantic.

Bavaria   One of the oldest states in Europe and part of Imperial Germany, which maintained its kingdom until November 1918.

Bilateral trade treaty   A trade agreement between two countries or parties.

Black market   The underground economy where goods are sold at unregulated prices.

Blanket bombing   The military policy of dropping large numbers of bombs so as to cause devastation of an area.

Blitzkrieg   Literally, 'lightning war'. The name of the military strategy developed to avoid static war. It was based on the use of dive-bombers, paratroopers and motorised infantry.

Blut und Boden   'Blood and soil.' Nationalist and racist romanticism which glorified the rural role of the peasantry.

Bolshevik Revolution   The term 'Bolshevik' means majority – which was used by Lenin as the leader of the majority Russian Socialist Party from 1903. In October 1917 Lenin and the Bolsheviks seized power to create a communist government.

Buffer state   The idea of separating two rival countries by leaving a space between them.

Cartels   An arrangement between businesses to control markets by exercising a monopoly.

Chancellor   Prime minister of the German government.

Coalition government   Usually formed when a party does not have an overall majority in parliament; it then combines with more parties and shares government positions.

Concordat   An agreement between Church and state. A concordat was signed by the papacy and the Nazi government in July 1933.

Conscription   Compulsory enlistment to military service by the state.

Constitution   The principles and rules that govern a state.

Constitutional monarchy   Where the monarch has limited power within the lines of a constitution.

Cult of personality   Using the power and charisma of a political leader to dominate the nation.

Deficit financing   The financial policy of a government to spend more than it receives as revenue, in order to stimulate the economy. In this way, it gives the people more money to spend and so, in theory, increases the demand for goods and thereby creates work.

Demagogue   A leader who plays on the prejudices of the masses with populist emotions.

Demilitarisation   The removal of military personnel, weaponry or forts.

Diktat   A dictated peace. The Germans felt that the Treaty of Versailles was imposed without negotiation.

Dualism   A government system in which two forces coexist, for example the Nazi Party and the German state.

Edelweiss Piraten   Edelweiss Pirates. The name given to a loose collection of youth groups who did not conform. Edelweiss is a white alpine flower which served as a symbol of opposition.

Ersatzkaiser   'Substitute emperor.' After Hindenburg was elected president, he provided the *ersatzkaiser* figure required by the respectable right wing: he was a conservative, a nationalist and a military hero.

Eugenics   The scientific programme for the genetic improvement of the race.

Euthanasia   Ending the lives of people suffering from incurable illnesses.

Expressionists   Artists who focus on expressing feelings through symbolism, exaggeration or distortion.

Federal structure   Where power and responsibilities are shared between central and regional governments, for example, the USA.

Final Solution   A euphemism used by the Nazi leadership to describe the extermination of the Jews from 1941, although in the earlier years the term had been used more loosely before there was any real overall plan.

First past the post   An electoral system that simply requires the winner to gain one vote more than the second placed candidate. In a national election it tends to give the most successful party disproportionately more seats than its total vote merits.

Freikorps   'Free corps.' Right-wing, nationalist soldiers who acted as paramilitaries and were only too willing to use force to suppress communist activity.

Führerprinzip   'The leadership principle.' Hitler upheld the idea of a one-party state, built on an all-powerful leader.

Fulfilment   The policy of conforming to the terms of Versailles Treaty, while aiming for moderate revision of the terms. It was initiated by Joseph Wirth in 1921–2, and later pursued by Stresemann.

Gauleiter   'Leader of a regional area.' The Nazi Party was organised into 35 regions from 1926.

GDR   Communist East Germany. Communist East Germany, 1949–90.

General Staff   A body within the German Army which was responsible for all military planning.

Genocide   The extermination of a whole race.

German romanticism   German classicism in art, literature and music.

Gestapo   *Geheime Staatspolizei*. Secret state police. A key policing organisation for surveillance and repression.

Ghetto   A term used to describe the historic area lived in by the Jews in a city.

Gleichschaltung   'Bringing into line' or 'co-ordination'.

GNP   Gross national product is the total value of all goods and services in a nation's economy (including income derived from assets abroad).

Gradualism   Changing by degrees; progressing slowly.

Great Depression   The severe economic crisis of 1929–33 that started in the USA with the Wall Street Crash. Marked by mass unemployment, falling prices and a lack of spending.

Guns or butter?   A question used to highlight the controversial economic choice between rearmament and consumer goods.

Hard currency   A currency that the market considers to be strong because its value does not depreciate. In the 1920s the hardest currency was the US dollar.

Hegemony   Political leadership and dominance.

High treason   The crime of betraying one's country, especially by attempting to overthrow the leader or government.

Hitler Youth   The Nazi youth organisation. In German: *Hitlerjugend* (*HJ*).

Holocaust   Term to describe mass slaughter – in this context it refers to the extermination of the Jews.

Horst Wessel   A young Nazi brownshirt killed in a fight with communists in 1930. The song he wrote became a Nazi marching song and later virtually became an alternative national anthem.

Hyperinflation   In Germany in 1923 this meant that prices spiralled out of control because the government increased the amount of money being printed. As a result, it displaced the whole economy.

Imperial Germany   Germany from its unification in 1871 until 1918. Also referred to as the Second Reich (Empire).

Indoctrination   Inculcating and imposing a set of ideas.

Intentionalists   Historians who interpret history by emphasising the role (intentions) of people who shape history.

Junkers   The landowning aristocracy, especially from eastern Germany.

Kaiser   Emperor. The last Kaiser of Germany was Wilhelm II, 1888–1918.

Kreisau Circle   Name given to the resistance group which met at the estates of Helmuth von Moltke.

Kripo   *Kriminalpolizei*. Criminal police responsible for the maintenance of general law and order.

Kulturkampf   A struggle for culture or civilisation. Bismarck's anti-Catholic policy of the 1870s aimed at reducing the role and power of the Catholic Church in Germany.

Labour exchanges   Local offices created by the state for finding employment. Many were created in countries to counter mass unemployment.

League of Nations   The international body to encourage disarmament and to prevent war.

Lebensborn   Literally, the 'spring' or 'fountain of life'. Founded by Himmler and overseen by the SS to promote doctrines of racial purity.

Lebensraum   'Living space.' Hitler's aim to create an empire by establishing German supremacy over the eastern lands in Europe.

Maginot Line   Extensive defence fortifications built on the Franco-German frontier by the French governments in the 1930s.

Mandates   The name given by the Allies to the system created in the Peace Settlement for the supervision of all the former colonies of Germany (and Turkey) by the League of Nations.

March converts   Those who joined the NSDAP immediately after the consolidation of power in January–March 1933.

Martial law   Government and control by military authorities over the civilian population.

Mass suggestion   A psychological term suggesting that large groups of people can be unified simply by the atmosphere of the occasion. Hitler and Goebbels used their speeches and large rallies to particularly good effect.

Mein Kampf   'My struggle.' The book written by Hitler in 1924, which expresses his political ideas.

Mittelstand   Translated as 'the middle class', but in Germany it represents the lower middle classes: shopkeepers, craft workers and clerks.

Mutual guarantee agreement   An agreement between states on a particular issue, but not an alliance.

Nacht und Nebel   'Night and fog.' Name given to a decree by Hitler in December 1941 to seize any person thought to be dangerous. They should vanish into *Nacht und Nebel*.

National Opposition   A title given to a group of various political forces that was forged out of the Young Plan in 1929 to oppose all reparations payments.

Nationalism   In general, the belief in – and support for – a national identity. The spirit of German nationalism helped to unify the German states in the nineteenth century. But many nationalists wanted to create a Greater Germany of all German speakers.

Nazi–Soviet Pact   A non-aggression pact of 1939 between the USSR and Germany that opened the way for the invasion of Poland by both countries.

Neue Sachlichkeit   A form of art that developed in post-war Germany which tried to express reality with a more objective view of the world.

New Order   A phrase given by the Nazis to the economic, political and racial integration of Europe under the Third Reich.

Night of the Long Knives   A crucial turning point when Hitler arranged for the SS to purge the SA leadership. About 200 victims were murdered, including Röhm, Strasser and Schleicher.

November criminals   Those who signed the November Armistice and a term of abuse to vilify all those who supported the democratic republic.

Operation T-4   The collation of information about mentally and physically ill patients in offices in Tiergartenstrasse 4 in Berlin as part of the euthanasia programme.

Pan-German League   A movement founded in the late nineteenth century, which campaigned for the uniting of all Germans into one country.

Paramilitary units   Informal non-legal military squads.

Paris Peace Settlement   The meeting by the Allies in Paris, 1919–20, which resulted in five peace treaties with the defeated enemies and the creation of the League of Nations. The Versailles Treaty was signed with Germany on 28 June 1919 and the St-Germain Treaty with Austria-Hungary on 10 September 1919.

Parliamentary democracy   A system of government where the political power is held by an elected parliament representing the people.

Passive resistance   Refusal to work with occupying forces.

Pearl Harbor   A US military base in the Pacific.

Phoney war   Used to describe the war period from September 1939 to May 1940 because there was no real aggressive activity on the Western Front.

Plebiscite   A vote by the people on one specific issue – like a referendum.

Pogrom   An organised or encouraged massacre of innocent people. The term originated from the massacres of Jews in Russia.

Polarised   The division of society into distinctly opposite views (the comparison is to the north and south poles).

Population policy   In 1933–45 the Nazi government aimed to increase the birth rate.

Progressive tax   A tax system in which those who earn higher incomes pay a higher percentage of their income than those with lower incomes.

Proletarian dictatorship   Marxist theory of a state created in which the working class control power.

Proletariat   The industrial working class who, in Marxist theory, would ultimately take power in the state.

Proportional representation   A system that allocates parliamentary seats in proportion to the total number of votes.

Public works   Employment schemes financed by the state to provide jobs.

Putsch   The German word for an uprising. Normally, a *putsch* means the attempt by a small group to overthrow the government.

Radicalisation   A policy of increasing severity.

Reactionary   Opposing change and supporting a return to traditional ways.

Real wages   The actual purchasing power of income when set against prices, taking into account inflation/deflation and also the effect of deductions.

Red Army   The name given to the Soviet army created in 1917.

Red threat   A 'Red' was a loose term used to describe anyone sympathetic to the left. It originated from the Bolshevik use of the red flag in Russia, which in turn had been based on its use in the French Revolution.

Reichstag   The German parliament. Although created in 1871, it had limited powers until the October reform of 1918.

Reparations   Payment of money (and gold) and the transfer of property and equipment from the defeated to the victor after war.

Revisionism   In general terms it is the aim to modify or change something. In this context, it refers specifically to a historian who challenges a well-established interpretation.

Revolution from below   The radical elements in the party that wanted to direct the Nazi revolution from a more local level rather than from the leadership in Berlin.

Ribbentrop Bureau   Office created by the Nazi Joachim von Ribbentrop, who ran his own personal 'bureau' to oversee foreign affairs.

Rote Kapelle   'Red Orchestra.' Name given to the communist spy network which passed information to the USSR.

RSHA   Reich Security Office, which amalgamated all police and security organisations.

Rule of law   Governing a country according to its laws.

SA   *Sturmabteilung*; became known in English as the Brownshirts after the colour of their uniform. They supported the radical socialist aspects of Nazism.

Schlieffen Plan   Its purpose was to avoid a two-front war by winning victory on the Western Front before dealing with the threat from Russia. It aimed to defeat France within six weeks by a massive German offensive in northern France and Belgium.

SD   *Sicherheitsdienst*. Security service.

'Second revolution'   The aims of Röhm and the SA were for social and economic reforms and the creation of a 'people's army' which would merge the army and the SA. These aims were more attractive to 'left-wing socialist Nazis' or 'radical Nazis'.

Self-determination   The right of people of the same nation to decide their own form of government. In effect, it is the principle of each nation ruling itself. Wilson believed that it was integral to the peace settlement and would lead to long-term peace.

Siegfriede   'A peace through victory.' Referring to Germany fighting the First World War to victory and making major land gains.

Social Darwinism   A philosophy that portrayed the world as a 'struggle' between people, races and nations. Hitler viewed war as the highest form of 'struggle' and was deeply influenced by the theory of evolution based on natural selection.

Socialist republic   A system of government without a monarchy that aims to introduce social changes for collective benefit.

Soviet   A Russian word meaning an elected council.

Soviet republic   A system of government that aims to introduce a communist state organised by the workers' councils and opposed to private ownership.

SS   *Schutz Staffel* (Protection Squad); became known as the Blackshirts after their uniform.

SS *Einsatzgruppen*   SS Special Action Units. First used during the invasion of Poland. After the invasion of Russia four units were launched in eastern Europe. They were responsible for rounding up local Jews and murdering them in mass shootings.

'Stab in the back' myth   The distorted view that the army had not really lost the First World War and that unpatriotic groups, such as socialists and Jews, had undermined it. The myth severely weakened the Weimar democracy from the start.

State within a state   A situation where the authority and government of the state are threatened by a rival power base.

Structuralists   Historians who interpret history by analysing the role of social and economic forces and structures. They tend to place less emphasis on the role of the individual in shaping history.

Tariffs   Taxes levied by an importing nation on foreign goods coming in, and paid by the importers.

Tenant farmer   A farmer who works land owned by someone else and pays rent either in cash or in a share of the produce.

Teutonic paganism   The pre-Christian beliefs of the Germans.

Toleration   Acceptance of alternative political, religious and cultural views.

Total war   Involves the whole population in war, economically and militarily.

Totalitarian   A system of government in which all power is centralised and does not allow any rival authorities.

Turn of the tide   The term used to describe the Allied military victories in the winter of 1942–3, when the British won at El Alamein in North Africa and the Russians forced the surrender of 300,000 German troops at Stalingrad.

Unconditional surrender   Roosevelt and Churchill's statement in 1943 that the Allies would not accept a negotiated peace.

Unilateral disarmament   The disarmament of one party. Wilson pushed for general (universal) disarmament after the war, but France and Britain were more suspicious. As a result, only Germany had to disarm.

Unrestricted submarine warfare   Germany's policy of attacking all military and civilian shipping in order to sink supplies going to Britain.

Untermenschen   'Subhumans.' Covered all races who, according to the Nazis, were 'inferior', or subhuman. Included Jews, Slavs and Gypsies (Sinti and Roma).

V-1 and V-2   The flying pilotless bombs and the long-range rocket developed by scientists in Germany. Used in air raids against Britain 1944–5.

Vernunftrepublikaner   'A rational (pragmatic) republican.' Used in the 1920s to define those people who really wanted Germany to have a constitutional monarchy but who, out of necessity, came to support the democratic Weimar Republic.

Volk   Often translated as 'people', although it tends to suggest a nation with the same ethnic and cultural identities and with a collective sense of belonging.

Völkisch   Nationalist views associated with Aryan racism (especially anti-Semitism).

Volksgemeinschaft   'A people's community.' Nazism stressed the development of a harmonious, socially unified and racially pure community.

Waffen SS   The armed SS: a paramilitary organisation of elite troops.

Wall Street Crash   The collapse of share prices on the New York Stock Exchange in October 1929.

War bonds   To pay for the war, Imperial Germany encouraged people to invest in government funds in the belief they were helping to finance the war and their savings would be secure.

Wehrmacht   The name of the combined armed forces 1935–45. From 1921 to 1935 the term *Reichswehr* had referred simply to the German Army. In 1935 the German armed forces were reorganised and given the term *Wehrmacht*. It consisted of the army, the navy and the air force.

Weimar Republic   Took its name from the first meeting of the National Assembly in Weimar, which had moved from Berlin because of many disturbances. Weimar was chosen because it was a town with a great historical and cultural tradition.

Welfare state   The idea of the state playing a key role in the protection and promotion of the economic and social well-being of its people.

Weltpolitik   'World policy.' The imperial policy of Kaiser Wilhelm II to make Germany a great power by overseas expansion.

White Russians   Opponents of the Bolsheviks after the creation of the Soviet state.

White Terror   The 'Whites' were seen as the opponents to the Reds. The term 'White Terror' originated from the suppression of the soviet republic in Bavaria in May 1919, although it became a general name for the murders and violence of 1919–22.

White-collar workers   Workers not involved in manual labour.

Zero hour   Used in German society to describe Germany's overall collapse at the end of the Second World War.

Further reading

Books relevant to the whole period

V. Berghahn, *Modern Germany,* **second edition (Cambridge University Press, 1987)**
Puts its emphasis on social and economic history with an excellent selection of statistics

W. Carr, *A History of Germany, 1815–1990,* **fourth edition (Edward Arnold, 1991)**
A clear and informative narrative that puts nineteenth- and twentieth-century German political history into perspective

G.C. Craig, *Germany, 1866–1945* **(Oxford University Press, 1981)**
Focuses on the continuity of German history from unification until 1945, with emphasis on the role of the traditional elites in Prussia

M. Fulbrook, *History of Germany 1918–2000: The Divided Nation* **(Blackwell, 2002)**
A broad summary of German history including the explanation of different interpretations

General texts on Weimar Germany

E.J. Feuchtwanger, *From Weimar to Hitler: Germany 1918–33,* **second edition (Macmillan, 1995)**
Highlights the positive achievements of the Weimar Republic and argues that Weimar's failure was not inevitable

E. Kolb, translated by P.S. Falla and R.J. Park, *The Weimar Republic,* **second edition (Routledge, 2004)**
A thorough and clear historical survey with an excellent overview of the main historiographical interpretations

A.J. Nicholls, *Weimar and the Rise of Hitler,* **fourth edition (Palgrave, 2000)**
The clearest and most accessible overview which emphasises how the weaknesses of Weimar paved the way for Nazism

D. Peukert, *The Weimar Republic: The Crisis of Classical Modernity* **(Penguin, 1993)**
An original and thought-provoking approach, but not an easy starting point

General texts on Nazi Germany

K.D. Bracher, *The German Dictatorship* **(Penguin, 1973)**
Still probably the best one-volume history of the Nazi dictatorship

M. Burleigh, *The Third Reich: A New History* **(Cambridge University Press, 1993)**
A recent – and demanding – analysis which radically re-examines the Third Reich, and puts emphasis on racial doctrine and policies

I. Kershaw, *The Nazi Dictatorship: Problems and Perspectives of Interpretation* **(Bloomsbury, 2000)**
A thorough review of historiographical interpretations

J. Noakes and G. Pridham, editors, *Nazism 1919–45,* **volumes 1–4 (University of Liverpool Press, 1983–98)**
A comprehensive coverage of documents with a commentary across the whole period of Nazism

Chapter 1

R. Bessel and E. Feuchtwanger, editors, *Social Change and Political Developments in Weimar Germany* **(Croom Helm, 1981)**
Ten detailed but interesting essays on Weimar Germany. The first one on the German Revolution is particularly helpful

F.L. Carsten, *Revolution in Central Europe* **(Wildwood House, 1988)**
Although it refers to Austria and Hungary, the study deals mainly with the German Revolution. He claims that the fear of Bolshevism ensured the failure of revolution in central Europe

Chapter 2

G. Feldmann, *The Great Disorder: Politics, Economics and Society in the German Inflation, 1914–24* **(Oxford University Press, 1997)**
A lengthy and detailed study of the causes and effects of the inflation

R. Henig, *Versailles and After* **(Methuen, 1984)**
A short narrative of the treaty with analysis of its consequences

Chapter 3

A. de Jonge, *The Weimar Chronicle* **(Paddington Press, 1978)**
Not really a historical interpretation, but more an attempt to explore the mood and culture of Weimar

J. Wright, *Stresemann, Weimar's Greatest Statesman,* (Oxford University Press, 2002)

A major recent biography of Stresemann's life and career which portrays him in a positive light

Chapter 4

W.S. Allen, *The Nazi Seizure of Power,* second edition (Penguin, 1989)

An engaging description of the early rise of Nazism in the small town of Northeim. It highlights the way the Nazi Party exploited social tensions and divisions

I. Kershaw, *Hitler 1889–1936: Hubris* (Allen Lane, 1998)

I. Kershaw, *Hitler 1936–1945: Nemesis* (Allen Lane, 2000)

A two-volume *tour de force* biography of Hitler, which aims to synthesise the intentionalist and structuralist interpretations

Chapter 5

T. Childers, *The Nazi Voter* (Chapel Hill, 1983)

A detailed analysis of the social foundations of Nazi electoral support during their rise to power

I. Kershaw, editor, *Weimar: Why Did German Democracy Fail?* (Weidenfeld & Nicolson, 1990)

An excellent collection of essays on the political and economic causes of the collapse of Weimar democracy

H. Mommsen, *The Rise and Fall of Weimar Democracy* (University of North Carolina Press, 1996)

A comprehensive analysis of the collapse of the Weimar Republic which focuses on the bringing together of domestic and international forces

H.A. Turner, *Hitler's Thirty Days to Power* (Bloomsbury, 1993)

An entertaining analysis of the details leading to Hitler's appointment, which supports the view that it was not inevitable

Chapter 6

M. Broszat, *The Hitler State* (Longman, 1981)

An authoritative study by the leading structuralist historian which examines the nature of government in the Third Reich

R. Gellately, *The Gestapo and German Society* (Clarendon Press, 1990)

A detailed study which shows the effectiveness of the Gestapo, despite its policing constraints

R.J. Overy, *The Nazi Economic Recovery, 1932–1938* (Cambridge University Press, 1996)

A concise and very clear overview of the economic material. He argues that, despite the expansion of the Nazi economy, it had become stagnant by 1939

Chapter 7

R. Bessel, *Life in the Third Reich* (Oxford University Press, 1987)

Eight essays of leading historians which provide clear and accurate pictures of how Germans lived under the regime

M. Burleigh and W. Wippermann, editors, *The Racial State: Germany 1933–45* (Cambridge University Press, 1991)

A thorough analysis of Nazi racial policies, which not only covers the Jews, but also gypsies, asocials and mentally handicapped people

D. Crew, editor, *Nazism and German Society 1933–45* (Routledge, 1994)

A collection of articles which questions the image of totalitarian control of the regime over the German people

D. Welch, *The Third Reich* (Routledge, 1993)

An account of the relationship between politics, public opinion and propaganda. It focuses on how the regime mobilised and controlled the masses

Chapter 8

R.J. Evans, *The Third Reich at War* (Penguin, 2009)

The best up-to-date text on the overall impact of the war. The last volume of his trilogy on Nazi Germany

L. Dawidowicz, *The War Against the Jews* (Weidenfeld & Nicolson, 1975)

An extensive account of the escalation of anti-Semitic persecution. It takes an intentionalist view which sees Hitler as central to the Jewish extermination

M. Housden, *Resistance and Conformity in the Third Reich* (Routledge, 1997)

A good study of the range of opposition forces in the Third Reich. Also contains an extensive range of primary sources

K. Schleunes, *The Twisted Road to Auschwitz: Nazi Policy towards German Jews, 1933–45* (Urbana Illinois Press, 1970)

In this structuralist account he believes that the rivalry in the unstable Nazi structure provided the momentum behind the 'Final Solution'

Index